The Kitchen Companion

The Kitchen Companion

BY POLLY CLINGERMAN

THE
AMERICAN
★ COOKING ★
GUILD™

GAITHERSBURG, MARYLAND

The Kitchen Companion

Acknowledgments:
—Edited by Joanne Leonard
—Design and Typesetting by Clara Graves Graphic Design
—Illustrations by Jim Haynes
—Cover photo by Burwell and Burwell

Printed in the United States of America

ISBN 0-942320-44-1

For a catalog of cookbooks write to:
The American Cooking Guild
6-A East Cedar Avenue
Gaithersburg, MD 20877
(301)963-0698

DEDICATION

To the wonderful pros: Surja, Papa Paul, Louie, Antoine, Enoch and Nellie, who graced our kitchens and our lives and taught me so much about cooking; to all the friends who read through the manuscript at various stages and contributed from their store of skill and experience; and, as always, to John.

Contents

101 CHAPTER 3: COOKING HELP FOR EGGS

How Do I Make a Perfect Omelet, What If the Soufflé Doesn't Rise, and How Many Small Eggs Equal a Large One?

115 CHAPTER 4: COOKING HELP FOR SHELLFISH, FISH, POULTRY AND MEAT

What Is Braising, Should I Roast at High or Low Temperatures, and How Do I Steam Fish?

401 Chapter 15: Entertaining

*How Soon Should I Start Cooking for a Party, How Many Hors D'Oeuvres
    Should I Make, and What's the Easiest Way to Serve a Crowd?*

427 Glossary of Cookbook Terms

Recipes

SEASONING MIXTURES

MISCELLANEOUS

Introduction

This is not a cookbook, it's a cooking book—for beginning cooks and experienced cooks, for curious cooks and hurried cooks.

It tells you the size of a medium onion and what to substitute when you run out of baking chocolate. It is full of charts and info-bytes and hints that tell how long to stir and beat and knead and roast and braise and bake and boil; at what temperature, in what size pan—and what pan to substitute if you don't have what the recipe wants.

If the soufflé swoons or the cake humps, *The Kitchen Companion* tells you how to bluff it out and delight your diners with a change of name and a sauce, and how to get a more expected result next time. *The Kitchen Companion* makes your kitchen and your recipe books user friendly and tells you what you need to know in order to alter existing recipes or follow your inspirations. It's all you need to fly on your own.

That's what today's busy cooks have to do. They don't have time to slavishly follow a recipe every time they belly up to the chopping block. They don't have Mom at their elbow or at the other end of the phone to answer questions. In fact, today's moms often know more about selecting a mutual fund than a ripe pineapple.

The Kitchen Companion is an expanded version of a painstakingly assembled, hand-written log that I carried with me to every post during 30 years in the diplomatic service when I lived, cooked and entertained all over the world. Far from phone and mother and familiar sources of help, I had to cook, and cook well. Bible, badge of office and security blanket, the indispensable notebook gradually filled with substitutes and equivalents, with tips and tricks and techniques and recipes from hundreds of books, scores of friends and acquaintances who knew their way around the kitchen, a passel of cooks, and a couple cooking teachers.

My notes and charts helped me to handle almost any sort of kitchen situation I encountered: what pan or ingredient to substitute when the prescribed one wasn't available, how many beans fed 16, and, when we hankered for a dish for which I had no recipe, a basic recipe pattern to build on.

One day I happened to mention my precious notebook to my publishers. They were curious. When I described it, their eyes lighted up. Every cook, every kitchen needed such a bible—a *cooking* book instead of a cookbook!

The Kitchen Companion doesn't give you all my original notes. I don't tell you how to make apple pie with green papaya. You don't need to know that. Or that radish tops are a good substitute for watercress. Or how to make catsup and mustard and tofu and cream cheese, all of which I had to make at one time or another. Or that two cigarette tins (an African village measure) equal one cup. However, you might well need to know about translating foreign ingredients, measures and oven temperatures into American ones, so I gave you that.

I originally wanted to tell you how to get ants out of raisins by placing the raisins on a cookie sheet in the sun, but I was informed that today's cook dumps anty raisins and buys fresh. Oh. In Zaire when our precious raisins had ants, anyone who suggested dumping them would have been greeted with stunned amazement and probably treated for sunstroke. So *The Kitchen Companion* doesn't tell you how to remove ants from raisins or weevils from flour (you sift it through a nylon stocking).

On the other hand, I added information which would fit the book to your kitchen and your needs so you can meet most cooking situations with aplomb and cook with confidence and joy. And because I don't like to do something when I don't know why, I included lots of reasons.

This is the book I wish I had had the day I started out on my long cooking adventure. Or, perhaps I don't, because then I would have missed the challenge of sleuthing out answers and the excitement of learning new things from all my wonderful cooks, cooking friends and books. I pass my bible on to you with my blessing. I wish I could pass on the adventure that went into creating it.

Bon appetit!

Polly

A Guide to Ingredients

Since without ingredients there is no cooking, it seemed like a good idea to start with a quick guide to those basic beginnings. Glance through it now to get an idea of what is there so you'll know where to look when you have questions.

You'll see it talks about how to choose, prepare, use, store, and even make some of your ingredients. For instance, it tells you how to make coconut milk, which pasta goes best with which sauce, why you shouldn't store potatoes in the refrigerator, and how to keep ginger root indefinitely. I didn't recommend the method of a Vietnamese friend who pokes it into the ground—a window pot in winter.

I didn't tell you about using yogurt plants, either. In Zambia I kept one in water in my kitchen window. Once a week I put it in milk, heated it, and fermented my yogurt. I didn't tell you how to do that because we don't have yogurt plants here.

Check this chapter when you meet a cooking surprise —Why didn't the flour work?—or when you wonder about using medium-grain instead of long-grain rice. Everything's listed alphabetically by ingredient. You'll find cooking suggestions for many of these ingredients in the Cooking Help chapters. Also, seasonings have their own chapter, so check Chapter 8 for things like paprika and parsley.

Acids From Sharp to Mild:

- Cider, malt or white vinegar
- Lime and lemon juice
- Wine vinegar
- Rice wine vinegar
- Balsamic vinegar
- Grapefruit and orange juice
- Dry red or white wine

Recipe

Louie's Baked Apples with Cognac

Louie, our cook in Benin, taught me to bake them this way. Don't peel, but core the apples almost down to the bottom. Place in an ovenproof dish. Pack the holes with sugar and bake at 400° for 20 minutes. Refill the holes with more sugar, top each with a pat of butter (maybe a teaspoon) and return to the oven. After 15 minutes start basting them with their own juice. Bake for 1 hour total. Remove from the oven, pour 1 tablespoon Cognac over each apple. Serve warm with cream.

Browse through this chapter and you'll know where to look when the need arises.

ACID INGREDIENTS (IN BAKING): Warning! When you modify a baking powder recipe (cookies, muffins) by adding buttermilk, yogurt, sour cream, molasses, chocolate, honey, vinegar, citrus fruit, tart apples, etc., you add an acid which has to be neutralized with a dose of baking soda. Otherwise, your muffin will be dense and gummy. For the amount to use, look up baking soda in the equivalents chart, p. 254. You will also need to decrease the recipe's baking powder, since baking powder is also acid. For every ½ teaspoon of soda you use, cut the baking powder by 1 teaspoon.

ACIDS (IN DRESSINGS, SAUCES, MARINADES): Cider vinegar is tarter than wine vinegar. Rice wine and balsamic vinegars are mild. It often makes a difference which one you use. In vinaigrette, for instance, a sharp acid needs a lot of oil to balance it while a mild one needs surprisingly little. Taste acid ingredients for sharpness before you add them. Lemon and lime juices, especially, can vary from mild-sweet to downright sour. See the box. You don't want a dressing or marinade that makes your teeth itch.

APPLES: It's always a puzzlement which apples to use for cooking, which for munching. In general Granny Smith, Northern Spy, Rhode Island Greening, Rome Beauty and York Imperial are the best for pies and cooking, but apples vary according to the region. Ask the produce manager at your store which apples in your area are best for cooking and which for eating. Scribble the names in the margin if you think you'll forget.

Apples give off a gas that turns carrots bitter so don't store them together.

ARTICHOKES: I used to be confused about artichoke *bottoms* and artichoke *hearts*. Which was what? In case you've had the same question, the bottom is the flat, dish-shaped piece of flesh at the stem end below the leaves and fuzzy choke. The *heart* is the small, bud-shaped piece that you buy marinated. It comes from the youngest artichokes and consists of the inner leaves, the bottom, and the soft, not yet fuzzy choke buried inside; it is available canned and frozen. You generally don't find it fresh unless you have a fancy Italian grocery in your neighborhood.

AVOCADOS: If you're lucky you may find one at the market that's soft at the stem end, which means you can use it right away. Usually, though, you have to buy avocados rock hard. Put them in a paper bag, punch a couple holes in it, and leave at room temperature. They'll be soft and unctuous in 2 to 5 days. I've heard people claim they can ripen avocados by microwaving or boiling them. I tried both—the avocados softened, but they didn't get buttery and yummy. Still, it's worth a try if you're intrigued or desperate.

Contrary to common wisdom, the pit does not magically prevent avocados from turning brown, except for where it touches the flesh and keeps out the air. (Someone did a scientific test to explode this common myth!) However, plastic wrap does a good job of keeping out air and holding color. Just wrap cut avocados or cover guacamole tightly with plastic wrap and they'll keep their lovely green.

BACON: If you don't use up bacon very fast, here's a how to keep it both frozen and accessible by the slice. Lay slices in a single layer on wax or freezer paper, roll up, and freeze in a plastic bag. When you need bacon, unroll, peel off what you want and put the rest back in the freezer.

My cousin goes this method one better. She cooks her bacon before freezing and then reheats the frozen slices. Here's how: Place raw slices side by side on a rack in a baking pan and bake at 400° for 12 minutes, or until not quite crisp. Cool, stack, wrap in foil and freeze. Reheat slices in a skillet over low heat.

ℛecipe Idea

Papa's Artichokes

Papa Paul, our cook in Zaire, used to serve artichokes with a warm sauce of half melted butter, half vinaigrette. Try it.

Preparing an Artichoke

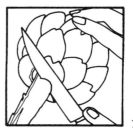
1

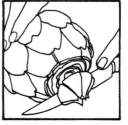

2

3

How Much Baking Powder?

Most modern American recipes are written for double-acting baking powder. The amount you need per cup of flour varies according to what you bake. As a rule:

To Make	Baking Powder Needed Per Cup of Flour
Cookies	½ teaspoon
Quick breads and muffins	1 teaspoon
Cakes, biscuits, waffles, pancakes	1½ teaspoons

BAKING POWDER: Sometimes it lets you down—the biscuits don't rise, the cake slumps in the pan. The problem is that baking powder starts working as soon as it meets liquid. Once you mix your batter, get it in the pan and the pan in the oven before too much rising gas is lost.

There are two kinds of baking powder, by the way: **double-acting** and **single-acting**, which can be either the tartrate or phosphate type. It's useful to know the difference. Double-acting, the one commonly used today, acts twice, as the name suggests. It starts bubbling when it gets wet, but doesn't get serious until the heat hits it, at which point it roars into action. Double-acting gives you a few minutes of grace. Single-acting is triggered immediately by liquid, and that's that.

If you use double-acting in a recipe written for single-acting, you won't use quite enough baking powder and the cake or muffin won't rise like it should. On the other hand, if you use single-acting in a double-acting recipe you'll use too much. Your muffin may overrise. It could even taste bitter from the extra baking powder.

When a foreign recipe doesn't specify the kind of baking powder, you can generally assume it's single-acting. If you want to be sure, compare the amount called for per cup of flour with the amount in the box. If greater, it is single-acting.

If you add an acid ingredient like buttermilk, molasses or chocolate to a recipe, you must add soda and reduce the baking powder. (See Acid Ingredients and chart on p. 255).

BARLEY, TO COOK: See p. 29.

BEAN CURD (TOFU): This could really be called "soy bean cheese". In Zambia we made our own from soy milk, which you make like coconut milk, but from ground soy beans. We curdled the hot milk with Epsom salts, dripped the curds through a dish towel, and had a tofu smooth as silk.

Tofu is high in protein and very low-fat. It comes in two varieties: firm (Chinese) and soft or "silken" (Japanese).

Both come packed in water. To keep it more than 24 hours, slit the package, drain, cover with fresh water and store in a covered container in the refrigerator. Change the water daily and it will keep for 10 days. Before you use it, drain the tofu briefly on paper towels—under a weight if you want to make it firmer. See the recipe in the box.

Use firm tofu for frying, braising and grilling. Dice it and add to tossed salads as you would cheese or ham, purée it for dressings, dips, spreads, sauces, soups. Use soft tofu in lighter dressings, fruit whips, mixed salads, desserts.

BEANS, DRIED, AND LEGUMES: Although this is technically the bean entry, I've included legumes like dried peas and lentils because you treat them pretty much like dried beans except that they don't have to be soaked.

Soaking makes dried beans cook more quickly. Modern culinary scientists have discovered that beans don't need to soak overnight after all—4 hours is plenty. Which is good news. But it won't hurt to do the long soak if that's more convenient. When you soak, first rinse, then pick through for small stones (yes, you find them—and you can break a tooth). Use 2 quarts of cold water per pound of beans.

If you want to shorten the soaking time even more, cover the beans with cold water by 2 inches, bring them to a quick boil and simmer over low heat for 2 minutes. Take the pot off the heat and let the beans stand covered for an hour. Discard the water and you're ready to get on with your recipe.

How do you know when beans have soaked long enough? Cut one lengthwise and take a look. The inside should have a single color and an even consistency—no white or hard bits. If time gets away from you and the beans oversoak—you'll know because the skins will be shrivelled and you'll see bubbles rising to the surface of the water—don't panic. Drain the beans in a colander and let them sit and dry out for half an hour. Then go ahead and cook.

─── *Recipe* ───

Thai Fried Tofu with Peanut Sauce

Use 1 pound of firm tofu. If it isn't extremely firm, wrap it in several layers of paper towel and press between two plates (weight the top one) for 30 minutes. Unwrap and drain.

Cut in ¾" squares. Roll in cornstarch and fry in deep oil at 365° for 5 to 6 minutes, until pale gold. Serve as an appetizer with toothpicks as is or better yet, with this snappy sauce.

Peanut Dipping Sauce: In a mortar make a paste of 2 coarsely chopped garlic cloves, 3 seeded, coarsely chopped small dried red chili peppers and ¾ teaspoon salt. Mix in ½ cup vinegar, ¼ cup sugar dissolved in ¼ cup hot water, and ¾ cup finely chopped peanuts.

Serves 6 - 8 as an appetizer.

Beans won't be as gassy if you change the soaking water several times and then boil them in fresh water. I change the water every hour for a 4-hour soak.

To fix delicious, tender beans, remember that **salt and acid make them tough.** Never salt until beans are almost done, and never add beans to any mixture containing salt or an acid like tomatoes until they are fully cooked.

For cooking instructions, see the chart below.

When you need to save time and bother, substitute canned beans for home-cooked. To make them taste best and cut the gassy effects, rinse them before you use them. A 15-ounce can will give you 1¾ cups of drained beans.

❧ COOKING DRIED BEANS AND LEGUMES ❧

To cook, first soak the beans as directed on p. 9, then drain and rinse thoroughly. Place them in a large (4-quart) pot with 8 cups of fresh cold water. Bring to a boil, reduce heat, cover and simmer for the time listed in the chart, or until tender. Just before the end of the cooking time, add 1 teaspoon of salt per original (dry) cup of beans.

All times and amounts in the chart are for 1 pound (2 cups) of dry beans.

Type	Cooking Time/Special Instructions	Yield in Cups
Black beans	1 to 1½ hours	6
Black-eyed peas or beans	Don't presoak. Simmer 45 to 60 minutes.	7
Boston beans	See Navy beans.	
Butter beans	1 to 1¼hours	6¼
Calico beans	1 hour	6
Cannellini	See Kidney beans.	
Chick peas	1½ to 2 hours	6¼
Cow peas	See Black-eyed peas.	
Cranberry beans	1¼ to 1¾ hours	7

Cooking Dried Beans and Legumes		
Type	**Cooking Time/Special Instructions**	**Yield in Cups**
Fava beans, with skins	Don't presoak. Instead, cover dry beans with 8 cups cold water, bring to a boil. Simmer 15 to 30 minutes or until skins soften. Let stand off heat, covered, for 1 hour. Drain and peel. Now cook per instructions for 45 to 50 minutes.	7
Fava beans, skinless	Soak as usual for dried beans, then cook per instructions for 1 to 1½ hours.	7
Garbanzos	See Chick peas.	
Great Northern beans	1 to 1½ hours	6⅔
Kidney beans, red and white	1 to 1½ hours	7
Lentils	Don't presoak. Cook per instructions 1 to 1½ hours.	5
Lima beans, baby	45 minutes to 1 hour	6½
Lima beans, large	1 to 1¼ hours	6¼
Mung beans	Don't presoak. Cook 45 minutes to 1 hour.	6
Navy beans	1 to 1½ hours	7
Pea beans	See Navy beans.	
Pearl haricot beans	See Navy beans.	
Pink beans	See Pinto beans.	
Pinto beans	1¼ to 1¾ hours	6 ½
Red American beans	1 hour	6
Soybeans	2 to 2½ hours	7
Split peas	Don't presoak. Cook 30 minutes.	6
Turtle beans	See Black beans.	
White haricot beans	See Great Northern beans.	

High Altitude Cooking

Dried foods like beans and peas take longer to cook at higher altitudes and will need more liquid.

When you cook at altitudes over 5,000 feet, you often have to adjust for the lowered air pressure, which affects time, temperature and moisture. I've scattered High Altitude Cooking hints like this throughout the book, wherever they apply, to help you.

BELGIAN ENDIVE: The little piece at the bottom of the stem end is very bitter. Always cut it off.

BERRIES: Store them in a colander in the refrigerator. They will keep fresh for several days as long as you resist the urge to wash them. A fastidious gardening friend used to send us huge, gorgeous berries which she had scrupulously washed. They always got squishy before we could finish them, but despite my pleas she continued to send them squeaky clean. One did *not* give dirty berries!

BREADCRUMBS: Which do you use in a recipe: soft or dry? If the recipe doesn't specify, use dry crumbs. Make your own from leftover bread. Cube it, place the cubes in a single layer on a cookie sheet and bake at 250° until they just start to color, 10 to 15 minutes. Cool and buzz in the processor or blender. **To make fresh crumbs,** omit the toasting step. Store tightly covered in the fridge for 2 to 3 weeks, or in the freezer.

BRITISH INGREDIENTS: The British turn out gorgeous cookbooks, a lot of which find their way into our book shops. Their seductive photos often send you straight to the kitchen, where you discover that some of the terms are puzzling, and a few that aren't should be. For instance, British *tomato purée* is our *tomato paste*, and their bacon is our ham—which is their gammon!

The books won't always send you rushing to the kitchen. Traditional recipes with intriguing names like "Bucks Bacon Badger" will catch your eye and you'll lean back in your lounge chair and imagine rolling suet pastry into a round, heaping it with ham, potato, onion and a flurry of herbs, gathering and sealing it over the top, tying it into a floured cloth and boiling it to moist succulence—as visions of Tiny Tim and Mr. Pickwick and Merrie Olde England dance through your head.

BRITISH INGREDIENTS

British Term	American Term
Single cream	Light cream
Double cream	Whipping cream
Lyle's Golden Syrup	Light Karo Syrup
Treacle	Molasses
Castor sugar	Superfine granulated sugar
Demerara sugar	Brown sugar
Mixed spice	Substitute apple pie spice or see p. 346 to make.
Dark cooking chocolate	Semi-sweet chocolate
Digestive biscuits	Graham crackers
Plain flour	All-purpose flour
Strong flour	Bread flour
Sultanas	Seedless white raisins
Morello cherries	Pie cherries
Tomato purée	Tomato paste
Courgettes	Zucchini
Aubergines	Eggplant
Haricot beans	Navy beans
Swedes	Turnips
Gammon	Ham
Streaky bacon	American bacon
Bacon	Canadian bacon or ham

Some Classic British Cookbooks You Might Enjoy

One of the delights of British cookbooks is the glorious recipe names—Bubble and Squeak, Singing Hinney, Star Gazey Pie, Spotted Dog, Roly Poly Pudding, Petticoat Tails, Fools, Flummery... Fun. Here are some classics:

- *Mrs. Beeton's Everyday Cookery*—the British Fanny Farmer. Traditional British food.

- Any by Jane Grigson, especially *Good Things*.

- Any by Elizabeth David. For creative cooks. Recipes are deliberately vague—British cooks don't like to be bossed around.

- Any by Marguerite Patton or Constance Spry. Precision recipes.

- Look for the current books. They are beautifully produced!

BROTH: See Stock.

BUCKWHEAT, TO COOK: See p. 30.

BULGUR: Bulgur differs from cracked wheat in that it has been steamed and dried. Two sorts are available—Ameri-

Recipe

Maggie's Tabbouleh

The best version I've tasted. If you don't know this parsley-speckled Middle Eastern delight, run out for a box of bulgur and try it. You'll thank Maggie.

Soak 1½ cups bulgur as directed on this page or according to package instructions. Measure 2 cups packed parsley, 1 cup cut-up spring onions and ¾ cup packed mint, chop it all finely, and add to the bulgur. Mix ¾ cup olive oil, ½ cup lemon juice and salt and pepper to taste and add all but ¼ cup of it. (Use the extra dressing for something else.) Mix well and refrigerate. Flavor will improve as it stands. This keeps well for 5 or 6 days.

Serve as a first course, a salad, or as a main course with some cooked chicken or shrimp mixed in. Makes 8 servings.

can: deep red-brown, made of hard wheat, and Middle Eastern: straw-colored, made of soft wheat, with a grassy-grainy aftertaste. Try both.

When soaked, this grain is used uncooked in dishes like tabbouleh (see the box). To use it without cooking, wash in several changes of cold water, letting it settle to the bottom before pouring off most of the water. When the water runs clear, drain in a sieve.

To soak, either cover 1 cup bulgur with 3 to 4 cups *boiling, salted water* and let stand for 40 minutes or cover with the same amount of *cold water* and let stand for 2 hours. (Expect it to swell to 3 or 4 times its bulk when soaked.) Drain in a cheesecloth-lined sieve, then twist the cloth to remove excess water.

Some boxed bulgur needs to soak only 30 minutes in twice its volume of boiling water. At the end of the time the water is absorbed, so you don't have to drain and squeeze.

To cook bulgur, see p. 30.

BUTTER: Careful cooks prefer **unsalted** butter because the amount of salt varies even within the same brand. If you cook with salted butter, ignore the recipe's salt and add to taste. I generally use salted butter because it keeps better. On the other hand, when the butter is a major ingredient (butter cakes, cookies, sauces), I use unsalted.

If you didn't get the butter out of the fridge in time, you can **soften it quickly** by grating it into the bowl or by microwaving it on *defrost* (# 5 or 50% power) in 10 second increments.

Whipped butter has been puffed with air to make it spread easily. If you use it for frying and such, you'll have to use more because of all the air. *Never* use it when you need a specific measure, as in baking—it won't come out right.

Butter not only adds flavor to food, it heightens the original flavor. More than that, it softens a sauce that tastes too intense, sharp or raw and adds silkiness to one that's harsh and thin. It adds tenderness to baked things.

See p. 71 for help in cooking with butter.
For substituting margarine, see p. 33.

CELERY: Use a vegetable peeler to get the tough strings off. Green celery has more flavor and nutrients than white. It crunches better between your teeth too.

CHEESE: A big hunk of cheese always starts to turn moldy before it's finished, but if you buy just a little piece you run out too soon. The answer is to buy big and **prevent the mold** by wrapping the cheese tightly in plastic wrap or a cloth dipped in vinegar water (½ cup water + 1 teaspoon vinegar + ½ teaspoon salt) and wrung out.

Cheese tastes its creamy best when it's at room temperature. Soft or semi-soft cheese needs 30 minutes to warm; hard cheese needs a good hour. When you're pushed you can **soften cheese** quite effectively in the microwave—but do it tiny increments, stopping constantly to give it a little test prod.

Before I grate soft cheeses like mozzarella, I brush the grater with a little oil so the cheese won't stick.

See p. 71 for help in cooking with cheese.

CHOCOLATE: For tips on working with chocolate, see p. 70. To substitute one form for another see p. 260.

There are many different sorts of chocolate. Each does something especially well. Here's a rundown.

Bitter or unsweetened chocolate has the strongest flavor. It's chocolate in the raw: no sugar or flavor added. Use it for cooking and baking.

Bittersweet, sweet-dark or semisweet has a rich flavor; the bitterness has been softened by a small amount of sugar. Use it for cooking and baking. Some people like to eat it; I find it too bitter. Good for baking, candy dipping, frosting, sauces.

Chips are generally semisweet chocolate. They have less cocoa butter, making them ideal for chocolate chip cookies where you want that firm nugget. For other cooking, the richer chocolates generally work better. If you substitute chips, add a bit of extra butter.

Cheese—How Much Fat?

Low

Cottage cheese (all)
Ricotta (reduced fat)

Medium

Camembert
Edam
Feta
Mozzarella
Reduced-fat
     varieties of
     regular cheeses

High

Blue-veined
Brie
Cheddar
Colby
Cream
Gouda
Parmesan
Swiss

═══ *Recipe* ═══

Chocolate Covered Apricots

Lay canned apricot halves on paper towel to drain thoroughly, then pat dry with paper towel. Place them on a cookie sheet in a 175° oven until they are dried (around 4 - 5 hours depending on the size of apricot). Remove apricots from the pan to a rack to cool thoroughly. Melt 6 tablespoons butter with 6 ounces of chocolate chips. Dip the apricots and lay on wax paper. When set, transfer to a rack to dry well. This will take a good 24 hours. Store covered.

I serve these with after dinner coffee.

Cocoa is only 10 to 12% cocoa butter. Dutch process cocoa, less acid and more mellow than regular cocoa, is preferred by most cooks. If you use regular cocoa, add a little extra sugar and/or cream or butter to the recipe to mellow it out. **Instant cocoa** has lecithin in it and lots of sugar. It won't work in recipes.

Couverture, or chocolate coating, is mostly sold by wholesale suppliers in huge blocks. It is rich and melts smoothly. The pros use it for dipping, coating, chocolate curls, ruffles, and other fancy garnishes. If you can't find it, a good-quality semisweet or bitter chocolate—one of the expensive European ones like Maillard or Lindt—is a fine substitute.

German's sweet chocolate is extra rich with added cocoa butter and is sweeter than semisweet. No, it isn't German, a Mr. German created it. Good for cooking, baking, eating. It's not as smooth as candy-bar chocolate.

Mexican chocolate contains sugar, ground almonds, cinnamon, salt. It's grainier than other chocolates. It's used in Mexican cooking and available where you buy Mexican foods.

Milk chocolate is made to be smooth on the tongue, and for that reason it's hard to work with and is best left for noshing.

White chocolate isn't really chocolate because it has no cocoa solids. It sets less firmly than real chocolate. If you substitute it for chocolate in a recipe, use more than the recipe measure or add extra butter.

COCONUT: The coconut that you buy in cans or bags is **sugared** and good only for baking. For **non-sweet recipes** like Thai and Indian, buy plain grated coconut in health food stores. Or buy a fresh coconut and grate your own—it's easy. Pierce the coconut eyes with a screw driver and drain off the liquid. (This isn't coconut milk. Throw it out, drink it, but don't cook with it. To make coconut milk, see below.) Bake the pierced coconut in a 400° oven for 20 minutes. Tap it all over with a hammer to loosen the shell, then split it with a whack of the hammer or a sharp knife and pry out the meat. Pare off the brown skin with a vegetable peeler and grate the meat by hand—a rotary grater is easiest—or in a blender or food processor.

COCONUT MILK: It's fun to make your own coconut milk. Put the **peeled, chunked meat** of 1 coconut in a blender or processor with 2 cups of very hot water. Whirl it at high speed until the coconut is pulverized. Dump it in a sieve placed over a bowl and press down hard with a spoon. Put the pressed coconut back in the blender/processor, add another 2 cups of hot water, and repeat. This time discard the coconut meat. It's pretty dead. Yield: 3 to 3¼ cups.

You can also make coconut milk with **dried, unsweetened coconut:** Put 2 cups of it in the blender or food processor with 2½ cups very hot water and blend 30 seconds. Strain and repeat as above. It will make about the same amount.

Both these methods give a rich coconut milk. If you want it even richer, substitute hot milk for water *in the first processing only*.

COFFEE: Coffee left at room temperature loses flavor surprisingly fast. Store beans, ground and instant in the refrigerator or freezer and it will stay rich and heady.

CORN: Here's a neat trick for cutting kernels off the cob. Place the bottom of the ear on the funnel of an angel cake pan. Hold the point of the ear with your fingers and shave down with a sharp knife. The kernels will fall into the pan. Voilà.

COTTAGE CHEESE: Use **small curd** for cooking, **large curd** for salads and cold dishes. Cottage cheese keeps longer if you store it upside down, the way painters store opened cans of paint, so air can't seep in under the lid.

How Do You Say It?

Pronunciations for foreign or unusual terms are provided in the glossary at the end of the book. I don't know about you, but I hesitate to do anything I can't pronounce.

Recipe Idea

Country Omelet

Have you ever filled an omelet with cottage cheese and chives? Keep it over the heat long enough to make the cheese gooey. Yummy.

Lighten-Up Trick: You can substitute milk for cream in a cooked recipe if you stabilize it so the heat won't make it separate. Before adding, beat cornstarch or flour into the milk—2 teaspoons cornstarch or 1 tablespoon flour per cup.

CREAM: The different types of cream vary a lot in fat content so it makes a difference which one you use. Here's the breakdown:

Heavy or whipping cream (40%)	Whips best. Won't curdle when boiled.
Light whipping cream (30%):	Whips but must be *ice cold*. Won't curdle when boiled.
Light, table or coffee cream (20%)	Won't whip, will curdle when boiled unless thickened with starch.
Half and half (10-14%):	Same qualities as light cream.

Don't try to substitute light cream or half and half for whipping or heavy cream in a sauce that's going to boil or simmer. They will separate. To lighten the dish, use a smaller amount of the heavy cream and make up the difference with another liquid from the recipe.

For more help in working with cream, see p. 71.

CRÈME FRAÎCHE: Sheer heaven—a cultured cream that's almost as dense as cream cheese only silkier, and has a slightly acid taste. The French use it more than they do regular cream. To make your own, see p. 297. Use it wherever you would use sour cream: in soups, salad dressings, sauces. Like heavy cream, *crème fraîche* can be boiled with no problem.

If you want to taste something good, sweeten *crème fraîche* a tad, and plop it over berries or other fruit. To experience pure joy, heap it on a little mound of canned, sweetened chestnut purée. (Patapouf, our cat in Paris, adored this treat and always demanded the last bite.)

EGGS: If you aren't careful when you separate them, you can lose a lot of egg and actually alter the proportions of a cake or soufflé. When you **separate yolks** into a small bowl before adding them to something, try to keep them whole so they'll slip out easily. Broken ones stick, leaving a lot behind. To make sure you get all the white, scrape out the shell with your finger. A baker told me that in a 6 or 8 egg recipe you can lose as much as an entire white if you don't scrape.

You so often use only the yolk or white in a recipe that it makes sense to freeze the other halves. I **freeze whites and yolks** in ice cube trays, one yolk or white per unit, and package them in plastic bags. If you freeze them in larger units (3 or 4 in a custard cup for instance) write the number on the package. Should you forget, or should the writing blur, remember: 1 large yolk = 1 generous tablespoon; 1 large white = 2 tablespoons. More often than not, I make my soufflés from frozen yolks and whites.

A caution. **Thawed egg yolks** tend to be grainy so don't use them in anything delicate like mayonnaise or custard, where you want a silken texture.

EGGPLANT: The smaller ones are sweeter and have fewer seeds. I often bake eggplants at 425° for 30 minutes, peel them, chop the meat and freeze it. Then I'm all set for cooking things like casseroles and spaghetti sauce.

FARINA, TO COOK: See p. 30.

FISH: Fish come in all categories: high to low fat, mild to assertive flavor, delicate and flaky to steak-like. If you keep this in mind, you can cook almost any fish almost any way. **When you substitute** one fish for another in a recipe—which we all do because fish counters are unpredictably stocked—choose one with similar fat content, taste and texture and your dish will be very like the original.

You can also substitute a quite different sort of fish in a recipe if you make allowances. For example, if you use a less fatty fish, baste a little more and cook a bit less. If you use a delicate fish it will cook faster, so place it farther from the heat.

The chart on the next page lists a wide assortment of fish and their characteristics so you can substitute intelligently.

━━ *Recipe* ━━

Eggplant Casserole

Fry up a chopped onion in 2 tablespoons oil. Add a 1-pound eggplant which has been baked, peeled and chopped (thawed if frozen—see text), a 6-ounce jar of roasted pimentos drained and chopped, 1½ teaspoons brown sugar, 3 tablespoons wine vinegar, a teaspoon or so of dried oregano, and salt and pepper. Toss in a handful of pitted black Greek olives if that sounds good. Serve as is or toss with spaghetti and top with grated mozzarella—feta or a mild goat cheese would also be good. Or serve cold with a few capers tossed in.

Serves 4.

Buy the Tender Cut

When you buy fish steaks, remember: one cut from the lazy middle is more tender than one from the muscular, hard-working tail. Center cuts have the deepest cavity in the center and a pronounced horseshoe shape.

===== TECHNIQUE =====

Filleting Fish

To fillet, cut round fish down to the spine, flat fish down *one side* of the backbone. Hold the knife flat to cut flesh from ribs and backbone.

To bone, cut the stomach opening and along backbone to tail. Slide knife between flesh and bones on each side. Snip backbone at tail and head. Peel out backbone.

You can keep fresh fish in the fridge up to 3 days without harming flavor or texture, even fish "previously thawed for your convenience". Ask the fish merchant to pack it in a bag of crushed ice, after first wrapping it in a protective layer of plastic. At home, store the fish, still in its plastic wrapping, in crushed ice in a tightly covered container. Renew ice as necessary.

Fish is fragile. A cooked fish can fall apart if you handle it too often or roughly *before* cooking!

My Chinese cooking teacher taught me that a little ginger juice sprinkled on uncooked fish removes any strong flavor. Put the ginger root in your garlic press and squeeze drops on all surfaces (inside and out if it's a whole fish). You don't need a lot. Sprinkle it as you would salt or pepper.

❦ SELECTING FISH ❦

Type	Fat Content	Flavor and Texture	Substitutes
Albacore		See Tuna.	
Angler		See Monkfish.	
Bluefish	High	Delicate flavor (stronger in large fish), soft flesh	Mackerel
Butterfish	Medium	Mild flavor, soft flesh	Catfish, mullet
Carp	Low to medium	Mild flavor, firm flesh	Haddock
Catfish	Medium	Mild flavor, tender flesh	Butterfish, mullet
Cod	Very low	Mild flavor, tender-firm flesh	Haddock, pike, pollock, sea bass, sea trout, striped bass
Croaker	Low	Mild flavor, tender flesh	Porgy, spot

Type	Fat Content	Flavor and Texture	Substitutes
		SELECTING FISH	
Flounder	Low	Delicate flavor, tender flesh	Ocean perch, sole, turbot, whiting
Grouper	Low	Mild flavor, tender-firm flesh	Mahimahi, red snapper, sea bass
Haddock	Low	Mild flavor, flaky, tender-chewy flesh	Carp, cod, pollock, sea trout
Halibut	Very low	Mild flavor, tender-firm flesh	Monkfish, red snapper, sea bass
Herring	High	Assertive flavor, tender flesh	Mackerel, shad
Kingfish	Medium	Assertive flavor, firm flesh	Salmon
Lingcod	Very low	Delicate flavor, tender flesh	Ocean perch
Lotte		See Monkfish.	
Mackerel	High	Rich, assertive flavor, fine-textured flesh	Bluefish, herring
Mahimahi	Very low	Mild, sweet flavor, tender, flaky flesh	Grouper
Monkfish	Low	Mild flavor, firm, meat-like flesh	Halibut, lobster
Mullet	Medium	Mild flavor, tender flesh	Butterfish, whitefish
Ocean perch	Very low	Mild flavor, tender, flaky flesh	Flounder, lingcod, sole, striped bass, turbot
Orange roughy	Medium	Mild, distinctive flavor, tender-firm flesh	Cod, flounder, sea bass, sole
Pike	Low	Mild flavor, firm flesh	Cod, sea trout, whitefish
Pollock	Low	Full flavor, tender-firm flesh	Cod, haddock, sea trout

SELECTING FISH

Type	Fat Content	Flavor and Texture	Substitutes
Pompano	Medium	Rich, distinctive flavor, firm flesh	Tuna
Porgy	Low	Mild flavor, tender, flaky flesh	Croaker, spot
Ray	Low	Delicate, distinctive flavor, gelatinous texture	——
Red snapper	Low	Mild flavor, tender-firm flesh	Grouper, halibut, sea bass, striped bass
Rockfish		See Striped bass.	
Sablefish	Medium to high	Buttery, mild flavor, very soft, melting flesh	——
Salmon	Medium	Rich, distinctive flavor, tender-firm flesh	Kingfish, sturgeon, swordfish
Scup		See Porgy.	
Sea bass	Low	Mild flavor, tender flesh	Cod, grouper, halibut, red snapper
Shad	Medium	Mild flavor, soft flesh	Herring
Shad roe	High	Strong flavor, firm, meat-like consistency	Fresh roe from flounder, herring, weakfish or other fish
Shark	Low	Assertive flavor, firm, meat-like flesh	Sturgeon, swordfish, tuna
Skate		See Ray.	
Smelt	Low to medium	Rich flavor, tender-firm flesh	——
Sole	Low	Delicate flavor, tender flesh	Flounder, ocean perch, orange roughy, turbot, whiting
Spot	Low	Mild flavor, tender flesh	Porgy, croaker

		SELECTING FISH	
Type	**Fat Content**	**Flavor and Texture**	**Substitutes**
Striped bass	Low to medium	Mild flavor, tender-firm flesh	Cod, ocean perch, red snapper
Sturgeon	High	Assertive flavor, firm flesh	Salmon, shark
Swordfish	Medium	Rich, distinctive flavor, firm, meat-like flesh	Salmon, shark, tuna
Trout: Lake	High	Mild flavor, firm flesh	Mullet
Rainbow	High	Mild, sweet flavor, firm flesh	Catfish
Sea	Low	Mild flavor, tender-firm flesh	Cod, haddock, pike, pollock
Tuna	Medium	Rich flavor, soft flesh, firm when cooked	Pompano, swordfish
Tilefish		See Sea bass.	
Turbot	Low	Mild flavor, tender, soft, flaky flesh	Flounder, ocean perch, sole
Whitebait		See Smelt.	
Whitefish	Medium	Delicate flavor, tender flesh	Mullet
Whiting	Low	Mild, delicate flavor, tender, flaky flesh	Flounder, sole

Very Low: Less than 2% fat
Low: 2 to 5% fat
Moderate: 6 to 9% fat
High: 10% fat and above

FLOUR: All flour is not the same. I wish I had known that when I started out baking. Some is made from soft wheat, some from hard. **Soft wheat,** grown in the southern states, makes wonderful, tender biscuits but, because it doesn't have much gluten, doesn't stretch well—which is what yeast needs. **Hard wheat** is grown in the rest of the U.S. It

Protein Content of Flours

Instant	1%
Cake	2 - 6%
Pastry	7 - 9%
All-purpose:	
National brands	10 - 11%
Southern brands	2 - 6%
Bread	11 - 12%
Semolina or durum	12.3% and up

is strong enough to stand the stretching and rising of yeast, but doesn't bake up as tender. Soft wheat flour weighs less and absorbs less liquid than hard wheat flour. This is why bread recipes give you an approximate rather than a specific amount of flour. (See p. 182 for more about moisture in flour.)

Cake flour is made from *soft* wheat, **bread flour** from *hard*, and **all-purpose** is a mix of the two.

So how do know you have the right flour for the recipe? Cake and bread flour are no problem since their name tells what they do. But how do you know whether you've got hard or soft all-purpose flour? Easy. It's on the package. Hardness and softness are a matter of protein content. The more protein, the harder the flour. And every package lists its protein content. See the box for guidance.

What flours do what:

Biscuits and cakes are lightest when made with soft wheat flour, bread does best with hard wheat. So millers have come up with **all-purpose flour**: a compromise mix of hard and soft, designed to do everything. Like most compromises, it doesn't do any one thing quite as well as the flour made for the purpose. There is no standard formula for the mix. Nationally distributed brands, designed with bread bakers in mind, have a high percentage of hard wheat; regional southern brands, designed for the biscuit baker, are mostly soft—little different from cake flour.

A savvy southern cook gave me this excellent advice. Make a geographical match between all-purpose flour and recipe. General recipes are written for a hard wheat mix, so when you bake from those, use nationally distributed brands of all-purpose. When you use native southern recipes, which assume a soft wheat mix, use a regional southern all-purpose flour. Non-southerners can substitute cake flour.

All flour is aged, usually artificially by bleaching, to strengthen the protein and give it longer shelf life. **Bleached flour** is whiter and perhaps bakes up a bit fluffier. **Unbleached flour**, which is aged naturally, has better flavor. It's excellent for pastry, making a tender, easy to handle dough.

Bread flour is mostly hard wheat. It makes a light, high, stretchy loaf, but it doesn't taste quite as good as soft wheat flour. French bread flour, with its high percentage of soft wheat, has a lovely taste. When I make French-style breads, which don't need to rise so high, I use unbleached all-purpose instead of bread flour. Some cooks I know soften their flour for French bread even more, using 2 to 2½ parts unbleached all-purpose to 1 part cake flour.

Cake flour is mostly soft wheat. It makes the tenderest cookies, cakes, biscuits and the like—things that don't need to do so much stretching when they rise.

Instant (granular) flour is processed so it won't lump when you mix it with cold water. It's ideal for lump-free sauces and gravies. It makes a gorgeous crisp coating on fried food and many cooks swear by it for crepes and food-processor pastry. In general, you can't substitute it for all-purpose flour, but there's a new instant flour on the market which was developed for baking and has a higher protein content.

Non-wheat flours. There are lots of these! See the chart on the next page for descriptions.

Pastry flour is used for flaky doughs like croissant, Danish, puff pastry and pie crust, where you need enough tenderness and elasticity to support all the buttery layers but not enough to make the dough rubbery. Unfortunately it's available mostly in the South, and is not as common there as it once was. In the rest of the U.S. you can often find it in health food stores. See p. 267 for some good, workable substitutes.

Self-rising flour, which is flour with added baking powder and salt, is used for cookies, cakes and biscuits. It's sold exclusively in the south. To make your own see p. 267.

Whole wheat and graham flour are terms used interchangeably, although technically whole wheat flour is a little more finely ground than graham. You can substitute

Substituting Whole Wheat Flour

In **pastry**, substitute whole wheat for *half* of the all-purpose flour and let the dough rest 5 minutes before you work it.

In **pancakes, waffles, dough-nuts** and **crepes**, substitute it for three-fourths of the all-purpose flour and increase the liquid slightly.

In **bread** and **pasta**, you can substitute whole wheat for *all* the bread, all-purpose or durum flour. It will make a more crumbly dough, so add a little more water and an extra egg yolk. Let the dough rest before kneading or rolling out.

To make oat flour, whirl rolled
oats in the blender until fine.

it for part of the all-purpose flour in a recipe. How
much you use depends on what you make (see box on
p. 25). When you add whole wheat flour to cakes and
breads you often have to bake them a little longer.

For more help in substituting one type of flour for
another, see p. 266.

❧ NON-WHEAT FLOURS ❧

You can use non-wheat flours for part of the wheat flour in most recipes. The third column
in the chart shows you how much of the wheat flour in a recipe may be replaced.

Type	Description	Substitute Per Cup
Barley	Nutty, malty flavor.	3 T
Brown rice	Has rice bran and germ, nuttier flavor than white rice flour.	4 T
Buckwheat	Earthy flavor.	4 T
Corn	Don't confuse with cornstarch or British cornflour, which is cornstarch. Slightly sweet flavor.	4 T
Millet	Nutty, slightly sweet flavor.	4 T
Oat	Sweet, earthy flavor. Lengthens keeping time of loaf.	5 T
Potato (Potato starch)	Primarily a thickener for sauces, but doesn't hold up over long periods or tolerate temperatures over 170°. Used for cakes and cookies in specific recipes.	——
Rye, dark and medium	Dark rye flour has bran; medium sometimes does. Both have light, full-bodied, bitter, slightly sour flavor.	Medium: 11 T Dark: All
Soy, Soya	Soy flour is made from raw beans, soya from lightly toasted beans. Slightly sweet, musty flavor. Improves keeping quality of loaf.	4 T

Non-Wheat Flours		
Type	Description	Substitute Per Cup
Triticale	A hybrid developed by crossing wheat and rye. Nutty, wheat-like taste, slightly sweet and slightly bitter.	All
White rice	Absorbs more liquid and absorbs it more slowly than wheat flour, so add extra liquid and increase mixing time. Slightly sweet flavor.	4 T

FRUIT, CANDIED: When you bake with candied fruit you have to first remove the sugar coating or the fruit will sink. Rinse it under cold water or steam it for 5 minutes in a strainer over (not touching) boiling water. Pat very dry. **Candied mixed peels** are recipe ready and don't need washing.

FRUIT, FRESH: The best way to ripen mangoes, avocados, pineapple, persimmons, peaches, quince, tomatoes, etc., is to put them in a paper bag with a lot of little holes punched in it (the holes let out the ripening gas), close tightly and store at room temperature. To speed ripening, add an apple. It gives off ethylene gas, a ripener.

GARLIC: The entire garlic bulb is called a *head*, and each section of the head is called a *clove*. (My Indian friends call it a "toe".)

The strength of garlic's flavor is determined by whether and how you cut and cook it. For very mild (and surprisingly sweet) flavor, cook or roast garlic whole, long and slow. For slightly more flavor, cook it in liquid. For medium flavor, sauté it just enough to soften and barely color. For pungent flavor use raw or sauté to a deep gold. (Warning: cooked darker than that it will taste bitter.)

To peel easily, lay the side of your knife blade on the clove and whack it with your fist. Peel.

❖❖❖

Controlling Garlic's Pungency

Mildest: Leave whole and roast or cook long and slow. Chop coarsely and cook in liquid.

Medium: Chop fine. Sauté just enough to soften but not color.

Strong: Crush with the flat of a knife blade.

Stronger: Crush peeled clove in garlic press.

Strongest: Crush *unpeeled* clove in garlic press. Sauté to a deep gold. Or use raw.

❖❖❖

To keep garlic from sticking to the knife, use some of the recipe's salt when you chop it.

Indian friends who use a lot of garlic often peel several bulbs of garlic cloves and refrigerate them, covered with oil, in a tightly covered glass jar. This also gives you a wonderful garlic-flavored oil to add to dishes. When you use it, remember to top the jar up with more oil.

Or turn garlic into garlic oil. Purée 10 to 15 garlic cloves with ½ cup olive oil in the blender or processor. It will keep several weeks stored tightly covered in the fridge. Brush it on food before you roast or grill, add it to stews, soups, vinaigrettes or marinades or use it to punch up a dish that still needs something.

GELATIN: There are two forms: powdered, the kind we generally use, and leaf, brittle sheets available at specialty stores and bakery supplies. Many European recipes call for leaf gelatin. Professionals use it because it has a purer flavor and makes a clearer gelatin. You can use the two interchangeably. One package (1 tablespoon) powdered gelatin equals 4 sheets. Before being added to any mixture, gelatin must be softened and melted. See p. 73 for details.

Gelatin dishes keep nicely for 2 to 3 days. However, they are really at their best during the first 12 hours because gelatin stiffens as it ages. If a gelatin dish is more than 12 hours old, let it sit at room temperature for 30 minutes before serving to soften it up.

Don't freeze gelatin dishes. They crystallize, separate and weep.

GINGER ROOT: Wrapped in plastic it keeps for 6 weeks in the fridge, indefinitely in the freezer. Immersed in sherry in a tightly covered jar, it will keep in the refrigerator indefinitely and give you a delightful, flavored sherry to cook with. Remember to top it up after you use the sherry.

However you store ginger, just grate off what you need —no need to peel it—from the fresh or frozen root and return the root to fridge or freezer.

Quick Hint

An envelope of unflavored gelatin is enough to jell 2 cups of fruit juice or other liquid, or to give a jellied consistency to 3 cups of soup.

Recipe

Ginger Chicken

Make a paste of ginger root and garlic (4 parts ginger to 1 part garlic), and rub it into a split broiler that has been seasoned with salt and pepper. Place the broiler skin-up in a pan, dot with butter and pour on ½ cup heavy cream. Bake covered at 400° for 20 minutes, then uncovered at 350° for 30 minutes more. Baste a couple times. Marvelous!
Serves 4.

Oriental markets sell beautiful little porcelain graters made just for ginger. Mine is white and shaped like a fish. They have raised bumps instead of knuckle-shredding holes. Cut ginger across the fibers and rub that edge against the grater. The long, coarse fibers that run the length of the root will stay with the piece in your hand. Neat. If you cut ginger lengthwise and grate the long side, you end up with a lot of stringy chunks.

Ginger Grater

I learned this Thai trick from a friend. Soak grated ginger root in cold water for 10 minutes, squeeze dry and use. The resulting ginger has a lovely, delicate flavor—pungent, but no fiery harshness.

If you want to flavor with ginger juice, here's an easy way to get it. Thaw a piece of frozen root. It will be soft and you can squeeze out the juice with your fingers.

GRAINS, TO COOK: See chart below.

❦ COOKING GRAINS ❦

All amounts and directions are for 1 cup of grain.

Use 1 teaspoon salt for each cup of grain. When water boils, reduce heat to a temperature that keeps the grain simmering and cover if directed.

Don't always use the traditional method given on the chart below; try cooking buckwheat, bulgur, barley, and millet *pilaf* fashion. In the pan it will cook in, sauté the grain for 3 to 5 minutes in 1 tablespoon butter or oil per cup of grain. (I like to add a minced onion and 4 ounces sliced mushrooms, both sautéed.) Add boiling beef, chicken or vegetable stock instead of water, cover and simmer on top of the stove or bake at 350°, using timing from the chart.

Type	Liquid in Cups	Directions for Cooking	Yield in Cups
Barley, pearl	4	Add to boiling water. Simmer covered 45 minutes. Drain if necessary.	3
Barley, quick cooking	1⅔	Add to boiling water. Simmer covered 10 to 12 minutes.	2½

COOKING GRAINS

Type	Liquid in Cups	Directions for Cooking	Yield in Cups
Bulgur	1½	Add to cold water, bring to a boil, cover, simmer 10 to 12 minutes.	3
Cornmeal (Polenta)	3 (firm) 4 (soft)	Add to cold water, bring to a boil, stirring constantly. Lower heat and cook uncovered for 15 minutes. Stir often.	3 4
Farina, quick cooking	5⅓	Add to boiling water, simmer, stirring constantly, for 2 to 3 minutes.	6
Hominy grits, quick cooking	4	Add to boiling water, simmer uncovered, stirring occasionally, for 5 minutes.	4⅔
Kasha (Buckwheat groats)	1½	Add to cold water, bring to a boil, cover, simmer 10 to 12 minutes. *Or* in ungreased skillet mix 2 cups buckwheat with 1 beaten egg. Cook over high heat, stirring, for 2 minutes. Add 1½ cups boiling water, cover, simmer 12 to 15 minutes.	2
Millet	2⅔	Add to boiling water, simmer covered 15 to 20 minutes. Let stand covered for 5 minutes.	4
Oats, rolled, quick cooking	2	Add to boiling water. Simmer 1 minute, stirring occasionally. Let stand off heat, covered, for 3 minutes.	1¾
Oats, rolled, regular	2	Add to boiling water. Simmer uncovered 5 to 7 minutes. Cover, let stand off heat for 3 minutes.	1¾
Oats, steel cut	2½	Add to boiling water. Simmer covered 20 to 25 minutes.	3
Quinoa	2	Rinse well. Add to boiling water. Simmer covered 12 to 15 minutes.	2¾
Rice		See chart on page 47	

		COOKING GRAINS		
Type	Liquid in Cups	Directions for Cooking		Yield in Cups
Rye berries	3⅓	Add to boiling water, simmer covered 1 to 1¼ hrs. Check as it cooks, adding more water if it gets dry. If it is still wet when done, drain well.		3
Triticale	3⅓	Add to boiling water, simmer covered 1 to 1¼ hrs. Check as it cooks, adding more water if it gets dry. If it is still wet when done, drain well.		3
Wheat, cracked	2¼	Add to cold water, bring to a boil, cover and simmer 30 to 50 minutes, depending on the coarseness of the grain. Let stand off heat, covered, for 5 minutes.		3¾
Wheat berries	3⅓	Add to boiling water, simmer 45 to 60 minutes. Drain.		3

GRAPEFRUIT: See Oranges and Grapefruit.

GREEN PEPPERCORNS: The ones packed in brine are better than those packed in vinegar. The vinegar can overwhelm the taste.

HAM: Ready-to-eat hams, especially canned ones, taste much better if you've given them a thorough heating in a 325° oven—even if you plan to serve them cold. Take canned hams out of the can before heating. Place whole hams fat-side up and half ones cut-side down in a shallow dish. Roast to an internal temperature of 130° or use the timing chart on p. 135.

Because country hams have been cured and aged, they are safe to eat when you buy them. Still, they're so hard and salty that most people prefer to soak and cook them first. The ones sold in supermarkets always come with directions.

— *Recipe Idea* —

Shave the Ham

Try eating your unsoaked country ham as is sometime. Shave off paper-thin slices and eat them like you would prosciutto: with melon or figs or on crusty bread with tomatoes and mozzarella.

Which Onion Should I Chose?

Bermuda: Large, usually white, slightly flat. Mild, delicate. Good raw in salads and sandwiches.

Red or Italian: Purple-red. Sweet, mild. Best used raw in salads, sandwiches, marinades.

Yellow Globe: Brown, medium size, round. The strongest flavored onion. This is the standard cooking onion. Long cooking caramelizes it and turns it sweet.

Spanish: Golden brown, round, very large. Stronger than the Bermuda, but still mild, sweet, juicy. Use for salads, sandwiches, fried onion rings. Good stuffed or baked. Not as good as a Globe for long-cooked dishes.

White: ("Silverskin") Small, strong-flavored. Use whole in soups, stews, creamed onions.

HAMBURGER: Expensive, lean ground beef does not necessarily make the best hamburgers. A good American hamburger needs about 15% fat if it's going to be moist and taste good. I could never make good hamburgers abroad until I learned to ask the butcher to grind in a little extra fat. Surprisingly, tests show that burgers, if they've been drained on paper towels, end up with about the same amount of fat after cooking no matter how much they started with.

Meat loaf, meatballs and stuffing mixtures are quite another matter, since here a pan or starchy filler holds in the fat. In this case you want your meat very lean—no more than 5 to 10% fat.

HERBS: To store fresh herbs, wash and dry carefully, place in a tightly closed jar and refrigerate. Parsley will keep up to 2 weeks; other herbs a week to 10 days.

To freeze them, do as above but dry *very well* so they don't stick together when they freeze. Pack airtight in plastic.

The microwave is the easiest way **to dry herbs.** Wash and dry 2 cups of loosely packed leaves or sprigs. Scatter them in an even layer on a double layer of paper toweling. Microwave uncovered on *high* for 4 minutes. Store tightly covered.

HOMINY GRITS, TO COOK: See p. 30.

IMITATION FOODS: There are many imitation products on the market now. If you decide to *cook* with them, remember you are sailing in uncharted territory—especially when baking. "Lite" butter, mayo and sour cream and no-fat sour cream and mayonnaise may not react like the real thing. Imitation cheese and chocolate melt and set up differently from the real stuff. If your recipe doesn't require cooking, you'll have fewer problems, but be prepared for differences in taste and texture. Remember, fat carries flavor, so the light versions have had to make a lot of compromises.

JERUSALEM ARTICHOKES (SUNCHOKES): Don't bother trying to peel these knobby little fists. You'll just frustrate yourself and use up time better spent on the tennis court. The peels are edible. Just scrub well.

LEEKS: The best ones have bright green tops and medium-size stalks; big ones can be woody and tasteless. I've found their quality is better during the cool months. Leeks are sandy and can be gritty. Here's the way to wash them: Trim off the root end and the dark green leaves. Split the leek, starting at the leaf end, to within a half inch of the root end. Push the layers apart slightly and wash under running water.

LEMONS: Rough skins are easier to grate, but smooth lemons have more juice. Room temperature lemons give the most juice. You can get even more if you soften the uncut lemon by rolling it on the counter while pressing down firmly. Or soften it this way: microwave the whole lemon on high for 10 to 20 seconds. If you need only a few drops of juice, try this chef's trick: stab the uncut lemon with a toothpick and squeeze out what you need.

Buy lots of lemons when they're cheapest and freeze them whole. Once thawed they're soft and the juice presses out easily.

MARGARINE: My niece who, for health reasons, had switched from butter to margarine phoned last Christmas to say her butter cookies weren't working right. She had run into the consequences of margarine having a different shortening power from butter. Most of the time recipes will work out fine with either. But, especially in baking, there are occasions when the difference matters. For instance, margarine can change the delicate balance of butter cakes and the consistency of croissant, puff and Danish pastry doughs, butter cookies and toffee. Most baking recipes indicate whether you can substitute margarine. If the recipe doesn't say you can, you may encounter some problems.

Cleaning Leeks

1

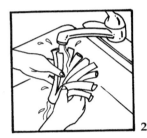

2

TECHNIQUE

Boning Tips

Boning sounds difficult, but it's not. Just think through what you want to accomplish, then:

- Use a very sharp, pointed knife.

- Keep the blade against the bone to avoid cutting into the flesh or skin.

- Locate the bones with the knife point.

- Scrape, don't cut, meat away from the bones.

- To help you see what you are doing, use your fingers to pull the meat away from the bones as you work.

- Use a sawing motion; don't use force.

The basic rule when baking with margarine is to use the hard variety. Diet or soft margarines are puffed with air and water, have less fat and never work properly in recipes.

MEAT: If you're looking for a tender cut of meat, here's your rule: The front half of the animal works hardest and is the least tender. Meat from the lazy rear end is more tender; meat along the spine is tenderest of all.

When you store meat in the fridge, remove the store wrapping. Don't wash the meat, just wrap it loosely, leaving it as flat as possible.

Partially frozen meat is easy to slice thin for scallopini and stir-fries.

To flatten meat for scallopini, place it between sheets of plastic wrap and whack gently with the flat side of a cleaver or the bottom of a small pan or skillet.

See also Ham and Hamburger, and Chapter 4 for help with cooking meat.

MELONS: The seeds hold in moisture, so don't remove them until near serving time.

MILK: What's the difference between evaporated and condensed milk? A lot of people get them confused. **Evaporated** has had the water taken out—that's all. **Condensed** has lost the water and also had sugar added, making it a thick, heavy syrup.

Don't let unused milk go sour. If you don't use milk often or in large quantities, divide the quart into 3 or 4 parts. Keep one part in the refrigerator to use right away and freeze the rest. Thawed milk is fine for cooking; give it about 4 hours to defrost in the refrigerator.

Another way to keep fresh milk on hand is to use **extended-life milk.** Give it a try if you haven't already. I got used to this milk-on-the-shelf when we lived in Africa and was delighted to find it on the grocery shelves here. It keeps for months without refrigeration, comes in both low- and full-fat varieties, and tastes good enough to use on your cereal.

MILLET, TO COOK: See p. 30.

MUSHROOMS: Use your egg slicer to slice a few quickly. The freshest mushrooms have tops tightly curled under; if you can see the gills underneath, the mushrooms are old. Don't scorn old mushrooms. They are wonderful for soups and dishes where you want a strong flavor. Freeze mushrooms, either raw or sautéed, to have them recipe-ready.

To use dried mushrooms, wash them to get out the sand, then soak in warm or hot water to cover for about 30 minutes. Don't discard the soaking liquid. It's loaded with flavor. Strain it through a sieve lined with a coffee filter or damp cheesecloth (it's usually sandy), and add to your dish. If you want only a rich mushroom flavor, soak dried mushrooms for at least 2 hours and use the liquid *instead* of the mushrooms, which will have given their all by then.

NOODLES: In general, you cook American noodles and all pastas according to box directions, although it's a good idea to start checking for doneness a little early.

If your recipe calls for one of the Oriental noodles, you may have problems because so many are packaged with no cooking directions. Here are descriptions and instructions for handling some of the most popular kinds.

Cellophane noodles (also called mung bean noodles, glass noodles, bean threads, bean starch noodles, transparent noodles or silver threads) are brittle, translucent and off-white. How to use: Soften by soaking in warm water for 10 minutes, drain, then mix into a stir-fried dish or pour hot soup over them.

Chinese egg noodles come in various thicknesses but are usually very fine. How to use: Drop them in soups or cook them *al dente* as you would pasta. Add the cooked noodles to stir-fried dishes at the last minute—or make them into a crunchy-edged pancake and top it with a meat or vegetable combo. See the box. You can substitute any thin Italian egg pasta for Chinese egg noodles.

Recipe

A Gorgeous Caramel Frosting

Put ½ cup condensed milk, ½ cup butter, ⅓ cup sugar and 2 tablespoons light corn syrup in a small pan and boil over low heat, stirring constantly, until a deep gold color—about 15 minutes. The darker it gets the chewier the frosting. Cool to spreading consistency.

Enough frosting to fill or top an 8" cake.

Recipe

Chinese Noodle Pancake

Cook and drain 1 pound of Chinese noodles and fry in a big cake over low heat in 2 tablespoons of oil. When the bottom is lightly browned, turn and brown the second side. The outside noodles will be crunchy, the inside ones soft. Ummmm. If you like, top with a stir-fry sauce.

RULE OF THUMB

When recipes call for nut pieces, how big should they be? A *broken* nut is about ⅓", *coarsely cut* about ¼", and *chopped* means just that.

Recipe

Oatcakes

We made these in Africa when nostalgia for the Scots ones got too strong.

Mix 1 c flour, ½ t baking powder, ½ t salt, 1 t sugar and 1½ c rolled oats. Rub in ½ c butter until crumbly. In a little bowl beat 1 egg with 2 T water. Add and work to a stiff dough. Roll out—not too thin—on lightly floured board, cut into 2- or 3-inch circles. Bake on a greased baking sheet at 400° for 12 minutes. Serve hot with butter, cream cheese and jam and a pot of hot coffee or tea.

Yield: 30 to 36

Rice vermicelli are thin, brittle and whitish. To use: soak as for cellophane noodles, then give them a quick boil (2 to 3 minutes). **Rice sticks,** the thicker version of rice vermicelli, and the big, 1- or 2-inch square **rice noodles** need to soak 15 instead of 10 minutes before the quick boil.

Some Oriental noodles, like dry (unsoaked) cellophane or rice noodles, can be fried. When you put them in hot oil they whoosh up into huge, crispy puffs. Once you've opened a package of these noodles, store them tightly covered. If they absorb moisture from the air they won't puff.

You can substitute very fine egg noodles for both cellophane and rice noodles in soups or stir-fried dishes, but you can't fry them dry—they won't puff.

NUTS: To get rid of bits of shell, dump shelled nuts into a bowl of cool water, then pour off the water along with the floating shell bits. Dry well.

To remove **pecans and walnuts** from their shells whole, cover nuts with boiling water and let stand until cold. Crack the nuts with a nut cracker—end-to-end.

To remove skins from almonds, blanch them by covering with boiling water. Let stand for 5 minutes, then drain and pop off the skins. If you're working with a lot, keep them damp because once dry the skins glue back on.

To remove skins from hazelnuts, toast for 10 to 15 minutes, cool slightly, and rub between your fingers or in a kitchen towel.

Toasting gives nuts a rich flavor. Skin them if necessary, then either spread in a single layer on a baking sheet and toast in a 350° oven for 3 to 5 minutes, or stir in a dry, heavy skillet over low burner heat for 2 or 3 minutes. Whichever method you use, *watch closely.* Be ready to snatch them out the minute they start to color.

Oats: Rolled oats are the same as oatmeal. In a recipe "rolled oats" usually refers to the old-fashioned ones that take longer to cook. However, you can use old-fashioned and quick-cooking interchangeably. To cook, see p. 30. To make flour, see p. 26.

OIL: Store oil in a cool place away from light. **Oriental sesame oil,** which is made from toasted seeds, keeps indefinitely. (See p. 245 for comments on sesame oil.) **Nut oils** (almond, hazelnut, walnut) lose flavor quickly after they are opened. They also go rancid quickly. So buy them in small amounts and store in the fridge. Do try the nut oils. They're light, sweet and delicate—a treat in salads or tossed with hot vegetables instead of butter. Buy other oils in amounts that you will use up in several months.

Virgin olive oil has a lower acidity than other olive oil. Oil from second and subsequent pressings has some fruit pulp in it and burns more readily. Virgin or extra-virgin oil is usually best for cooking; other olive oils, which have more flavor, are good in salads and uncooked dishes.

OLIVES: Pit olives with a cherry pitter, if you have one. When they are too large for this (as the fat, black Greek ones might be), place them on a paper towel or wax paper and roll gently with a rolling pin. A press with the heel of your hand will pop the pit.

That lacy white scum that sometimes forms on olive brine is harmless.

If you find that your oil-cured olives are too bitter to use in a recipe, simmer them in water for 10 minutes or so to gentle the taste.

ONIONS: The notes under Garlic on how cutting and cooking affect flavor apply to onions as well. Also see the box.

Unless otherwise specified, when a recipe says "onion" it means a round, yellow onion.

If the onions you want to serve raw are too strong, all is not lost. You can mute their flavor by soaking them for an hour in sweetened cold water (1 teaspoon sugar per cup of water). Drain and pat dry before using.

Everyone has a pet way to prevent tears when cutting onions. I know a cook who holds a kitchen match between his teeth which, if it doesn't stop the tears, at least gives him a rakish look while he weeps. Another friend puts onions in the freezer for 15 minutes before cutting them.

Controlling Onions' Pungency

Mildest:	Leave whole and roast or cook long and slow. Chop coarsely and cook in liquid.
Medium:	Slice thin or chop small. Sauté just enough to soften but not color.
Strong:	Grate or chop super fine. Sauté to a deep gold. Use raw.

Recipe

A Nifty Onion Relish

Slice 2 large onions thin and put them in a screw top jar with ⅓ cup olive oil, 3 tablespoons vinegar and a teaspoon of anchovy paste. Shake well and let marinate at least an hour. Especially good heaped on ham or beef in sandwiches.

Instant Pasta

I always keep a box of capellini on hand. I like the way the mesh of thin strands sponges up the sauce; even better, it cooks in about 3 minutes! Perfect for the night when dinner's about ready and you suddenly realize it needs a starch.

Quick Hint

When you hold pasta for saucing at table, how do you keep it from sticking in nasty clumps? While the pasta cooks, warm the serving bowl and melt a tablespoon or two of butter or olive oil in the bottom. Add pasta and toss. Or grate the butter on top and toss. Then grind on a little pepper, grate on some Parmesan (maybe ¼ cup) and toss again.

Then there's the Mexican I encountered who chops a little first and sticks it on her head! Do what works for you.

When onions sprout, they start drying out, the layers separate, and the onions lose flavor. *But* the green sprouts are tasty. Use them instead of chives or green onions.

Potatoes and onions give off gases that mold each other. Don't store them together.

ORANGES AND GRAPEFRUIT: An easy way to peel them and get rid of the white membranes is to pour boiling water over the fruit before peeling and let it stand 5 minutes off the heat. *Caution:* If you plan to grate the peel, remember to do that first!

PASTA: The pasta with the finest flavor and texture is made with 100% semolina (Italian imports) or durum wheat (American pasta). Check the package when you buy.

Dried vs. fresh: Most pasta lovers don't find any difference between fresh pasta and the better brands of dried. The two cook differently, however. Fresh pasta absorbs more sauce and takes on a bit more flavor. It expands less when it cooks, so prepare about a fourth more. Finally, it cooks a lot faster than dried, so start checking after only a minute or two.

Whole wheat pasta has a lovely texture and flavor. Give it a try. But never use egg noodles in pasta dishes. You'll be disappointed if you do.

Suit your pasta to the sauce. Delicate butter and cream based sauces go well with fresh pasta because they let the pasta flavor come through. Team tangy tomato and sturdy meat sauces with sturdy pastas: spaghetti, mostaccioli, rigatoni or rotini.

Fettuccine or linguine are good with cream and butter based sauces, herb sauces and light tomato sauces because they offer so much clinging surface. Clam and other seafood sauces seem to go best with thin pasta like linguine, thin spaghetti, capellini and vermicelli.

Sauces with chunky ingredients need a pasta that catches the chunks. Try shells, rotini, elbows, wagon wheels or rigatoni with these. Pasta size should suit ingredient size: match small shells, elbows or tubes with peas and small vegetable pieces; pair rigatoni or mostaccioli with big chunks like broccoli flowers.

Some pastas improve if they steep in the sauce for a few minutes. Add pastas with hollow centers, holes, or indentations to the sauce in the pan, toss lightly using two forks, then let sit over low heat for 2 to 3 minutes to absorb the flavor. Lovely.

Pasta dishes made with cream and vegetable bits are also better if you mix them before serving. Just before they go to table, spoon some of the solids on top.

When I serve **long, solid pastas** like spaghetti with chunky sauces, I don't sauce them ahead because the good stuff always slides off the strands and not everyone gets a fair share. It's best to have diners sauce their own at table so no one is slighted.

See also Noodles and, for cooking help, p. 87.

PEAS: To test whether peas are fresh, rub two pods together. They should squeak.

PEPPERS, CHILE: When you work with a quantity of hot peppers, wear gloves to protect your hands from burns; they can be serious! Even when you are cutting a single pepper, keep your hands away from your face. I once rubbed an eye and it was blinded for several minutes.

To tone down the heat of hot peppers remove the seeds and membrane, which are the heat producers. Gentle them even further by soaking the trimmed peppers in water for an hour or parboiling them for 5 minutes.

To prepare dried peppers for use in a recipe, toast them briefly in a dry skillet or on a griddle, turning once or twice, until fragrant. Remove stems and seeds and tear peppers into pieces. If the recipe calls for using them dry, they are now ready to grind. For sauces, chiles are usually simmered or soaked in hot liquid until soft (30 minutes to an hour), then puréed in some of their soaking liquid.

Recipe

Pasta with Four Cheeses

This pasta dish is rich and silky, pure heaven on the tongue. Cook 1 lb. pasta, al dente. Drain and set aside. In a heavy saucepan over low heat, melt 6 tablespoons butter. Stir in 3 ounces Fontina cheese, 3 ounces Gorgonzola cheese, 3 ounces Bel Paese cheese and ¼ teaspoon white pepper. Cook and stir over low heat until cheeses have melted (do not boil). Stir in 1¼ cups whipping cream and ⅔ cup Parmesan cheese. Heat through. Toss the hot pasta with the sauce until coated. Serves 4.

RESCUE

Meltdown!

You've bitten into a hot pepper, your mouth is on fire, your eyes are streaming—**Don't Reach For Water!** It will act like a blowtorch. A bite of banana, bread or rice is what you want. Yogurt, as Indians know, will also damp the flames.

🌶 CHILE PEPPER VARIETIES 🌶

Type	Description	Hotness
Fresh		
Anaheim	Slender, elongated; light green color	Mild
Cubanel	Looks like an Anaheim, but not as flavorful.	Mild
Fresno	Small, slender; green to greenish red	Very, very hot
Green	See Anaheim.	
Habanero (also dried)	Yellow, round	Pure fire
Hungarian wax	Medium length; turns from yellow to salmon to red.	Hot
Jalapeño	Short, fat, oval; green to reddish green	Hot to very hot
Korean	Slender, elongated; green or red	Medium-hot
New Mexico	See Anaheim.	
Poblano	Long, irregular bell-pepper shape; deep green	Mild to medium-hot
Scotch bonnet	Lantern shape, yellow	Very, very hot
Serrano	Tiny, slender; deep green sometimes ripening to red	Very, very hot
Thai (also dried)	Very small, elongated; red or green	Very hot
Yellow banana	Short, fat, oval; pale yellow	Very hot
Dried		
Ancho	Dried poblano; dark reddish brown	Mild to medium-hot

CHILE PEPPER VARIETIES		
Type	Description	Hotness
Cascabel	Small, round; fairly smooth skin; dark red	Medium-hot to hot
Cayenne	Tiny, narrow; red; usually sold ground	Very hot
Chipotle	Smoked and dried jalapeño; wrinkled skin; dull reddish-brown	Hot
de Arbol	Long, thin; red	Very hot
Pasilla (Chile negro)	Long, slender; wrinkled skin; brownish-black	Very hot
Pequin or Tepin	Tiny, round or oval; slightly wrinkled skin; orange-red	Very, very hot

PEPPERS, ALL VARIETIES, TO PEEL: Why do recipes direct you to peel peppers? To soften them and make them better able to absorb flavor. Also to get rid of those pesky bits of skin that stick to your teeth.

Peeling is no big deal and it's fun to do. Place the peppers on a foil-lined cookie sheet under the broiler in a 450° oven or lay them over the flame of a gas burner. Turn them as they char. When the skins are completely blackened and the peppers look ruined (this will take 15 to 20 minutes in the oven), they are ready. Place them in a tightly closed plastic bag and leave for at least 10 minutes. When they are cool enough to handle, remove their stems and seeds and slip off the skins. You'll be surprised how quickly this goes.

Resist the urge to rinse the peppers while peeling. That washes away flavor. If you're working with hot chiles, remember the caution to wear rubber gloves and keep your hands away from your face.

RESCUE

I Put In Too Much Hot Pepper!

If the dish is liquid, drop in a couple chunks of raw potato and simmer for 15 minutes. Remove the potato which, with luck, will have absorbed some of the fire.

Next time remove the seeds and veins of the peppers before using since they carry most of the heat. And try the trick used by some canny Mexican cooks. Soak peeled, roasted chiles in salted water for several hours. Rinse before using.

——— *Recipe* ———

Polenta Treats

For a dynamite first course, toast polenta slices under the broiler or in a 425° oven, turning once to brown both sides. Spread, hot and steaming, with Gorgonzola or another blue-veined cheese, or top with curls of canned roasted red peppers and drizzle with olive oil. Serve warm or at room temperature. Pure heaven.

A splendid supper or side dish: Stir ¾ cup grated Parmesan cheese and 3 table-spoons of butter into 3 cups hot cooked polenta. Chill, slice and place slices overlapping in a shallow baking dish. Drizzle on 3 tablespoons melted butter. Bake at 400° until browned (10 to 15 minutes). You can gild this lily by topping it with 2 cups of cheese sauce before baking—spoon it down the center of the dish. Delicious with roasts and chops.

Serves 6 as a side dish.

PIMENTOS (CANNED): An opened jar of pimentos molds quickly. Cover pimentos with vinegar or oil and they'll last a week in the fridge. For longer storage, wrap in plastic and freeze. They thaw in a few minutes.

PINEAPPLE: Contrary to what your mother taught you, pulling out a leaf tells you nothing about ripeness; leaves will pull out of any pineapple that isn't rock-hard. The best way to judge ripeness is by how sweet the pineapple smells. Another good test is to press its sides. A little give is a good sign. To ripen a pineapple further, put it in a paper bag with a lot of little holes punched in it. Close tightly and keep at room temperature.

POLENTA: Polenta is cornmeal mush Italian style. It can be soft and creamy or firm and molded. Make it according to the directions on p. 30 (see Cornmeal) and serve hot with butter and cheese. Dishes with rich gravies, like stewed or braised meat or poultry, are heavenly on polenta, as are spaghetti sauces. You can chill firm polenta, cut it in squares, and fry, broil or bake it. See the box.

POPCORN: The moisture in the kernel makes it pop. As popcorn ages, it dries and loses its kick. To ensure that yours pops, buy it where turnover is fast and store in an airtight container in the fridge. If you're stuck with corn that won't pop, soak it in water for 5 minutes, drain and try again. This often works and keeps the kids from grousing.

POTATOES: The way you store potatoes makes a big difference. Store them in a cool dark place so they don't sprout or develop greenish skins, but *never* in a plastic bag (they'll mold) and *never* in the fridge. Cold changes the starch to sugar and gives potatoes a weird, sweet taste. This, fortunately, can be reversed—return the potatoes to room temperature and the sugar will reconvert to starch. Also, don't store potatoes with onions. Each gives off a gas that rots the other.

❧ Potato Varieties ❧

Ask your produce manager about the best potato varieties in your area.

Type	Description	Basic Use
Long white	Oblong, tan skin, few eyes, mealy	All-purpose
Idaho or Russet	Long, slightly flattened cylinder, brown leathery skin, mealy	Baking
Mature (any potato left longer in the ground)	Thick skin, low moisture, mealy	Baking
New (any potato harvested young)	Thin, fragile skin, low starch, high moisture, waxy	Boiling
Round red	Smooth, thin skin, waxy	Boiling
Round white	Tannish skin, somewhat mealy	Boiling

Poultry: When you buy poultry, here are things to watch for:

Chicken and turkeys should have little visible moisture, unbroken skin, no dark patches, and plump breasts. A pliable point on the breast bone of a chicken means it's still young and tender. Poultry pieces should have little moisture and no smell.

Ducks and geese should have little moisture, light colored skin, and be plump but not too fat. A goose should have a pliable backbone. Don't let a duck's apparent size fool you; it has a lot of bone and fat. A big-looking six pounder will serve only three! Most people learn this after they serve their first duck dinner to company.

Wild game birds vary depending on their age and where they come from. Birds that have lived by the sea can taste fishy and elderly birds will turn to rubber if you roast or barbecue them. Braising is best.

Which Potato Do I Use?

Waxy, smooth-skinned potatoes and new potatoes are best for boiling, frying and using in scalloped potatoes and potato salad; **mealy, rough-skinned potatoes** are best for baking, French fries and mashed potatoes. If you're not sure which you have, rub two cut edges together. The mealy, starchy ones will froth.

❦ Selecting Poultry ❦

This chart will help you select the right bird for the recipe.

Type	Age	Size	Best Way to Cook
Chicken			
Poussin	Under 6 weeks	1 lb	Broil, grill, roast, sauté
Rock Cornish game hen	4 - 5 weeks	1 - 1½ lbs	Broil, grill, roast, sauté
Broiler	7 - 9 weeks	1½ - 2 lbs	Broil, grill, roast, sauté
Fryer	9 - 12 weeks	3 - 4 lbs	Broil, grill, fry, roast
Roaster	10 - 20 weeks	Over 5 lbs	Braise, fry, roast, stew
Capon	16 - 20 weeks	6 - 9 lbs	Roast
Stewing chicken	Over 10 months	4 - 6 lbs	Braise, stew, make stock
Turkey			
Fryer-roaster	Under 16 weeks	4 - 8 lbs	Roast
Young turkey			
Hen	14 - 22 weeks	7 - 15 lbs	Roast
Tom	14 - 22 weeks	Over 15 lbs	Roast
Mature (yearling) turkey	Over 15 months	12 - 15 lbs	Stew, make stock
Other Poultry			
Duckling	6 - 8 weeks	3 - 4½ lbs	Broil, roast
Young goose	Over 6 months	4 - 14 lbs	Roast
Pheasant	6 weeks	2 - 3 lbs	Bake, roast
Quail	Under 6 weeks	¼ - ½ lb	Broil, grill, roast, sauté
Squab	Under 6 weeks	¾ lb	Broil, grill, roast, sauté

A note on safe handling: Poultry often carries salmonella bacteria. Cooking completely destroys it, so there's no need for concern as long as you take these simple precautions: Keep raw poultry chilled. Wash your hands and anything else—the knife, the cutting board—which has touched it or that you touched before washing your hands. Make sure frozen birds are completely thawed before cooking so there are no rare spots in the done bird. Stuff poultry loosely so heat can penetrate to the center of the bird.

RAISINS: Years ago I saved the raisins left in the bottom of the Christmas Glögg bowl and used them in baking. They were sensational, but friends who begged for recipes were disconcerted when I added, "but you have to use glögg-soaked raisins." I finally came up with a solution and told them to store raisins covered with a mix of red wine and ruby port, with a clove and a cinnamon stick, in a jar. When I ran out of glögg raisins that's what I did. You can use rum or brandy if that appeals to you. These raisins are wonderful for baking and also for non-sweet recipes (Middle Eastern and Mexican dishes, for example).

RICE: Here's a guide to some common and more exotic types:

Arborio is a fat short-grain rice from Italy with a white spot on each kernel. It will absorb a sauce and become creamy without turning mushy during long cooking. Use it for risotto (see the box on the next page).

Basmati rice is imported from India, expensive, and worth every penny. When we first arrived in India I was enchanted by flavor of the rice. What I had eaten all my life was pale and starchy compared to this nutty, perfumy and utterly wonderful grain. Because it has been aged, you have to cook basmati rice a little differently. See the box.

Brown rice still has the bran layer and takes longer to cook than white.

Converted (parboiled) rice is sold under the brandname Uncle Ben's. It's long-grain rice processed to force B

RESCUE

The Raisins Are Stuck!

If raisins are stuck together, heat them for a few minutes in a 300° oven or freeze them and rub the frozen raisins between your palms.

Recipe

Basmati Rice

Wash 2 cups rice well and drain. Then soak for 30 minutes in 5 cups water with ½ teaspoon salt. Drain well. Melt 1 tablespoon butter in a heavy-bottomed pan over medium heat. Add rice and stir for 1 minute. Add 1¼ cups water and ¾ teaspoon salt. Bring to a boil, cover, and cook over *very* low heat for 20 minutes. Lift the lid and mix rice gently with a fork. Cover and cook 10 minutes more or until tender.

Recipe

Arborio Rice, Italian Style

Heat 4 cups of any stock and keep it at a low simmer. Over medium-high heat melt 4 tablespoons butter in a saucepan. Add 1¼ cups arborio rice and stir until well coated and white. Add 1 cup of hot stock and stir hard with a fork. Simmer uncovered, stirring now and then to prevent sticking, until stock is almost absorbed. Add a second cup of stock; cook and stir until it's almost absorbed. In the same way, add the remaining stock ½ cup at a time (you may not need it all). Rice will be done in about 25 to 30 minutes, but start tasting early so you stop cooking when it is creamy but still chewy-tender. Stir in 1 or 2 tablespoons of Parmesan cheese.

Note: If you add ingredients like peas, mushrooms, onions, bits of cooked meat, poultry or seafood, sauté them in the butter before adding the rice.

vitamins from the bran into the kernel before milling. It never gets sticky and may take a bit longer to cook. Same uses as long-grain.

Long-grain rice is the "Carolina rice" often called for in recipes. Cooked grains are tender, fluffy and separate. Good for salad, pilaf and all general use. Many people use it for risotto although it doesn't cook up quite as creamy.

Medium-grain rice is plumper, moister, stickier and chewier than long-grain. Use it now and then for a refreshing change. Some new varieties have a distinctive flavor. Same uses as long-grain rice. Especially good for soup.

Short-grain rice, also called pearl, round and pudding rice, is almost as wide as it is long. It has more starch than the other rices and becomes quite sticky as it cooks. Perfect for molds, puddings, paella and risotto, although the classic risotto rice is Italian arborio. See above.

Texmati rice (brown and white) is grown in the U.S. It has a nutty flavor, and is cooked like long-grain rice.

Wehani rice is a California strain of Indian basmati rice. Brownish red color, earthy flavor. Cook like brown long-grain rice.

Wild rice is actually the seed of a grass that grows in Minnesota lakes. True *wild* rice is chewy, with a very earthy flavor. The *cultivated* grains have a milder flavor and are less expensive. Wash before cooking in several changes of cold water.

Wild pecan rice is from the U. S. South. A quick cooking brown rice with an elusive pecan flavor. Cook like white long-grain rice.

This chart gives instructions for cooking the different rice varieties. If you want a fluffy texture rather than a creamy one, wash the rice before boiling.

❦ THREE WAYS TO COOK RICE ❦

Standard Method

Bring water to a boil (see below for amount, depending on kind of rice). Add 1 cup rice and 1 teaspoon salt and stir once with a fork. Reduce heat to low and cook, covered, for the amount of time given. Remove from heat and let stand, covered, for 5 minutes. Fluff with a fork.

Type	Liquid in Cups	Cooking Time in Minutes	Yield in Cups
Arborio	See p. 46.		
Basmati	See p. 45.		
Brown, long-grain	2	45 to 50	3½ to 4
Brown, short-grain	3	30 to 40	3
Converted	2	18	3½
Texmati	1½	18	3½
Wehani	1½	18	3½
White, long-grain	1½	18	3½
White, medium-grain	1½	23	3½
White, short-grain	1½	15 to 20	3
Wild	4	40 to 50*	3 to 4
Wild pecan	1½	18	3½

*Water may not be completely absorbed. If not, drain.

Chinese Method

Place 1 cup of rice in a saucepan with 2 cups *cold* salted water. Bring to a boil over high heat. Simmer uncovered over medium heat until the water evaporates down to about the level of the rice. (Fish-eye bubbles will appear on top of the rice.) Cover and turn heat to lowest setting. Cook short-, medium- or long-grain white rice 20 minutes more, long-grain brown rice 45 minutes more.

Three Ways to Cook Rice

Pilaf Method

Melt 2 tablespoons oil or half oil and half butter in a saucepan over medium heat. Add 1 cup rice, stir to coat the grains, and sauté and stir for 2 to 3 minutes until the grains turn opaque. Add amount of liquid (water or broth) shown in chart, cover, reduce heat to low. Cook for time given below. Let stand covered, off heat, for 5 minutes. Fluff with a fork.

Type	Liquid in Cups	Time in Minutes	Yield in Cups
Brown, long-grain	2	30 to 40	3½
White, long-grain	1½	15	3½
Wild	3	45 to 60	4

Quick Hint

Thump the core end of lettuce briskly on the counter and the core will twist out easily.

To slide bulky lettuce heads into plastic bags, turn the bag inside out over your hand, pick up the lettuce in that hand and pull the bag right-side out over it, the same way your mother showed you to put on pillow cases.

Rye Berries, to cook: See p. 31.

Salad Greens: The secret of perfect salads is dry greens. Dressing won't cling to wet leaves; it just pools in the bottom of the bowl and dilutes in the water that drips down. So after you wash your greens, spin them in a salad spinner and roll them in paper towels or a dish towel. Store in a tightly closed plastic bag and chill in the refrigerator for at least 1 hour so they crisp up. They will keep nicely for 4 to 5 days.

If head lettuce you've brought home from the market looks droopy, try this trick I learned from a Belgian housewife. Fill a large pan with very hot water. Plunge the lettuce in for a few seconds, drain, plunge into ice water. It works like a charm.

Walnut oil makes a delicious dressing on bitter greens like arugula, radicchio and watercress.

To know how many cups of greens you'll get per pound of leaves, see the chart on the next page.

❦ MEASURING SALAD GREENS ❦

Type	Weight in Ounces	Amount, Torn and Loosely Packed in Cups
Bulk packaged salad mix	4	6 (fluffed)
Butterhead lettuce, medium head	12	4
Curly endive, medium head	12	10
Escarole, medium head	8	7
Iceberg lettuce, medium head	18	10
Leaf lettuce, medium head	9	8
Romaine, medium head	16	6 to 8
Spinach, loose	16	12 (stemmed)
Spinach, prewashed package	10	12 (stemmed)

Also see "Choosing Salad Greens," page 50

SALT: In addition to the familiar table salt, here are some of the varieties you see on the grocery store shelf:

French *gros sel* is unprocessed. It has a grayish color and a distinctive, fresh taste.

Kosher salt has large, irregular crystals. It is about half as salty as table salt, so use twice as much.

Rock salt is the coarse gray stuff you use to freeze ice cream, prop up snail shells, and de-ice the porch steps. It's not usually eaten.

Sea or bay salt comes in either small grains or large crystals. It can be much more or less strong than table salt, so taste when you open a new pack to know how much to use.

Coarse salt is wonderful on corn on the cob because the little jagged edges cling to the kernels. Because it doesn't melt quickly, bakers sprinkle it on pretzels and breads before baking.

Choosing Salad Greens

Try combinations of textures and flavors: mild with bitter and/or spicy, crisp with tender, deep green with pale or red.

Mild

Soft
Bibb
Boston (butterhead)
Corn Salad (mache, lambs lettuce)
Leaf (green & red-tip)

Crisp
Iceberg
Romaine

Coarse
Spinach

Assertive, all crisp

Bitter
Escarole
Belgian Endive
Chicory (curly endive)
Raddichio

Tart
Arugula (rocket)

Peppery
Watercress

Coarse salt is also easier to pick up with the fingers. Most chefs season this way instead of using a shaker or measuring spoon. You can easily work out your finger measures. Pick up all you can hold with your 5 fingertips and measure that amount. (I get ⅛ teaspoon.) Then measure what you can hold between thumb and fore or middle finger.

SHALLOTS: When a recipe says 1 shallot, it means one shallot *clove*, not the two or three that bunch on a single root.

SHELLFISH: Before you cook **clams** and **mussels** you have to eliminate the sand and grit clinging to them. To do this, put them in a large bowl, cover with cold water and give a vigorous stir. After 5 minutes lift the shellfish out. (Watch for unusually heavy ones—they'll probably be filled with mud.) Repeat, using fresh water, until you don't see any more sand in the bowl. Discard opened ones that don't close when tapped gently. Don't let the shellfish soak for an extended period. They're not used to fresh water and may die.

Pull the stringy beards off **mussels.** Scrub both **mussels** and **oysters** with a stiff brush under cold running water.

Rinse **crayfish** and **lobster** in cold water before you cook them.

If you need to thaw frozen **langoustines** (also called small spiny lobsters) or **shrimp** in a hurry, do it under cold running water.

You can shell **shrimp** before or after cooking, depending on how you plan to serve them.

Should you remove the black vein on the outside curve of the shrimp? Certainly, if you can see it. On a lot of medium shrimp, the ones most commonly used in recipes, the vein isn't obvious and many good cooks don't remove it. Since the vein is perfectly harmless, it's up to you. To remove the vein before shelling, cut the shell along the back with sharp-pointed scissors. Run a knife point or punch-type can opener or your fingernail down the vein. To remove after cooking, peel the shrimp—with your fingers; they're faster than the gadgets—and with a small, sharp knife make a shallow slit down the outer curve. Pull out the vein.

Shrimp come in all sizes. *Medium* or *medium-large* (26 to 30 per pound) suit most recipes. *Large* or *jumbo* are best for grilling, broiling or butterflying.

The little crescent-shaped muscle on the side of **sea scallops** (the big ones) is pure rubber. It takes just a second to nip it off and it makes an enormous difference in the eating. The smaller **bay scallops** don't seem to have these.

Rinse scallops thoroughly before you use them; they can be sandy.

SOUR CREAM: Remember, sour cream won't tolerate high heat. Like light cream, it breaks down and curdles if it boils. If your recipe calls for cooking after you add the sour cream, you might want to use *crème frâiche* instead. It has a similar taste and consistency and isn't bothered by high heat. Directions for making *crème frâiche* are on p. 297.

STOCK, TO MAKE: Homemade stock is much better than bouillon cubes, but most of us don't make it often enough. I didn't until I learned that respected chefs use quickly-made chicken stock for *everything*—including beef and veal stock!—and that I could make chicken stock in the microwave in a quick 30 minutes. So homemade stock is now a staple in my kitchen. See pp. 293 and 294 for recipes.

Freeze stock in recipe amounts—2 tablespoons (ice cube tray compartments), 1 cup and 1 pint—and pack the frozen blocks in plastic bags.

SUGAR: Recipes use sugar in many forms. Here are some of them:

Brown sugar contains some molasses, which makes it moist. **Light brown** has a smaller amount of molasses and a mild flavor. **Dark brown** has more molasses and a

How to Clean Shrimp

1

2

3

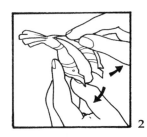

4

RESCUE

The Brown Sugar Is Like Granite!

Soften it by sprinkling it with a very little water and heating uncovered in a shallow pan in a 200° oven. Once it is softened, crumble with a fork or whiz in blender or processor. You can also soften it in the microwave oven. See p. 369. Store it tightly covered in the refrigerator or freezer so it stays soft.

stronger flavor. This extra molasses makes it burn more easily in baked goods. It also makes the sugar just acid enough to affect the texture of baked goods (see Acid Ingredients) and to curdle milk or cream if heated with them.

Brownulated sugar is granulated brown sugar. It's dry, doesn't lump, and is easier to handle than moist brown sugar. It's especially handy for sprinkled toppings and the crust on Crème Brulée.

Confectioners, powdered or icing sugar is ground to a fine powder. Use it in uncooked foods like cake frosting where regular sugar would be grainy. Because some manufacturers add cornstarch to prevent caking, this sugar can make whipped cream gummy. Use **superfine** sugar for whipped cream.

Corn syrup is made from cornstarch and comes in two colors: **light,** which is clear and mildly flavored, and **dark** which has a stronger, molasses-like flavor. Both are used in making candy, jam, frosting, cookies and desserts. Their big advantage is that they don't crystallize like white sugar does. Use them interchangeably depending on the flavor you like.

Cube or lump sugar is used to sweeten hot drinks. Bakers have a trick you should try: Rub the cubes on skins of citrus fruits. The cubes act like little sponges to absorb the tasty oils and are then added to recipes. I like to dip them into a liquor or juice and stick them on top of biscuits, muffins and cakes before baking. See the Orange Biscuit recipe on p. 311.

Granulated (regular white table sugar) is the all-purpose sugar. When a recipe calls for sugar without saying which kind, it's this one.

Maple sugar is made from maple syrup. It's a bit sweeter than white sugar.

Molasses is the dark brown syrup left behind after white sugar has been refined. **Light** (Barbados) molasses has the lightest color and is the sweetest. **Dark** molasses is stronger flavored. **Blackstrap** is very strong flavored, less sweet, almost bitter. Most supermarket molasses is a combination of light and dark and is blended with corn syrup. Molasses is used in gingerbread, plum pudding, Boston baked beans and barbecue sauce. Some cooks find molasses too bitter and use dark corn syrup instead.

Superfine or extra fine is finely ground granulated sugar. It is the preferred sugar for baking because it dissolves quicker than granulated. Superfine is especially good for meringues and whipped cream, where graininess is the enemy.

Turbinado sugar is partially refined, containing 15% molasses. It's usually sold in coarse crystals and served with coffee and tea by hosts who like a special touch.

For more on sugar, see p. 245.

TOMATOES: Ripen them in a sunny spot or place in a paper bag with holes punched in it and leave at room temperature. Once they are ripe, store them in a cool place or, if you must, in the refrigerator. Out of season you'll be happier cooking with canned tomatoes instead of fresh. If you have to cook with out-of-season tomatoes, punch up their flavor with a little tomato paste or purée and a little sugar.

Tomatoes used in recipes should first be peeled and seeded. It takes just a minute. Cut an *x* on the smooth bottom, cover the tomato with boiling water for 15 seconds (plum tomatoes may take a little longer), lift out and cool under cold water for a second. Use a paring knife to cut out the stem end; the skin will then slip off easily. Cut the tomato in half across its equator, hold it over the sink, and gently squeeze out seeds and the watery stuff.

TOFU: See Bean Curd.

VEGETABLES: See Chapter 5 for help in cooking all kinds of vegetables.

WHEAT: Don't overlook this wonderful, nutty-tasting whole grain. Cooked cracked wheat and wheat berries are delicious added to breads. To cook, see p. 31.

WINE: What wine do you cook with? Any good, drinkable table wine—jug or fancy bottle. A lot of cooks use the

Quick Hint

Crisp up limp carrots, celery, cucumbers, radishes by placing them whole in a bowl of very cold water in the fridge for anywhere from 30 minutes to 3 hours.

wine they plan to serve with the dish. Don't use a sweet wine unless the recipe specifically calls for it. And don't use one of those "cooking wines" they sell at the supermarket. They have added salt (originally, to keep you from swigging while you cooked!) and are pretty dreadful. If your recipe doesn't specify the wine to use, or if you are winging it, check the box below for guidance. For more on cooking with wine, see p. 80.

❧ Some Cooking Wine Suggestions ❧

White wine	Use something strong, dry and not fruity such as a Pinot Blanc, Chardonnay, Mâcon, or a dry white vermouth.
Red wine	Use something young and full-bodied like a Pinot Noir, Cabernet Sauvignon, Burgundy, a Bordeaux like St. Émilion or Mâcon.
Rosé	Don't use a rosé unless the recipe specifically calls for it. Rosés don't have enough acidity or depth for cooking.
Sherry	Use a medium dry for cooking; dry and very dry are often too sharp. Use a sweet sherry for dessert recipes.

YEAST: There are three forms: **fresh compressed, active dry,** and **active dry quick rise.** They all have the same leavening power per package, enough for 3 to 4 cups of flour. A package of dry yeast measures about 1 tablespoon.

Fresh and dry yeast are activated by liquid. Quick rise yeast takes half the rising time of the others and is mixed in with the dry ingredients instead of the liquid. I do the same with regular dry yeast when I'm in a hurry and it rises just fine, but I'm careful to have the liquid super hot.

YOGURT: It will curdle when it gets hot. When you cook sauces with yogurt, keep them silky by stirring a little cornstarch or flour into the yogurt first to keep it from separating. Use 2 teaspoons cornstarch or 1 tablespoon flour per cup yogurt.

CHAPTER 1

Measuring

What Can I Substitute for a 1-Quart Casserole, How Much Is a "Pinch", and What's the Difference between a Fluid Ounce and a Dry Ounce?

The information in this chapter can spare you a lot of head scratching and frustration. Measuring is an important part of cooking, especially in areas like baking where you are dealing with a chemical balance. The pages that follow offer tips on measuring and on what pan to substitute when you don't have the one the recipe specifies. There's a list of can sizes for those infuriating recipes that call for such things as a #303 can, and, for your ventures into the exotic, charts to translate foreign measurements into our familiar ones.

MEASURING INGREDIENTS

You need different kinds of cups for measuring dry and liquid ingredients. Cups for measuring dry ingredients are made to be filled to the top and levelled. Liquid measuring cups come in 1- to 4-cup sizes. They have measures marked on the side, a pouring spout, and extra space at the top to ensure against spilling. If you level off dry ingredients in one of these, you'll be a good quarter cup over the measurement.

Quick Hint

Use large containers for flour, sugar, salt, etc., and keep a set of measuring cups or spoons in each. They're cheap and it saves a lot of digging around and spoon washing.

A Musical Measure

In an old recipe for Indian Pudding, molasses is measured this way: "Let the molasses drip in as you sing one verse of 'Nearer My God to Thee'; sing 2 verses in cold weather."

Here are some tips on measuring common ingredients.

Flour and White Sugar

Spoon *lightly* into the measuring cup. Don't tap or shake down. Level off the surplus with the straight edge of a knife or spatula. Today's flour doesn't need to be sifted before measuring, except for delicate cakes or when a recipe written in the last 10 years specifically says to do so. In this case, sift the flour onto a piece of wax paper, then measure as above.

I like to sift already measured flour with other dry ingredients like baking powder to insure that everything is evenly mixed.

Brown Sugar, Coconut, Dried Fruit, Nuts

Pack these into a dry measuring cup up to the top.

Shortening, Butter, Margarine

Pack into a dry measuring cup and level off. If the fat is cold and hard, here's an easier way to measure: Pour cold water into a liquid measure, leaving empty the amount you want to measure. (For example, to measure ⅓ cup fat in a 1-cup measure, add water to the ⅔-cup mark.) Keep adding chunks of fat until the water reaches the 1-cup mark when all fat is submerged.

The wrappers of butter and margarine sticks can help. Most are marked at tablespoon intervals; they also show where to cut for ¼ cup and ⅓ cup. A whole stick equals ½ cup. Before you cut, be sure the first mark is at the edge of the stick; sometimes the paper is a bit off.

Honey, Molasses, Corn Syrup

Grease the cup or spoon before filling and they will slide out cleanly.

Grated Cheese, Chopped Fresh Herbs, Shredded Greens

These must be packed lightly to get the full measure, but not so tightly they form a compact mass.

Other Tips

Never measure over the bowl or pot you are adding to. Do it over the empty counter or sink. Your hand can shake, someone can jog your elbow, or something thick and sticky like honey can give a sudden plop and overflow the measure.

Sometimes you do things to the ingredient before you measure, sometimes you do them afterwards. Read the recipe carefully because it makes a big difference. For example, *1 cup of heavy cream, whipped* means that you measure 1 cup of cream and *then* whip it, whereas *1 cup whipped cream* means you measure out 1 cup after it's whipped. Generally the recipe is clear, but it's easy to miss these small details.

Pouring Tip

To pour powder from a jar, use a rotating motion. Slant the jar until the contents *almost* fall out. Then rotate from left to right. Powder will pour in a controlled stream.

MEASURING PANS

Some cooking and baking pans have their sizes clearly marked when you buy them. Others, unfortunately, you must measure yourself.

To measure the capacity (what it holds) of a baking dish or mold, add water by the cupful until filled to the brim.

To measure the dimensions (inches) of a casserole or pan:

> **Bakeware:** Measure length and width across the inside edge at the top. Measure depth from the inside, coming straight up from the bottom.

> **Skillets and Griddles:** Measure diameter across the top—excluding the pouring lip, of course.

Once you know the size and capacity of a baking dish or pan, mark it on the bottom with a permanent marking pen or nail polish.

Pan Arithmetic

An 8" *square pan* holds 1 cup more than an 8" *round one.*

If the depth is the same, a square pan holds the same amount as a round one measuring *1 inch more across.* For example, an 8" square pan holds the same amount as a 9" round one!

❦ Capacities of Some Standard Pans ❦

When a recipe calls for a 1-quart casserole or a 10" pie plate and your cupboard doesn't have one, check the chart below to see what containers hold the same amount. If you don't see the exact size you're looking for, find one that's close and go with that.

If you need this capacity:	Use this size:
2 tablespoons	1½" muffin tin cup
¼ cup	2" muffin tin cup
⅓ cup	2½" muffin tin cup
½ cup	3" (standard size) muffin tin cup
¾ cup	6-ounce custard cup or ramekin
⅞ cup	4¼" tartlet pan
1 cup	5¼" tartlet pan
1¼ cups	10-ounce custard cup
2 cups	7" pie pan 5½" x 3" x 2½" loaf pan
3 cups	8" pie pan 6½" x 4½" x 3" loaf pan
3½ cups	6¼" x 2½" ring mold
4 cups (1 quart)	9" pie plate 8" x 1¼" round layer cake pan 8" x 4" x 2½" loaf pan 1-quart soufflé dish 8 3" muffin tin cups 8" skillet (6" bottom) 11¾" x 7½" x ¾" jelly roll pan
4½ cups	8½" x 2½" ring mold
5 cups	8½" x 4¼" x 3⅛" loaf pan

CAPACITIES OF SOME STANDARD PANS

If you need this capacity:	Use this size:
6 cups (1½ quarts)	8" x 1½" square layer pan 9" round layer cake pan 10" x 6" x 1¾" rectangular pan 7" tube or 7½" x 3" bundt pan 7" x 5½" x 4" melon mold 12 3" muffin tin cups 10" pie pan
8 cups (2 quarts)	8" x 8" x 2" square pan 11" x 7" x 1½" baking pan 9" x 5" x 3" loaf pan 9½" brioche pan 9½" x 2¾" ring mold 10" skillet (8" bottom)
9 cups	9" x 3¼" tube pan (bundt, kugelhopf, angel cake)
10 cups (2½ quarts)	9" x 9" x 2" square pan 15" x 10" x 1" jelly roll pan
12 cups (3 quarts)	11" x 5" x 3½" loaf pan 9" x 3½" angel cake pan 10" tube or bundt pan 8" x 3" springform pan
13 cups	11½" x 17¼" x 1" jelly roll pan
14½ cups	12¼ x 17¼ x 1" jelly roll pan
15 cups	9" x 13" x 2" baking pan 8½" x 13½" x 2" baking pan
16 cups (4 quarts)	10" x 4" tube or kugelhopf pan 9" x 3" springform pan 12" skillet (10" bottom)
18 cups (4½ quarts)	10" x 4" angel cake pan
19 cups	14" x 10½" x 2½" roasting pan

Surface Measures
❦ of Some Standard Pans ❦

The ideal pan to substitute is one that keeps the ingredients the same depth as the original; in other words, a pan that is the same size on the bottom. To help you do this, the chart below gives the bottom surface of some commonly used pans. Look up the square-inch measure of the pan you are replacing and find one with the same or approximately the same bottom dimensions. (For example, a 9" round layer pan has 64 square inches of bottom surface; so does an 8" square pan.) You may have to use a combination of pans. (An 8" round (50 square inches) plus a 7¾" x 3⅝" (28 square inches) for a 9" square (81 square inches)).

Pan Size	Square Inches
7¾" x 3⅝" x 2¼"	28
9" x 5" x 3"	45
8" x 1½" round	50
11" x 4½" x 2¾"	50
9" x 1½" round	64
8" square	64
11" x 7" x 1½"	77
10" x 1½" round	79
16" x 5" x 4"	80
9" square	81
13" x 9" x 2"	117
15" x 10" x 2"	150
15½" x 10½" x 1"	160

When you substitute pans, your finished dish will often have a different shape from that in the original recipe. In fact, you may choose to bake a soufflé in a shallow dish rather than a high one. (You can, and they are lovely. See p. 207.) Whenever you change the shape, you have to make adjustments. It might be helpful to read Choosing the Right Pan Size in Chapter 9 before plunging ahead.

Quick Hint

You don't have to have a pie tin to bake a pie. You can use a deeper dish of the same diameter—just make sure to keep the crust at pie depth (about 1" deep).

MEASURING BY VOLUME AND WEIGHT

Perhaps you haven't given it much thought, but you should keep in the back of your head that a fluid ounce is not the same as a weighed-out ounce. Standard American measuring cups hold 8 *fluid* ounces; that is, the amount of water that weighs 8 ounces. When an American recipe calls for 1 cup of something, it means that 8-ounce cup, even though what you put in it may not weigh 8 ounces at all. A cup holds, for instance, about 4 ounces of flour or ⅓ ounce of popped corn.

How to Measure

The trap comes with our measuring cups which print both volume measurements (¼ cup) *and* fluid ounces (2 ounces) on their sides. If your recipe calls for a cup of milk and a cup of flour, no problem—fill that 8-ounce measuring cup. But if a recipe asks specifically for 8 ounces of a *dry ingredient* like flour, the cup is no help. Those dry ounces *must be weighed out on a scale.* (Europeans always weigh their dry ingredients.)

Butter and margarine weigh about the same as water, so 4 weighed ounces of butter exactly fits a ½ cup or 4 fluid ounce measure. But don't let that coincidence make you forget that most other ingredients weigh either less or more than water. See the chart on p. 66 for the weights and corresponding volumes of a few common ingredients.

❧ Volume Measurement ❧

The chart below shows, in the first column, some American measures that are equivalent to each other, and in the second column the *fluid* ounces they hold, where that applies. The third column lists rough metric equivalents, so you can convert recipes that call for milliliters (ml), deciliters (dl) and liters (l).

American Measure	Fluid Ounces	Fluid Metric Measure
Pinch (the amount you can hold between thumb and forefinger), less than ⅛ teaspoon		
Dash, 3 drops, ¼ teaspoon		
1 teaspoon		5 ml
3 teaspoons, 1 tablespoon	½	15 ml
2 tablespoons, ⅛ cup, 1 pony	1	30 ml, ¼ dl
3 tablespoons, 1 jigger	1½	45 ml
4 tablespoons, ¼ cup	2	60 ml, ½ dl
5⅓ tablespoons, ⅓ cup	2½	80 ml, ¾ dl
8 tablespoons, ½ cup	4	120 ml, 1 dl
10⅔ tablespoons, ⅔ cup	5⅓	160 ml, 1½ dl
12 tablespoons, ¾ cup	6	180 ml, 1¾ dl
14 tablespoons, ⅞ cup	7	210 ml, 2 dl
16 tablespoons, 1 cup	8	240 ml, ¼ l
2 cups, 1 pint	16	480 ml, ½ l
4 cups, 2 pints, 1 quart	32	950 ml
1 quart + 3½ tablespoons		1000 ml, 10 dl, 1 l
8 quarts, 1 peck		
4 pecks, 1 bushel		

If you want to do your own metric conversions, here are some formulas. They are close approximations, which are all you need for most cooking.

- *Fluid Ounces to Milliliters:* Multiply ounces by 30.

- *Milliliters to Fluid Ounces:* Multiply milliliters by .03.

- *Liters and Quarts:* A liter is .95 of a quart. That's close enough to allow you to exchange them one for one in the kitchen.

❦ WEIGHT MEASUREMENT ❦

This chart is handy for translating foreign weight measurements to American ounces. Again, the metric equivalents are rounded off. Also see the chart on p. 66. Do get a scale if you use foreign recipes often.

Ounces	Pounds	Grams	Kilograms
1		30	
2		60	
3		85	
4	¼	115	
5		140	
6		180	
7		210	
8	½	225	
9		250	¼
10		285	
12	¾	340	
14		400	
16	1	450	
18	1⅛	500	½
20	1¼	560	

WEIGHT MEASUREMENT			
Ounces	Pounds	Grams	Kilograms
24	1½	675	
28	1¾	900	
32	2	900	
	2¼	1000	1
	3	1350	1⅓
	3½	1500	1½
	4	1800	1¾

T, t and c

I haven't always spelled out the words *tablespoon, teaspoon and cup*. Here's an explanation of my shorthand:

T = tablespoon
t = teaspoon
c = cup

FOREIGN MEASURES

Here are some terms that will help you adapt recipes from foreign friends and British or continental cookbooks and magazines. Watch out for the spoon measures. Foreign recipes often call for "rounded" and "heaped" measures. There is a difference. For a rounded measure, the ingredient rises above the rim in a neat dome. A heaped measure holds as much as you can pile on without its toppling over. Unless the recipe specifies a level measure, you probably should assume heaped measures. Until I learned this, recipes I tried from foreign books and friends never worked out right.

You may see these measures in French recipes:

Bol: 10 fluid ounces

Verre: 6 fluid ounces

Cuillère à café: 1 teaspoon

Cuillère à soup, cuillère à bouche or verre à liqueur: 1 tablespoon

The following terms may appear in **British recipes** written before the 1970s, when Britain went metric.

British	US
Teaspoon	1½ teaspoons
Dessertspoon	1 tablespoon
Measuring tablespoon	1½ tablespoons
Coffee cup (demitasse)	⅓ cup
Gill	⅔ cup
Teacup	¾ cup
Cup or breakfast cup	1¼ cups

Keep the following overall differences in mind when using British recipes:

- A standard British measuring cup equals *10 fluid ounces*, not 8 like our American cups.

- A British Imperial pint equals *20 fluid ounces*, not 16 like our pints.

Australian measuring tablespoons hold 4 teaspoons.

You may also want to check deciliter and milliliter equivalents on p. 62.

Old-Time Measures

These measurements are the sort you find in old church and club cookbooks, and in hand-written family recipes. They were used well into the 1930s.

Butter the size of a walnut: 2 tablespoons

Butter the size of an egg: ¼ cup

A rounded cup, teaspoon or tablespoon: Fill your measure so that the ingredient is slightly rounded above the rim.

A heaping teaspoon: 1¾ to 2 teaspoons

A heaping tablespoon: 1½ to 2 tablespoons

A heaping cup: 1 cup and 1 tablespoon

TRANSLATING COMMONLY USED
❧ INGREDIENTS TO AMERICAN MEASURES ❧

Ingredient	Metric Weight (approx)	American Weight (approx)	American Volume
Bread crumbs:			
Fresh	60 grams	2 oz	1 cup
Dry	90 grams	3 oz	1 cup
Butter, margarine, vegetable shortening	15 grams 115 grams	½ oz 4 oz	1 T ½ cup
Cornstarch (cornflour, maizena)	30 grams	1 oz	¼ cup
Dried fruit	180 grams	6 oz	1 cup
Flour, all-purpose, unsifted	100 grams	4 oz	1 cup
Nuts, ground or chopped	120 grams	4 oz	1 cup
Rice	30 grams	1 oz	2 T
Sugar:			
Brown	160 grams	5 oz	1 cup
Confectioners	125 grams	4 ½ oz	1 cup
Granulated	200 grams	7 oz	1 cup
Syrups (honey, molasses, treacle)	40 grams	1 ½ oz	2 T

❧ CAN SIZES ❧

If your recipe specifies a 5-ounce or 14-ounce can of something and all you have are 8- or 28-ounce cans, or if you want to substitute a cooked leftover for the canned product, it's helpful to know how much you need to measure out. This chart will tell you.

Can Size	Volume in Cups
5-ounce	⅝
5⅓-ounce (small evaporated milk)	⅔
6-ounce	¾
8-ounce	1
#1 (11½ ounces)	1⅓
12-ounce	1½
13-ounce (evaporated milk)	1⅔
14-ounce (condensed milk)	1⅔
15-ounce	1¾
#300 (14 to 16 ounces)	1¾
16-ounce	2
#303 (16 to 17 ounces)	2
#2 (18 to 20 ounces)	2½
#2½ (29 ounces)	3½
#3 (46 ounces)	5¾
#10 (6 pounds)	12

Quick Hint

How much is a dollop? Cook-book writers love this word, which has a breezy, offhand ring to it. It probably means 1 or 2 rounded tablespoons.

How to Achieve
Some Tricky Measures

Here's how to measure amounts for which there aren't any standard spoon or cup measures. You'll run into this when you double or halve recipes. For additional help in multiplying and dividing recipe amounts, see the chart on p. 249.

⅛ teaspoon	Fill the ¼ teaspoon measure and level it off. With the point of a knife, mark off half and remove.
⅓ tablespoon	Measure 1 teaspoon.
½ tablespoon	Do as for ⅛ teaspoon using the 1 tablespoon measure, or measure out 1½ teaspoons.
⅔ tablespoon	Measure 2 teaspoons
⅛ cup	Measure 2 tablespoons.
⅜ cup	Measure ¼ cup plus 2 tablespoons.
⅝ cup	Measure ½ cup plus 2 tablespoons.
⅞ cup	Measure 1 cup less 2 tablespoons.

General Cooking Help

What Makes Chocolate Act Funny, What Is Simple Syrup, and Is It Safe to Flame a Dessert?

When you cook you're playing with fire. Heat is what cooking's all about. Heat is magic. It brightens color and deepens flavors. It turns solid chocolate liquid and liquid eggs solid. It tenderizes tough chuck roast and stiffens soft sweetbreads. It inflates batter, it browns, it crisps—and it makes those wonderful aromas.

In this chapter we get to the heat and the cooking, the fun of transforming raw ingredients into what gets applause at the table. There is help for cooking temperamental or unusual ingredients and a quick rundown of basic cooking techniques which will be dealt with in detail later in the book.

Boiling and baking and beating and basting... If something has stumped you, you may find the answer here. Often one little trick or bit of information is all you need to breeze through like a pro. So let's get on with it.

═══ RESCUE ═══

The Melted Chocolate Stiffened!

If melted chocolate stiffens, you can reliquify it by stirring in 1 teaspoon of vegetable shortening or oil for each ounce of chocolate.

If the cocoa butter separates, cool the mixture over ice, stirring vigorously.

═══ *Recipe* ═══

All-But-Instant Chocolate Sauce

Melt 6 ounces semisweet chocolate with 2 tablespoons butter and ¼ cup water. Stir well. Flavor with vanilla or replace 2 tablespoons of the water with rum, cognac, coffee, orange juice, etc. Make it sweeter with ¼ cup light corn syrup.

Yield: 1 cup.

BEFORE YOU START TO COOK

First of all: Read the recipe and note the ingredients you may have to buy and the utensils and pans you will need.

Well ahead, you can: Make stock, grate and measure cheese, peel, slice and chop ingredients. (I do vegetables up to a day ahead.) Store in containers if they will wait more than a few hours.

Immediate preparation: Remove from the fridge ingredients that should come to room temperature. Assemble the major ingredients, measured into bowls or onto pieces of wax paper on a cookie sheet. That way you can really enjoy the process of putting things together.

HELP WITH SOME INGREDIENTS

Cooking with Chocolate

Chocolate must be melted over very low heat. It starts melting at 80° (this is lower than body temperature!) and is fully melted by the time it reaches 110 to 115°. If exposed to higher heat, it can turn grainy, become too thick, separate or scorch.

Melt chocolate in the microwave, over hot water, or over very low heat.

To microwave, heat an ounce of chocolate at 50% power for 1 minute. The chocolate will start melting, but its shape won't change until you touch it with a spoon. Stir it to distribute the heat and microwave another minute. As the chocolate softens, shorten the heating time, stirring at each pause until smooth.

To melt over hot water, put chocolate in the top of a double boiler over very hot *tap* water (130° to 140°) and stir steadily until melted.

To melt over direct heat, put chocolate in a pan directly over *very low burner heat*—this means the pilot light of your range or on a heat diffuser (see p. 380) over low heat, or on a steam radiator. Just keep in mind: heat murders chocolate.

Never cover melting chocolate. If even a drop of water from condensing steam falls into it the chocolate will stiffen and refuse to combine with other ingredients.

Combining a liquid like milk, cream, melted butter or margarine with melted chocolate, as many recipes direct, is very tricky. If the liquid ingredient is hotter than the chocolate the cocoa butter will separate out; if it's cooler, the chocolate will stiffen. Avoid this temperature conflict by melting the chocolate with the other ingredient in a double boiler over very low heat. To do this, there must be at least one tablespoon of liquid per ounce of chocolate.

Cooking with Dairy Products

Butter: When you add butter to a sauce or to a pan for frying, cut it into small chunks. Otherwise the part that melts first may burn while the rest is melting.

Butter has milk solids in it that scorch easily in frying or sautéing. Eliminate the problem by replacing half the butter with oil, which has a better heat tolerance. Another solution is to *clarify* the butter by removing the scorchable solids. See the box.

Cheese: High heat turns cheese rubbery and makes the oil separate out. Always cook with room temperature cheese. Shred or cut it into small cubes so it melts quickly, and melt it over very gentle heat. When you add cheese to a sauce, shred or crumble it and add it at the end, stirring steadily over *low* heat for only as long as it takes the cheese to melt. When you use cheese as a topping, put it on at the end of baking, allowing just enough oven time to melt the cheese.

Cream: When you whip cream, make sure that cream, beaters and bowl are all ice cold. To insure success, chill everything in the freezer for 30 minutes before you start. You can whip even light (20%) cream if you follow this rule. It will have more volume than whipped heavy cream, but will feel less velvety and dense in your mouth.

TECHNIQUE

How to Clarify Butter

To clarify butter, melt it over gentle heat or in a microwave. Skim off and discard the foam. Pour into a bowl and chill. When it is hard, discard the milky residue on the bottom. Store clarified butter in the refrigerator or freezer. (I freeze it in 1 and 2 tablespoon amounts.)

Extra whipped cream? My Austrian friends always serve a bowl of it with coffee. Yum!

Handling It Like a Pro

My Belgian cooking teacher stressed that you never apologize for a dish; you pretend it's what you intended all along. Whenever a dish went awry in her kitchen, she simply renamed it, and got away with it every time. Who was to know that the lemon sauce on the cake was originally the filling which refused to thicken? Or that the velvety cheese timbale was a soufflé that fell?

Of course, some things can't be remedied. That's part of the game, too. If it was all victory, there wouldn't be any challenge—or any thrill when you hit a real winner.

To turn unexpected results into triumphs, look for help in the **Handling It Like a Pro** charts, which are scattered throughout the book.

If you plan to add sugar and a flavoring like vanilla or a liqueur, whip the cream until it's foamy before you add the flavor. Added at the beginning, it could hinder the whipping process; added at the end, it might cause you to overbeat.

When you fold whipped cream into a heavier mixture, first stir about ¼ to ⅓ of the whipped cream into the mixture to lighten it. The rest will fold easily into the lightened batter.

How long you whip cream depends on what you intend to do with it:

- **To fold into a mixture** like a mousse or cold soufflé, whip cream only until it begins to thicken. You've reached this point when a track drawn through the cream with a spoon handle fills back in quickly.

- **To top a dessert,** whip the cream until it clings softly to the beater and is thick enough to make swirls in the bowl when you lift the beaters.

- **To use for frosting or spreading on cakes,** whip the cream until it forms soft peaks that hold when you lift the beaters.

- **To pipe through a pastry tube,** whip the cream stiffly, to the point where a track drawn across it with a spoon handle stays in place.

Whipped cream should stick to the beaters.

Stiff whipped cream can be piped through a pastry tube.

❦ Handling Cream Like a Pro ❦

If	Next Time You'll Know	Turning It Into a Winner
Cream won't whip.	Not enough fat in the cream; should have at least 20%. Or, cream was too warm.	Chill bowl and beaters and try again. Or beat in ½ teaspoon gelatin softened and melted in 1 tablespoon water + 9 to 10 drops lemon juice. Chill. Makes a very softly whipped cream.
Develops butter lumps.	Whipped too long. Warning sign: just before it turns, cream will get granular and yellowish. Stop!	Keep beating, pour off liquid. You have sweet cream butter. Enjoy.
Curdles while being cooked with other ingredients.	Cooked at too high a temperature; using a double boiler might help. Or, too much acid (tomatoes, wine, citrus fruits) in the dish.	Whisk in a little cornstarch dissolved in water and cook gently until it thickens slightly.

Cooking with Gelatin

Both powdered and leaf gelatin must be softened in cold liquid, usually water. (For information on leaf gelatin see p. 28)

To soften powdered gelatin, sprinkle over a little cold liquid (¼ cup for a 1 tablespoon package) and let sit for 5 minutes until spongy.

To soften leaf gelatin, cover with cold water and soak 5 minutes or until very soft. Then lift out with your fingers, squeeze out the excess water and put the gelatin in a small dish.

If the liquid to which it will be added won't be hot enough to dissolve it, the softened gelatin must then be melted in a water bath.

To melt both types, put the dish holding the gelatin in a pan of hot water and heat over the burner until melted. Shake gently but *don't stir*. If you stir gelatin while it soaks or melts it may form strings. To see if it is completely dissolved, take up a little in a spoon. You shouldn't see any crystals. Never dissolve gelatin over direct heat—it will stick to the pan and burn.

When you add melted gelatin to any mixture, the mixture must be warm enough to keep the gelatin from starting to set immediately. Stir gelatin into the warm mixture thoroughly to distribute it evenly. Gelatin tends to separate out of fluffy mixtures like cold soufflés, so stir them gently but frequently while the mixture cools.

❧ GELATIN STAGES ❧

In order to do the steps of a recipe at the right time, you need to recognize the setting stages.

Stage	Characteristics	Time to
Partially set	Syrupy, with texture of beaten egg whites	Fold in whipped cream, beaten egg whites. Add solids like nuts, fruit and vegetable pieces. Pour onto almost firm layer of gelatin.
Almost firm	Looks set but will flow sluggishly if pan is tilted. Feels tacky.	Ready to receive additional layer of partially set gelatin.
Firm	Won't move when pan is tilted. Holds an edge when cut.	Serve.
Loosened from mold	When mold is moved from side to side after being dipped in warm water, gelatin moves slightly and edges are slightly melted.	Unmold.

To set gelatin quickly, place the filled mold in the freezer for 25 minutes (no more or it may crystallize and get watery—gelatin doesn't freeze well.) Then move it to the refrigerator. Another way: Dissolve 1 tablespoon unflavored gelatin or a small-size box of the flavored variety in 1 cup boiling water. Substitute 2 cups of ice cubes (about 10) for the remaining cup of liquid. If you use a large box of gelatin, double the amounts of water and ice. Stir until syrupy, then remove any ice lumps and, if the recipe has solid ingredients, mix them in. Chill as directed.

To test whether a gelatin mixture will be stiff enough for aspics and the like, pour ¼ inch into a small dish and place it in the freezer. If it's right, it will jell in 5 minutes.

If gelatin jells past the stage you want, place the bowl in a pan of hot water and stir until it melts. Then chill again to the correct stage.

Gelatin won't set if it's mixed with fresh ginger root or *uncooked* pineapple, figs, mangoes, kiwi fruit or papaya or their juices. All those things contain an enzyme that prevents jelling. Since 5 minutes of cooking destroys the enzyme, cook the fruits or juices first or use them canned. Note: Forget about using kiwi fruit in gelatin. Cooking wrecks its color, texture and flavor.

Too much sugar also keeps gelatin from setting firmly. If you have a setting problem, that could be your answer.

To unmold gelatin: Dip the mold in very warm water to the depth of the gelatin mixture for a few seconds. Lift out and loosen the edges with a thin knife blade. Rinse a serving plate in cold water, leave it wet, and invert it over the mold. Turn mold and plate upside down. Shake gently and the gelatin should slip out. Because the plate is wet you can easily slide the gelatin to the center.

TECHNIQUE

Gelatin Tricks

Here's a neat trick for coating a platter of sliced meat or fish with aspic. Chill a ¼" layer of aspic in a shallow, rimmed cookie sheet that is about the size of your platter. Arrange the food you plan to coat on the platter, pretty-side up. When the aspic has *almost* set, invert the cookie sheet over the platter and tap the aspic out onto the arranged food. Chop any extra bits in little pieces and arrange them in a sparkly heap around the edges.

❧ HANDLING GELATIN LIKE A PRO ❧

If	Next Time You'll Know	Turning It into a Winner
Gelatin got stringy when melted.	Was stirred while softening or melting; allowed to boil.	Not much you can do for this one.
Gelatin won't set.	Ingredient used which prevents jelling. See p. 75.	Add a cornstarch/water paste and cook until thick. Pour over cake as a sauce.
Fluffy part separated into a layer.	Whipped ingredients added too soon. Not stirred frequently as it cooled.	Call it Ribbon Pudding or Layer Loaf. It will taste good, but different.
Fruits and nuts sank.	Added before gelatin reached right stage.	Melt until syrupy. Stir several times while it sets.
Set up too fast.	Melted gelatin was added to cool rather than warm mixture. Mixture must be warm enough to prevent quick jelling.	If it contains no beaten egg or whipped cream, melt over low heat and rechill. Soften egg and cream mixtures at room temperature.
Set too firmly.	Chilled too long.	See above.
Gelatin formed strings in mixture.	Not carefully stirred into the warm mixture.	Buzz it in blender or processor. You'll get a fluffy dish.
It came out rubbery.	Too much gelatin.	Melt and add more liquid.
Was awfully stiff the next day.	Gelatin dishes keep for 2 to 3 days but get stiffer after 12 hours.	Let it soften at room temperature for 30 minutes before serving.
Broke down, got watery	Left too long in the freezer for quick chilling.	Melt down and treat like gelatin that won't set.

Cooking With Sugar

Sugar attracts water from the air, so it keeps foods moist. It makes cakes lighter because it slows the stiffening of gluten. It lowers the freezing point of a liquid, so it keeps ice cream from freezing rock hard. It helps tenderize meat and keeps ham and bacon from getting over-hard when cured. It tastes good, too.

Sugar syrups are used a lot in the kitchen—for mixing drinks, poaching fruit, soaking rum babas, and making boiled frosting, Italian meringue and candy.

Too many of us have run into recipes that called for **simple syrup** and wondered what on earth it was and where to buy it. You don't buy it, you make it in a saucepan, like this:

Simple Syrup

Thin (for soaking babas, poaching fruit, adding to mixed drinks)	1 cup sugar to 2 cups water
Medium (for candied fruit, brushing on cake layers)	1 cup sugar to 1 cup water
Heavy (for liqueur syrups to soak cakes and for sorbet)	1 cup sugar to ¾ c water— may be part liqueur

Heat and stir sugar and water over low heat, making sure the sugar dissolves before boiling starts. When the mixture starts boiling, stop stirring and boil uncovered for 1 minute. If you want to flavor the syrup, you can add lemon or orange juice before cooking or add flavor extracts after it has boiled. This recipe yields 1 to 2½ cups of syrup, depending on the consistency.

Candy syrups, which cook longer than simple syrup, can crystallize, forming gritty little sugar crystals. The enemies here are: the tiniest speck of grit or fat on the side of the pan; failing to dissolve the sugar completely before it

Quick Hint

When you cook a sugar syrup, use the bubbles as a guide: they get smaller as the syrup thickens.

RESCUE

I Overcooked the Syrup!

If you overcook a sugar syrup—say it cooks to the hard ball instead of soft ball stage—just stir in boiling water. For a 1-2 cup recipe, use ¼ cup water. Then cook the syrup again to the stage you want.

boils; and stirring or agitation during boiling. Here are the rules:

1. Use a clean, smooth-sided pot (copper and enamel are best).

2. Stir steadily over low heat to dissolve the last tiny grain of sugar before boiling starts.

3. Don't stir once boiling starts.

4. During boiling, wash pan sides frequently with a pastry brush dipped in water or cover the pan and let condensed steam do the washing.

5. If called for by your recipe, corn syrup, cream of tartar, or lemon juice will discourage crystal formation.

To caramelize sugar for candies and desserts: To 2 cups sugar add ½ teaspoon cream of tartar and a scant ½ cup of cold water. Stir over low heat with a metal spoon until the sugar dissolves. Raise the heat, bring the mixture to a boil and cook *without stirring* until the syrup turns amber (8 to 10 minutes). Watch it closely. Once it starts to darken it goes like the wind. Lift the pot off the heat and set it in cold water to stop the cooking. I use a heavy-bottomed, light-colored pan (so I can watch the color change) and I keep a large bowl of cold water ready by the stove.

❦ A Guide to Cooking Sugar ❦

You can test syrup for doneness with a candy thermometer or by dropping a little syrup into cold water to see how it behaves.

If You're Making	Done Stage	Done Temperature	Test
Syrup for fruit paste and candies	Thread	230° - 235°	Spins soft, 3" thread when dropped from fork or spoon. If dropped in ice water, threads can't be forced into a ball.
Buttercream frosting, fondant, fudge, penuche	Soft ball	235° - 240°	Bit of slightly cooled syrup dropped in ice water forms soft ball which loses shape when removed.
Seven-minute frosting (1 egg white per cup sugar)	Medium ball	238° - 242°	When dropped in very cold water, forms a slightly firmer ball.
Caramels, seven-minute frosting (2 egg whites per cup sugar)	Firm ball	244° - 248°	When dropped in very cold water, forms firm ball that will not flatten by itself when removed.
Italian meringue, almond paste, divinity, marshmallows, nougat, syrup for popcorn balls, taffy.	Hard ball	250° - 265°	When dropped in very cold water, forms hard ball as above that can be flattened between thumb and finger.
Butterscotch	Soft crack	270° - 290°	When dropped in very cold water, separates into bits which are hard but not brittle.
Praline, pulled and spun sugar, brittles, glacés	Hard crack	300° - 310°	In very cold water, separates into hard, brittle threads.

A Guide to Cooking Sugar

If You're Making	Done Stage	Done Temperature	Test
Barley sugar candy	Clear liquid	320°	Sugar liquifies.
Caramel for crème caramel, cakes	Brown liquid	338°	Sugar liquifies and turns brown.

Quick Hint

Wine hinders the cooking of vegetable fibers, so onions should always be cooked soft or transparent *before* wine is added to the pan.

Wine curdles milk, cream, butter and eggs. Put wine in pan first, reduce it slightly, then add the fragile items off the heat. From then on, no high heat.

Cooking with Beer

Use light beer unless directed otherwise.

Start with *still* beer. Open it 15 minutes ahead.

Cooking With Wine

When you cook with wine, you must allow enough cooking time for the alcohol to evaporate or the dish will taste harsh. To lose the raw taste, red wine must reduce by half, white by a little more. In a shallow pan, alcohol will cook out of a dish in about 2 minutes; in a deeper pan it can take 15 to 20. **Fortified wines** (sherry, port or Madeira) are different. When you add them or Cognac to dishes like soups, you want the full, uncooked flavor, so you add them in small amounts, just before serving. For amounts to add, see the chart on the next page.

If you use a wine that isn't as full-bodied as the one called for in the recipe (for example, a regular wine in place of a fortified wine or a light Beaujolais instead of a rich Burgundy or Pinot Noir), beef it up with a teaspoon of sugar or currant jelly per cup of wine.

When a recipe calls for a bottle of wine, it means about 3 cups.

Always use a dry wine unless the recipe specifies a sweeter one.

You can substitute dry white vermouth for any dry white wine. Use about ¼ less since the flavor is a bit stronger, and make up the difference in liquid volume with water or stock.

Stop to think before you decide to braise meat or poultry in red wine. The long, slow cooking concentrates the wine flavor, making it very dominant. You want this in a Beef à la Mode or Coq au Vin, and most game can stand up to the competition. However, in general, don't use red wine for more than half the recipe's liquid. You may find you prefer food braised in white wine.

A non-wine note: when a recipe calls for rum, use dark or golden rum. The light doesn't have enough flavor.

❧ COOKING WITH WINE ❧

Food: Amount to Use	Suggested Wine	When to Add
Cream soups: 1 tablespoon per serving	Sherry, dry white wine	Add just before serving.
Meat and vegetable soups: 1 tablespoon per serving	Dry or medium sherry or dry red wine	Add before serving.
Fish, broiled or baked: equal parts wine and butter or oil	Dry white wine or vermouth	Baked: add at beginning and baste. Broiled: use as basting liquid.
Fish, poached: equal parts wine and water	Dry white wine or vermouth	Add at beginning.
Chicken, broiled: equal parts wine and melted butter	Dry red or white wine, vermouth or sherry	Use for basting every 10 minutes.
Chicken fricassee: about half of total liquid	Dry white or red wine or vermouth	Add after browning.
Chicken and duck, sautéed: ½ cup per bird	Dry red or white wine, vermouth or sherry	Add after browning.
Game, duck, pheasant: ¼ cup per pound	Dry red wine. For pheasant, add dry white wine or sherry	Use as basting liquid or add after browning.
Baked ham: 1 to 2 cups	Any dessert wine (port, muscatel, sherry) or table wine	Use for basting at start of glazing period.

COOKING WITH WINE

Food: Amount to Use	Suggested Wine	When to Add
Pot roasts, braises and stews: ¼ cup per pound	Beef or lamb: dry red wine Lamb or veal: dry white Ham: Madeira	Add after browning meat.
Cream sauces: 1 tablespoon per cup	Dry or medium sherry, dry vermouth or dry white wine	Add with liquid ingredients.
Brown sauce or tomato sauce: 1 tablespoon per cup	Sherry or dry red wine	Add with liquid ingredients.
Gravies for meat or poultry: about 2 tablespoons per cup	Dry red or white wine or sherry	Add with liquid and boil well.
Fruit, fresh, canned, or frozen in syrup or juice: 1 tablespoon per cup	Port, muscatel, sherry, rosé, sweet sauterne	Add early to macerate or at serving time for fresher flavor.
Fruit, drained	Sparkling or still wine	Pour over fruit at table.

Flavoring With Wine

Two tablespoons fortified wine and ½ cup table wine have the same flavoring power. Boost the flavoring strength of table wine by reducing. Ten minutes uncovered boiling will reduce 1 cup to ¼ cup...A good trick when you don't want to further dilute a sauce.

HOW TO FLAME FOODS

You flame food (Cherries Jubilee, Steak au Poivre) with burning alcohol, generally from brandy or whiskey. This not only enriches the flavor but, done in front of guests, makes a great impression.

For success and safety, you must follow a few rules:

- Always pour the liquor into a ladle and *then* into the pan. If you pour liquor from a bottle into a pan near an open flame, the flame can follow the liquor stream back up into the bottle and make it explode. Which creates more drama than you had in mind.

- Both food and liquor must be warm. Heat the liquor in a metal spoon, ladle, or small pot over a burner or candle flame until it is warm to the touch. You can also heat it in the microwave oven for 15 seconds on high (100%).

Then, either:

1. Pour it over the heated food and immediately light it with a long match,
2. Light it in the ladle or pan and pour it flaming over the food, or
3. If the food is in a chafing dish over an open flame, pour the liquor on the food while tilting the pan so the flame ignites the liquor. (Avert your face because liquor can ignite with a whoosh.)

- **Cook long enough to burn off the raw taste and mellow the flavors**—this is where many flambé artists blow it.

Customarily you let the flame go out on its own. However, if you want still more drama, turn out the lights and serve the dish while it's still flaming. Just be careful. Remember, you're playing with fire.

Flaming Foods

MARINADES AND RUBS

A marinade has 3 essential ingredients: oil, acid, and flavoring. The first two tenderize, and the last one improves taste.

In general, use equal parts oil and acid (vinegar, lemon juice, dry wine) plus flavoring (garlic, onion, herbs, spices or seeds). Figure ⅓ to ½ cup marinade per pound of food.

The more acid in the marinade and the warmer the environment, the less time you need. In general, marinate half as long at room temperature as in the refrigerator. Don't marinate too long or you can ruin both flavor (too strong) and texture (meats get mushy and crumbly). If food has marinated in the refrigerator, let it come to room temperature (30 minutes) before cooking.

When marinating, use a nonreactive container such as

——— *Recipe* ———

Louie's Wonderful Marinade

Louie marinated thick fish steaks for 8 hours in the fridge in this delicious marinade. Good for meat, fish and fowl.

¼ cup lemon juice
¼ cup olive or salad oil
½ medium onion, minced
2 cloves garlic, minced
crushed red pepper to taste
salt and pepper to taste
Mix all ingredients.

Yield: About ¾ cup, enough for 1½ pounds of meat.

Recipe

Teriyaki Marinade

This Oriental-style marinade is good for beef, poultry, fish and vegetables. It is enough for a 9- to 10- pound turkey.

½ cup vegetable oil
½ cup soy sauce
3 tablespoons sugar
2 teaspoons grated fresh ginger,
   or 1 teaspoon ground
1 large clove garlic, minced
2 tablespoons dry sherry
Mix all ingredients.

Yield: About 1¼ cups, enough for 1 or 2 pounds of meat.

glass or stainless steel or a large zip-lock plastic bag. The acid in the marinade can pit aluminum and give the food an off taste. Turn the food often if the marinade doesn't completely cover it.

In the boxes are two marinades our household likes. The first came from Louie, our cook in Benin, who grilled the crustiest, moistest, most glorious fish steaks you ever tasted. The second is a Japanese one we use for everything. Some Thanksgivings we marinate turkey parts in it and grill our bird. It's spectacular.

A dry rub of herbs and spices will flavor the outside of the meat as it cooks. It doesn't tenderize, but because it is dry it helps produce a crisp exterior. Use it for bulky pieces that would need gallons of marinade or for days when there's no time to marinate. Rub it into big pieces and sprinkle it over small or delicate ones.

See pp. 355 and 360 for a couple of ideas.

❦ How Long to Marinate ❦

Food	At Room Temperature	In the Fridge
Delicate-textured, like fish, or in small chunks	15 - 30 minutes	——
Poultry, small pieces of meat	1 hour	4 hours
Large, tough cut of meat	——	2 days

Cooking Methods

Basically, you cook with two sorts of heat: moist and dry.

Moist heat (boiling, parboiling, simmering, poaching, steaming, stewing, braising) adds the flavor of herbs, wine, and vegetables from an aromatic liquid or its steam. You poach and steam delicate items for a short time; you slowly simmer, stew and braise tougher things since cooking in moist heat tenderizes.

Dry heat (baking, broiling, grilling, roasting, sautéing, deep frying) caramelizes sugar and starch and gives food that lovely browned flavor and golden surface; it's the way to cook tender foods. Because it has a drying effect it's good for doughs, batters and casseroles, but it's not so good for meats, poultry and vegetables. These need protecting, either by their own internal fat, a light coating of butter or oil, or a couple strips of bacon. **Food cooked in fat** generally needs protection from the hot fat, which might scorch the outside before the inside cooks. You coat these foods with breading, batter or flour.

Once you get a feel for what heat does, you'll be comfortable cooking just about anything by just about any method.

Blanching and Parboiling

With both of these methods, you cook in boiling water for a very short time, then plunge the food immediately into cold water to stop the cooking.

Blanching has many uses. It softens strong flavors (cabbage) and sharp flavors (onions, eggplant); it removes excess salt from salt pork or bacon and an overly smoky taste from ham. Blanch greens to fix their color, and tomatoes, peaches and almonds to loosen their skins for easy peeling. Recipes sometimes call for blanching to firm up delicate meats like sweetbreads or to soften cabbage leaves for stuffing. Blanching precooks vegetables so they need only a quick toss in hot butter before serving.

Technique

When Should You Cover a Pot?

Never when frying.

Never when roasting.

Never when reducing.

Never when boiling green vegetables (the cover traps acids given off by the vegetables and they turn gray).

Initially when you add pasta to boiling water. Uncover the minute water returns to the boil.

Partially when simmering, to eliminate the risk of boiling over and to allow the liquid to concentrate slightly.

Tightly when steaming or braising. To ensure a really tight cover, lay a sheet of foil on the pan before putting on the cover.

Rule of Thumb

For boiling all vegetables except potatoes:

Cover what grows below ground.

Don't cover what grows above.

Parboiling is the same as blanching but is done for a little longer. Parboil longer-cooking vegetables that are to be deep-fried or grilled so they will be fully cooked by the time their outsides are crisp and golden; parboil tough vegetables like celery root to prepare them for further cooking.

You can blanch or parboil food for further cooking and refrigerate it up to 24 hours ahead. **To reheat blanched vegetables** for serving, bring to room temperature, then toss in butter until their color turns bright and they are crisp-tender (2 to 6 minutes).

❦ Blanching and Parboiling ❦

There are three ways to blanch or parboil, depending upon the food:

1. Pour boiling water over the food and let it stand for 15 to 60 seconds. Then drain and plunge into cold water to stop the cooking.

2. Place the food in a large pot of cold water, salt lightly, bring to a boil. Start timing when the boiling begins. When the time is up, drain and plunge the food into cold water.

3. Same as method 2 except the food is added to already boiling water and the timing starts when the food hits the water.

Ingredient	Method	Time
Almonds (to peel)	1	1 to 2 minutes
Root vegetables	2	1 minute
Tomatoes (to peel)	1	15 seconds
Spinach	3	Less than a minute
Cabbage	3	Less than a minute
Other vegetables	3	1 minute
Peaches (to peel)	1	1 to 2 minutes

Boiling

Dozens of everyday cooking tasks make use of boiling. It's a way to cook foods that don't need particularly gentle treatment, and to reduce and concentrate large volumes of stock or sauce. Since cooking at a full boil toughens most protein foods, it's not a good way to cook eggs, shellfish, fish, poultry or meat.

At a normal boil, which you use for most purposes, the surface of the liquid is bubbling and in constant movement. **At a rolling boil**, the liquid actually rolls on top of itself; bubbles form rapidly, rise, and break before they reach the surface. This is what you want for cooking green vegetables and pasta, reducing stocks and making preserves and syrups.

Some hints for boiling foods:

Pasta: Don't depend on the cooking times on the package. Start testing early, after about 2 minutes for thin pasta, up to about 15 for thick. It's done when the raw flour taste and hard white center are gone, but the pasta is still chewy.

Add a tablespoon of oil to the water to prevent boil-overs and keep pieces from sticking together. If you add the pasta gradually, so the water keeps its rolling boil, the movement of the water will keep it from clumping. If, by chance, the boil subsides, turn up the heat and stir until the water boils again.

See p. 38 for more about cooking pasta.

Sugar Syrups: See p. 77.

High Altitude Cooking

Liquids evaporate faster at high altitudes, so allow a little more liquid and check often that food isn't going dry. Cooking time will be longer—this is true in the microwave, too.

TECHNIQUE

To Salt Water or Not?

Do salt water for things that have a short, furious boiling time, like vegetables and pasta.

Don't salt water for corn; it toughens it. Add a pinch of sugar to the water instead.

Don't salt water for foods that cook long and slowly, like stocks, stews and beans. Stock may become too salty when it reduces, beans get tough. Salt these dishes when they are almost done.

Stack Your Steamers

If you use stackable steamers like the Oriental bamboo ones, you can steam things for different times over the same pot.

If you have foods to cook for 15, 10 and 5 minutes, put on the 15 minute one, cover and steam 5 minutes. Uncover, top with the 10 minute one in its basket and cover again. After 5 minutes add the last basket and cover.

If you don't have a rack, you can steam on a plate set on a heatproof cup or empty tuna fish can to keep it above the water.

Steaming

Steaming means cooking on a rack above gently simmering liquid. This is a healthful way to prepare many light foods such as shellfish and fish.

Indirect Steaming: This is a cross between cooking in a water bath and steaming, where a food, usually a pudding, steams in a tightly covered mold. The mold can be stainless steel, ovenproof glass, ceramic or aluminum. Fill it ⅔ full so the mixture can expand. Cover tightly to keep out water, using the mold's cover or a double thickness of foil pressed around the edges or tied tightly with string. A 1-pound coffee can makes a good mold. For individual molds use custard cups, metal gelatin molds, or 3" cans.

Set the mold on a trivet in a heavy kettle and add boiling water to come up ⅓ of its height. Cover the kettle tightly and place over high heat until steam starts escaping. Then lower the heat to keep a gentle boil for the rest of the cooking time. Before unmolding, remove the mold cover and let the pudding rest until it has stopped steaming. This way it isn't so likely to break up when you unmold it.

Poaching and Simmering

These methods involve cooking in a generous amount of liquid that is hot but not quite boiling, either covered or uncovered. Poaching and simmering are perfect for delicate foods like eggs, shellfish, fish and chicken breasts. They tenderize sturdy meats like stewing hens, beef chuck, tongue and corned beef brisket. And they're a less common, but glorious way to cook large, luxury cuts like beef rib eye, beef tenderloin (a magnificent dish!), leg of lamb or pork, hams and turkey.

When you're poaching small, quickly cooked foods like seafood and poultry, the choice of liquid is important because it flavors the food and the food flavors it. Poach poultry in chicken stock and seafood in fish stock or court bouillon.

When you poach large pieces of meat, the starting liquid isn't so important because the long cooking produces a flavorful stock. Still, you may like to use a mix of broth, wine, herbs and spices.

See Chapter 10 for stock and court bouillon recipes.

Cooking in a Wrapper (En Papillote)

In this method individual portions of delicate or quickly-cooked foods are seasoned and/or sauced, sealed in a wrapper and baked, trapping all the flavor and juices inside.

In classic cooking you cut parchment in a heart, butter it, place food on one half, fold it over and crimp the edges to seal. It's easier to use a large square and gather the edges to make a pouch. Before closing, add any liquid you may be using. Tie the neck with string or a wire twist. Brush the outside with butter, or use foil. Enclose the food loosely, crimp or fold to close. Bake packets on a baking sheet in a 375° oven for 15 to 20 minutes. (Parchment will puff and brown.) Diners break open the packages at table, letting out a puff of aromatic fragrance. You can fill the packets with meat, poultry, seafood, vegetables—whatever. Add seasoning, a little wine or butter...A bed of pilaf is elegant.

Deep Fat Frying

Deep-frying is a tasty way of cooking poultry, fish, vegetables and sweet treats, but many people avoid it because it seems to involve so much fat. However, when food is properly fried, surprisingly little fat penetrates the crisp outer crust.

Food to be deep-fried should be at room temperature so it won't cool the fat, and should also be protected from the hot fat with breading (see p. 90), seasoned flour, or a batter like pancake or tempura batter (see p. 150). (Beer makes an excellent liquid for frying batters—it makes a crispy coating.) Items to be fried should not be more than ¾" thick. If they are thicker, you'll get undercooked food in a golden crust or cooked food in a burnt one.

When you fry moist vegetable slices without a coating, salt them ahead of time and let them stand 15 minutes

⸻ *Recipe* ⸻

Chicken in a Wrapper

Brown 8 chicken thighs or small breast halves in 2 tablespoons each of butter and olive oil. Place two pieces on each of four pieces of parchment. In the skillet sauté a small chopped onion and a clove of minced garlic until golden. Put ¼ of this mixture on each portion. Divide among them 1 teaspoon each rosemary, oregano, thyme and fennel seed. Sprinkle with salt and pepper. Dot with butter. Close up the packages. Bake at 350° for 45 minutes. Serves 4.

⸻ *Recipe* ⸻

Fruit in a Wrapper

Peaches, plums, strawberries, bananas, kiwi. All work well. Sauté them lightly in a little butter. Sprinkle with sugar and any flavoring you like. Add very little extra liquid. Enclose in packages, seal and bake at 350° for 15 minutes.

RULE OF THUMB

Deep Fat Temperature

You can fry almost everything—meat, poultry, vegetables, fritters, or doughnuts—at 365°.

High Altitude Cooking

Deep-fried food will brown faster at high altitudes, so use slightly lower frying temperatures—3 degrees less for every 1,000 feet above sea level.

to draw off some of their moisture. Pat very dry before slipping them into the oil. (If they are wet the fat will explode.)

When you are ready to fry, place enough fat or oil to cover the food in a deep, heavy pan. Never fill the pan more than half full of fat or oil, especially when frying things that swell, like doughnuts or fritters. Always heat fat *slowly*, usually to 365°, to allow the moisture in the fat to evaporate before the fat gets hot enough to spit. Once the fat is heated, adjust the burner to hold the temperature.

Temperature is very important. When it's right the coating seals out oil and the food fries up crisp and greaseless. When it's too low, the coating absorbs oil and is greasy; when too high, the outside burns before the inside cooks. Fry in small batches. This keeps the oil temperature from dropping and allows fat to bubble around each piece. When you add to the oil, don't do it while food is in the pan, and always allow the oil time to reheat before you put in the next batch of food.

To reduce grease fallout, use a spatter screen or invert a large colander over the pan. When you aren't worried about spatters you can fry at a properly brisk temperature so the food comes out crisp and absorbs a minimum of fat.

Try to turn food only once, always using a spoon so you don't puncture the seal of the crust.

Drain fried food on paper towels before serving.

You can reuse frying oil. Strain it through a sieve lined with a paper towel or a coffee filter and store it covered in the refrigerator.

Breading for Fried Foods

Breading makes a particularly nice crust for fried food. To do it, you'll need three shallow dishes, one holding seasoned flour (about ¾ cup for a 3½ pound chicken in parts), one with about the same amount of dry bread crumbs, and a third containing one or two eggs beaten with a little water, or just egg whites beaten frothy.

Here's chef's trick to avoid gluey hands. With your

right hand turn the piece of food in flour to coat it. With your left hand dip the coated food in the egg mixture and lay it on the crumbs. Now use your dry hand to flip crumbs over it and turn it. This keeps one hand doing dry things, the other doing wet. No goo. Neat.

The secret to breading that clings tightly is to have the food absolutely dry when it is dipped in the beaten egg, then to let the coated food sit on a rack and dry for 15 to 30 minutes before frying.

If you want to bread small or thin pieces of frozen food, thaw them just until the surface moistens and is soft enough for the breading to stick. Bread and cook without the drying step, until the breading is golden.

Sautéing and Stir-Frying

When you sauté, stir-fry or pan-fry, thin pieces of food are cooked quickly over direct, high heat in a small amount of fat. Since the heat is high, the food must be kept in motion, either by frequently shaking the pan or by stirring and flipping the food. As soon as the food is brown, it is removed and kept warm while you pour liquid into the pan and scrape up the browned bits to make a sauce.

WHEN IS IT DONE?

One of the most important cooking skills is knowing when food is done. The most glorious ingredients prepared to perfection will turn greasy, mushy, tough, floppy, dry, bitter, or tasteless if they're overcooked. Temperature is probably the most accurate—at least it's the most scientific—way of judging. But the best cooks learn better ways. They poke and pinch, they jiggle dishes to see how much looseness is left in a mixture. They smell. They listen to the way the fat sounds—is it singing briskly? And all these things tell them something. So use the thermometers, but at the same time, be aware of how things are looking and feeling as they cook. When you bake, roast and braise,

---

RESCUE

The Oil Caught Fire!

If the fire is in the pan, smack a large lid on it pronto! If the fire has spilled onto the burner, *don't lift the pot!* Clap on the lid and shake lots of salt or baking soda on the fire.

RULE OF THUMB

Sautéing Temperature

The *thicker* the piece, the *lower* the heat—to give heat time to reach and cook the food's center before the outside burns.

trust your nose. When you start to smell something, it is time to start checking for doneness. You'll enjoy cooking more, and you'll gradually develop your own instincts for knowing when something is done.

A Few Thermometer Notes:

Meat thermometer: Be sure the tip doesn't touch a bone or a pocket of fat, both of which are a lot hotter than the meat you're testing. Try to place the thermometer in the thickest part of the meat.

Always remove roasted meat from the oven when it registers 5 degrees below the done temperature. The internal temperature of meat will continue to rise while the meat rests—which it must do to allow the juices the heat pulled to the surface to be absorbed back into the center.

Candy thermometer: Before and after plunging into a seething pot of fat or boiling sugar syrup, let it stand in a little hot tap water.

Check your thermometer's accuracy now and then by sticking it in boiling water. It should read 212°. If it doesn't, note the difference and allow for that when you use it.

SAUCES

Here are ways to defat a sauce, or the cooking liquid that goes into one.

- Chill until the fat solidifies and lift it off.

- Pour into a clean wine bottle. When the fat rises into the bottle's neck, pour it off.

- Tilt the pan off the edge of the burner. When the fat accumulates on the low side, spoon it out.

- Toss in ice cubes and remove them along with the fat clinging to them. You may have to repeat this several times, but it's very effective.

- If the liquid is thin, you can use one of the special cups with a long spout at the bottom that allows you to pour off the liquid while the fat remains in the cup.

Thickening Sauces

Most sauces are thickened with a starch such as flour, cornstarch, potato starch or arrowroot. If you stir dry starch directly into hot fat or liquid, the sudden heat shrivels the starch into rubbery lumps. Always protect starches by mixing them to a paste with a little cool liquid before stirring the paste into the hot fat or liquid. See chart for amounts.

THICKENING A SAUCE WITH A STARCH PASTE

For every cup of liquid:

Cornstarch*	Water	Sauce Consistency
½ tablespoon	1 tablespoon	Thin
1 tablespoon	2 tablespoons	Medium
2 tablespoons	3 tablespoons	Thick

*Use the same measure for potato flour or arrowroot, double the measure for flour.

Two Ways to Thicken With Flour

Beurre manié: Knead together equal amounts of soft butter and flour and drop it by bits into boiling liquid while you stir. Use 2 tablespoons of paste per cup liquid for medium thickness.

Roux: Stir flour into an equal amount of warm, *not hot* fat in the pan. Cook and stir for 2 to 3 minutes to cook out the starch taste. Add hot liquid to cooked *roux*, not the other way around. For a white sauce, cook the *roux* for

Thickening Tips

Cornstarch, potato starch and arrowroot have little protein so they make clear sauces.

You thicken with them using the water paste method at left. To ensure success:

- Warm the paste by adding a little of the hot liquid to be thickened before you stir it in.
- Don't stir the sauce too hard. Furious stirring can make it thin out.

Flour has more protein and makes an opaque sauce.

Flour thickens best when mixed with fat rather than water. See the two methods at left. A flour-water paste generally makes lumps in the sauce and leaves a taste of raw flour. Still, the flour-water paste is quick. Here's how to minimize problems:

- Stir steadily and the minute those lumps appear, stir hard with wooden spoon or whisk. (Fast stirring doesn't thin flour sauces.)
- If lumps remain, buzz the sauce in the processor or blender.
- Cook the sauce at least 3 minutes to reduce the raw flour taste.

Technique

Stirring Tip

If you stir or whisk sauce in a figure 8 pattern you will reach all areas of the pan.

Rescue

I Scorched the Sauce!

If a dessert sauce burns, a little extra vanilla or almond essence often covers the taste.

2 to 3 minutes. To add color and deeper flavor to brown sauces, cook to the color of a brown paper bag.

Or thicken a sauce by whisking in one of the following: a grated cheese like Parmesan, cream, sour cream or plain yogurt. Keep the heat low when you use these dairy products; too much heat makes cheese string and turn rubbery, and curdles light and sour cream. Even very low heat can make yogurt act up unless you first stir in 2 teaspoons of cornstarch or 1 tablespoon of flour for every cup of yogurt.

Here's a last, old-fashioned thickening technique. Cut the crusts from a slice of bread (the Belgians spread it with butter and chopped herbs or prepared mustard). Drop this, seasoned side down, into the pan or casserole and leave it for 10 minutes. Then stir it in until blended. It will thicken the sauce and, if you fancied up the bread, add flavor.

Reducing Sauces

You can also thicken a sauce or liquid that's too thin by cooking it down over high heat until it's syrupy. Reduce sauces uncovered in a wide pan over high heat, so you get maximum evaporation, or in a 350° oven. The oven will take from 15 minutes to an hour, depending on the amount. You can also reduce sauces in the microwave, uncovered, in a wide, shallow dish, for 20 to 40 minutes. Check them often.

When you reduce a sauce, how do you know when it is down to the specified half or third? Before you start, rest a wooden spoon, handle-down, on the pan bottom and mark the sauce level on the handle. Then you'll know how much you started with.

Because reducing concentrates flavors, season sauces after they reduce.

To Pep Up a Sauce

A little meat glaze like Bovril, Kitchen Bouquet or Maggi can give spunk to a sauce that "needs something". Add them to taste, using very small (½ teaspoon) amounts at a time. My favorite combination, for 1 to 2 cups of meat or poultry sauce, is a teaspoon of meat glaze, another of tomato paste, and 1 to 2 teaspoons of red currant jelly. I often add a tablespoon or two of Cognac or sherry, in which case I boil the sauce at least 5 minutes to cook out any raw alcohol taste.

❦ HANDLING SAUCES LIKE A PRO ❦

If	Next Time You'll Know	Turning It into a Winner
Lumps in the sauce.	Unprepared starch was added to hot liquid or fat (see p. 93). Water/starch or butter/flour mixture not mixed smooth; liquid added too quickly; not constantly stirred.	Whisk furiously with wire whisk; whirl in blender or processor; press through strainer.
Sauce too thin.	Too little flour or other starch.	See Thickening Sauces, p. 93.
	Too much liquid; sauce not cooked long enough.	Cook some more.
Sauce too thick.	Too much flour; too little liquid; cooked too long; stood too long after cooking.	Whisk in more liquid.
Butter in sauce separates.	Cooked too long or over too high heat. If Hollandaise, butter was added too quickly.	Quickly pull pan from heat, swirl in an ice cube for 3 or 4 seconds to lower temperature, remove it and beat sauce well. If this doesn't work, it will look odd but taste fine. Call it something else.

Handling Sauces Like a Pro

If	Next Time You'll Know	Turning It Into a Winner
Egg-based sauces curdle.	Egg yolk added too quickly; heat too high; sauce cooked too long	Add a couple ice cubes and whisk. If that doesn't do it, buzz the sauce in the processor or blender.
Sauce in casserole turns watery when baked.	Sauce not made extra thick to compensate for an ingredient that oozed liquid while cooking (like mushrooms or raw seafood); casserole baked covered so water collected under cover and dripped in.	If it won't disturb the casserole, stir in a flour/water paste or bread crumbs. Or sprinkle top with lots of bread crumbs to absorb liquid and run under broiler to toast them.
Skin formed on top.	Air dried it. Next time lay a piece of buttered wax paper or plastic wrap on surface of a sauce made in advance, or float a film of melted butter on it when lukewarm.	Warm the sauce and push through a strainer or whirl in processor or blender. If it won't hurt the texture, whisk the thick part in, breaking it up well.

Cooking Ahead

With no maids, cooks and butlers around these days, it makes sense to cook ahead. When you're busy, rushed, or just plain tired you can put something on the table that was made at a leisurely pace rather than in a slam-bang dash. Cooking ahead is also the answer to frazzle-free parties.

Here are some tips on holding food prepared a short time ahead and reheating what you prepared last week.

Holding Food until Serving Time

The home equivalent of the restaurant steam-table is putting food in a pan over hot water. For more than one dish, pour boiling water into a large shallow pan, place it over the lowest heat setting and set covered containers of food in the hot water. Water must stay very warm but mustn't approach a simmer. You don't want the food to cook!

Keep **fried foods** warm on a pan lined with paper towels in a 300° oven while you cook the rest.

To keep **pancakes** warm, place them on and between cloth towels in a 200° oven. Arrange waffles, which must stay crisp as well as warm, in a single layer on a wire rack on a baking sheet and place in a 300° oven. (If you stack them they'll be soggy.)

Keep **poached eggs** in a pan of cold water. Just before serving, slip them into gently simmering water just long enough to to warm through (about 30 seconds).

You can hold a traditional **Hollandaise sauce** in a tightly covered wide-mouth thermos jar for up to 4 hours.

To keep **cooked rice** at serving temperature, put it in a colander over a saucepan containing 2 inches of gently simmering water. Cover the rice with a layer of paper towel and it can sit for up to an hour.

To prepare a **tossed salad** ahead and hold it until serving time, place the dressing in the bottom of the salad bowl, add any ingredients that would benefit from marinating (cucumber, mushrooms, onion), and pile greens lightly on top. If there are no bulky items to marinate, invert a saucer over the dressing before adding greens so the leaves won't sog in the dressing. *Do not toss until serving time.* Don't worry about the dressing separating; tossing will mingle it again.

Keep **rolls** warm in your electric casserole or skillet, covered, with heat set at low.

Quick Hint

When you cook a casserole or roast the day before: cool it quickly by placing the pot in a container or sinkful of cold water for 15 minutes or so, then refrigerate.

—— RULE OF THUMB ——

How Fast Do Things Reheat?

The thicker the liquid and the more solid food it contains, the more slowly you should heat a dish to give it time to warm evenly. So:

- Heat clear liquids quickly over high heat.
- Heat thick soups or stews at a simmer over low heat and stir often.

Reheating

It's the oxidation of fat that gives leftovers that warmed-over taste. To minimize oxidation, don't reheat food in aluminum or iron or add salt early. Also, try to keep out air. When you wrap food, cover it with foil, pressing to eliminate air pockets. Plastic wrap is not so good for this purpose because oxygen can penetrate it.

If you've refrigerated something in the dish it was cooked in, transfer it to another pot when you reheat to prevent starchy ingredients from sticking to the pot bottom. If the dish has a thick sauce, film the bottom of the new pan with water before you add the food. Always give the food an occasional stir while it reheats to prevent sticking.

Liquids like **sauces and gravies** should cook gently for 1 or 2 minutes after reaching a simmer. But don't recook the food or it will taste tired.

Reheat **creamed soups** by bringing them slowly to the boil and simmering gently for 2 minutes. Serve immediately.

If you want to make **Hollandaise sauce** ahead and not worry about it separating when you warm it later, mix 1 tablespoon cornstarch with 2 tablespoons cold milk in a little bowl. Add to the finished sauce one tablespoon of this paste for every 3 yolks in the recipe.

Reheat **meat or poultry** in liquid or sauce with care. High heat shrinks and toughens the fibers. If you heat it in boiling liquid or over high heat it will be tough, dry and tasteless, because sauce and gravy can't penetrate stiffened fibers. Here's how to do it:

- **Roasted meat and poultry:** Warm a reheating liquid such as leftover meat juices, gravy, a sauce, or small amounts of butter or meat drippings *slightly*. Then slide in the food and heat gently (no peppy bubbling) until thoroughly heated.

• **Moist-cooked meats** like boiled beef and pot roast tolerate longer heating in their liquids—just be sure to keep the heat low.

A **whole roast** should be at room temperature when you place it in a 350° oven to reheat.

Chilled meat doesn't have much flavor. Reheat rare meat and keep it rare by placing thin slices of *room temperature* meat on warmed plates and covering them with *very hot* gravy or meat sauce. Serve instantly. If, instead of reheating, you serve roast meats cold, be sure they have warmed to room temperature.

When you reheat **dishes containing meat chunks**, the 10-minutes-per-inch timing used for cooking fish works perfectly. A stew or ragout with 2-inch pieces of meat will take about 20 minutes to reheat.

Reheat a **room-temperature casserole** for about 30 minutes in a 325° oven. A cold casserole will take up to 1 hour to heat to the center. To know when it is heated through, hold a paring knife blade in the center for 20 seconds. When pulled out, the blade should feel hot.

If you are reheating a dish with ingredients such as **cheese or cream** that separate or toughen with too much heat, the safest way is in a water bath. Set the dish in a larger container and add water to come about halfway up the sides of the casserole. Reheat creamed and egg-sauced dishes over hot water.

To reheat a **cold baked potato**, dip it in cold water and bake for 10 minutes at 350°.

Cook **rice** in the morning and place it in a greased casserole. When it is cool, cover it tightly with foil and reheat from room temperature in a 350° oven for about 20 minutes. Or use the microwave.

Don't try to keep **steamed or boiled vegetables** warm until serving time. Cook them ahead, but the instant they are crisp-tender drain and run cold water over them to stop the cooking. Now they can wait as long as overnight,

Quick Hint

To quickly cool cooked food such as boiled potatoes for salad, spread it out on a clean dish towel.

covered in the fridge. Just before serving, reheat them very briefly in hot water or, bring them to room temperature and toss in hot butter or any sauce.

To reheat **deep-fried foods** place them, not touching each other, on racks, *uncovered*, in a 250° oven until heated through.

BLAME IT ON THE WEATHER!

It's a comfort to know that you can legitimately blame some cooking mishaps on the weather:

- On a humid or very hot day yeast doughs are hard to knead, rise too fast and lose elasticity.

- Candy made on a hot, humid day won't set. You need a room temperature of 60° to 68° and low humidity to make chocolates, fudge, nougats, fondant, hard candy and divinity.

- Jam and jelly won't jell on a rainy day or in high humidity.

- Meringues made in damp weather fall and come out limp.

- Noodle and pasta doughs are difficult for beginners to make on rainy days.

- Puff pastry and brioche doughs need cold, dry weather. In a hot, humid room, the butter gets too soft, the dough becomes greasy, and so does the finished baked pastry.

- Mayonnaise won't thicken if made during a thunderstorm. Heat and high humidity make mayo heavy and greasy.

Cooking Help for Eggs

How Do I Make a Perfect Omelet, What If the Soufflé Doesn't Rise, and How Many Small Eggs Equal a Large One?

Cooking eggs is fun. They cook so fast that you can see the results as you stir or flip. You can cook eggs so many ways: poached, boiled, fried, scrambled, baked. They are delicious on their own with just a tad of pepper from the grinder and a sparkle of salt crystals. Or dress them up. Cover poached ones with buttery creamed spinach, lay three or four, soft-poached, in a cheese soufflé before baking. Lay a fried egg on a tortilla, top with a Mexican-style tomato sauce (see p. 302) and grated cheese. Roll scrambled eggs in a crepe, fill an omelet, or bake eggs in little ramekins with a swirl of cream and a dot of butter. Equally delicious for breakfast or supper.

The cholesterol publicity scared a lot of us off eggs for a while, but now we know we can enjoy them in moderation.

WAYS TO COOK EGGS

Baking Eggs
Baking is a good method for cooking egg dishes, but we don't think of it as often as we should.

Recipe

Archie's Baked Eggs

When my husband read in a Rex Stout novel that Archie had breakfasted on eggs baked with sausages, cream and chives, he couldn't rest until he had tasted it. So I got out little flat dishes and in each put an egg, two breakfast sausages fried to get rid of some fat, a spoonful of heavy cream and a sprinkle of chives. Bake at 325° (300° for glass) for 10 to 12 minutes. Archie knew how to live! Try it.

Baked or Shirred eggs: Butter individual ramekins (little custard cups—small for 1 egg, larger for 2), sprinkle with salt and pepper. If you're feeling festive, add something extra: a western omelet mix of minced onions, green peppers and tomatoes; a bed of creamed spinach, minced sautéed mushrooms, or a thin slice of prosciutto browned in butter. Break the egg on top. Add a tablespoon of cream. Cover loosely with foil.

Set the ramekins in a skillet (if the handle isn't oven-proof, wrap it in several thicknesses of foil) and add boiling water to reach halfway up the sides of the cups. Bake at 375° for 7 minutes or until the whites are set and yolks soft.

You can sprinkle the eggs with chopped chives, bacon, sour cream or grated cheese. If you want a treat, top them with a blob of sour cream and a spoonful of caviar. Wonderful.

To bake eggs in a shallow dish *(sur le plat):* Use shallow oven-glass or porcelain casseroles (the shape of small pie plates), either individual size or one that holds up to 6 eggs. Proceed as for the ramekins but, if you use a bed of seasoning ingredients, make a well in the center for the egg. (For a large dish, make as many wells are there are eggs.) Sprinkle with salt and pepper. Bake in a 325° oven (300° for glass) without a water bath for 8 to 12 minutes.

Boiled Eggs

First of all, that's a misnomer, since eggs should be simmered, not boiled.

For soft-cooked eggs, use room-temperature eggs so you can trust the timing. If you're forced to use eggs straight from the refrigerator, add 2 minutes. Put the eggs in a pan with cold water to cover by 1 inch and bring to a boil over high heat. Lower heat so bubbles barely break the surface. For a solid white and thickened yolk, simmer 4 to 5 minutes. Serve immediately.

For hard-cooked eggs, simmer for 10 minutes. Immediately plunge them in cold water to stop the cooking. If you won't peel the eggs right away, leave them in the water for an hour to cool.

❦ Handling Eggs Like a Pro ❦

If	Next Time You'll Know	Turning It into a Winner
Hard-cooked eggs have a greenish ring around yolk.	Cooked too long or at too high a temperature.	Cover with a little mayonnaise or parsley. With deviled eggs, no one will notice.
Hard-cooked eggs difficult to peel.	Eggs were too fresh. Older eggs peel easiest.	If they're really messy, chop them.
Poached eggs break up in water.	Water was salted. (Salt loosens protein.)	Rescue what you can for egg salad.

Fried Eggs

For old-fashioned fried eggs, melt 1 or 2 tablespoons of butter per egg over medium heat. When the butter foams, add the eggs. They cook best when they don't touch, but if they do, you can separate them with a spatula when they are done. Turn the heat to medium-low. Cook the eggs, spooning the hot butter over them, until the whites are set and the yolks have a white film.

Don't cook too long or over too high heat, or the whites will toughen. The underside should barely brown. But cook to your taste. Some people like the edges a bit crisp and lacy.

The eggs are now sunny-side up, a stage which, at present, isn't considered safe because the yolk isn't cooked enough to kill salmonella. So, turn the eggs and cook them a little more to set the second side and thicken up the yolk to your liking.

Another way of frying is to cover the eggs as soon as you put them in the butter and cook until done to your taste—safe sunny-side up will take about 1 minute. Or use less fat, and steam-fry by the next method.

Salt and Eggs

Salt toughens egg whites. Salt fried eggs just before serving.

Salt in poaching water loosens protein and can make egg whites break up.

— Recipe Ideas —

A Few Omelet Fillings

Before folding the omelet, add 3 to 4 tablespoons of any of the following:

Grated Swiss, Cheddar, or Parmesan cheese

Lumps of blue, mozzarella, cream or cottage cheese

Feta cheese and a pinch of garlic

Caviar, sour cream and a little minced onion

Creamed mushrooms, seafood or chicken livers

Sautéed pimento, tomato, garlic and parsley

Sautéed mushrooms, ham and tomato

Sautéed boiled potato, bacon and a little onion

For dessert:
Canned, thawed or fresh fruit, in smallish pieces

Jam, jelly or preserves

Flambé! Sprinkle the filled, folded omelet with 1 to 2 tablespoons liqueur and flame. See p. 82.

Steam-fried Eggs: This is "fried eggs lite". Use 1 teaspoon fat per egg (or spray a cold skillet with non-stick coating). Begin to cook as for fried eggs. When the bottoms are set, add 1 to 2 teaspoons of water to the pan, clamp on a cover, and cook until done to taste. Press a yolk gently with your finger to test.

Omelets

Read this through a couple of times before you start. It's surprisingly easy; the explanation looks long because I wanted to make it clear. This serves one. Making an omelet is the only time you cook eggs over high heat.

With a fork, whisk 2 eggs with salt and pepper just enough to mix whites and yolks. For a dessert omelet, add 4 teaspoons of sugar and omit the salt and pepper. Over high heat, melt 2 teaspoons butter in a 7" or 8" omelet pan or skillet (non-stick is best). When the butter foams and is just starting to brown, add the eggs and count 3 seconds (one elephant, two elephants, etc.) Then stir with the underside of a fork.

When the bottom begins to set (a matter of seconds), pull the set egg from the sides toward the center while tipping the pan to let uncooked egg flow on the bare pan bottom. When the eggs are almost set (15 to 30 seconds), stop stirring. The top will be moist and creamy. Now add seasoning or a filling (see the box).

Let the omelet sit a moment to set the bottom. Then tip the pan away from you and with your fork fold the near (high) edge of the omelet halfway down to the lower edge. With the pan still tipped, whack the base of the handle a couple times with the fist of your free hand. The lower edge of the omelet will jump up, overlap the top edge, and make a neat package. Use your fork to press the omelet closed at the seam. Roll it out onto a plate, seam down. Voilà!

Julia Child very sensibly suggests that you invest in a dozen eggs and make six practice omelets. Stir, whack and roll with abandon. Feed the results to the cat, throw them out, make a sandwich of them. As she says, a carton of eggs costs a heck of a lot less than a cooking lesson.

Flat Omelets (Fritattas)

Italians call them *fritattas*, Spaniards *tortillas*. Put the eggs in the pan mixed with any additions and seasonings. Stir until the eggs start to thicken. Let the omelet sit for a moment, then lift the edges with a fork to let the uncooked egg run underneath. When it is almost done—30 to 45 seconds—stop lifting and give it 20 to 30 undisturbed seconds to brown the bottom. Then run it under the broiler to brown the top (30 to 60 seconds).

If you make a 6-egg *fritatta* to serve 4, you're back to the low-heat rule. Use a 12" skillet, turn the heat to the lowest setting as soon as you add the eggs. It will take about 15 minutes to set the eggs with just the top still runny.

To Poach an Egg

Put 1½ to 2 inches of water in a large skillet (it's easier to lift eggs out of a shallow pan). If the eggs aren't super fresh (the whites of older eggs are thin) you can add a little vinegar—1 tablespoon per quart of water—to help keep the whites in a tight, tidy shape, but it's not necessary, and if you overdose, it could flavor the eggs.

Bring the water to a full boil. Break each egg into a cup. Holding the rim just below the water's surface, slide the egg into a bubbling area so the bubbles spin the egg and set the white around the yolk. Add up to 6 eggs to the pan. Immediately lower the heat so the water barely shivers. Cook the eggs uncovered for about 4 minutes or until whites have solidified and yolks are runny-firm. (Lift one out and press gently with your finger to test it.)

Remove eggs with a slotted spoon and trim their edges with a scissors. Drain for an instant on a folded paper towel, season and serve.

Scrambled Eggs

Count on 2 eggs per person. Whisk them with salt and pepper. Use a heavy pan that will make the eggs at least ¾" deep. Over medium heat melt 1 to 2 teaspoons of butter per egg (use the lesser amount if you are cooking

Poached Egg Trick

You can poach eggs ahead. Just slip them into a bowl of cool water for up to one hour. To hold for 24 hours, put the bowl of eggs and water in the refrigerator. To reheat, place eggs in water hot to the touch for 10 minutes, and be sure to drain well before serving.

───Recipe Idea───

Elegant Eggs

Scrambled eggs can be glamorous. A Belgian friend starts her elegant dinners with a large crouton heaped with soft-scrambled eggs topped with smoked salmon. Delicious.

❖ ❖ ❖

Thickening With Eggs

To thicken one cup of	Use
Soup	1 yolk
Baked custard	1 whole egg + 1 yolk
Soft (pouring) custard	2 yolks
Custard for quiche	2 to 4 whole eggs

❖ ❖ ❖

a big batch). When the butter stops foaming, turn the heat to medium-low and add the eggs.

Let them sit 1 to 2 minutes until they begin to set on the bottom—scrape the pan a couple times to test. Then scrape and stir, lifting the thickened egg so the uncooked egg runs underneath. Scrape, stir and fold until you have glossy, moist curds. For small curds in a soft, semi-set mass (the French way) scrape and stir steadily; for big, fluffy curds (my preference), don't stir steadily. Just scrape the bottom of the pan at intervals.

When you're judging doneness, remember, the eggs will continue cooking after they leave the heat. You won't like them if they get too dry.

For a lighter texture add 1 tablespoon milk, water or cream per egg. Jazz them up by swizzling onions, sliced mushrooms, ham, etc., into the butter before you add the eggs. Or sprinkle grated cheese on top just before the eggs are done, or top with snipped fresh herbs when they're finished.

EGGS AS INGREDIENTS

Eggs, like most other ingredients, yield the best results when properly handled. It helps to know that cold eggs are easiest to separate, while room temperature eggs beat to the highest volume. Here are some specifics:

Egg Custard

Custard is just milk thickened and set with eggs. Egg whites set the custard, egg yolks make it creamy. The usual proportions are 3 to 4 eggs to 2 cups of milk for firm (baked) custard and 4 yolks per cup of milk for soft (boiled or "stirred") custard. Soft custard is made on top of the stove. Thick, creamy and soft, it's used for sauce or pudding. Firm custard is baked in a dish or a crust. Dessert custards have about ¼ cup sugar added per cup of milk.

For a richer, smoother custard, add extra egg yolks and substitute half and half or light or heavy cream for the milk. Some recipes for the real French *Pôt de Crème* use all yolks and cream. Deadly but pure heaven.

For a lighter custard, substitute 1 teaspoon cornstarch for each egg or egg yolk.

Cooking custard: Like all egg mixtures, custards are delicate and don't like high heat. They thicken at a low temperature. If you hurry and raise the temperature, they won't be creamy. If you cook them too fast or too long they get curdled and nasty. Egg whites are more delicate than yolks, so a custard made with whole eggs will curdle even more easily.

How do you handle such delicate ingredients? You'll have beautiful, trouble free custards as long as you insulate the eggs from the heat: first, when you add the eggs to the hot liquid and second, when you cook the mixture.

To prepare the eggs to withstand hot liquid, beat them slightly in a small bowl. Then beat in a little of the hot liquid. Now they are warmed and you can safely beat them into the rest of the hot liquid.

To protect custard from heat, cook *soft custard* mixtures over (not touching) hot water in a double boiler and *baked custards* in a hot water bath covered with a sheet of foil (unless you want the tops to brown) or insulated in a crust, as for custard pie and quiche.

Checking for doneness: *Soft custard* coats the back of a spoon thickly (if you run a finger down the coated spoon the empty track won't fill in again). You'll know when it is about to break into a boil when bubbles start to reach the surface. Allow just two (no more) and stop the cooking. Temperature on an instant-read thermometer will be 165°. A knife inserted midway between the edge and center of a *baked custard* comes out clean. Done temperature for baked custard is 180°.

Tips for Cooking Soft Custards

If custard gets too hot and starts to curdle, pour it into a cold bowl and whisk for 10 to 15 seconds. Then finish cooking over gentlest heat.

It's All Custard

All these things are made with custard mixture:

Soft:
Custard Sauce
Floating Island
Bavarian Cream
Pastry Cream

Baked:
Crème Caramel
Bread Pudding
Rice Pudding
Custard Pie
Quiche
Some casseroles

...and French Toast

Keep the top soft: When you take soft custard from the heat, sprinkle it with a little sugar. This will melt as the custard cools and keep a skin from forming.

Keep it thick and rich: Beat custard as it cools to release steam which could condense and make it watery.

❧ HANDLING CUSTARDS LIKE A PRO ❧

If	Next Time You'll Know	Turning It into a Winner
Baked or soft custard curdles.	Too much heat. Bake in a water bath or cook over hot water. Eggs not pre-warmed with a little of the hot milk.	Strain soft custard into a cold bowl. If it didn't overcook, a whirl in the blender will re-emulsify it. Turn baked or soft custard into a trifle: mix with cake cubes, a slosh of sherry and a little jam, and top with cream.
Soft custard grainy.	Too much heat. Used frozen egg yolks.	Strain it.
Doesn't seem as rich as usual.	Too much heat. Custards need very slow cooking to be rich and silky.	Make trifle as above.
Baked custard has tunnels and weeps.	Too much heat. Cooked too long.	Drain off liquid, cube and mix with canned fruit and its syrup and a little almond flavor. Or try the trifle trick above.
Soft custard starts to curdle.	Too much heat. Don't let it touch the hot water below.	Snatch from heat source, pour into a bowl or set pan in cold water and beat for 10 seconds. If you caught it in time you're okay. If it curdled, try buzzing in the blender or push through a strainer.

Handling Custards Like a Pro		
If	**Next Time You'll Know**	**Turning it into a Winner**
Soft custard is watery.	Steam condensed in it while it cooled. Next time beat it while it cools.	Whisk in some cocoa or ground nuts and use as a sauce.
Skin formed on soft custard.	Didn't sprinkle top with a little sugar before cooling.	If skin is thin, whisk it into the cool custard. If thick, lift off. If a pudding in its serving dish, hide the uneven top with cream or a film of melted jelly.

Egg Whites

Egg whites swell from 3 to 7 times their original size when whipped, so use a large enough bowl. Even a hint of grease keeps egg whites from whipping well; they can lose as much as two-thirds of their expected volume. So make sure bowl and beaters are dry and squeaky clean and that no trace of yolk (it's fatty) gets into the whites when you separate them.

If you're going to fold them into a batter or whipped cream, beat the egg whites before you use the beaters for anything else. This way you won't have to wash them for the next step. (By the way, don't combine raw egg white with anything that won't be cooked, because of the risk of salmonella.)

Millions of teeny, even-sized bubbles give beaten egg whites the greatest volume and stability. To get them, use a large whisk with a lot of fine wires or your mixer on high speed, and beat in an acid like cream of tartar (⅛ teaspoon per egg white) to stiffen egg white protein. The easiest way to beat one egg white is to use a small, deep bowl and only one of the mixer's beaters.

An unlined copper bowl is the chef's choice for beat-

RESCUE

I Overbeat The Egg Whites!

If you overbeat egg whites, beat in 1 unbeaten white for every 3 or 4 overbeaten ones.

What's Magic About a Copper Bowl?

Copper's a demon heat conductor. When friction from the whisk heats the egg whites the heat, which hinders formation of tiny, stable bubbles, is instantly absorbed by the copper. Copper's second trick: it releases ions during beating that strengthen and stiffen egg white protein. No need for cream of tartar.

ing egg whites (see the box). However, any metal except aluminum (it turns egg whites gray) works well and is a lot cheaper. Porcelain, ovenproof glass and plastic bowls won't give you as much volume because the egg whites can't cling to the slippery sides. Plastic has a second disadvantage. Being porous, it may have absorbed grease from a previous use.

Sugar stiffens egg whites the way acid does. It makes egg whites pliable, so don't add sugar until the whites have become foamy with no liquid in the bowl bottom, or they will be too stretchy to hold the air well. Undissolved sugar causes uneven, fragile bubbles. Add the sugar gradually, beating to dissolve before adding more.

A recipe often tells you to beat egg whites to a specific stage. Here is how to know when you're there.

Foam: Big bubbles and lots of white suds on still-liquid whites. This is the stage where you add salt and cream of tartar if they are used. Use foamed egg whites to clarify stocks and to coat food for breading.

Soft foam: Smaller bubbles, soft peaks with bent tops when you lift the beater. This is the stage where you start gradually adding sugar for meringues.

Stiff foam: Small bubbles, moist and shiny, soft pointed peaks when you lift the beater. This is what you fold into mixtures like soufflés or cakes. If you beat any further the egg whites will be dry and granular and won't rise well, because at that point the air pockets are destroyed. If you're not sure you've reached this stage, opt for underbeating.

When you fold egg whites into a heavier mixture, first stir about ¼ to ⅓ of the beaten whites into the mixture to lighten it. Now it's much easier to fold the rest into the lightened batter.

EGG SIZES

Most recipes are based on the "large" egg. You can substitute any size with the following chart:

For this many	Use this many			
Large	Jumbo	Extra Large	Medium	Small
1	1	1	1	1
2	2	2	2	3
3	2	3	3	4
4	3	4	4	5
5	4	4	6	7
6	5	5	7	8

―Recipe Idea―

Cheese Puff

If you are lucky enough to have leftover soufflé, cut it in strips and put them in a buttered gratin dish. Sprinkle with cheese and milk and broil for 10 minutes or until puffy. (For half of a 4-egg soufflé, use ¼ cup cheese and ¼ cup milk.)

Soufflés

A soufflé is a light, fluffy dish made of egg yolks and stiffly beaten egg whites. Enlivened with savory ingredients like cheese, vegetables or seafood, it makes a luscious main dish. Sweetened, it becomes a heavenly dessert.

Here are a few hints for making perfect soufflés.

Adding cheese: Grate it finely and add it to the warm soufflé base so it will melt into the sauce before you fold in the egg whites.

Choosing a dish: The uncooked mixture should reach about an inch below the top of the dish.

Temperature: You can bake a soufflé at almost any temperature. If you choose the standard high temperature (375° to 400°) the soufflé will rise fast and have a soft center. It must be served immediately because it will start collapsing within 10 minutes. If you choose a lower temperature (325° to 350°) and use a water bath to lower the temperature around the soufflé, it will cook as it rises, end up sturdier with a completely cooked center, and hold up for as long as 30 minutes without collapsing. Dense soufflé mixtures made with seafood, vegetables or fruit purées take longer for the

Bake Your Soufflé Ahead

You can bake a soufflé ahead if you alter recipe proportions (see recipe on p. 328) to 4 tablespoons butter, 8 tablespoons flour (yes!) and 1⅓ cups milk and bake in a water bath. Cool it and chill. Baked in a 350° oven for 30 minutes, it repuffs like magic. I often make one in the morning for an easy meal when we come in late from golf or tennis. By the time the salad's tossed, the soufflé's ready.

centers to set, so always bake them at the low temperature or in a water bath.

Timing: Depends on how you like your soufflé. If you like it with a soft center, French style, it is ready when the top is a little concave and the center wobbles when you shake the pan gently. If you want it firm, bake until the top is flat and the center doesn't wobble.

Don't be nervous about time and temperature. If you're at all uncertain, just stay near the oven and watch so you can stop the cooking when you like.

You can freeze a fully-prepared, uncooked soufflé. Put it frozen into the oven, adding 15 minutes to the cooking time. Be sure to use a freezer-to-oven dish or line your original dish with foil, so you can lift out the frozen block of soufflé and wrap it for freezing, then replace it in the dish at baking time.

To serve a soufflé: Hold a large spoon and fork back to back, cut straight down to the bottom and gently pull the soufflé apart. Repeat this a couple inches away, then lift out the cut portion.

HOW DONE DO YOU WANT YOUR SOUFFLÉ?

For	Bake at
Very soft center (soft center acts as a sauce for the rest.)	400°
Medium soft center	Preheat the oven to 400° and turn it to 375° when you put in the soufflé.
Slightly soft center (good for savory soufflés)	Bake in a water bath at 400°.
Firm center (best for sweet soufflés)	Bake in a water bath at 325° to 350°.

❦ HANDLING SOUFFLÉS LIKE A PRO ❦

If	Next Time You'll Know	Turning It into a Winner
Soufflé browns on top before sufficiently risen.	Oven temperature was too high.	Lower oven temperature and lay foil on top for the rest of cooking. If top has burned, remove before serving.
Didn't rise properly.	Egg whites insufficiently beaten or not immediately folded into soufflé base; egg whites stirred instead of folded into base.	Texture will be dense and velvety instead of puffy, but the taste will be rich and good. Call it a timbale, and give it a sauce.
Soufflé fell while baking.	Oven door slammed or was opened too often.	Same as above. Top it with a sauce.
Soufflé collapsed before serving.	Waited too long after baking.	Return to a hot oven. Some times it will repuff. If not, see above.
Soufflé not done in time.	Oven temperature too low.	Bake it longer, until it tests done.

Cooking Help for Shellfish, Fish, Poultry and Meat

What Is Braising, Should I Roast at High or Low Temperatures, and How Do I Steam Fish?

This chapter deals with cooking fish, poultry and meat. There are charts giving times, temperatures and a sprinkling of useful information. How long to simmer a 2-pound lobster, for instance, and how long and how far from the heat to broil a lamb chop, or how long and at what temperature to roast the beef.

I organized it according to categories of cooking methods we're all familiar with:

Cooking in a pot (moist heat): Steaming, poaching, simmering, braising, stewing;

Oven and grill cooking (dry heat): Baking, oven-frying, roasting, broiling, grilling;

Cooking in fat on the stove-top (dry heat): Pan-broiling, sautéing, stir-frying, pan-frying, deep-frying.

As you know, the cooking method greatly influences the taste and texture of food. In general, low, moist heat,

Recipe

Pasta with Smoked Salmon and Caviar

Another recipe from my artist friend, Ellen. A heavenly flavor combination. Cook 8 ounces angel hair or fettuccine pasta, al dente. Drain and keep warm. In an 8" skillet over medium heat sauté 2 finely minced green onions in 2 tablespoons butter for 2 minutes. Stir in 1 cup sour cream and stir and cook until heated through and 1 or 2 bubbles break the surface. Gently stir in 4 ounces thinly sliced smoked salmon and plenty of coarsely ground black pepper. Heat through. Remove from heat and stir in 2 ounces of red caviar. Pour over cooked pasta. Garnish with parsley. Serves 4 as first course, 2 as main course.

which softens and turns tough connective tissue to gelatin, will make older birds and tough meats tender and succulent. If you're unsure of a wild bird's age, braise or pot roast it.

Use dry heat for poultry and tender meats. Remember, while the heat is softening connective tissue it is stiffening muscle fibers and cooking out moisture. So the trick to keeping the meat juicy and tender is not to overcook. Marbling, the little bits of fat sprinkled through tender cuts of meat and some fish, is the friend of dry heat cooking. Along with adding rich flavor as it melts, it tenderizes and moistens. All game birds are lean and need moistening. When you roast, grill or broil them, cover breasts and legs with a thin layer of fat (bacon, a sheet of pork fat, etc.) to keep them succulent. Marinating also moistens and tenderizes--see p. 83.

Shellfish can go either way—simmer, steam, broil or grill them. Fish vary so much in fat content and texture that any method can be suitable depending on the fish.

If you understand the methods and how they work, you can upset the applecart at will. That's what makes cooking fun. Poach a tender beef fillet, roast a well-exercised piece of chuck, or stew a fish! You'll see what I'm getting at as you use the charts.

COOKING IN A POT

Blanching and Parboiling

Quick blanching or longer parboiling is a first step in some meat recipes. It removes excess salt and strong flavors from ham, salt pork, bacon, smoked meats and tripe; it firms up sweetbreads and brains so they can be sautéed or braised.

To blanch meat, place it in a large pot of cold water, lightly salted unless the meat is already salty, and bring to a boil. As soon as the water boils start timing, using the chart below. When time is up, drain the meat and plunge it into cold water to stop the cooking.

❦ Blanching and Parboiling Meat ❦

Type	Time
Cured tongue	10 minutes
Salt-cured (country) ham	20 minutes per pound or to an internal temperature of 150°
Salt pork:	
Chunk	3 minutes
Diced	Remove just after water returns to a boil.
Bacon	Remove just after water returns to a boil.
Brains:	
Veal	20 minutes
All others	25 minutes
Sweetbreads	1 to 3 minutes, depending on size

Steaming

Steaming, which is cooking on a rack above gently simmering liquid, is a healthful way to prepare shellfish and fish.

Shellfish: For up to 5 pounds of crab or lobster, or 2 pounds of shrimp or crayfish, use a steamer or a large pan with a rack that sits at least 2 inches above the pan bottom. Pour 1 inch of water in the steamer and bring to a boil. Place the shellfish on the rack and cover tightly. When steam starts to escape under the lid, reduce the heat to medium. Cook crab, lobster and crayfish until bright red, shrimp until they turn pink. See the chart on the next page for approximate cooking times.

To steam live oysters, mussels, and clams, pour ¼ inch of water in a 5- to 7-quart pan. Add the shellfish, cover, and boil over medium high until the shells open. See the chart for estimated times. Oysters should open enough for you to be able to insert a knife; discard any that don't open.

— *Recipe Idea* —

Steamed Shellfish

Try steaming oysters in beer instead of water. Toss in a crushed garlic clove and a bay leaf. Mussels and clams can be steamed in a simple court bouillon (1 cup water and ¼ cup lemon juice), or white wine. To either, add 6 chopped green onions and ¼ teaspoon dried thyme and thicken the boiling liquid with a paste made of 1 teaspoon butter and 1 teaspoon flour.

—Recipe Idea —

A Gourmet Feast

Accompany steamed fish with vegetables steamed over the same broth. Carrots, zucchini, fennel, cucumbers, celery root and broccoli are good choices, singly or in combination.

Fish: Steaming works well for fish fillets, steaks and small whole fish. Steam them over plain water or, even better, a richly-flavored broth (see the recipe for court bouillon, p. 295). You'll need only a little concentrated broth because the steam is so hot that the fish cooks very quickly. Make your broth with assertive vegetables like fennel and dill. Add extra flavor by putting the fish on a bed of fresh herbs. (Some cooks use seaweed.) When you steam over an aromatic liquid, use a perforated rack so the steam comes up through the fish.

On the lightly greased rack, lay fish flat, fillets skin-upwards, without overlapping so they cook evenly. Place the rack in the pot *after* the liquid starts boiling and giving off its aromas. Cover tightly.

Unlike poaching liquid, the broth from steamed seafood is sometimes too concentrated for a sauce. If that is the case, sauce steamed fish with an herb butter instead.

❧ How Long to Steam Seafood ❧

Shellfish are done when the shells open or the color changes: pink for shrimp, red for crabs, crayfish and lobster.

Type	Minutes
Clams	5 to 10
Crab	5 to 10
Crayfish	5 to 8
Lobster	5 to 10
Mussels	4 to 8
Oysters	8 to 10
Shrimp	3 to 5
Fish	See poaching times, p. 120.

Poaching and Simmering

Poaching and simmering involve cooking in a generous amount of liquid that is hot but not quite boiling, with the pot either covered or uncovered. These methods are perfect for delicate foods like shellfish, fish and chicken breasts. They tenderize sturdy meats like stewing hens, beef chuck, tongue and corned beef brisket. And they're a less common but glorious way to cook large luxury cuts like beef rib eye, beef tenderloin (a magnificent dish!), leg of lamb or pork, and turkey.

When you poach small, quickly cooked foods like seafood and poultry, the liquid is important because it flavors the food and the food flavors it. Poach poultry in chicken stock and seafood in fish stock or court bouillon.

When you poach large pieces of meat, the starting liquid isn't so important because the long cooking produces a tasty stock. Still, you may like to use a mix of broth, wine, herbs and spices.

See Chapter 10 for stock and court bouillon recipes.

Now for some specifics.

Shellfish: To simmer up to 5 pounds of crab or lobster, or 2 pounds of shrimp or crayfish, pour enough liquid (water or water and wine) into a pan to generously cover the shellfish. Add 2 teaspoons salt per quart of liquid and bring to a boil. Add the shellfish. (Put a live lobster in head first and tuck the tail under to prevent a muscle reflex which could splash you). Cover, return to a boil, reduce heat and simmer according to the time on the chart on p. 120.

When cooking shellfish in water, be sure to immerse them briefly in cold water the minute they are done to stop the cooking.

Fish, Chicken and Meat: Place in a large pot and add liquid to barely cover. Cover and simmer over very low heat (water should just tremble with a few small bubbles rising now and then) until done. For fish this is a matter of minutes; for ham, several hours.

Steaming Sausages

Steam sausages anywhere from 15 to 30 minutes, depending on diameter.

RULE OF THUMB

How Long to Cook Fish

For all methods of cooking:
- Measure the fish at its thickest point.
- Cook fresh fish 10 minutes per inch if cooked alone, 15 minutes if cooked in a sauce.
- Simmer frozen fish 6 to 9 minutes per ½" of thickness.
- Time a poached fish from the moment the liquid starts bubbling again, and start testing early.

RULE OF THUMB

Rule for **seasoning fish:** Herbs point up the fish taste; spices tone it down.

So: Season non-fishy fish with herbs.

Season fishy fish with spices (also see page 20).

If vegetables are to be added to your simmered dish, (for Beef à la Mode, for instance), add them near the end, separately, according to the time each one takes. This way they don't overcook.

The cooking liquid for long-cooked meats is often served first as a soup or used to sauce the thinly sliced meat or pieces of poultry.

When you poach chicken for salads, cool it in the poaching liquid for rich flavor and velvety moist flesh.

To poach fish fillets or steaks, bring 1½ cups water, wine or broth to a boil in a large skillet. Slip the fish in, return liquid to a boil and lower heat to a bare simmer.

Sausage: Simmering is a good way to cook sausage (links, not patties). Place uncooked breakfast links, Italian sausage, etc., in a pan with just enough lightly salted, boiling water to cover. Cover and simmer 10 to 30 minutes, depending on the diameter of the sausage. For links purchased fully cooked, use cold water and cook 5 to 10 minutes to heat through.

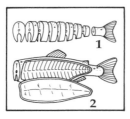

1. Fish steaks
2. Fish fillets

HOW LONG TO POACH
🍒 OR SIMMER 🍒

Shellfish

Crab, Dungeness, 1 to 1¼ lbs	20 to 25 mins
Crayfish	5 to 7 mins
Lobster, Northeastern:	
Small (¾ to 1¼ lbs)	10 to 15 mins
Large (1½ to 2½ lbs)	15 to 20 mins
Lobster, spiny:	
Whole 1 to 1½ lbs	12 to 15 mins
1½ to 2 lbs	15 to 18 mins

How Long To Poach or Simmer

Tails	2 to 4 oz	3 to 5 mins
	4 to 6 oz	5 to 7 mins
	6 to 8 oz	7 to 9 mins

Shrimp:
Large or jumbo (6 to 15 per lb)

Shelled		4 to 5 mins
Unshelled		5 to 6 mins

Medium (30 to 32 per lb)

Shelled		3 to 4 mins
Unshelled		4 to 5 mins

Fish

Whole, any size, per inch thick		9 to 11 mins
Fillets:	½"	4 to 6 mins
	¾"	6 to 8 mins
	1"	9 to 11 mins
Steaks:	¾"	6 to 8 mins
	1"	9 to 11 mins

Chicken

Whole, 3½ to 4 lbs	35 + mins
Breasts, boneless	8 to 10 mins
Tenders (fillet)	4 to 6 mins

Pork

Hocks, ¾ lb each	3 hrs

Ham:

Whole, 12 to 16 lbs	18 to 20 mins per lb
Shank, 5 to 6 lbs	25 to 30 mins per lb
Butt (boneless), 2 to 3 lbs	40 mins per lb

Recipe

Corned Beef—A Simmered Dish

Rinse a corned beef brisket. Put in a kettle with ½ cup celery tops, a couple quartered onions, a quartered turnip and a sliced parsnip. Drop in 5 allspice berries, 6 peppercorns and a bay leaf, cover with cold water and bring slowly to a boil. Simmer 10 minutes, then skim off any foam. Cover, cook over very low heat (just a bubble now and then) for 4 to 5 hours or until very tender. Remove the meat and keep warm, then cook red potatoes, carrots and cabbage in the broth: cook the first two uncovered for 20 minutes, then add the cabbage and cook 15 minutes more. Slice the meat and heap everything on a platter, drizzle some cooking liquid over the meat, and serve with mustard.

A brisket serves at least 8. Figure on 4 carrots, a potato and a couple wedges of cabbage per person.

TECHNIQUE

Browning Meat

Always brown in a preheated pan over brisk heat.

To brown well, meat must be dry. Moisture creates a layer of steam between fat and food that prevents browning. For this reason don't salt food until after browning, since salt draws moisture to the surface. Also, always leave a little space around each piece of meat. If pieces touch, juice oozes out and the meat doesn't fry, it steams and turns gray.

The wonderful color and flavor of browned foods come from caramelized meat juices. To caramelize, food has to stick slightly to the pan, so don't stir or move it around too often.

You can brown meat under the broiler or in a 450° oven—keep turning until all surfaces are brown and crusty, about 15 to 20 minutes. This also eliminates spattering oil.

HOW LONG TO POACH OR SIMMER	
Picnic, 7 to 8 lbs	35 to 40 mins per lb
Beef	
Fresh brisket or plate, 8 lbs	4 to 5 hrs
Corned brisket, 4 to 8 lbs	4 to 6 hrs
Crosscut shanks, 4 lbs	3 to 4 hrs
Fresh or smoked tongue, 3 to 4 lbs	3 to 4 hrs

Braising

Braising, or cooking food in a small amount of liquid with the lid on, makes the less tender varieties of poultry and meat moist and succulent. It is often easier to braise in the oven than on the stove top because the oven holds a more even temperature and you don't risk burning the bottom.

Choose a heavy pan that's *just the right size* for the food to be cooked, otherwise the braising liquid might cook away too fast. Brown the meat or poultry on all sides in a small amount of oil (see box), and spoon out any excess fat. Season. If you plan to use vegetables for flavor (onions, garlic, carrots), brown them before adding. Pour in a small amount of liquid—it shouldn't come more than halfway up the meat or poultry.

Don't add too much liquid; the sauce must end up a concentrated essence of meat and vegetable, not of the added wine and stock.

Cover tightly. You want as little space as possible between the lid and the top of the meat. If your pot is deep, set a dish-shaped piece of foil on the meat or poultry to catch condensing liquid so it won't drop in the pot and dilute the pan juices.

Bring the liquid quickly to a boil. *Immediately* lower the heat (high heat toughens meat fibers) or put the pot in a 300° to 325° oven, and simmer gently until the meat is fork tender. The chart below will help you estimate cooking time, but remember that meat pieces vary in shape. A short fat piece will take longer than a long thin one of the same weight. If a range of times is given, start checking at the earliest time.

Near the end of the cooking time, when the sauce has reduced, turn and baste the meat or poultry several times so it will stay moist. When it's done, remove from the liquid. If the pan juices need thickening, boil them down rapidly or add a flour or cornstarch paste.

Braising Fish: The French do this. Gently sauté equal amounts of carrot, celery and onion strips plus some minced garlic in a little butter until soft. Place in a baking dish or stove-top pan. Lay fish on top and add liquid to half cover fish. Bring to a boil, cover. Count cooking time from the minute liquid starts to boil. Use the vegetables and cooking juices to make a sauce.

❧How Long to Braise❧

Fish	
All varieties	10 mins per inch thickness
Chicken	
Young, 3 to 3½ lbs	35 to 40 mins
Stewing, 5 to 6 lbs	2 hrs
Fricassee, 2" pieces	1½ to 2½ hrs
Turkey	
Drumsticks	1½ hrs
Thighs	2 hrs
Wings	1½ hrs

Recipe

Traute's Goulash

For Beef or Pork Goulash: use equal weights of meat, cut into 2-inch pieces, and sliced or coarsely chopped onions. Brown the onions to a deep gold. Push aside, add meat and brown. Stir in 1 tablespoon paprika per pound of meat and pepper to taste. Add a glugg or two of catsup. Cover tightly. Cook over lowest possible heat for 1½ to 2 hours—up to 4 if needed—until utterly tender-tender!

For Chicken Goulash, let onions equal half the chicken's purchased weight. Skin the chicken and whack it (bones and all) into 2" to 3" chunks. Omit the catsup and add 2 cups water. Cook till the meat falls off the bones.

My Austrian friend Traute served these with French bread for mopping the sauce. You could serve potato, rice, or noodles, but try it with just bread first.

Serves 3 people per pound of beef, 2 per pound of chicken.

How Long to Braise

Wing drumettes	2 hrs
Veal	
Rolled shoulder, 4 to 5½ lbs	2 to 2½ hrs
Pork	
Rib or loin chops, ¾" to 1½"	35 to 60 mins
Shoulder steaks, ¾"	45 to 60 mins
Spareribs	1½ hrs
Back ribs	1½ to 2 hrs
Country style backbones	1½ to 2 hrs
Tenderloin: Whole, ¾ to 1 lb	45 to 60 mins
Fillets, ½"	30 mins
Cubes, 1" x 1¼" pieces	45 to 60 mins
Ham	25 to 30 mins per lb
Lamb	
Rolled shoulder, 3 to 5 lbs	2 to 2½ hrs
Shoulder chops, ¾" to 1"	35 to 40 mins
Neck slices, ¾"	1 to 1¼ hrs
Shanks, 1 lb each	1½ to 2 hrs
Breast, stuffed, 2 to 3 lbs	1½ to 2 hrs
Breast, rolled, unstuffed, 1½ to 2 lbs	1½ to 2 hrs
Riblets	1½ to 2 hrs
Beef	
Arm pot roast, 3 to 4 lbs	2 to 3 hrs
Blade roast, 3 to 5 lbs	1¾ to 2¼ hrs
Rump or heel of round, 3 to 5 lbs	3½ to 4 hrs
Round steak: 1"	1 to 1½ hrs
Round steak, 1½" to 2½"	2 to 3 hrs

How Long to Braise	
Flank steak, 1½" to 2"	1½ hrs
Short ribs	1½ to 2½ hrs
Oxtails, 1 to 1½ lbs	3 to 4 hrs

Stewing

Stewing usually refers to long, slow cooking of less tender cuts in a moderate amount of liquid; less than simmering, more than braising.

To stew poultry or meat, first coat it with seasoned flour, then brown on all sides in a little oil in a heavy pan. (See Browning Meat, p.122) Pour off drippings. Barely cover the meat with liquid (water, stock, tomato juice, a little wine, etc.,) and add any desired seasoning.

Cover tightly and simmer over low heat. If the liquid seems to evaporate too quickly, add a little more. See the chart for stewing times. Add vegetables toward the end. Figure how long each vegetable needs to cook tender and add each at the appropriate time. This way they won't be mushy.

When the meat is fork tender, the liquid should have reduced but should still cover from half to two-thirds of the meat. If the sauce lacks flavor boil it down rapidly, uncovered, until it is rich and tasty. If the flavor is well concentrated but the sauce is thin, thicken it with a flour or cornstarch paste. See p. 93. You can also thicken by puréeing some of the vegetables with part of the liquid in a blender or processor and stirring it back in—while you're at it, why not add a little cream to the purée?

To stew fish use seasoned broth (see the recipe for court bouillon on p. 295) with whatever vegetables you like. The cooking time will be short. Start the vegetables in the broth first; add fish near the end, allowing appropriate time to cook it. Use the chart on p. 120 for cooking times.

RESCUE

The Meat is Overdone!

If meat braised in sauce is overcooked, make toast croutons in the toaster or toast buttered bread in a 325° oven. Put servings of the meat on the crisp croutons, which will give them some texture, and pour the gravy around them.

RESCUE

The Pot Lid Is Stuck!

If lids and pots are precision matched, you often get an airtight seal that is almost impossible to break. If that happens, place the pot over moderate heat for a few seconds to a minute, to let the pressure in the pan rise, and the lid will lift off.

I Burned the Stew!

If the stew burns, quickly remove all of the unburned part you can, and put it in a clean pot. Taste it. If it tastes burned, cover the pot with a damp cloth for 30 minutes. This often does it. If not, my favorite remedy, when it suits the recipe, is to add cream until the burned taste vanishes. I happened on this when desperately trying to salvage a burned chicken casserole while the unsuspecting guests waited at table. The result was so good that from then on I always added cream to the dish. Another remedy is to add a full-bodied seasoning like curry, chutney, mustard or chili powder—whatever suits the flavors. The trick in using these additions is to go slowly, tasting as you go.

❦ HOW LONG TO STEW ❦

Pork

Spareribs	2 to 2½ hrs
Country style back ribs	2 to 2½ hrs
Hocks	2½ to 3 hrs

Ham, old-style and country:

Whole, 10 to 16 lbs	4½ to 5 hrs
Half, 5 to 8 lbs	3 to 4 hrs
Picnic or shoulder, 5 to 8 lbs	3½ to 4 hrs
Shoulder roll, 2 to 4 lbs	1½ to 2 hrs
Hocks	2 to 2½ hrs

Veal and Lamb

Cubes from shoulder or breast, 1" to 1½" pieces	1½ to 2 hrs

Beef

Cubes from neck, chuck, or heel of round, 1" to 1½" pieces	2½ to 3½ hrs
Brisket, fresh or corned, 4 to 6 lbs	3½ to 4½ hrs
Shank cross cuts, ¾ to 1¼ lbs	2½ to 3 hrs

Chicken

Whole:	3½ to 4 lbs	1 to 2 hrs
	5 to 6 lbs	2 to 2½ hrs

OVEN AND GRILL COOKING

Baking

The main difference between baking and roasting, which are both done in the oven, is that in roasting you expose food to heat on all its sides whereas in baking you use containers with higher sides. Baking is a good method for cooking fish, chicken and meat dishes that don't need or want complete exposure to dry heat. You can bake uncovered for a browned finish, or cover to hold in steam, moisten the food, and help the cooking along.

To Bake Fish: Bake uncovered at 450°. Line the baking dish with a double layer of heavy-duty foil. Butter it well.

Wash **whole fish,** dry, season inside, and stuff if you like. Rub the skin with butter, sprinkle the fish with salt and pepper and place in the pan. Use a rack for oily fish to keep them out of the cooking juices.

Arrange **fish fillets** or **steaks** on the pan and brush with melted butter or a basting mixture. Baste once or twice during baking. For stuffed fish steaks, sandwich the stuffing between two large steaks and place in the pan.

Bake all fish for 10 minutes per inch thickness (measure the thickest point of the fish; for stuffed steaks, measure stuffing and all). You can bake **frozen fish fillets or steaks** uncovered in a 450° oven for 9 to 11 minutes per ½" of thickness.

To Bake Chicken or Pork: Brown **chicken pieces** and place in a shallow dish. Pour on sauce if you like— barbecue, mushroom, tomato or cream. Bake 1 hour at 350° to 400° or until done.

Don't brown **short ribs.** Cover tightly with foil and bake 2½ hours at 350°, uncover and skim off fat, cover and bake 30 minutes more.

Coat **thick pork chops** with flour and brown. Bake covered at 350° for 25 to 30 minutes.

Baking in a Wrapper: A fun use for kitchen parchment (see p. 381) is baking single portions of food in a wrapper,

Recipe

Easiest Chicken

In an ovenproof casserole that will hold chicken in one layer, place one cut-up chicken, ¼ cup oil, and any seasonings: herbs, spices, Italian mix, curry—or just salt and pepper. Bake uncovered at 400° for one hour. That's it! Serves 4.

Baking in a Wrapper

1

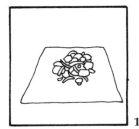
2

3

───── *Recipe* ─────

Deviled Beef Bones

Crunchy and heavenly. Next time you carve a rib roast, leave some meat on the bones and devil them this way.

Dip 4 or 5 meaty, cooked rib bones in melted butter. Mix 2 cups dry breadcrumbs with 1 teaspoon each salt, pepper and dry mustard, plus cayenne pepper or hot pepper sauce to taste. Pat this mixture on the ribs, coating them well. Drizzle on a little more melted butter. Bake at 450° to 500° for 15 minutes until browned and crispy, or broil about 6" from heat for 10 minutes, turning to brown and crisp both sides.

Serves 2 - 3.

or *en papillote*. The parchment browns and swells dramatically, trapping all the moisture and flavors inside until diners open their aromatic packages at table. This is dynamite party fare: easy, tidy, and terribly impressive. You can use foil instead of parchment; the package won't do the dramatic puff, but the flavors will be trapped and wonderful. If you want to try it, see the full directions on p. 89.

BAKING TIMES FOR CASSEROLES	
Size	**Minutes at 350°**
Individual bakers, custard cups or ramekins	20 - 30
Medium casseroles (8" - 10" diameter)	30 - 45
Large casseroles	30 - 60

Oven-Frying

Oven-frying uses the roasting principle of lots of exposure to dry heat. It gives a crisp coating with a minimum of fat, and is a good way to cook small pieces of meat, poultry or fish. To oven-fry, coat the pieces with a dry coating or batter and place them in a shallow metal pan that has ⅛" of hot fat in it. Roll the food in the fat to coat it evenly. Then bake in a 400° to 500° oven. Meat and poultry often need to be turned after their tops brown. Don't turn fish. The trick with oven-frying is to use as little fat as possible.

To Oven-Fry Fish: Coat fish pieces with crumbs and drizzle each with oil, butter, or margarine. Place, not touching, in a greased shallow pan and bake uncovered at 500° for 10 minutes per inch inch of thickness.

Or, put ⅛" of vegetable oil in a pan and heat in a 450°

oven for 5 minutes. Dry fillets well with paper towels. Dip in a mixture of 1 egg beaten with 1 tablespoon of milk, then in crumbs. Place in the hot pan. Turn to coat both sides. Bake until done, timing as above.

Whole fish and steaks don't oven-fry as well as fillets.

To Oven-Fry Poultry: Cut small birds in half, chicken and other poultry in quarters or pieces. If pieces are very large, parboil for 3 to 5 minutes. Coat poultry in something to make crumbs stick—melted butter, mayonnaise, mustard, or an egg beaten with a tablespoon of water—then in seasoned crumbs, patting them on firmly. Pour up to ⅛" oil (or half oil, half butter) in a pan just large enough to hold the poultry without crowding and place it in a 450° oven until the oil sizzles. Using tongs, turn each piece in the oil to coat all sides. Place them skin down and bake uncovered until the tops are brown, then turn and bake until the second side is brown and crisped.

Roasting

When you roast, food is cooked by the hot air surrounding it in the oven. No liquid is needed, except that used for basting. No cover. It's an excellent way to cook large cuts of meat and poultry. In order to roast to the doneness you want, you need an instant-read thermometer (See p. 383).

To Roast Poultry: The best roasting chickens weigh from 3½ to 4½ pounds. Turkeys have better flavor if they weigh at least 10 pounds. To prepare them, remove the lumps of fat from the cavity. Sprinkle the inside with seasoning.

If you're using stuffing, allow ¾ cup per pound for birds up to 14 pounds; for larger birds allow ½ cup per pound. Never stuff until just before roasting. Stuffing deteriorates rapidly in an unroasted bird and can be dangerous.

If you don't stuff the bird, put a couple pieces of butter inside and any seasoning you like—slices of onion or orange, herb sprigs.

Always truss a bird. It will cook more evenly, be moister, and look better. To do this, cut a 3-foot piece of

High Altitude Cooking

Roasting times at high altitudes will be longer. Ignore the times on the charts and roast to the desired internal temperature.

RESCUE

The Roast Isn't Done!

If dinner is ready and the roast isn't done, slice the undone meat and heat it *gently* in its sauce or gravy. If the meat has no sauce, put the slices on buttered foil on the broiler pan and heat under the broiler. *Watch it closely.* This goes zip-zip so you have to guard against overcooking and drying the meat out.

You can also slice the meat and microwave it in 30 second increments.

If the roast is overcooked, cut it into thick steaks rather than neat slices.

How to Truss a Chicken

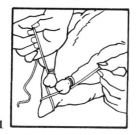

1

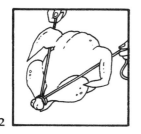

2

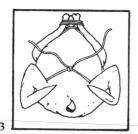

3

cotton kitchen string. Lay the bird on its back and tuck the wing tips behind its shoulders. Loop the middle of the string around the tail and knot. Cross the ends of the string and loop each end around an ankle bone so when you pull the ends the ankles pull together. Tie a knot. Bring the string ends straight up toward the wings and run them under the armpits. Flip the bird over and tie the string across the bird's back.

Place the trussed bird breast up on a rack in a shallow roasting pan. Don't cover it. Some cooks roast chickens one third of the time lying on the left side, one third on the right side, and the last third breast up.

Remember to place the neck end toward the back of the oven where heat is most intense. If the skin starts looking dry, **baste with fat: butter, margarine, olive oil, etc.** When roasting duck or goose, both of which are very fatty, spoon fat out of the pan as it collects.

Use the chart on p. 133 to estimate cooking times.

Let roast poultry rest for 15 minutes before you cut into it or you'll lose all the juices. A large turkey (over 20 pounds) can be left at room temperature for up to an hour with no problem.

I have a friend who roasts turkeys breast down; they turn out wonderfully juicy and the method is bother-free since there is no need to baste. If you want to try it, roast the bird breast-side down at 325° until the breast reaches an internal temperature of 170°. Turn it breast up and roast for 20 to 30 minutes or until the internal breast temperature reaches 175° and the bird is brown. If necessary, increase the oven heat to 450° or turn on the broiler for a few minutes to finish browning.

To Roast Meat: Remove meat from the refrigerator and place it, fat side up, on a rack in a shallow, open pan. Season it. Don't cover or add water.

As with poultry, let the roast stand for 15 minutes, loosely covered with aluminum foil, after you remove it from the oven. Roast to an internal temperature 5 degrees below what you want—the meat will continue to cook the extra degrees while it rests.

The cooking chart is based on low roasting temperatures. This insures that the outside doesn't overcook before the inside is ready, and that the meat is juicy all the way through. Low temperature roasting also helps tenderize, which is important with less tender cuts like chuck, rump or round. For the high temperature method of roasting luxury cuts such as leg or rack of lamb, tenderloins and rib roasts as well as chickens, see the next page.

The chart gives you the time to *begin* checking for doneness, so you're sure not to overcook. Smart cooks start checking for doneness soon after they start to smell the meat, especially for small roasts.

Note: Roasting time will vary with the diameter of the roast. A long, thin one cooks quicker than a short thick one. **If you want to roast cuts like rump, round or sirloin tip** buy Prime or Choice grade, or marinate them first to tenderize them.

To roast meat from the frozen state, multiply the times given in the chart by 1½ to 2.

Roasting Sausage: Many people don't think of roasting sausage, but it is a delicious way to prepare fat links. Spread them out in a shallow roasting pan, and roast at 400° for 25 to 30 minutes. Keep turning them so they get brown and crusty all over.

Internal Temperatures for Pork	
Boneless roasts	160° to 170°
Other uncured pork (shoulder, etc.)	170°
Fully cooked hams and picnics roasted to enhance flavor	130° to 140°
Uncooked hams, loin, picnic shoulder, shoulder roll, Canadian bacon	160°

Cooking Today's Lean Pork

Modern pig raising has all but eliminated the deadly trichina parasite which, in any case, we now know is killed at 130°. Today's leaner pork turns tough and dry when cooked well done, so cook it only to medium.

Cooks and pork lovers don't agree on the preferred done temperature for pork. Some love it cooked to 160°. At this temperature boneless roasts are slightly pink (bone-in roasts very pink) near the bone and the meat is succulent and juicy. Pork cooked to 170° has no pink color; it is less juicy, but the flavor is better developed. The timing I give on the roasting chart is for a done temperature of 170°, but do experiment with 160°. You may prefer your pork that way.

Because of its muscle content, pork shoulder is always best cooked to 170°. See the chart on this page for other temperatures.

TECHNIQUE

Carving Tips

- Use a sharp knife. The carving fork should have a guard to protect you if the knife slips.

- When carving a leg of lamb or pork, it's often easier to forget the fork and hold the bone end with your hand. Wrap the bone with foil to keep your hand clean, and carve *away* from your hand.

- Try to learn where the bones are in the various cuts of meat. Feel them out on the raw meat. Carve toward or between bones.

- Whenever possible, carve across the grain—this will usually be vertically with large cuts, horizontally with smaller ones. A sawing motion gives the tenderest slices.

- In general, cut beef into thin slices; pork, lamb and poultry into thicker slices.

- Carve a large bird—goose or turkey—like you would a chicken. Remove wings and legs, but cut breast, leg and thigh meat into thick slices.

- Duck is a problem because of its awkward shape. Poultry shears help. Also use poultry shears to cut up game birds and Cornish hens.

High-Temperature Roasting: When you invest in a piece of prime beef or lamb, give it the luxury, high-temperature treatment. If the meat you're roasting is top quality with a lot of marbling, not previously frozen, and at room temperature, you can give it a crisp brown outside and a juicy inside this way.

Preheat the oven to 500°. Put in your *room-temperature* meat and roast for 15 minutes. Reduce the temperature to 350° and continue roasting for these times:

Rare: 15 minutes per pound plus an extra 15 minutes.
Medium: 20 minutes per pound plus an extra 20 minutes.
Well done (not recommended): 25 minutes per pound plus an extra 25 minutes.

The oven cooking bag is a way to roast in a wrapper. It comes in three sizes and tolerates oven heat up to 400°. To keep the bag from bursting, you have to shake a tablespoon of flour in it before adding the food. Once the food is enclosed, make six half-inch slits in the bag to let the steam escape. If you use a thermometer, put it through one of the slits.

You can roast whole birds in a cooking bag. My friend Carol, who is a marvelous cook, roasts all her holiday turkeys that way. The bag is porous enough to let the bird brown and get a crisp skin. Roasting-size chickens and ducks come out brown, crisp-skinned and succulent. Place ducks on a rack inside the bag because you won't be able to spoon out accumulating fat during roasting.

Cooking seems to go faster in the cooking bags, so start checking for doneness a good 15 to 30 minutes before the time given on the chart.

Carving Techniques

 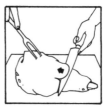 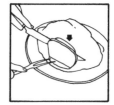

❦ ROASTING POULTRY AND MEAT ❦

The times given for poultry are for *unstuffed* birds; a stuffed chicken, capon or turkey up to 12 pounds will take a total of 30 minutes longer to roast than an unstuffed one. (For stuffed turkeys above 12 pounds, you don't have to make any allowance.)

   If you roast in a covered, dark enamel pan, roasting time will be less. A stuffed bird will cook in the time given on the chart for an *unstuffed* one; an unstuffed bird will take about 30 minutes less.

Type	Weight in Pounds	Oven Temp	Approximate Time
Poultry			
Chicken	4 to 7	400°	18 mins per lb
Chicken breasts		350°	20 to 30 mins
Capon	7 to 9	375°	25 mins per lb
Cornish game hen		400°	25 to 40 mins
		350°	60 to 75 mins
Duck		325°	15 to 20 mins per lb
(for crisper skin)		400°	15 mins per lb
Goose		325°	20 to 25 mins per lb
Grouse		350°	60 to 75 mins
Guinea hen		350°	20 to 22 mins per lb
Partridge		350°	30 to 40 mins
Pheasant		325°	15 to 20 mins per lb
Quail		350°	35 to 30 mins
Squab or pigeon		325°	45 to 60 mins
Turkey:			
Whole	9 to 12	325°	3 to 3½ hrs
	12 to 16	325°	3½ to 4 hrs
	16 to 20	325°	4 to 4½ hrs
	20 to 24	325°	4½ to 5 hrs

ROASTING POULTRY AND MEAT			
Type	**Weight in Pounds**	**Oven Temp**	**Approximate Time**
Drumsticks		325°	1¾ hr
Thighs		325°	2 to 2½ hrs
Wings		325°	2 hrs
Wing drumettes		325°	2½ hrs
Tenderloins		350°	1 hr
Breast half		325°	1¾ hrs
Hindquarters		325°	1¾ hrs
Pork, fresh			
Loin:			
Center	3 to 5	325°	35 mins per lb
Half	5 to 7	325°	40 mins per lb
End	3 to 4	325°	45 mins per lb
Rolled	3 to 5	325°	40 mins per lb
Boneless top	1½ to 2	325°	42 mins per lb
	2 to 4	325°	35 mins per lb
Crown	4 to 6	325°	40 mins per lb
Picnic shoulder:			
Bone in	5 to 8	325°	35 mins per lb
Rolled	3 to 5	325°	40 mins per lb
Boston			
shoulder	4 to 6	325°	45 mins per lb
Leg (fresh ham):			
Whole, with bone	12 to 16	325°	26 mins per lb
Whole, boneless	10 to 14	325°	28 mins per lb
Half, with bone	5 to 8	325°	40 mins per lb
Tenderloin	½ to 1	325°	45 to 60 mins per lb
Back ribs		325°	1 ½ to 2½ hrs
Country style			
backbones		325°	½ to 2½ hrs

ROASTING POULTRY AND MEAT					
	Weight in Pounds	**Oven Temp**	**Approximate Time**		
Spareribs		325°	1½ to 2½ hrs		
Pork, cured					
Ham (uncooked):					
Whole	10 to 14	300°	20 mins per lb		
Half	5 to 7	300°	25 mins per lb		
Shank portion	3 to 4	300°	40 mins per lb		
Butt portion	3 to 4	300°	40 mins per lb		
Ham (cooked):					
Whole	7 to 10	300°	18 mins per lb		
Half	5 to 7	300°	24 mins per lb		
Loin	3 to 5	300°	30 mins per lb		
Picnic shoulder, cook before eating	5 to 8	300°	35 mins per lb		
Picnic shoulder, fully cooked	5 to 8	300°	30 mins per lb		
Shoulder roll, butt portion	2 to 4	300°	40 mins per lb		
Canadian bacon	2 to 4	300°	40 mins per lb		
			Approximate Mins Per Pound		
			(Rare)	**(Med)**	**(Well)**
Lamb					
Leg:					
Whole, with bone	5 to 9	325°	20	25	30
Whole, boneless	4 to 7	325°	25	30	35
Shank or sirloin half	3 to 4	325°	20	25	35
Crown	2 to 3	325°	30	35	40
Shoulder, square cut	4 to 6	325°	*	25	30
Shoulder, boneless	3½ to 5	325°	30	35	40

* Not recommended.

ROASTING POULTRY AND MEAT					
Type	**Weight in Pounds**	**Oven Temp**			
			Approximate Mins Per Pound		
			(Rare)	**(Med)**	**(Well)**
Shoulder, cushion	3½ to 5	325°	*	*	30
Ribs, rack	2 to 3	375°	25	30	35
Beef					
Rib roast	4 to 6	325°	26	34	40
	6 to 8	325°	23	27	32
Tenderloin:					
Piece	1	425°	30		
Half	2 to 3	425°	17		
Whole	4 to 6	425°	10		
Boneless rump rolled**	4 to 6	325°	*	25	30
Round rump roast**	3 to 6	325°	*	36	42
Eye of round or rib**	3 to 6	350°	*	16	18
Tip**	3⅓ to 4	325°	*	38	40
	6 to 8	325°	*	32	35
Round tip roast**	3 to 5	325°	*	32	40
Meat loaf	1½ to 2½	325	*	40	45

* Not recommended.

** Can be roasted if Prime or Choice grade, or if tenderized with a marinade.

Broiling

Broiling is cooking directly under a flame or other heat source. It's a wonderful way to bring out flavor of shellfish, fish, poultry and meat without using too much fat.

Gas broilers don't need preheating but electric ones do. When you broil any food, always preheat the broiler but not the pan, or the food will stick. Broil in a gas oven with the oven door closed. In an electric oven leave the door ajar, otherwise the thermostat will switch the broiler off.

To broil shrimp, scallops or fish, season them first, then dot with butter or margarine and place on an oiled rack or in a shallow pan under the heat source. Here are some suggestions:

Shrimp: Marinate peeled or in the shell for two hours. Broil *without shells* in a shallow pan in the marinade or *with shells* on skewers, and boil the marinade for dipping.

Soft-shell crabs: Clean and flour lightly. Dot with butter, baste often.

Lobsters: Halve, dot with butter. Broil shell-side down, baste frequently.

Oysters: Wrap in bacon or thread on skewers and brush with butter.

Split fish and fillets: Place on rack with skin side away from the heat source.

Frozen fish fillets or steaks: Place 4 inches from the heat for 5 to 9 minutes per ½" of thickness. Turn at half time if fish is 1" thick or more.

To broil poultry requires a little more preparation. With shears, cut the bird (no larger than 3½ pounds) in half down the breastbone and along both sides of the backbone. Leave a small bird in one piece by cutting the backbone out and spreading it open like a book. I like to press the breastbones of halved birds with the heel of my hand to flatten them (the British call this shape "spatchcock"). They brown more evenly this way because they lie flatter.

Place the bird on a cold pan or broiler rack, skin side down. Broil under medium-high heat for a little less than half the time given on the chart. Turn. The second side, being meatier, will take a little longer than the first, bony side. Lower the heat if the skin browns too fast.

Meats to broil include steaks and other tender cuts, either whole or cubed for kebabs, and ground meat patties. You can broil less tender cuts (flank, top or eye round, chuck

Seafood: What and When to Turn

Turn medium or large shrimp, soft-shell crabs, oysters, very large scallops, fish steaks and whole fish halfway through the cooking time.

Don't turn lobster, fish fillets, split fish and smaller items; they're thin enough to cook through by the time the top is browned.

Quick Hint

Line both bottom and rack of the broiler pan with heavy-duty foil. Extend the foil in the bottom pan well up the sides. Mold foil over the rack and cut openings with a knife over the slots so that fat can drain down where it won't catch fire.

Quick Hint

Always roast fat-side-up so the fat drips down and bastes the meat as it melts. Remember, a turkey has most of its fat in its back—another reason for roasting it breast down (also see p. 130).

steak, short ribs) if you marinate them first for 6 to 8 hours to tenderize them.

Place the meat on the cold broiler pan rack, positioning the pan so the top of the meat is the right distance from the heat. (See the chart below.) When you broil small steaks or chops, you don't need to use the broiler pan. Use a small pan with low sides set on the broiler pan.

Broil meat half the suggested time, or until brown. Season and turn. Cook the second side until the meat is done as you like it. The second side usually cooks faster than the first. **Watch for the juices to bead on the surface.** This tells you it's about done. Season the second side. Serve immediately.

To broil frozen steaks, chops and hamburgers, place them 1 to 2 inches farther from the heat source than for unfrozen meat and increase the cooking time by 1½ to 2 times.

❧ BROILING ❧

This chart will give you an idea of the right broiling time and distance from the heat for various foods. Start checking for doneness at the earliest time given on the chart, since cooking times are always approximate. For beef and lamb, times are given for rare (140°) and medium (160°). The government recommends that ground meat patties be cooked to 160°. If you add such things as egg, bread crumbs, onions or liquid though, cook them to 170°. Undercooked ground meat can carry still-potent bacteria.

Food	Inches From Heat	Approximate Total Minutes
Shellfish		
Lobster, split, 1½ to 2 lbs	5	12 to 15
Oysters	3	5 to 8
Scallops, sea	3	3 to 5

BROILING		
Food	**Inches From Heat**	**Approximate Total Minutes**
Shrimp:		
Medium	3	5 to 8
Large	3	7 to 9
Soft-shell crabs	3	5 to 8
Fish		
Fillets:		
Thin	3	5 to 8
Thick	3 to 4	6 to 10
Steaks, 1"	3 to 4	8 to 10
Whole:		
Small	3 to 4	8 to 13
Large	6	8 to 13
Medium, split	3 to 4	10 to 15
Chicken		
Breasts	6 to 8	10 to 20
Broiler halves, 1 to 1½ lbs	6 to 12	25 to 35
Turkey		
Breast tenderloins	6 to 8	10
Veal		
Loin chops, 1"	3 to 4	15 to 20
Pork		
Loin chops, 1"	3 to 4	15 to 20
Ham slices (cooked):		
½"	3	10 to 12
¾"	3 to 4	13 to 14
1"	3 to 4	18 to 20

BROILING

Food	Inches From Heat	Approximate Total Minutes	
Ham cubes (cooked), 1" to 1½"	4	12	
Bacon	3	4 to 5	
Pork sausage links, 12 to 16 per lb	4	12 to 15	

Lamb		**(Rare)**	**(Medium)**
Shoulder chops:			
¾" to 1"	3 to 4	7	14
1½"	4 to 5	12	22
Rib or loin chops:			
1"	3 to 4	7	14
1½"	4 to 5	15	22
Sirloin chops, ¾" to 1"	3 to 4	12	22
Leg steaks, ¾" to 1"	3 to 4	14	20
Cubes, ¾" to 1"	4 to 5	8	15
Liver	3	4	8

Beef		**(Rare)**	**(Medium)**
Porterhouse, T-bone, rib and eye steaks:			
¾"	2 to 3	8	12
1"	3 to 4	10	15
Sirloin steaks, boneless:			
¾"	2 to 3	10	15
1"	3 to 4	16	30
Sirloin cubes, 1" to 1¼"	3 to 4	9	12
Tenderloin steak, 1"	2 to 3	10	15

BROILING			
	Inches From Heat	**Approximate Total Minutes**	
Beef		**(Rare)**	**(Medium)**
Top loin steak, boneless:			
¾"	2 to 3	8	12
1"	3 to 4	12	17
Chuck shoulder steak, boneless, 1" *	3 to 4	14	18
Chuck blade steak, ¾" to 1" *	2 to 3	11	14
Eye round roast, butterflied, 2 to 3 lbs*	5 to 7	20	25
Eye round steak, 1"	2 to 3	9	11
Top round steak, 1" *	3 to 4	15	18
Flank steak, 1 to 1½ lbs*	2 to 3	12	14
Short ribs*	2 to 3	10	12
Ground beef patties:			
½"	3 to 4		10
¾"	3 to 4		13
Liver (calf, beef), ½ "	3	5	9

* For best results, marinate for 6 to 8 hours before broiling.

Quick Hint

Use your microwave to pre-cook meat and poultry for faster, moister grilling. Figure about 3 minutes per pound on high.

Slash, or score, thick slices of fish for even cooking.

Grilling

Your backyard barbecue can produce wonderful grilled fish, poultry and meat.

Before you start cooking, let the charcoal burn for at least 30 minutes to form a gray ash over the coals. See the box below to know when the coals are hot enough. Oil the grill if the food you're cooking isn't already oiled.

CHARCOAL TEMPERATURE

Count the number of seconds (say "one elephant, two elephants") that you can hold your hand at the grilling level before pulling it away.

Temperature		Seconds you can stand the heat
Low	(250°)	6
Medium low	(275°)	5
Medium	(300°)	4
Medium hot	(325°)	3
Hot	(350° - 375°)	2

To grill fish, grease the rack. Don't turn thin fillets, and turn thicker ones halfway through the cooking time. Baste with oil or melted butter. Slash a whole fish in two or three places so it cooks evenly.

To grill chicken or other poultry, prepare as for broiling. If the pieces are very large, parboil them first for 3 to 5 minutes and rinse in cold water to stop the cooking. Or pre-cook in the microwave for half the recommended cooking time.

Marinate the chicken, or coat lightly with oil and season all over. Place small pieces 4 to 5 inches from the heat, larger pieces 5 to 6 inches away. The skin side should be away from the heat to start, the bone side toward the heat. Start cooking pieces that take longest (legs and thighs) 3 to 5 minutes before you add the quicker-cooking ones (breasts, wings, backs). Turn and baste frequently, especially during the last 10 minutes.

To grill turkey parts, prepare as for chicken, above. Grill 6 to 8 inches from the heat, turning occasionally, either uncovered or in a covered kettle-type grill. Allow the same time as you would for roasting.

To grill meat, trim off the excess fat, leaving a ¼" rim to provide flavor. Slash the rim at 1-inch intervals so the meat won't curl. Marinate less tender cuts like flank, chuck, blade and top round. Coat all surfaces lightly with oil, butter or margarine. Turn meat halfway through cooking time, or when juice beads on the surface. **Spareribs,** which cook over a lower heat, need to be turned every few minutes. Baste occasionally with marinade or sauce, or with fat.

To avoid burned edges, brush on barbecue sauce only during the last 10 to 15 minutes of cooking. (The sugar in it burns easily.)

To grill frozen meat, cook 5 to 6 inches from the coals, turning often, for about half again as long as for unfrozen meat.

See the chart on the next page for cooking times and distance from the heat.

Don't Throw Out The Marinade

Leftover marinade makes a delicious sauce to serve with grilled food, but first you must boil it for 2 to 3 minutes to kill any bacteria it picked up from the raw meat. This is important!

Quick Hint

When you grill, use an oil can with a long spout to drizzle oil on the food. Keeps you from getting burned, and the food from sticking.

❧ GRILLING ❧

Food	Heat of Coals	Approximate Total Minutes
Shellfish		
Clams, mussels, oysters	Medium hot	3 (or as soon as shells open)
Lobster:		
Split, 1 to 1½ lbs	Medium hot	12
Tails: 6 oz	Medium hot	8
8 oz	Medium hot	12
Scallops, sea (kebabs), 12 to 15 per lb	Medium hot	6
Shrimp, peeled (kebabs):		
20 per lb	Medium hot	7
12 to 15 per lb	Medium hot	10
Fish		
Fillets or steaks, ½"	Medium hot	5
Fillets, steaks or cubes, 1"	Medium hot	10
Whole, ½ to 1½ lbs cleaned weight	Medium hot	8 mins per lb
Chicken		
Broiler-fryer half, slightly flattened, 1¼ to 1½ lbs	Medium	45
Breasts, skinned and boned, 4 to 5 oz	Medium hot	12
Breast half with bone and skin	Medium	15 to 20
Thighs, drumsticks	Medium	40
Kebabs (boneless meat in 2" x ½" strips threaded on skewers)	Medium hot	8

GRILLING

Food	Heat of Coals	Approximate Total Minutes	
Turkey			
Breast steak, 4 to 6 oz	Medium	14	
Drumstick, ½ to 1½ lbs	Medium	50	
Hindquarter, 2 to 4 lbs	Medium	1¼ hrs	
Thigh, 1 to ½ lbs	Medium	55	
Ground, ¾" patties	Medium hot	16	
Other poultry			
Cornish game hen half, slightly flattened, ½ to ¾ lb	Medium hot	45	
		(Med)	**(Well)**
Duck, split, 5 to 6 lbs	Medium low	20	38
Veal		**(Med well)**	
Steak or chops:			
1"	Medium	20	
1½"	Medium	26	
Pork		**(Med well)**	
Steak or chops:			
½"	Medium hot	10	
¾"	Medium hot	14	
1½"	Medium	35	
Spareribs	Very low	60	
Canadian bacon:			
¼"	Med hot	4	
1 to 1½"	Medium	35	

GRILLING

Food	Heat of Coals	Approximate Total Minutes		
Ham slice, 1"	Medium hot	22		
				(Well)
Fresh sausages, 1"	Medium hot			12
Hot dogs	Medium hot			4

Lamb		**(Rare)**	**(Med)**	**(Well)**
Chops, 1 "	Medium	12	14	
Cubes, 1½" square	Medium hot	12		

Beef				
Steak (tender cuts like top loin, tenderloin, T-bone, porterhouse, sirloin, rib, rib eye):				
1"	Medium hot	10	12	18
1½"	Medium hot	16	20	26
2"	Medium	32	36	50
Steak (less tender cuts like chuck, blade, top round):				
1"	Medium	14	18	22
Flank steak, 1 to ½ lbs (Not tender if cooked past medium)	Hot	12		
			(Med well)	
Ground, 1" patties	Medium hot	14		

RULE OF THUMB

Sautéing Temperature

The *thicker* the piece, the *lower* the heat—to give heat time to reach and cook the food's center before the outside burns.

Reminder: butter burns easily. If you use half butter and half oil for sautéing you'll have no problems.

Scallops Defined

Scallops, escalopes, cutlets, scallopini, schnitzels—whatever you call them—are thin pieces of meat, chicken or turkey flattened to between ¼" and ½" thick.

To flatten meat for scallopini, place it between sheets of plastic wrap and whack gently with the flat side of a cleaver or the bottom of a small pan or skillet.

COOKING IN FAT

Sautéing

When you sauté (pan-fry), thin pieces of food are cooked quickly over direct, high heat in a small amount of fat. Since the heat is high, the food is kept in motion either by frequently shaking the pan or by stirring and flipping the food. As soon as the food is brown, it is removed and kept warm while you pour liquid into the pan and scrape up the browned bits to make a sauce.

Sautéing is the ideal way to cook chicken breasts, veal chops, pork chops, and liver, to keep them moist during cooking. Season them and either bread them or sprinkle them with flour so they keep their juices. (See p. 90 for how to bread.)

Brown and cook meats quickly so they are done and out of the pan before they can tighten and lose any juice. Brown them for 2 minutes on each side over medium-high heat, then add other ingredients. Cover and simmer over medium-low heat for 6 to 12 minutes, depending on their thickness, or until just cooked through. Scallops (see box) need only 1 minute per side and no simmering. All of these lean meats are done when the tip of a knife slides in easily.

Fish and Seafood: Sautéing is ideal for fish. If you are cooking fillets, choose a firmer-fleshed fish. Cut long fillets crosswise so they won't break when you turn or lift them out. You can sauté fish steaks up to 1" thick as well as small whole fish, shrimp and scallops.

Heat about ⅛ inch of margarine or butter or a mixture of butter and oil in a skillet. Dip lean fish into seasoned flour or crumbs—fatty fish doesn't need the protection of a coating. Always fry first the *non-skin* side of a fillet, which will be served uppermost. (The first-cooked side always looks best.) Cook the fish in the hot fat a total of 4 to 10 minutes, depending on the thickness. (Remember the rule: 10 minutes per *inch* of thickness.) Turn once during cooking.

What Are Chicken Tenders?

Chicken breasts consist of two large pieces and two small fillets. The fillets are called tenders. Use in stir-fries, put them in salads, or bread and fry.

TECHNIQUE

Partially frozen meat is easier to slice thin for stir-fries and scallops.

Chicken: You can sauté small and medium-sized (under 3½ pounds) chickens, cut up. Coat them first or not. Brown on all sides, lower the heat, season to taste (add things like chopped onions and garlic now) and cook gently for 6 to 8 minutes. Put light meat on top of dark (dark takes longer to cook), add about ¼ cup of any liquid, and herbs if you like. Cover tightly and cook until just tender. This will take anywhere from 5 to 20 minutes depending on the size of the chicken.

Meat: Sauté thin (no more than 1" thick), tender cuts of meat which will cook through in the short time it takes for the outside to brown.

To sauté beef steaks or lamb chops, heat ⅛ inch or less of oil or fat in a heavy skillet over high heat until rippling hot. Place the meat, *unseasoned and unfloured*, in the pan. If the pan is the right temperature, the meat will sizzle instantly. As soon as juices start to bead on the surface, turn the meat and season the browned side. The second side will brown faster than the first. When juices start to bead on the browned side, the meat is rare. Continue cooking for medium or more done—just don't cook too done or the meat will be dry, tasteless and tough.

To sauté frozen steaks, chops and meat patties, brown both sides quickly in a very hot skillet before they get a chance to thaw. (When thawing starts, the surface turns wet and won't brown nicely.) Reduce heat to medium low and cook as for unfrozen meat, turning more often. Cook one and a half to two times as long.

To sauté ½-inch thick raw sausage patties, place them in an unheated skillet and cook over medium-low heat until juices run clear—10 to 12 minutes. Turn once to brown both sides.

To sauté uncooked sausage links, poach them first by placing in an unheated skillet with cold water to barely cover. Bring to a boil, reduce heat, cover and simmer until juices run clear—5 to 10 minutes for small links, 15 minutes for breakfast sausages, 20 minutes for Italian sausage.

Then drain and sauté over low heat in the fat they give off, turning often, until browned. To make them crispy, dry well after poaching, dust lightly with flour and brown in a little butter.

Stir-Frying

When you stir-fry, you toss small, thin, uniform-size pieces of meat, poultry, fish, shellfish and/or vegetables over high heat in very little fat. Often a little liquid is added at the end and the pan is sometimes covered then for a quick steaming.

Cut the meat into thin, uniform slices, strips or pieces. To add extra flavor, marinate the meat while you prepare the other ingredients. Cut, measure and assemble all ingredients before you start frying because the cooking goes very quickly.

Place a wok or skillet over medium-high to high heat. When the pan is hot, add a small amount of oil and let it heat briefly. Drop in a piece of meat or vegetable. If the oil sizzles, it's ready. Fry meat in batches if necessary, but never more than 12 ounces at a time. A crowded pan lowers the temperature and meat stews instead of frying. Lift and flip the meat as it browns.

If your dish has vegetables in it, stir-fry them separately. Start with the longest-cooking ones. Combine them with the cooked meat and toss together to heat through.

Deep Fat Frying

We deep-fry more seafood and chicken than meat, but a golden, crisp-coated Wiener Schnitzel is a thing of wonder. Properly fried food seals its surface immediately and absorbs a minimum of fat, so you can comfortably indulge now and then in these crispy pleasures. Read the discussion of deep-frying on p. 89 and the hints below.

- Temperature is the key to perfectly fried food. It's like Goldilocks's porridge: If the oil is too cool, the coating soaks it up. If it's too hot, the outside of the food burns before the inside cooks. But ah, when it's just right, the

---

TECHNIQUE

Pan-Broiling

Pan-broiling is like frying, except that you use little or no fat. It is an excellent method for cooking thin pieces of tender meats and fatty meats like bacon and hamburger patties.

To pan-broil: Heat a heavy skillet over medium heat. Cast iron works beautifully, especially the skillets with raised ridges that make grill marks. Leave the skillet dry for fatty meats; lightly oil it for lean ones.

High Altitude Cooking

Deep-fried food will brown faster at high altitudes, so use slightly lower frying temperatures—3 degrees less for every 1,000 feet above sea level.

═══ Recipe ═══

British Fish 'n Chips

Gourmets who spend time in England become fanatical fans of fish and chips (chips are British for French fries). Here's how to do your own. You wouldn't fix it every day, but a treat now and then makes you a nicer person.

Marinate 1½ pounds cod or halibut fillets in ⅓ cup lemon juice and a little finely chopped onion for 1 hour. Cut 6 potatoes for French fries and fry only until pale yellow. Remove, drain on paper towels, and reserve. Dip fish in seasoned flour (paprika, salt, pepper and cayenne), then in **beer batter:** Mix ¾ cup flour and ½ cup beer until slightly lumpy, cover, let rest 1 to 2 hours, then stir in 1 egg yolk and fold in 1 stiffly beaten white. Dip the drained fillets in this batter and fry golden and crisp (3 to 5 minutes). Drain on paper towels. Reheat oil and refry potatoes in small amounts until deep gold. Drain. Serve with lemon wedges. To do it right, you should wrap each serving in *The Times.*

Serves 4.

coating crisps immediately, seals out the oil, and the food fries up crisp, greaseless—perfect.

• Always coat the food. Coating protects food from the intense heat of the oil. It also insures that the food is dry when it hits the fat so it doesn't spit and prevent the hot oil from forming a quick seal.

• Turn a piece when the bottom is brown and fry until the second side browns. Don't overcook—especially seafood, which cooks done within 3 minutes.

Deep-Frying Fish: Small fish are best fried whole; larger fish should be filleted or cut in steaks or fingers—none more than ¾" thick. If you fry a biggish whole fish, as Oriental cooks do, make 1" to 2" slashes an inch apart and ⅛" deep on both sides to keep the fish from curling and to help the thick part to cook as fast as the rest.

Seasoned cornmeal or fine oatmeal (whirl it in the blender or processor) are tasty alternatives to a flour coating. Also, see the box for a tasty batter.

Fish is done as soon as the coating turns golden. If you have a lot to fry, hold the early batches in a 200° oven on a paper towel-covered cookie sheet. And if you save the oil for reuse, mark it so you'll use it only for fish!

Deep-Frying Chicken: If you want to deep-fry chicken Colonel-style, you can parboil the pieces for 3 to 5 minutes before frying. I don't do that because I was taught differently by Emily, a southern army wife. I like her way. See the box.

Some people finish up fried chicken in the oven. Bread the chicken and fry it just until golden, transfer to a casserole, season, and bake uncovered at 350° for 20 to 25 minutes.

Deep-Frying Meat: Pieces should be thin or small. Flour steaks or chops, dip in an egg and water mixture and coat with fine, fresh bread crumbs. Fry in 360° oil until golden. These are surprisingly delicate, although you won't want them for breakfast as your grandfather did.

The classic **Wiener Schnitzel** is made with veal, but Germans often use juicy slices of pork. Some adventurous souls use pounded turkey breast. Pound pork or veal scallops to ¼" thickness and bread (see p. 90). Chill for 20 minutes. Fry two pieces at a time in 365° oil, until golden on both sides—2 or 3 minutes total. Drain on paper towels. Serve with a wedge of lemon. Gourmets top this golden delicacy with sautéed, thickly-sliced forest mushrooms in a silky cream sauce. Rich, but so is chocolate-chip cookie dough ice cream. You have to choose your sins.

DEEP-FRYING HELP

Temperature: Almost always 365°
Timing: Until golden

For:	About:
Coated large pieces of chicken or chops	10 to 20 minutes
Coated small chicken pieces:	5 to 7 minutes
Coated fish	10 minutes per inch of thickness
Shrimp, oysters, clams	3 minutes

Recipe

Emily's Southern Fried Chicken

Soak a cut-up frying chicken in cold salted water (4 cups water, 1 tablespoon salt) for 2 hours, then drain and pat dry. Coat with seasoned flour. In a deep frying pan, heat enough oil to cover the chicken to 365°, slide the chicken into it, skin-side down. Turn the heat down a little. When the chicken starts to brown underneath, reduce heat and partially cover the pan. When the underside has turned a lovely deep gold, (about 15 minutes), turn with tongs. Don't cover. Cook until the second side is browned. Drain on paper towels.
    Serves 4.

WHEN IS IT DONE?

One sign of the good cook is being able to judge when things are done. Overdone meat, poultry and fish lose their flavorful juices—they're dry, tasteless and tough.

The more delicate the item, the more attention it needs. When you cook delicate foods, stay nearby and watch for the signs that tell you they have reached their succulent best.

Checking Doneness With a Thermometer

Beef, lamb	140° (rare)
	160° (medium)
	170° (well)
Chicken, duck, goose	175° - 180°
Meat loaf	160°
Pâté	170° - 175°
Pork:	
Fresh	160° - 170°
Cured	130° - 140°
Poultry stuffing	165°
Turkey:	
Breast	170°
Thigh	180°

Watch for changes in:

Color: Fish, scallops, veal, pork and chicken breasts turn opaque; some shellfish turn pink or red; beef goes from blue-red to walnut brown.

Shape: Oyster edges curl; meat and casserole edges shrink and sharpen.

Resilience: Most food stiffens—prod with a finger.

Smell: When the aroma tickles your nose, food is about done.

Here are some specific tests for doneness:

Chicken (roasted or broiled): Juice running out of the tail end is clear; when tapped lightly, leg feels springy rather than soggy; drumstick feels loose when you wiggle it. Professionals protect their fingers with a thick pad of paper towel and squeeze the thick part of the thigh to see if it feels tender. When your chicken tests done with a thermometer, give the thigh a squeeze to learn the "done" feel.

Chicken breast: The thickest part turns from pink to white. Press it lightly with your index finger. As soon as it feels springy instead of squidgy, it's done. Get it off the heat fast so it stays moist and tender.

Chicken livers: Cut one open. The center must have lost all but a slight pink cast. If *no* pink remains, it's overcooked and you won't like it. Cut up these dry livers and serve them in a creamy sauce, or mash them with butter, herbs, and a tad of Cognac for lovely pâté.

Clams: Edges are firm, centers soft. If steamed in the shell, shells open. Discard unopened ones.

Crabs: Turn red.

Crayfish: Turns red. Tail meat is firm and opaque in the center; pull off one tail to check.

Fish: Has to be moist and juicy. When it is almost done, flesh feels *very* springy; when it is done it feels *slightly* springy, looks opaque and has lost all shininess. You should just be able to nudge the flesh cleanly from the bone. Don't wait until it flakes easily or the fish will be dry.

Liver: When pricked with a fork, juices run pale pink. Don't overcook!

Lobster: Turns red.

Meat loaf: Pulls from the side of the pan and juices run almost clear with just a pink tinge.

Meats (broiled, pan-fried or grilled): Test the springiness of steaks, chops, liver and kidneys with your finger. Here's what to feel for: hold your left hand limp and pinch the soft muscle between thumb and forefinger. It should feel spongy. That is how *very rare* meat feels. Now make a loose fist and feel the spot again. It will resist pressure and feel springy. That's how *medium-done* meat feels. Tighten your fist until there is almost no resistance. That is how *well done* meat feels.

A less artistic test: make a little cut near the bone, (near the center for a boneless piece) just before you think the meat should be done and peek at the color. *Very rare* meat will be bluish red, *rare* will be a deep pink, *medium rare* will be pink in the center area, and *well done* will have no pink at all.

Steaks and chops are *ready to turn* when drops of juice begin to appear on the surface. **Steaks** are rare when juices bead on the *browned* (first cooked) surface.

Meats (braised, stewed): Chops and cubes fall easily from a two-tined fork.

Meat patties: When *well done* (safest), there is no pink in the centers at all. For medium, centers are brownish pink. Patties with additions such as eggs, bread crumbs, onions or liquid should be cooked until *no pink* remains in the center.

Mussels: Edges curl and centers are soft. If steamed in the shell, shells open. Discard unopened ones.

Oysters: Edges curl and centers are soft. If roasted in the shell, shells open. Discard unopened ones.

Pâté: A skewer inserted in the center for 30 seconds feels hot when withdrawn. A crustless pâté will have clear liquid bubbling around it like a meat loaf.

Sausages: A skewer inserted in the center for 30 sec-

Recipe

Pasta with Chicken and Feta Cheese

A version of the wonderful Greek shrimps with feta. This is yummy.

Put 3 tablespoons of butter, 2 tomatoes (peeled, seeded, coarsely chopped) and 1 tablespoon finely minced onion in a small saucepan. Simmer uncovered over medium-low heat for 20 minutes. Add salt to taste. While it cooks, sauté 4 skinned, boned chicken breast halves in 1 tablespoon butter for 3 minutes on each side. Pour the sauce over, lay thin slices of feta cheese on the breasts (use 8 ounces total). Cover the pan and cook gently for 20 minutes, basting several times. Serve over pasta. Serves 4.

onds is hot to the touch when withdrawn; meat is tender, no longer pink in the middle.

Scallops: Opaque but centers are still slightly transparent.

Shrimp: Turn pink but are still open and relaxed, not tightly curled.

Snails: Firm but tender.

Cooking Help for Vegetables

How Do I Roast Garlic, Can I Really Grill Asparagus, and Aren't Artichokes a Bother to Prepare?

At last vegetables are getting the credit they deserve. They're no longer just something to dress up the meat or give the plate color. Of course there were always the superstars: spring asparagus with browned butter; the first new potatoes and peas sauced with thick cream; corn on the cob twinkling with coarse salt and melted butter; thick slabs of vine-ripe beefsteak tomatoes.

Now all vegetables are getting the star treatment, and it's about time. We microwave them and steam them and they turn out tender-crisp, brightly colored and delectable. We grill them so they get crispy little charred edges, moist, creamy insides, and a scrumptious smoke flavor mingled with herbs and garlic. We snuggle them next to the meat or poultry roasting in the oven, casserole them, and stuff them with crumbs and meat, nuts or cheese. Today, vegetables can carry the meal.

Serve vegetables plain; sauce them with butter or cream; dust them with a flurry of grated cheese, nutmeg, and paprika; drizzle them with fruity olive oil; or give them a slam bang topping. And never again have to tell the kids, "Eat your vegetables or you don't get any Triple Chocolate Fudge Cake."

Flavor and Cooking Time

Onions and their relatives (garlic, shallots, leeks) develop sharp flavors when they start to cook (see box p. 37), whereas long, gentle cooking or roasting turns them sweet and mild.

Cabbage and its relatives (broccoli, Brussels sprouts, turnips, rutabagas, kohlrabi), develop mild and gentle flavor when cooked a short time, but long cooking turns them strong and unpleasant. Six minutes is plenty for cabbage—45 minutes is disaster.

Blanching and Parboiling Vegetables

You blanch vegetables as a preliminary step to other preparation. Blanching softens the strong flavor of cabbage and the sharp flavor of onions. It fixes the bright color of greens like spinach. It loosens the skins on tomatoes and softens cabbage leaves so you can stuff them. It pre-cooks vegetables so that later you can give them a quick toss in butter and serve them hot and crisp-tender.

You parboil long-cooking vegetables before grilling, roasting and deep-frying so they will be fully cooked by the time their outsides are crisp and golden. Some tough vegetables like celery root must be parboiled before the next cooking step.

Blanching and Parboiling Vegetables

At the end of cooking, plunge vegetables into cold water or, for tomatoes, run under cold water to stop cooking immediately.

Vegetable	Method
Root vegetables	Place in large pot of lightly salted *cold* water. Bring to boil. Boil 2 minutes.
Tomatoes	Pour boiling water over. Let stand 15 seconds.
Leaves (cabbage, spinach)	Drop into boiling water. Boil less than a minute—until leaves soften.
Other vegetables	Drop into boiling water. Boil 1 minute.

BOILING VEGETABLES

Some vegetables should start in cold water, some in boiling. Here's the rule:

Place all root vegetables (except for new potatoes) in *cold* salted water and bring to a boil. Drop all others, including new potatoes, into rapidly boiling water. Start timing both when the water returns to a boil.

It's a good idea to use a shallow pan and as little water as possible, to conserve vitamins. See the chart below for cooking times and an idea of how much water to use.

Quick Hint

Perk up old or tired vegetables by adding a pinch of sugar and ¼ teaspoon salt to each cup of water you will use to cook them.

❦ BOILING VEGETABLES ❦

Type	Minutes	Amount of Water	Cover?
Artichokes	30 to 40	To cover	Yes
Asparagus:			
Spears	7 to 10	1"	Yes
½" to 1" slices	2 to 5	½"	Yes
Beans (green, wax, Italian), 1" pieces	5 to 10	1"	Yes
Beans, lima	12 to 20	1½"	Yes
Beets, whole, 2 to 3"	20 to 45	To cover	Yes
Belgian endive, halved lengthwise	5 to 7	½"	Yes
Broccoli:			
Spears	7 to 12	1"	Yes
1" pieces	3 to 6	½"	Yes

BOILING VEGETABLES

Type	Minutes	Amount of Water	Cover?
Brussels sprouts	7 to 10	1"	Cover after 4 mins
Cabbage (green, savoy, red), in wedges	8 to 12	1"	Cover after 2 mins
Carrots:			
Whole baby or ¼" slices	5 to 10	½"	Yes
Whole large	10 to 20	1"	Yes
Cauliflower:			
Whole medium	15 to 20	1"	Yes
Flowerets	5 to 9	½"	Yes
Celery hearts, halved lengthwise	8 to 12	½"	Yes
Celery root, whole medium	40 to 60	To cover	Yes
Corn on the cob	3 to 5	To cover	Yes
Eggplant, peeled, in ¾" cubes	4 to 5	To cover by 1"	Yes
Fennel:			
Halved lengthwise	8 to 10	1"	Yes
½" slices	5 to 8	½"	Yes
Greens (collards, kale, mustard, turnip), coarsely chopped	5 to 15	1"	Yes
Jerusalem artichokes (Sunchokes):			
Whole	10 to 20	1"	Yes
½" slices	5 to 10	½"	Yes

BOILING VEGETABLES

Type	Minutes	Amount of Water	Cover?
Kohlrabi:			
Whole	30 to 40	1"	Yes
Sliced	12 to 15	½"	Yes
Leeks, halved lengthwise	5 to 8	½"	Yes
Okra, whole	5 to 10	To cover	Yes
Onions, small white	15 to 20	To cover	No
Parsnips:			
Whole medium	10 to 20	1"	Yes
¼" slices	5 to 10	½"	Yes
Peas (edible-pod)	30 secs	Lots	No
Peas (green, shelled)	5 to 10	½"	Yes
Potatoes (white or red thin-skinned):			
Whole, 3"	20 to 30	½"	Yes
½" slices	8 to 10	½"	Yes
Potatoes (sweet), 3"	20 to 30	2"	Yes
Rutabagas:			
Whole (3" to 4")	25 to 30	2"	Yes
½" slices	7 to 10	½" to 1"	Yes
Spinach	2 to 4	Water that clings from washing	Yes
Squash (pattypan, sunburst, yellow, zucchini):			
Whole	8 to 12	½"	Yes
¼" slices	3 to 6	½"	Yes

BOILING VEGETABLES

Type	Minutes	Amount of Water	Cover?
Squash (acorn, banana, butternut, Hubbard, pumpkin, turban), ½" slices	7 to 9	½"	Yes
Swiss chard, stems in ¼" slices, leaves shredded	Cook stems 2 mins, add leaves and cook 1 to 2 mins more.	¼"	Yes
Turnips:			
Whole (2" to 3")	20 to 30	2"	Yes
½" slices	6 to 8	½"	Yes

STEAMING VEGETABLES

Steaming, or cooking on a rack above gently simmering liquid, is a healthful way to prepare vegetables.

Use a steamer or a collapsible metal steaming basket. A metal colander also works if your pan is large enough to hold it with the cover on. Whatever you use, the steaming rack should be large enough to hold whole vegetables in one layer and small or cut-up vegetables in a layer no more than 1½ to 2 inches deep.

Put the rack in the pan, add 1 to 1½ inches of water (it should not touch the rack), and bring to a boil over high heat. Place the vegetables on the rack, cover the pan, and adjust the heat to maintain a steady boil. Begin timing when you add the vegetables. Add more *boiling* water as needed to maintain water level. The chart gives you cooking times for each vegetable.

RESCUE

The Vegetables Are Overcooked!

Purée them and:

- Stir in a little butter or cream for an elegant side dish.
- Thin with broth and/or cream for soup.
- Add to pan juices for a delicious sauce.

❧ STEAMING VEGETABLES ❧

Type	Minutes
Artichokes	25 to 35
Asparagus spears	8 to 12
Beans (green, wax, Italian), 1" pieces	10 to 15
Broccoli spears	15 to 20
Brussels sprouts	15 to 25
Cabbage (green, savoy, red), wedges	9 to 14
Carrots:	
Whole baby	8 to 12
Slices	5 to 10
Whole large	12 to 20

STEAMING VEGETABLES

Type	Minutes
Cauliflower:	
Whole	20 to 25
Flowerets	10 to 18
Celery hearts, halved lengthwise	10 to 14
Corn on the cob	8 to 10
Eggplant, peeled, in ¾" cubes	4 to 5
Fennel:	
Halves	18 to 22
Slices	10 to 12
Jerusalem artichokes (Sunchokes):	
Whole	15 to 20
½" slices	12 to 15
Leeks, halved lengthwise	5 to 8
Okra	15 to 20
Onions, small white	20 to 25
Parsnips:	
Whole	15 to 25
Slices	7 to 15
Peas (edible-pod)	3 to 5
Peas (green, shelled)	8 to 12
Potatoes (white or red thin-skinned):	
Whole small	30 to 35
½" slices	8 to 10
Potatoes (sweet), 3"	30 to 40
Rutabagas:	
Whole	30 to 45
Slices	9 to 12

STEAMING VEGETABLES	
Type	**Minutes**
Spinach	3 to 5
Squash (pattypan, sunburst, yellow, zucchini):	
Whole	10 to 12
Slices	4 to 7
Squash (acorn, banana, butternut, Hubbard, pumpkin, turban), ½" slices	9 to 12
Swiss chard	Stems 3 minutes. Add leaves and cook 2 to 4 minutes more.
Turnips:	
Whole	25 to 35
Slices	7 to 9

BRAISING VEGETABLES

Braising is a wonderful way to cook root vegetables and sturdy leaves (cabbage, Boston lettuce, escarole, etc.), either on the stove top or in the oven.

Leave vegetables in big pieces—split celery hearts, quarter fennel bulbs or cut in thick slices. Leave lettuce in whole or half heads, cut cauliflower and broccoli in flowerets, shred cabbage. Line the braising pot or baking dish with sliced bacon or butter it well. Add the vegetable and pour on broth to barely cover. Top with a piece of buttered wax paper, then cover tightly and bring to a boil. Cook over low heat or in a 350° oven for 30 to 40 minutes, depending on the vegetable. If the juices aren't well reduced, pour them into a small pan and boil until thickened. Spoon them over the vegetables.

Recipe

Savory Braised Vegetables

Place 1½ pounds fennel, celery, Boston lettuce, escarole or endive in a dish. Sprinkle with 3 tablespoons lemon juice, ½ cup stock, ½ teaspoon salt and 1 teaspoon sugar. Dot with 2 tablespoons butter. Cover, bring to a boil and cook as in general instructions. Makes 4 servings.

Red cabbage is lovely cooked this way. Toss in a couple of diced apples.

MICROWAVING VEGETABLES

A few reminders about microwaving.

- Always pierce the skin of vegetables to be cooked whole and unpeeled, otherwise you risk a messy explosion.

- Cook vegetables on 100% power (high).

- Vegetables cooked with water should be covered so they steam—cover any vegetables you're cooking by the chart below.

- Halfway through cooking, stir vegetables, rearrange them, or give the dish a half turn.

- Don't omit standing time, which lets insides and center areas finish cooking without further bombarding the already done exterior with microwaves.

- Check for doneness at the end of the *minimum* time given. Times are approximate because vegetables vary in shape, size, and age.

❧ MICROWAVING VEGETABLES ❧

All vegetables should be cooked covered.

Type and Size	Amount	Cooking Time in Minutes	Standing Time in Minutes
Artichokes, 6 - 8 ounces each, top third cut off, each wrapped in wax paper. Place on dish upside down.	1 2 4	5 - 8 8 - 10 12 - 14	5 5 5
Asparagus, stalks pared unless very thin	1 lb + 2 T water	4 - 7	1

MICROWAVING VEGETABLES

Type and Size	Amount	Cooking Time in Minutes	Standing Time in Minutes
Beans (green, wax, Italian), 1½" pieces	1 lb + 2 T water	5 - 7	2
Beets, whole. Pierce skin. After cooking, cool, remove skin under running water	1 lb + 2 T water	9 - 12	5
Broccoli, cut in spears, stalks pared	1 lb + 2 T water	6 - 8	2
Brussels sprouts, larger ones cut in half	1 lb + 2 T water	8 - 10	3
Cabbage:			
Chopped or shredded	1 lb + 2 T water	6 - 8	0
Wedges	1 lb + 2 T water	5 - 7	2
Carrots, sliced in rounds	1 lb + 2 T water	6 - 8	1
	1 - 1½ lbs + 2 T water	6 - 8	2
Cauliflower, flowerets, whole	1 lb + 2 T water	11 - 13	3
Celery, cut in ½" slices. Cook only till crisp tender.	4 cups + 2 T water	11 - 13	0
Corn on the cob, in husk. If husked, brush with butter, wrap each in wax paper, twist ends.	1	3 - 4	3
	2	4 - 6	3
	4	10 - 12	3
Eggplant:			
Whole, skin pierced	1 - 1¼ lb	4 - 7	3
Peeled, cubed	1 lb + 2 T water	6 - 8	1
Fennel, cut in quarters lengthwise	2 bulbs + ¼ c water	6 - 8	0
Jerusalem artichokes (Sunchokes), sliced ¼" thick	2 cups + 2 T water	5 - 7	2

MICROWAVING VEGETABLES

Type and Size	Amount	Cooking Time in Minutes	Standing Time in Minutes
Mushrooms, sliced. Don't overcook; remove as soon as they start to darken.	1 lb + 2 T water or 2 T butter	4 - 6	2
Onions, small, whole	1 lb + 2 T water	4 - 8	2
Parsnips, peeled and cubed	1 lb + 2 T water	8 - 10	3
Peas: Edible-pod Green, shelled	1 lb + 2 T water 1½ lbs + 3 T water	4 - 6 5 - 7	1 1
Potatoes, Russet baking, 6 to 8 ounces each, skin pierced. If still hard at end of cooking time, cook 1 or 2 minutes more. Same standing time.	1 2 4	4 - 6 6 - 8 12 - 16	5 5 5
Potatoes, New, skin pierced	1 lb + 3 T water	8 - 12	3
Potatoes, Sweet, 6 to 8 ounces each, prepared as for baking potatoes	1 2 - 3 4 - 5	4 - 5 6 - 7 8 - 12	5 5 5
Rutabagas, peeled, cubed	1 lb + 2 T water	11 - 13	3
Spinach, whole leaves. Wash, do not dry.	1 lb + water clinging to leaves	4 - 6	0

MICROWAVING VEGETABLES			
Type and Size	Amount	Cooking Time in Minutes	Standing Time in Minutes
Squash, Pattypan, sunburst, yellow or zucchini, sliced ¼" thick	1 lb + 2 T butter	5 - 6	3
Squash, Spaghetti, cut in half lengthwise. Remove seeds. Place cut side down.	1 squash (4 - 5 lbs) + ¼ c water	15 - 20	5
Squash, Acorn, banana or butternut, halved, seeds removed. Place cut-side down on plate in dish. Cover with wax paper. At half time, turn over and brush with butter.	1 to 2 squash (1 lb each)	9 - 14	5
Turnips, peeled and cubed	1 lb + 2 T water	10 - 12	2

GRILLING VEGETABLES

To grill vegetables, first either marinate them or brush with oil or melted fat. Because grill heat is uneven, move them around the grill and turn slower cooking vegetables at least four times.

You can also cook vegetables on the grill without exposing them directly to the coals. To do this, rinse vegetables but leave the moisture clinging to them. Place up to 4 servings on a sheet of heavy-duty foil (wrap potatoes and corn individually) and dot with butter. Wrap tightly. Grill 4 - 6" above medium coals for the time indicated on the chart.

❧ GRILLING VEGETABLES ❧

Type and Size	Heat of Coals	Approximate Total Minutes
Asparagus, tied in bundles, precooked 3 - 4 minutes.	Medium hot	3 - 5
Beans (green, Italian, wax), in foil packets	Medium	20
Carrots:		
Baby, whole, precooked 3 - 5 minutes	Medium hot	3 - 5
1" slices, in foil packets	Medium	25 - 30
Corn on the cob, large ears, no husk or silk, in foil packets.	Medium	15 - 20
Eggplant, small, split lengthwise, or cut into 1" crosswise slices	Medium hot	8
Fennel bulb, precooked 10 minutes, then cut into 6 wedges	Medium hot	8
Leeks, green top, root end, and 2 layers white skin removed, precooked 10 minutes, halved lengthwise	Medium hot	5
Mushrooms, large caps	Medium hot	3
Onions, ½" thick slices	Medium hot	9
Peas (green, shelled), in foil packets	Medium	20
Peppers (bell), halved or quartered	Medium hot	9
Potatoes:		
New, halved, precooked 10 minutes	Medium hot	11
Russet, ½" slices in foil packets	Medium hot	12
Squash:		
Yellow crookneck, split lengthwise	Medium hot	8
Zucchini, small, split lengthwise	Medium hot	6

ROASTING AND BAKING VEGETABLES

Roasting mellows and sweetens the flavor of vegetables. You can roast them alone according to the chart below, or roast them in the pan alongside meat or chicken. When you cook potatoes with a roast, parboil them for 5 to 10 minutes first, and baste them now and then as they roast.

❧ ROASTING AND BAKING VEGETABLES ❧

Type and Size	Procedure
Beets, 2" to 3", unpeeled, scrubbed, dry	Wrap each in heavy foil. Bake at 375° for 1 to 1¼ hrs.
Carrots, peeled, 1" diagonal slices	Arrange in shallow layer in baking dish, dot with butter. Bake at 325° covered for 40 to 50 minutes. Stir several times.
Corn on the cob, large ears, no husk or silk	Rub with butter. Wrap each in heavy foil. Bake at 375° for 30 to 35 minutes.
Eggplant, large, unpeeled, ½" slices	Brush all sides with oil. Arrange in single layer in shallow baking pan. Bake uncovered at 425° to 450° for 20 to 30 minutes.
Onions, medium, peeled	Stand upright in close-fitting baking dish. Drizzle with melted butter. Bake uncovered at 350° for 30 to 45 minutes. Baste several times with butter.
Parsnips, medium, peeled, ½" x 3" sticks	Arrange in shallow layer in baking dish. Dot generously with butter. Bake covered at 325° for 45 to 60 minutes. Stir several times.

ROASTING AND BAKING VEGETABLES

Type and Size	Procedure
Peppers (green and red bell), stemmed, seeded, quartered lengthwise	Place skin-side down in greased, close-fitting dish, drizzle with oil. Bake at 375° uncovered for 40 to 45 minutes.
Potatoes (russet and white baking), unpeeled, washed, dried, skin pierced with fork	Bake uncovered on oven rack at 375° for 1 hr 15 minutes. A done potato will register 210° on your instant-read thermometer.
Potatoes (sweet) unpeeled, washed, dried, skin pierced with fork	Bake not touching on rimmed baking sheet at 400°, uncovered, for 45 to 50 minutes.
Pumpkin, 9 to 11 lbs, halved lengthwise, seeded and stringed	Place cut-side down on greased, rimmed baking sheet. Bake at 350°, uncovered, 1¼ hrs.
Rutabagas, peeled, ¼" slices	Arrange in shallow layer in baking dish. Dot with butter, sprinkle with water. Bake covered at 400° for 30 to 45 minutes.
Squash, spaghetti, medium, rinsed, pierced in 2 or 3 places	Bake on rimmed baking sheet at 350°, uncovered, for 1½ hrs. Turn over at half time.
Squash (acorn, butternut, banana, Hubbard), halved or in large pieces, seeded and stringed	Place cut side down on greased baking dish. Bake uncovered at 425° for 30 to 40 minutes.
Tomatoes, medium, cored, halved, juice and seeds squeezed out	Arrange in one layer, cut side up in baking dish. Drizzle with oil or dot with butter. Bake at 400°, uncovered, for 20 to 25 minutes.

❦ STIR-FRYING VEGETABLES ❦

When you stir-fry a single vegetable, check this chart. Some can be stir-fried in either oil or butter, some only in butter. Most need water added and a final steaming. Quantities of oil and liquid are for 2 cups vegetables.

Type and Size	Procedure
Asparagus, ½" diagonal slices	Stir-fry in 1 tablespoon oil or 2 tablespoons butter for 1 minute. Add 1 to 2 tablespoons liquid, cover, cook 2 to 3 minutes.
Bean sprouts	Stir-fry in 1 tablespoon oil or 2 tablespoons butter for 30 seconds. Cover, cook ½ to 1½ minutes.
Beans (green, wax, Italian), 1" pieces	Stir-fry in 1 tablespoon oil or 2 tablespoons butter for 1 minute. Add 4 tablespoons liquid, cover, cook 4 to 7 minutes.
Beets, whole, 2" to 3", greens shredded	Stir-fry beets or greens or both in 2 tablespoons butter for 1 minute. Add 1 to 2 tablespoons liquid. Cover, cook beets 5 to 6 minutes, greens 2 to 3 minutes.
Broccoli flowerets, ¼" slices	Stir-fry in 1 tablespoon oil or 2 tablespoons butter for 1 minute. Add 3 to 5 tablespoons liquid, cover, cook 3 to 5 minutes.
Brussels sprouts, halved	Stir-fry in 2 tablespoons butter for 1 minute. Add 3 to 5 tablespoons liquid, cover, cook 3 to 5 minutes.
Cabbage (green, savoy, red), shredded	Stir-fry in 1 tablespoon oil or 2 tablespoons butter for 1 minute. Add 2 tablespoons liquid, cover, cook 3 to 4 minutes.
Carrots, ¼" slices	Stir-fry in 1 tablespoon oil or 2 tablespoons butter for 1 minute. Add 2 to 3 tablespoons liquid, cover, cook 3 to 5 minutes.
Cauliflower flowerets, ¼" slices	Stir-fry in 1 tablespoon oil or 3 tablespoons butter 1 minute. Add 3 to 4 tablespoons liquid, cover, cook 4 to 5 minutes.

Stir-Frying Vegetables

Type and Size	Procedure
Celery hearts, ¼" slices	Stir-fry in 1 tablespoon oil or 2 tablespoons butter for 1 minute. Add 1 to 2 tablespoons liquid, cover, cook 1 to 3 minutes.
Celery root, ¼" slices	Stir-fry in 2 tablespoons butter for 1 minute. Add 3 to 4 tablespoons liquid. Cover, cook 2 to 4 minutes.
Eggplant, ½" slices cut into strips, peeled	Stir-fry in 2 tablespoons oil and 2 tablespoons liquid for 2 minutes. Add 2 tablespoons more liquid, cover, cook 10 minutes. Add chopped herbs and a shot of well flavored vinegar if you like.
Fennel, ¼" slices	Stir-fry in 1 tablespoon oil or 2 tablespoons butter for 1 minute.
Jerusalem artichokes (Sunchokes), ¼" slices	Stir-fry in 2 tablespoons butter for 1 minute. Add 2 to 3 tablespoons liquid. Cover, cook 3 to 5 minutes.
Kohlrabi, ⅛" slices	Stir-fry in 3 tablespoons butter for 1 minute. Add 7 tablespoons liquid, cover, cook 6 to 8 minutes.
Leeks (white only), ¼" slices	Stir-fry in 1 tablespoon oil or 2 tablespoons butter for 1 minute. Add 3 to 4 tablespoons liquid, cover, cook 3 minutes.
Lettuce (iceberg), shredded	Stir-fry in 2 tablespoons butter for 30 seconds. Cover and cook 2 to 3 minutes.
Mushrooms, ¼" slices	Stir-fry in 1 tablespoon oil or 2 tablespoons butter for 3 to 4 minutes.
Onions, ¼" slices	Stir-fry in 1 tablespoon oil or 2 tablespoons butter for 1 minute. Cover, cook 3 to 4 minutes.
Parsnips, ¼" slices	Stir-fry in 2 tablespoons oil or 4 tablespoons butter for 1 minute. Add 6 to 8 tablespoons liquid, cover, cook 4 to 6 minutes.
Peas (edible-pod)	Stir-fry in 1 tablespoon oil or 2 tablespoons butter for 1 minute. Add 1 tablespoon liquid, cover and cook 30 seconds.

STIR-FRYING VEGETABLES

Type and Size	Procedure
Peas (green, shelled)	Stir-fry in 1 tablespoon oil or 2 tablespoons butter for 1 minute. Add 3 to 4 tablespoons liquid, cover, cook 30 seconds.
Peppers (bell), 1" pieces	Stir-fry in 1 tablespoon oil or 2 tablespoons butter for 1 minute. Add 2 to 3 tablespoons liquid, cover, cook 3 to 5 minutes.
Rutabagas, ¼" slices	Stir-fry in 1 tablespoon oil or 2 tablespoons butter for 1 minute. Add 4 to 5 tablespoons liquid, cover, cook 5 to 6 minutes.
Spinach, whole or coarsely chopped	Stir-fry in 1 tablespoon oil or 2 tablespoons butter for 30 seconds. Cover, cook 2 to 3 minutes.
Squash (pattypan, sunburst, yellow, zucchini), ¼" slices	Stir-fry in 1 tablespoon oil or 2 tablespoons butter for 1minute. Add 2 to 4 tablespoons liquid, cover, cook 3 to 4 minutes.
Squash (acorn, banana, butternut, Hubbard, pumpkin, turban), 1" cubes	Stir-fry in 2 tablespoons butter for 1 minute. Add 3 to 5 tablespoons liquid, cover, cook 3 to 5 minutes.
Swiss chard, stems in ¼" slices, leaves shredded	Stir-fry stems in 1 tablespoon oil or 2 tablespoons butter for 1 minute. Add 1 tablespoon liquid. Cover, cook 3½ to 4½ minutes. Add leaves for last 2 minutes of cooking.
Turnips, ¼" slices	Stir-fry in 1 tablespoon oil or 2 tablespoons butter for 1 minute. Add 4 to 5 tablespoons liquid. Cover, cook 4 to 5 minutes.
Turnip greens, shredded	Stir-fry in 2 tablespoons butter for 1 minute. Add 1 to 2 tablespoons liquid. Cover, cook 3 to 5 minutes.

Recipe

A Nifty Frying Batter

Use ¾ cup flour or pancake mix; ¾ cup beer, water or milk; 1 egg; 1½ teaspoons salt and 2 tablespoons oil. Add wet ingredients slowly to dry. Let stand at least 2 hours to let flour absorb liquid and eliminate air bubbles—overnight is okay.

Quick Hint

Protect the color in purple and red vegetables (cabbage, beets, etc.) by adding acid to the cooking water. One tablespoon citrus juice or vinegar or a handful of chopped apple per 2 cups water will do the trick. The acid also improves the flavor.

Pale vegetables like cauliflower and artichokes won't discolor if you add a pinch of cream of tartar to the cooking water or cook them in milk. Two tablespoons of vinegar also works well for artichokes.

DEEP-FRYING VEGETABLES

You can deep-fry vegetables coated or uncoated. If you don't coat them they must be absolutely dry before you drop them into the fat, or they will spit dangerously and the moisture will keep them from browning.

A crisp batter or crumb coating makes fried vegetables delicious. Use the breading technique on p. 90 or make a thin batter of equal parts liquid and flour—some people add egg and oil. See the box. My Japanese friends insist that water makes batter cook up crispest.

Fry vegetables at 365° until golden. Turn when one side forms a crust and starts to brown.

For utterly glorious French fries, try the Belgian method. Fry in 330° oil for 2 minutes. Drain and cool. Rev up the fat to 365° and fry for 3 minutes. Drain. Crisp, light, heavenly! In Belgium you buy fries in a paper cone from street vendors and dip them in mayonnaise to munch while you stroll.

MORE WAYS WITH VEGETABLES

Here are some comments on cooking a few specific vegetables by traditional methods:

Artichokes: New cooks hesitate to prepare them because they look tricky. They're not. Trim the bottom so it sits flat. With a sharp knife slice off the top third. I like to snip the prickle off the remaining leaves with kitchen scissors, but it's not necessary. Boil uncovered in lots of salted water with a slice of lemon and optional clove of garlic for about 40 minutes. (Weigh them down with a plate to keep them submerged.)

When a center leaf pulls out easily they are done. Drain upside down. To remove the fuzzy choke, cool slightly, spread the leaves and twist out the center cone of pale leaves. Scrape the fuzz from the artichoke bottom with a teaspoon and throw it out.

Cabbage: Cook it just to the crisp-tender stage and cabbage will have a mild, delicate flavor and no "boarding house" smell. Cooked until limp and soggy, it will taste and smell strong.

Canned Vegetables (as an ingredient): Remember, they've already been cooked, so add them to soups, casseroles, etc., near the end of cooking, allowing only enough cooking time for flavors to mingle and the mixture to heat through.

Eggplant: When you fry eggplant, it drinks oil like a blotter. It will absorb much less if you first place the slices in boiling water in a covered pan for 1 to 2 minutes. Drain them immediately in a colander and pat dry. Then fry uncoated (for dishes like Moussaka) or dredged in flour (for Eggplant Parmigiana) in a thin film of oil. You can also paint raw slices with olive oil and broil them, but this uses a little more oil.

Here's a way to keep fried eggplant from tasting bitter or absorbing too much oil. Peel and slice. Sprinkle the cut surfaces with coarse salt, place in a colander and allow to drain for at least 30 minutes. Pat slices dry with several layers of paper towel to get rid of excess salt. Now dredge the eggplant in flour and fry over moderately high heat. Drain well on paper towels.

Garlic: It's so easy to burn garlic and turn it bitter. When you sauté garlic, put it in the pan at the same time as the oil so it heats gently. If it goes directly into hot fat it can burn before it has time to soften. Also, garlic cooks faster than onion. When you sauté them together, add the garlic when the onions are nearly ready.

Keep in mind that garlic cooked in water will have a milder flavor than garlic cooked in fat. For the strongest flavor, sauté garlic to a deep gold color, but no further.

Whole garlic cloves roasted, braised or boiled are incredibly sweet and mild. Do at least one head, separating the cloves or not. Remove the papery outer skin of the head but leave the cloves unpeeled. *Boil* for 20 minutes, or

RESCUE

The Cooked Vegetables Look Faded!

Pep up their looks with parsley, chopped greens, butter-browned crumbs, toasted nuts or grated cheese.

A Mashed Potato Trick

When you mash potatoes, moisten them with a little of the cooking liquid for a lighter texture and deeper flavor. This works well with all mashed veggies.

**How to
Slice Onions**

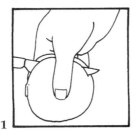

1

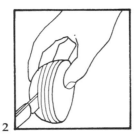

2

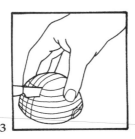

3

4

roast until golden (1 hour) at 350° with 2 teaspoons butter and 1 tablespoon water per head in a baking dish just large enough to hold them, basting every 10 minutes. Scatter the cooked cloves over roasted or grilled meats or season with pepper and coarse salt and serve. Let diners pop them out of their skins and spread them on bread.

Toss whole raw cloves into dishes that will braise—40 is the standard dose for Provençal-style chicken.

Onions: When you sauté or fry onions to a deep brown color you caramelize the sugar in them. That's what gives them that wonderful sweet, rich taste. However, once onions begin to darken, watch carefully. Indian cooks, who use deeply caramelized onions in their curries, keep adding dribbles of water as the pan dries to prevent the caramelized sugar from burning.

Like garlic, onions have a stronger flavor when cut small and cooked in oil.

To keep onions whole when cooking them in liquid, leave the root end intact and cut a ¼-inch deep cross in it.

Potatoes: *Boil* the waxy ones (round, with smooth, thin skins, often red); *bake* the starchy ones (oblong, with rough, thick skins).

Opinions abound on the best way to bake a potato fast. Some people find microwaved potatoes too moist. Another way to speed cooking is to parboil the whole, unpeeled potato for 5 minutes, then run it through with an aluminum nail or purchased "potato nail" and bake 20 minutes at 400°. Foes of this technique claim the nail lets moisture escape and ruins the finished potato. Clearly, you can't please everyone.

My quick method is a compromise: I cut the potatoes in half lengthwise, oil the cut sides, place them cut-side down in a pan and bake at 400° for half the usual time, or about 30 minutes.

Tomatoes: Unless you have peak-season, vine-ripe tomatoes, you'll do better to cook with canned ones. If you must use winter tomatoes, give them a boost with a little tomato paste or purée. Because most tomatoes are somewhat acid, I generally toss in a little sugar—not enough to sweeten, but enough to remove the sharp edge.

WHEN IS IT DONE?

Most vegetables are done if they are tender when pierced. Here are some other tests:

Asparagus: Bright green; thick end pierces easily with a fork; when held by the thick end the stalk bends. Stop cooking immediately to preserve the bright color.

Cauliflower (whole): Slides off a knife blade inserted near the core.

Onions and seasonings sautéed for curry and goulash dishes: They're ready for the next step when the liquid given off by the onions has evaporated and the cooking oil starts to separate out.

Potatoes (boiled or baked): A paring knife blade slides easily to the center.

Spinach: Wilted and bright green.

Squash, spaghetti (whole): The shell gives under pressure.

CHAPTER 6

Baking Help

Can I Use Margarine in Butter Cookies, How Do I Knead Dough, and Why Doesn't the Bread Recipe Tell Me *Exactly* How Much Flour?

This chapter is called Baking Help even though it has some non-baking things in it. I couldn't think where else to put information on doughnuts and pancakes and waffles. Flour-Based Cooking might have been more accurate, but that sounds high-tech and un-tasty, and I couldn't call the chapter Sweet Things because there's a section on yeast breads. I think you get the idea of what's in here.

The Handling It Like a Pro boxes will help with the questions that always seem to arise when you're working with yeast and baking powder and batters, so you won't have to run for the phone to ask Mom or a friend.

THINGS YOU SHOULD KNOW ABOUT BAKING

Don't crowd your oven. I blamed my small oven for not baking evenly until I changed to smaller cookie sheets and pans that gave the heat enough space to circulate. The oven bakes perfectly now.

The fuller the oven, the slower things will cook. When you roast or bake in a full oven, allow more cooking time

Before You Start to Bake

Well ahead: Read the recipe and note the ingredients you may have to buy and the utensils and pans you will need.

At baking time: Move chilled ingredients (eggs, butter, milk) from the refrigerator to the counter. Break eggs into a bowl; separate them if necessary.

Prepare pans (grease, flour, etc.) Sift or measure flour and other dry ingredients onto a piece of wax paper. Measure other important ingredients into small bowls.

Adjust oven racks and preheat oven. Grab your spoon and start.

RULE OF THUMB

Ingredient Temperatures

Everything *cold* for pastry; everything *warm* for bread.

---

and raise the heat by 25 degrees.

The areas where pans touch each other or touch the side of the oven will burn. Leave at least 1 inch of clear space around each pan. Also, never place one pan directly above or below another. Heat absorbed by the top one will reflect down and burn what's in the pan below.

The oven is hottest at top and bottom. Bake pies in the lower third of the oven to give them a crisp bottom crust, and casseroles in the top third to brown them. To roast or bake, place food in the center.

The back of the oven is hotter than the front (doors have teeny cracks). Halfway through the baking time, turn pans and dishes.

As for peeking in at other times, control your curiosity or get an oven with a window. **Every time you open the oven door the temperature drops about 25°,** and it could take up to 5 minutes to regain that heat. With this in mind, when baking delicate foods some bakers preheat the oven 25° higher than the recipe specifies, and lower the temperature when they put the food in to bake.

Try to use the size pan recommended in the recipe. If you don't, make adjustments. See p. 58 for help in substituting one pan for another.

Always place batter or dough in/on *cooled* pans. A warm pan melts the fat in the dough too quickly and you'll be disappointed with the result.

Baking sheets aren't just for cookies. Ovenproof glass and ceramic bakeware conduct heat evenly, but they heat very slowly. If you place them in the oven on a *heated metal baking sheet*, they will heat up faster and the cake or pie will have a nice crisp bottom. An old battered cake pan set on a baking sheet will bake a lovely cake. A soufflé set on a baking sheet will get hotter on the bottom and rise better. The sheet also keeps boil-overs off the oven floor.

❦HOW TO TELL BATTERS FROM DOUGHS❦

The proportion of flour to liquid is what changes a mixture from thin batter to stiff dough.

Used For	Consistency	Amount of Flour per Cup Liquid (Including Eggs)
Crepes, popovers, batter for fried foods	Thin batter (pours easily from spoon, like heavy cream)	1 cup
Griddle cakes, waffles	Medium batter	1 ½ cups
Muffins, quick breads, fritters, dumplings	Thick batter (drops from spoon in 1" - 2" splats)	2 to 2½ cups
Biscuits	Soft dough	3 cups
Yeast breads	Stiff dough	3½ cups or more

YEAST BREAD

You used to have to proof yeast (mix it with warm water and let it sit for 10 minutes until it foams) to make sure it was still active. This is no longer necessary, although most recipes still call for it.

Heat starts yeast growing so, except for quick-rise yeast, dissolve it in very warm (110°) liquid. You can get the right temperature by using 1 part boiling water to 2 parts cold tap water, but be careful, because liquid hotter than 130° kills yeast. Sugar feeds yeast, so a little is generally added to the liquid to get it started.

If you mix the dry yeast in with the flour, the liquid you add to the dry ingredients has to be especially warm.

Yeast is more active in large quantities of dough. If you double a recipe, use only 1½ times the yeast.

Try using the water potatoes have boiled in for your liquid. It gives a unique flavor and some claim it keeps the bread fresh longer.

⎯RULE OF THUMB⎯

Always Preheat

The oven must be preheated for all baking unless the recipe says differently. Batters and doughs have to encounter immediate heat to start expanding the gas formed by baking powder or the air beaten into egg whites before it leaks away.

Where to Put the Rack

Upper third: Most cookies.

Center: Most cakes.

Lower third: Anything in a deep container, such as tube and Bundt cakes, and soufflés, or things in a crust whose bottom should brown.

Knead on Wood

Experts agree that wood is the best kneading surface because it is slightly tacky. Smooth formica and plastic lack this grabbing quality. Use a large wooden cutting board or a plain piece of ¾-inch plywood, lightly sanded.

Kneading

Work on the lowest surface you can so your arms don't get so tired. Form the dough into a ball. Place it on a lightly floured surface and sprinkle with flour. The best way to do this is to use a shaker or throw a couple tablespoonfuls horizontally 3 inches above the dough. This creates a "snowfall" that drifts down and scatters evenly.

Flour your hands and with the heels, push the dough down and away from you. Fold it over and give it a quarter turn. Continue pushing down, turning, and folding until the dough feels smooth, silky and elastic and springs back into shape when you poke it lightly with two fingers. This usually takes 4 to 10 minutes. If your hands get sticky in the process, dip them in flour and rub them together.

You can also knead with the dough hook of an electric mixer or a food processor using the metal blade.

The first two minutes of kneading decide the bread's texture, so try not to add any more flour after that. As you knead, stickiness will disappear. A sweet dough, however, will always be sticky to work with. Don't try to make it completely unsticky by adding flour, or the bread will be hard and dry instead of moist and tender.

Butter also makes dough sticky. Again, don't be tempted to add extra flour. If the dough is too warm it may be sticky because its butter is oversoft; remedy this by by chilling the dough.

Moisture in the Flour: Ever wonder why you have a baking failure when you've made a recipe exactly as you did a million times before? It could be the moisture in the flour. All flour does not have the same moisture content, and there's no way to tell what you've got by looking at it. Flour takes on moisture from the air; it loses moisture in high altitude, cold weather, or during long storage.

Once when I was making bread, I measured the usual amount of flour out of a new package and got pancake batter instead of dough. I had a bag of wet flour. It took almost half again the amount called for before my dough stiffened up. (The bread turned out fine!)

This was a worst-case instance, but flour can vary by as much as 20% in the amount of moisture it absorbs, which is why bread recipes always call for a range (2½ to 2¾ cups) rather than a specific measure. Since your flour can change from one day to the next, always start with the smallest amount.

Rising

Yeast dough rises best at 80°. If your kitchen is too cool, try these places: an oven with a pilot light; a heating pad set at medium; the top of the TV, if the TV is on and the spot is draft-free.

Cold slows yeast action, so always use room temperature ingredients. Let cold work for you. When you want to interrupt the rising, put the dough in the refrigerator with plastic wrap over the bowl to slow it down. When you are ready to resume, punch the dough down (it will have risen a little) and continue where you left off.

Salt flavors bread to a surprising degree, but slows fermentation. In very hot weather when dough tends to rise too fast, a little extra salt added to the dough will slow it down.

The speed of rising makes a great difference in the flavor of bread. The longer it takes to ferment, the better flavor the yeast develops. Bread that rises too fast is flavorless; bread whose rising has been rushed with artificial heat will have an unpleasant beery taste.

Dough has risen sufficiently if it has doubled in bulk and holes remain when you poke it gently with two fingers.

Unless the recipe directs otherwise, remove bread from the pan as soon as it comes from the oven and place it on a rack to cool completely. If left in the pan or wrapped while even a little warm, it will steam and get wet.

Rising Times for Bread Doughs

Warm place (75° - 85°)
45 - 60 minutes

Room temperature (65° - 70°)
1½ - 2 hours

Refrigerator
12 - 24 hours

Kneading Dough

1

2

❧ Handling Yeast Bread Like a Pro ❧

If	Next Time You'll Know	Turning It into a Winner
There are lumps in the dough.	Not enough mixing or kneading; too much flour; dry ingredients like milk powder added to the *dough* instead of being first blended with the flour.	Mix or knead some more. Work in liquid by spoonfuls if needed.
Didn't rise enough before baking.	Yeast too old; liquid too hot for yeast; ingredients or rising area too cold; dough insufficiently kneaded (it should feel resilient and alive).	Try placing in a warmer area; if that makes no change but it has risen somewhat, go ahead and bake. It will be good enough for toast, French toast, and soup dippers.
Loaf didn't rise enough in oven.	Dough rose more than double before baking; oven not hot enough.	You can still serve it; the texture will just be different.
Crust too pale.	Oven temperature too low; pan not in the middle of the oven; insufficient sugar (sugar makes crust golden, so you need at least 1 tablespoon).	Brown it quickly under the broiler, watching every second!
Bottom and sides of the loaf are pale.	Baked in shiny pan which didn't absorb and pass on enough heat. See p. 377.	Remove bread from pan and return to the oven for 5 to 10 minutes.
Slices break up, bread is crumbly.	Too much liquid for amount of flour; insufficient kneading.	How about a bread pudding? Or make crumbs. Every kitchen needs them.

Handling Yeast Bread Like a Pro

If	Next Time You'll Know	Turning It into a Winner
Slices sag and are soggy.	Too much liquid; not enough kneading; not baked long enough. (Whole grain breads need more baking time than white breads.)	Slice and toast.
Loaf has big holes.	Too much yeast; didn't punch dough down sufficiently between risings; too little salt. (Remember, you *want* holes in French bread!)	Even with big holes, it's fine for everything except sandwiches with wet fillings.
Thick top crust has air space beneath.	Dough didn't rise enough before baking, so too dense to rise properly. Loaf not tightly formed so, as it cooled, moisture trapped beneath the crust turned it hard and left the space.	Cut off the loose top.
Crust too thick.	Baked in a glass pan without reducing oven temperature by 25°. See p. 374.	If really bad, cut off all the crusts like the British do for their sandwiches.
Loaf smaller than expected.	Too much salt; not enough rising time; oven not hot enough; pan too large. If heavy, whole grains are used, the loaf will always be smaller and denser.	Because it's denser, it will make lovely thin slices to butter for a tea party.
Loaf higher on one side than the other.	The oven baked unevenly. Next time, turn the loaf around at half time.	Whack off the top and eat it hot with butter and brown sugar. You now have a square loaf for symmetrical sandwiches.

Handling Yeast Bread Like a Pro

If	Next Time You'll Know	Turning It into a Winner
Loaf denser at the bottom.	Oven giving too much heat from the bottom so that part baked too quickly. Next time, place the bread pan on a cookie sheet to insulate the bottom from the heat.	Slice off and discard the bottom and use the rest.
Loaf cracked on one side.	This is not a fault. The crust hardened before the loaf had fully expanded so it had to burst somewhere. If you don't like the look, next time slash across the top of the loaf before baking so loaf can expand evenly.	Serve it proudly. It looks very French.
Free-form loaf (one baked on a baking sheet instead of in a container) flattens out too much.	Not enough flour.	Perfectly good loaf, just makes a shorter slice.
Bread has strong yeast flavor.	Too much yeast for the amount of flour; dough was too long rising or forced to rise super-fast.	Not much help for this, but don't throw it out immediately. Some folks like the yeasty flavor.

Quick Breads

Quick breads like biscuits and muffins are usually leavened with baking powder. Unlike yeast breads, which like to be slapped around, quick breads take badly to vigorous handling. Mix them with the fewest, lightest strokes, get them quickly into a hot oven, and they'll be tender and feather-light.

Popovers are an exception. You should stir them hard—old-fashioned recipes say to "beat several hundred times"! Popovers have no leavening except eggs—which work like magic. One of my favorite kitchen entertainments is hovering at the oven window when popovers get ready to rise to watch them shiver, crack, and shoot straight up. I'd make them for the drama even if they weren't so luscious.

Biscuits

Cut in the fat with a pastry blender or two knives, only until the mixture looks like small peas. A food processor will do the job, if you use a very light touch. Biggish pieces of fat melt and expand in baking, leaving biscuits flaky; if the fat is cut too small, the biscuits will be dense. Using a fork, stir in the liquid just until the flour is dampened—no more than 20 seconds. Knead 8 strokes on a lightly floured board to finish blending the ingredients. The dough should still be soft, almost sticky. Too little liquid makes biscuits hard. Soft wheat flour makes the best biscuits. See p. 23.

Who says biscuits have to be round? When you're in a hurry, cut patted-out dough into squares with a couple swift knife strokes. I pat and cut right on the baking sheet and then separate them slightly. Bake at 425°. A lower heat will let biscuits dry before they are done.

Popovers

If you like popovers, invest in a real popover pan. In the widely separated individual cups, popovers pop and puff to perfection. Or use the trick a friend taught me years ago and fill every other well in a standard muffin pan. (Put a little water in the empty wells.) Fill the preheated pans two-thirds full and bake at 450° for 10 minutes, then at 350° for 25 minutes. If you use a muffin tin, fill the wells only half full and reduce the last 25 minutes to 15. Prick each popover when it comes from the oven to let out steam so it stays crisp.

Some Foods Like It Moist

Muffins, cakes and quick breads bake best in high humidity. Electric ovens, which don't vent as well as gas ovens, provide the ideal atmosphere. If you have a gas oven, leave a muffin well empty and fill it with an inch of hot water. When baking small cakes and gift-size loaves, stick a custard cup of water in the back of the oven. You can do the same for normal-size cakes and loaves, but it's not necessaary.

Quick Hint

Buttermilk makes baked things tender. You can substitute it for regular milk in most recipes that use baking powder. Rule: for each cup of buttermilk, add ½ teaspoon baking soda and omit 2 teaspoons baking powder.

Quick Hint

Don't throw out butter and margarine wrappers. Use them to grease your baking pans. You'll be surprised how much fat remains on some of them—it keeps fingers from getting all greasy, too.

Muffins

Overmixed muffins are tough and full of tunnels. Leave the batter lumpy; ingredients will continue to blend during baking. Twelve to fifteen stirs are plenty. If the batter doesn't fill all the muffin cups, fill the empty ones with water so the pan won't warp.

You can bake muffins in custard cups. Set them on a baking sheet and reduce the oven temperature by 25°. The giant muffins that are so popular now are baked in 4½-inch glass baking dishes. Bake them a bit longer.

Muffins have the best flavor if they stand 10 minutes before serving.

Loaves

Like muffins, quick loaves get tough if mixed too much. If you leave a few lumps in the batter the bread will be light and tunnel-free. Check the loaf 10 to 15 minutes before done time. If it is browning too fast, lay a piece of foil over it. Loaves taste and slice best the second day.

❦ HANDLING QUICK BREADS LIKE A PRO ❦

If	Next Time You'll Know	Turning It into a Winner
Biscuits		
Not flaky.	Oil substituted for shortening (tiny lumps of cold fat make the flakiness); dough overmixed so no fat lumps remained.	They'll make a good base for a creamed something. Or split, toast under the broiler and butter while hot.
Dry and crumbly.	Too much flour or too little liquid.	Biscuits may just be too cold—try warming them up.
Tough.	Too little shortening; dough overmixed; too much flour (perhaps when rolled).	Slice, top with grated cheese, brown in the broiler and serve with soup or salad.

Handling Quick Breads Like a Pro

If	Next Time You'll Know	Turning It Into a Winner
Heavy.	Too much shortening; insufficient baking.	See above. Both of these would please a snack-hungry kid if toasted, buttered and jammed.
Misshapen.	Dough not rolled or patted out evenly. Next time press straight down with the cutter.	Call them Ragged Robins and serve cheerfully.

Popovers

Collapsed.	Removed from oven before they were done; oven was opened during baking; small instead of large eggs used. Next time, bake until they are firm.	Try returning to the oven; sometimes they repuff. If not, they are still edible—in fact some may prefer the unctuous, custardy texture.
Stuck to pan.	Pans not greased generously enough. Use ½ teaspoon fat for each popover cup or lots of nonstick spray.	They'll look funny, but the family will enjoy them.
Soggy.	Popover not pricked with fork when removed from oven to let out steam.	Prick and return to the oven for 10 minutes. That may help; if not, you may like the custardy texture.

Muffins

Uneven shapes.	Muffin cups too full (½ to ⅔ is enough); temperature too high.	They'll still taste good. Call them Ragamuffins.
Tunnels, dry.	Too much flour or too little liquid; batter overmixed; overbaked or oven too hot.	Slice, dip in egg batter and make French toast. Or toast golden and butter generously.

HANDLING QUICK BREADS LIKE A PRO

If	Next Time You'll Know	Turning It into a Winner
Loaves		
Crack down the middle.	That's what you want! It rose correctly.	Serve with pride.
Dry and crumbly.	Too much flour or flour not well incorporated; baked too long (it's done as soon as the top center is not sticky and resists finger pressure).	Bread will moisten and improve a bit after 24 hours. If not, slice with a serrated knife and serve buttered.
Tough and gummy.	Too much liquid (a big problem with fruit breads—next time decrease the recipe's liquid); insufficient shortening, too much flour; batter overmixed.	Slice and toast. Or cube and fold it into any pudding with a compatible flavor.
Wet, falls apart.	Too much liquid (batter should fall in heavy plops); bread cut before it cooled.	Slice with serrated knife and toast.
Streusel topping sinks into batter.	Streusel chunks were too large.	Rename it Streusel Swirl Bread. It may taste even better than the topped one.

❖ ❖ ❖

Quick Hint

To grease a pan without gooing up your fingers, slide your hand into a small plastic bag and use it as a glove.

❖ ❖ ❖

COOKIES

Grease your baking sheets with oil, solid shortening or cooking spray. Butter and margarine can burn, and the cookies may stick.

To keep cookies from spreading too much, don't grease the sheet unless the recipe says to and never put unbaked cookie dough on a hot baking sheet.

Butter cookies require special attention. When you make a large batch or if the kitchen is very warm, keep the extra dough in the refrigerator while it waits to be rolled. If the dough sits at room temperature, the butter will begin to melt and the baked cookies will be greasy and crumbly.

Margarine makes a softer dough than butter. This is no problem for drop and bar cookies. However, dough for other cookies must be stiffened by extra chilling before you use it. Chill dough for rolled cookies at least 5 hours in the refrigerator, dough for slice-and-bake cookies at least 5 hours *in the freezer.*

When you bake delicate butter cookies, use bright, shiny baking sheets—they don't get so hot. Dark metal drinks up heat and zaps it to the cookies so fast that they burn before the tops are done.

If you don't have a shiny cookie sheet, or if your dark sheets are burning even sturdy cookies before the centers are done, place one cookie sheet on top of another of the same size to make a double layer. Or invest in air-cushioned cookie sheets. Those who use them swear by them. When you "double-pan" you may need to add a few minutes baking time.

If you line cookie pans with parchment or heavy-duty foil, you can shape the cookies on that, without waiting for pans. When one batch is done, slide cookies along with parchment or foil onto a cooling rack and pull a filled sheet of unbaked cookies onto the pan.

As they cool, cookies must dry, not steam. A rack holding big or thick cookies should be a good six inches above the kitchen counter to prevent steaming. Set the rack on a pan or bowl.

After they are baked, keep soft cookies in an airtight container with something moist, like a slice of fresh bread or small chunk of apple. Change the bread or apple every 2 or 3 days to prevent mold.

Recipe Idea

Cookies From a Cake Mix

You can make soft drop cookies with a cake mix. Prepare as directed, but use only enough water to make a dough and don't beat.

Bake at 375° for 8 to 12 minutes.

Margarine and Butter

Margarine and butter have different shortening powers. This can affect the delicate balance of butter cakes and the consistency of butter cookies and croissant, puff and Danish pastry doughs.

Most recipes indicate whether it's safe to substitute margarine. If the recipe doesn't say you can, you may encounter problems.

❦ Handling Cookies Like a Pro ❦

If	Next Time You'll Know	Turning It into a Winner
Cookie bottoms are browned and tops are undercooked.	Cookie sheet was of dark instead of shiny metal; cookie sheet placed too low in oven; too much sugar in recipe (sugar caramelizes and burns fast on hot metal).	Brown tops quickly under the broiler for a few seconds to a few minutes. Watch like a hawk! Or, while they are still warm, form each into a ball. If they look bumpy, roll in powdered sugar, cocoa or nuts.
Tops are browned and bottoms are under-cooked.	Heat circulation was blocked from below by another pan; oven rack too high or heat too high.	If you notice the problem in time, lower the rack or oven heat. Otherwise, make ball cookies as above.
Cookies spread too much.	Dough was placed on a warm cookie sheet; oven not hot enough; cookie sheet greased even though recipe didn't say to.	If you see it happening in time, pull the cookie sheet out of the oven and, with a knife, quickly push the edges toward the center into a neat shape. Then continue baking. If you were too late, you now have a crisp, delicate cookie.
Cookies are gummy.	Underbaked; cookies cooled on the sheet instead of a rack; bar cookies were cut before thoroughly cooled.	Return cookies to the oven for a few more minutes. Watch carefully. If you discover it after they have cooled, change their name to *Chattanooga Chews* or *Chewy Delights*. You may be asked for the recipe.

HANDLING COOKIES LIKE A PRO

If	Next Time You'll Know	Turning It into a Winner
Hard and dry.	Oven too cool (cookies need high heat because they are so thin); baking time too long; not enough liquid or egg; too much flour—a problem with rolled cookies. Try rolling them between pieces of plastic wrap or roll on board dusted with powdered sugar instead of flour.	Sandwich two together with a frosting or jam. Or break them up and fold into a pudding. Or crumble for a crumb pie crust.

PIES AND PASTRIES

For light, crisp pastry, chill the dough before rolling: 30 minutes in the refrigerator or 15 minutes in the freezer. A day in the fridge will make it even crisper. Then give the dough a few minutes at room temperature before rolling. Dough is ready to roll as soon as it gives under pressure.

Rolling Dough

The way you roll dough affects your crust. First, flour the rolling surface. With your hands, shape the chilled dough into a flat, round cake about 1 inch thick. Flour the rolling pin and place it on the center of the dough. With light strokes, roll away from you to within half an inch of the edge. Give the dough a quarter turn and roll out from the center again—always away from you. Keep doing this until the dough is ⅛ to ¼ inch thick.

For an 8-inch pie, roll both top and bottom crusts to 10 inches in diameter; for a 9-inch crust, to 11 inches.

To avoid a soggy bottom crust on a pie that will bake filled, chill empty pie shell and filling separately. After you add the filling, bake immediately.

Recipe Idea

Flavor Your Pastry

Consider adding flavors to your pastry dough. For a meat or chicken pie, try a pinch of curry or chili powder or a tablespoon of sesame seeds. For a sweet pie use cinnamon, nutmeg, grated orange or lemon peel, or some chopped nuts (¼ cup for a single crust).

WHAT SIZE PIE CRUST
❧ WILL MY RECIPE MAKE? ❧

If recipe calls for this much flour or crumbs:	It will make:
⅓ cup	One 4-inch tart shell
1 cup	One 8-inch crust
1¼ - 1½ cups	One 9-inch crust Four 4-inch tart shells
2 cups	Two 8- or 9-inch crusts One 10-, 11-, or 12-inch crust
2½ cups	Eight 4-inch tart shells

Baking

For a well browned bottom crust use a pan of dark metal or ovenproof glass. Both absorb more heat than shiny metal. Metal transfers heat rapidly to the crust but glass heats more slowly, so place a glass pie pan on a dark metal baking sheet to heat it up faster. When using a glass pan be sure to reduce the oven temperature by 25°.

Always slit the top crust to let out steam or the steam will burst out through a seam and the pie will run over.

Pre-Baked Crusts (Baking Blind)

To insure a crisp bottom crust when you use a very wet filling (for quiche, for instance), pre-bake it. Line the chilled crust with a piece of wax paper or buttered foil, buttered side down, and weigh down the lining with rice or dried beans. You can keep these in a jar and use them over and over. Bake at 450° for 8 to 10 minutes until the pastry is just firmed up. Then lift out the liner and weights, bake 5 minutes more and the crust is ready for filling. If you brush the crust with lightly-beaten egg white before that last 5 minute of baking, it will be even crisper and more waterproof.

You can use this method when you need a baked crust for a filling that won't be cooked—just continue the last baking until the crust is lightly browned, 10 or 15 minutes more.

Quick Hint

Good, juicy fruit pies always ooze a little, so bake them on a baking sheet to catch the drips.

❦ HANDLING PIES LIKE A PRO ❦

If	Next Time You'll Know	Turning It into a Winner
Crust too hard or tough.	Too much water in dough; too little shortening; handled dough too much; over-rolled the dough.	Lift filling and top out of bottom crust. Serve filling as a pudding with a little top crust on each serving. Top with cream.
Crust shrinks.	Too much shortening; pastry was stretched to make it fit pan.	It will still taste fine, so cover the skimpy edges with something like cream or fruit.
Unfilled crust puffed and bumpy.	Failed to prick unbaked crust; crust baked without being weighted down; oven too cool.	Gently break the pastry bubbles with your fingers and then put in the filling.
Juice leaked out of pie.	Bottom crust pricked (you don't do this for a filled pie); top crust not slashed to let steam escape; top crust not well sealed to lower crust.	A good fruit pie always oozes a little (see box). If it was a real Vesuvius, serve it like a hot pudding with cream or soft custard sauce.
Soggy bottom crust.	Filling was not cool when put into crust.	If really soggy, lift out filling and serve as in first hint.

HANDLING PIES LIKE A PRO		
If	**Next Time You'll Know**	**Turning It Into a Winner**
Crumbly pastry.	Too little water; too much shortening.	Crumbly pies are a bother to serve neatly, but they taste rich and wonderful. Don't apologize.
Edge of crust too brown.	Edge not covered with strip of foil during last 15 minutes of baking. (Do this when you see that it is browning too soon.)	If really burned, cut it off. French pastries never have a raised edge. Disguise if necessary with whipped cream.

Quick Hint

To cut a meringue pie easily and tidily, dip your knife in water before cutting each slice.

MERINGUE

Meringue is made by beating sugar into egg whites. See the hints for beating egg whites on p.109.

Beat the whites until foamy. Add cream of tartar to help them stiffen and swell, then beat until they form soft peaks. Start beating in the sugar. If you add it earlier, you'll get less volume. Add sugar a tablespoon at a time, beating until you don't feel any grains when you rub meringue between your fingers. Superfine granulated sugar works best.

Crisp (hard) meringues that you fill, top, or use for tortes are really dried at a very low temperature rather than baked. Pipe or spoon these onto parchment or aluminum foil so they're easy to remove after baking. Here's a trick for making sure hard meringues come out crisp and don't weep: leave them in the turned off, closed oven until the oven has completely cooled.

For meringues with crisp-chewy outsides and soft, marshmallow-like centers, beat in ¼ t vinegar for each egg white. The Australian Pavlova is one of these. See p. 325.

You can add nuts, candied fruits, or grated chocolate to meringues. Stir them in gently—and add the chocolate gradually. If you want to flavor your meringue with an extract, fold it in with the last spoonful of sugar. You can also sprinkle unbaked meringues with grated coconut or candied fruit. Try a marbleized effect by substituting a tablespoon of chocolate syrup for the last tablespoon of sugar. Stir it in slowly in a thin stream so it makes a swirling pattern.

Soft meringue which goes on pies and desserts won't shrink if you anchor it well by making sure it touches the crust all the way around. Unlike hard meringue, soft meringue is baked at a medium temperature and emerges brown on top and moist inside.

Light cooking may not entirely destroy the salmonella bacteria that may be in egg whites. To be safe, put the meringue atop *hot* pie filling, spread it evenly to touch all edges, and bake in a 350° oven for 12 to 15 minutes—or until golden brown.

If you cool it at room temperature, soft meringue won't get little wet drops on top. Then you can refrigerate it if you like.

Some Foods Like it Dry

Notice how your glasses steam when you open the oven door? All that trapped moisture isn't doing your meringues any good.

When baking foods that must dry, like hard meringues and cream puffs, prop the oven door open during the last half of baking time with a wine cork or wooden spoon handle. This gives steam a chance to escape. The temperature will drop about 50 degrees, which will help, since you aren't baking so much as drying at this point. This is especially useful if you bake in an electric oven, which doesn't vent as much as a gas one.

❦ Handling Meringue Like a Pro ❦

If	Next Time You'll Know	Turning It into a Winner
Hard meringue		
Sticky, not dry and firm.	Too much sugar; egg whites insufficiently beaten; not baked long enough; weather too humid.	Put back in the oven. If meringues won't bake dry, rename them Ardent Kisses and fill as usual. Chewy meringues can be yummy. Or break them up and fold into whipped cream or a pudding.
Soft meringue		
Shrinks from pie shell.	Meringue didn't touch crust *all* the way around	No problem. It will still taste good.
Is tough.	Overcooked; oven too hot.	Lift the meringue off and discard it. Top pie with whipped cream or topping.
Weeps.	Meringue not put on *hot* filling (the filling's heat helps cook the meringue as it bakes); sugar not completely dissolved in beaten egg whites.	If it's not too bad, serve it anyway. It will still taste good. If it's really bad, lift off and top the pie with whipped cream or topping.

CREAM PUFFS

Cool your dough a little before beating in the eggs (always one by one) so the heat doesn't curdle them. Break the final egg into a cup, beat lightly with a fork, and add only as much as you need. The dough should be just stiff enough to hold a peak when you lift out the spoon. Sometimes you will need slightly less, on rare occasions slightly more egg than the recipe calls for. My friend Ellie, who bakes the world's fluffiest cream puffs, claims the secret is to do this step in the food processor.

Bake puffs at 375°, large ones for 40 to 50 minutes, small ones 25 to 30 minutes. When cream puffs are done, pierce the side of each with a knife so steam can escape and the centers won't be soggy. Some good bakers turn off the oven and leave the puffs in the closed oven for 15 to 20 minutes more to dry out. (Tiny puffs need 10 minutes). Try it.

To fill, slice shells in half horizontally and remove any uncooked dough from the inside. Heap the filling above the rim. Put on the top. If you use a sweet filling, dust tops with powdered sugar or spread with icing.

A Good Turn

Get in the habit of turning pans during baking. This ensures that all areas get equal heat and that hot spots don't overheat.

❦ HANDLING CREAM PUFFS LIKE A PRO ❦

If	Next Time You'll Know	Turning It into a Winner
Puffs didn't rise enough.	Dough overcooked; eggs not beaten in well; dough balls too flat; too much egg added; oven not hot enough; puffs not sufficiently baked.	If they feel soft and moist, bake a little longer. If they remain flat, split in half, scoop out uncooked dough and fill sandwich style.
Soggy inside.	Insufficiently baked; once baked, steam couldn't escape (slits not cut in side when taken from oven).	Return to the oven for a little longer. If still wet inside, cut in half, scrape out the damp part. Fill puffs as usual.

═ RULE OF THUMB ═

The rule for adding wet and dry ingredients alternately: start with dry—end with dry.

═══ RESCUE ═══

The Cake Stuck!

If cakes or muffins stick to their baking pans, place the pans on a wet towel. The cakes will steam away from the sides and bottoms and lift out nicely.

CAKES AND FROSTING

To make a good cake, start with room-temperature ingredients. Take them out of the fridge an hour ahead—eggs only 30 minutes ahead.

Before adding the sugar, cream the fat until it is the consistency of stiff mayonnaise. When you add the eggs, the mixture might curdle. That's okay. Ignore it.

After you fill pans with layer cake batter, hold each pan 6 inches above the countertop and drop it to burp out large air bubbles. Angel food and sponge-type cakes are too delicate for this treatment. You can accomplish the same thing by running a metal spatula through the batter.

Cool layer cakes on a rack for 10 minutes, then remove from the pans to finish cooling. Turn angel and sponge-type cakes upside down to cool. Some pans have legs to help with this. If yours doesn't, invert the pan over a long-necked ketchup or wine bottle.

❧ HANDLING CAKES LIKE A PRO ❧

If	Next Time You'll Know	Turning It into a Winner
Top crust of cake is hard.	Oven temperature too high, or cake baked too long.	A moist icing will help soften it. If really hard, cut off the top, invert cake and frost.
Top crust is sticky.	Too much sugar or liquid; it didn't bake long enough; the oven wasn't hot enough; weather was humid.	Dust with powdered sugar instead of an icing. If really gummy, remove crust and treat as above.

HANDLING CAKES LIKE A PRO

If	Next Time You'll Know	Turning It into a Winner
Top is humped or cracked.	Too much flour or too little liquid; batter overmixed (4 minutes with an electric beater or 300 strokes is plenty); oven was too hot; the batter wasn't spread evenly. *Sponge cakes:* perhaps too much sugar in the batter.	Cut it in the kitchen and top each serving with whipped cream or a nifty sauce—hot fudge, melba, whatever. Or cut off the top and frost.
Higher on one side.	Batter not spread evenly; an uneven pan; uneven oven heat; pan placed too near one oven wall. Also, check that the oven is level.	See above.
Soggy layer on bottom.	Too much liquid or eggs too big (most recipes are written for large eggs); butter too soft when added; batter not thoroughly mixed; cake not baked long enough. *Sponge cakes:* too many eggs or underbeaten yolks.	Cut off soggy bottom and serve a thinner cake. The soggy bottom often makes a good pudding served warm with a sauce or a little cream.
Fallen cake, collapsed center.	Too much sugar, liquid or leavening; too little flour; oven not hot enough; cake didn't bake long enough; pan too small, making cake so thick that center couldn't bake done. *Sponge or angel food cakes:* overbeaten egg whites.	Cut out collapsed center, creating a ring cake, and frost. Slice center part, dip in french toast batter and fry in a little butter. Sprinkle with sugar. Yum.

Handling Cakes Like a Pro

If	Next Time You'll Know	Turning It Into a Winner
Coarse grain.	Used all-purpose instead of cake flour; too much leavening; shortening too soft when added; fat and sugar not creamed together sufficiently; oven not hot enough. *Sponge and angel food cakes:* cream of tartar omitted.	Cut in squares and top with sauce or fruit. Also good toasted. Think of the wonderful bread pudding it will make!
Cake is tough.	Too much flour; too many eggs; too little sugar or shortening; batter overmixed. *Sponge or angel food cakes:* too much sugar; overbeaten egg whites.	Slice and toast. Serve warm with a warm lemon sauce. (See Lemon Sauce, p. 344). Slice thinly and assemble with frosting between layers.
Heavy, compact texture.	Too much liquid or shortening; too many eggs; too little leavening or flour; batter overmixed; honey substituted for sugar. *Sponge or angel food cakes:* underbeaten yolks or overbeaten egg whites	Slice and toast. Top with ice cream. Also use suggestions above.
Tunnels.	Too many eggs; batter undermixed or air pockets in batter. (Did you burp the batter?)	Serve warm with warm sauce.
Angel food or sponge cake falls out of pan before completely cooled.	Too much sugar; pan *greased* (the cardinal sin!); cake not baked long enough.	Cut in small cubes and fold into a chocolate mousse (one 8-egg mousse recipe to a cake). Or fold into any pudding. You may be glad this happened.

❧ How Much Frosting? ❧

Size Cake	Top Only	Top and Sides	Top, Sides and Filling
8" 2-layer	——	1½ c	2 c
9" 2-layer	——	2 c	2½ c
9" 3-layer	——	2½ to 3 c	3½ to 4 c
8" square	¾ c	1½ c	——
13" x 9"	2 c	2½ c	——
9 or 10" tube cake	——	3 to 4 c	——
9" x 5" x 3" loaf	1 c	——	——
12 cupcakes	¾ to 1 c	——	——

How Much Glaze?

9" or 10" cake	1 c	——	——
10" x 15" sheet cake	1⅓ c	——	——

When is it Done?

Without mom or grandma at your elbow the first time you bake something (assuming mom and grandma were bakers and not career women who patronized cookie boutiques and cake shops), it's hard to be sure when something has baked to the right stage. That's as much a part of good baking as stirring, folding and mixing.

Born cooks don't seem to have these problems. One famous southern cook *listens* to her cakes! They're done when she can't hear liquid bubbling in the batter. My mother-in-law patiently explained to me that you used the amount of soda in your buttermilk that made it sound

High Altitude Baking

When you bake at altitudes over 5,000 feet, make these adjustments for the lowered air pressure:

Baking powder batters: Reduce each teaspoon of baking powder by ¼ teaspoon. You don't have to reduce soda.

Batters containing beaten egg whites: Beat the egg whites only to soft instead of stiff peaks.

Cakes that contain a large amount of fat or chocolate: These may fall. If this happens, next time decrease the shortening by 1 to 2 tablespoons and add an extra egg. Serve the fallen cake in bowls topped with lots of custard sauce or pudding

Yeast doughs: Shorten rising time. Start checking early. As soon as the dough has risen, punch it down and let it rise an extra time before shaping. This improves flavor. When yeast rises rapidly it doesn't develop much taste.

Oven time and temperature: For cakes and cookies, increase the oven temperature by 25 degrees and decrease baking time slightly.

soft when beaten in a china cup next to your ear! Unfortunately, most of us don't have these instincts.

Ways to Judge Doneness

Biscuits: Tops and bottoms are golden. (Lift an edge and peek underneath.)

Cake: Feels springy on top but finger leaves no imprint; a toothpick inserted near the center comes out clean; edges start to shrink from the sides of the pan.

Cookies: Crisp, thin cookies will feel firm to the touch; edges will be a delicate brown. Drop cookies won't show a lasting imprint when you press the center lightly.

Cream puffs: Puffed and golden, sound hollow when tapped lightly with fingertip. At this point, puncture the sides to let out the steam.

Doughnuts: Golden on both sides.

Muffins: See Cake.

Pancakes: Turn when the tops are full of tiny bubbles, before the bubbles start to break. The second side will take only half as long as the first. They are done when they stop steaming.

Pie: Crust is golden and fruit filling tender; berry filling starts to bubble up through steam vents; meringue topping is golden; custard or pumpkin filling leaves knife blade clean after it's inserted near center.

Quick breads: See Cake.

Waffles: Golden brown and have stopped steaming.

Yeast bread: Starts to pull away from the sides of the pan; the top and sides are brown; sounds hollow when you thump the bottom with your fingers; a thin, sharp knife blade inserted in bottom of loaf and well up into center comes out clean; an instant-read thermometer poked in near the bottom registers 200°.

Yeast rolls: Tops are golden; bottoms and sides lightly browned.

❦ BAKING TEMPERATURES AND TIMES ❦

Item	Oven Temperature		Minutes
Breads			
Biscuits	425° - 450°		10 - 15
Cornbread	400° - 425°		30 - 40
Muffins	400° - 425°		20 - 25
Popovers: start at	450°	and bake for	10
then reduce to	350°	and bake for	15 - 25
Quick loaf	350° - 375°		60 - 75
Gingerbread	350°		40 - 50
Yeast:			
Loaf, non-sweet:	400°		35 - 50
or start at	450°	and bake for	10
then reduce to	350°	and bake for	25 - 30
Individual loaves,			
6" x 3" pans	375°		25 - 30
Yeast rolls	400° - 425°		15 - 20
Yeast rolls, sweet	375° - 400°		12 - 18
Cakes			
Cupcakes	375°		20 - 25
Layers	350° - 375°		25 - 35
Square	350°		35 - 45
Loaf	350°		45 - 60
Sheet cake	350° - 400°		20 - 30
Fruitcake	250° - 275°		3 - 4 hours
Angel	325° - 350°		50 - 75

Baking Temperatures and Times

Item	Oven Temperature	Minutes
Sponge	325°	60
Tube or bundt	350°	75
Cookies		
Fruit, molasses or chocolate	325° - 350°	10 - 15
Rolled ⅛" thick	400°	6
Rolled ¼" or drop	375° - 400°	8 - 15
Refrigerator	400°	8 - 10
Bars, strips, squares	325° - 350°	25 - 40
Macaroons	300° - 325°	20 - 30
Meringues, hard	275°	45 - 60
Pastry		
Empty pie shell	450°	10 - 12
Crumb crust	375°	8 - 10
1-crust pie, custard	400° - 425°	30 - 40
2-crust, uncooked filling	400° - 425°	45 - 55
2-crust, cooked filling	425° - 450°	30 - 40
Meringue, soft, on cooked filling (filling must be hot when meringue is put on)	350°	15
Deep-dish dessert pie:		
start at	450° and bake for	10
then reduce to	350° and bake for	30 - 35
Meat pie, biscuit top	450°	15 - 20
Meat pie, pastry top:		
start at	450° and bake for	15
then reduce to	350° and bake for	30

BAKING TEMPERATURES AND TIMES

Item	Oven Temperature	Minutes
Tarts	450°	10 - 15
Turnovers	450°	15
Egg Dishes		
Custard, baked, any size	350°	30 - 45
Soufflé (Heat oven to 450° and turn down as soon as dish is in oven.)		
8-cup dish	350°	40
6-cup dish	350°	30
Shallow 6-cup dish	350°	20 - 25
1½-cup dish	350°	13 - 15
Individual (1-cup dish)	375°	20
Flat soufflé in a jelly-roll pan (to be rolled)	425°	12 - 15

❦ DOUGHNUT HINTS ❦

- Don't roll dough too many times or the last ones will be tough.
- Most doughs fry at 365°.
- Pot shouldn't be more than half full—doughnuts expand as they cook.
- Fry for 45 seconds to 1 minute per side.
- When doughnuts float to the surface, they're usually ready to turn.
- Turn only once.
- Sugar doughnuts by shaking in a bag with granulated or powdered sugar.
- For a recipe, see p. 308.

How Phyllo Is Used

Phyllo sheets are lightly buttered or oiled, then rolled, folded or stacked to enclose fillings in a million buttery, flaky layers. For small pastries, place filling at one end of a narrow strip of phyllo and roll up or fold into triangles as you would a flag. Popular fillings are seasoned spinach, cheese or ground meat bound with egg. For strudels, place the filling in a thin log across one end then roll up the whole sheet of phyllo around the filling. For pie-type pastries (both sweet and non-sweet) layer the sheets in a baking pan to form the top and bottom crust. A supper we love is made with 6 or 8 buttered sheets, a filling of creamed chicken, seasoned ground meat, or feta in a thick white sauce with 6 - 8 more buttered layers of phyllo for the top. A stack of lightly oiled sheets makes a delicious, low-cholesterol, low-fat top crust for meat and chicken pies, fruit cobblers and such.

PHYLLO DOUGH HINTS

Phyllo is sold in the freezer section of most supermarkets. It generally comes in 1-pound packages containing 20 to 25 11" x 15" sheets. Frozen phyllo keeps for 6 to 8 months.

Thaw phyllo in the refrigerator overnight, then leave it at room temperature, unopened, for 2 hours before you use it. Phyllo doesn't refreeze very well—though I have done it.

Because phyllo dries out quickly, don't open the package until all other ingredients are ready to go. Unroll phyllo and cover it with waxed paper topped by a damp towel. (Don't let the towel touch the dough because moist spots will stick together.)

To layer phyllo in a pan, remember to make bottom and top sheets large enough so you can extend the bottom sheet up the sides of the pan and tuck the top sheet down the sides.

Don't paint the entire surface with the butter or oil; just streak lightly. Use a little more on surfaces that will touch moisture (filling) so they don't get soggy. Dribble the butter on and smear it lightly with your palm, or paint it on with a brush—a 2-inch one with natural bristles from an artists' or restaurant supply is perfect.

When you make small pastries, cover the finished ones with a cloth while they wait to go into the oven or freezer.

When you make a larger pastry, turn the pan as you put on butter or filling so you do it evenly. You'd be surprised how right-or left-handed we are.

If your pastry will be cut for serving, make the cuts before baking, scoring deeply with a sharp knife through the top layers almost to the filling. Cut baklava right to the bottom. If you don't cut first, even a sharp knife will smash the pastry layers rather than cut them.

Phyllo pastries can be frozen baked or unbaked.

Temperatures

When Is Milk Scalded, How Do I Know the Fat Is Hot Enough, and How Long Does It Take to Defrost a Duck?

This chapter tells you things like the temperature your refrigerator and freezer should be, the difference between a simmer and a boil, and the difference in degrees between a slow, a moderate and a hot oven. These are all things we think we know, but really don't. How do you know when your pan is hot enough to start frying? This matters. If it's not hot enough your steak just lies there oozing juice.

I've included charts to tell you how long food will keep refrigerated or at cool temperatures; how and how long to freeze prepared food like doughs, cakes, pies and casseroles; and how to thaw them for serving. If you buy and cook ahead, and we all do these days, this section is for you. Give it a close look.

NICE TO KNOW

The coldest area of the refrigerator is at the bottom near the back; **the warmest** is in the door shelves.

The hottest areas of the oven are the top and bottom thirds. The back is hotter than the front (doors don't seal 100%).

❦ TEMPERATURES YOU SHOULD KNOW ❦

What temperature should your freezer be? What is a safe refrigerator temperature? Where should the oven be set to bake at "low", "moderate" or "hot"? What are the equivalent Celsius or British or French gas temperatures? Check this chart to find out.

	Fahrenheit	Celsius	British Gas Mark (Regulo)	French Gas Setting
Freezer	0	-18		
Refrigerator freezer	10	-12		
Refrigerator	34 - 40	1 - 4		
Wine storage temperature	55	13		
Room temperature	68	20		
Room temperature needed for dough to rise	80	25		
Water simmers	180	80		
Water boils	212	100		
Keep food warm	225 - 250	105 - 120	¼ - ½	2 - 3
Very slow oven	275 - 300	135 - 150	1 - 2	3
Slow oven	325	165	3	4
Moderate oven	350 - 375	175 - 190	4 - 5	4 - 5
Moderately hot oven	400 - 425	205 - 220	6 - 7	5 - 6
Hot oven	450	235	8	6
Very hot oven	475	245	9	6
Extremely hot oven	500	260	10	
Broiling	550	290		

Heat

Checking Doneness With a Thermometer

A cooking thermometer will contribute a lot to your success at the stove. You need several kinds: an instant-read meat thermometer, a thermometer that clamps on the pot to keep tabs on the temperature of sugar syrups and deep fat, and an oven thermometer to check that your oven is giving the temperature you set.

Professional chefs are always poking a thermometer into a sauce, a custard, or a chicken thigh. Use yours not just for the obvious roast beef or poultry, but also to check doneness of meat loaves, tricky things like pâtés whose cooking signals might be hidden under a crust, and custards that have to cook thick but not boil. Some people even check their bread with a thermometer. See the box.

Judging Temperature Without a Thermometer

A thermometer isn't the only way to judge temperature. You can learn a lot with your other senses when you know what to look, listen and feel for. Here are some time-honored clues to telling temperatures.

Deep or shallow fat: A Chinese friend holds a chopstick upright on the bottom of the pan. When bubbles climb the stick, the oil is ready. Another way: drop in a small piece of raw vegetable. It should sizzle.

Fat for sautéing: When the surface wavers and small bubbles appear on top of the fat, it is very hot but just short of smoking. (Heat the oil in a pan over medium-high heat. When it is ready, lower the heat to medium and fry.) Another test: the meat should sizzle briskly when it hits the fat.

For searing meat: The fat should be a little hotter than for sautéing; it must flirt with the smoking stage.

Sautéing in butter: Butter foams when it melts. As soon as the foam dies down, the butter's moisture has evaporated and it is ready for the food to be added.

Checking Doneness With a Thermometer

Beef, lamb	140° (rare)
	160° (medium)
	170° (well)
Chicken, duck goose	175° - 180°
Custard:	
Soft	165°
Baked	180°
Meat loaf	160°
Pâtè	170° - 175°
Pork:	
Fresh	160° - 170°
Cured	130° - 140°
Potato	210°
Poultry stuffing	165°
Turkey:	
Breast	170°
Thigh	180°
Yeast bread	200°

RULE OF THUMB

Charcoal Temperature

Count the seconds that you can hold your hand over the grill.

Temperature		Seconds
Low	(250°)	6
Med low	(275°)	5
Med	(300°)	4
Med hot	(325°)	3
Hot	(350°-375°)	2

Pan-broiling and pancakes: Place the dry pan over high heat. The pan is ready when a drop of water sprinkled on it bounces, skitters about, and dries almost instantly.

Waffle iron: When it's ready, a drop of water sprinkled on the hot iron forms a ball instantly. If it just sizzles madly, the iron isn't hot enough. Another method: Put a teaspoon of water on the cold iron, close the iron and turn it on. When the steaming stops, the iron is ready.

HOW TO TELL A SIMMER FROM A BOIL

To know your liquid is the right temperature for:	Look for these things:
Stock-making	Water trembles; surface begins to shake but no bubbles appear around the edge of the pan.
Scalding milk	Bubbles appear around the edge of the pan.
Poaching, delicate sauces	Water "smiles"; small bubbles begin to pop on the surface.
Slow cooking, soups, stews, braises	Water simmers. A continuous stream of bubbles slowly rises to the surface.
Most normal cooking	Water boils: the surface is agitated but it doesn't roll on top of itself.
Cooking green vegetables or pasta, reducing stocks, making preserves and syrups	Rolling boil: now water rolls on top of itself. Bubbles form rapidly, rise, but break before they can reach the surface.

Judging Fat Temperatures

At this temperature:	A 2-inch square of white bread will turn golden brown in this many seconds:
345° - 355°	65 (will sizzle slowly)
355° - 365°*	60
365° - 375°*	50
375° - 385°	40 (will sizzle instantly)
385° - 395°	20

* Optimum frying temperature

Rule of Thumb

When a recipe uses the term *cool*, it means that the ingredient no longer feels warm. The bottom of a pan containing cooled food can rest comfortably on your hand.

Cold

Refrigerating Food

Don't refrigerate onions, shallots, garlic (the cold encourages sprouting), potatoes (the starch turns to sugar), or tomatoes (unless so ripe they're threatening to spoil).

Some cooks decant milk and cream into glass bottles; glass gets much colder than cardboard or plastic.

Remove plastic wrap from meat, fish, poultry, fruit and vegetables. Rewrap fish, meat and poultry loosely in wax paper. (Remove anything in the cavity of poultry and wrap it separately.) Store fruits and vegetables in the vegetable drawers.

Quick Hint

If a recipe directs you to chill something for 2 hours or overnight and you can't wait, chill it in the freezer for 30 minutes or in the freezing section of the fridge for 1 hour.

❧ How Long Will It Keep? ❧

Food — Where to Store	How Long
Fruit — In the crisper	
Berries, cherries, grapes, pineapple	3 to 5 days
Soft fruits and melons	5 days
Cranberries	1 week
Citrus fruits	2 weeks
Apples	1 month
Vegetables — In the crisper	
Corn on cob, in husks	1 to 2 days
Green leaves and salad vegetables	5 days
Asparagus, beans, broccoli, brussels sprouts, cabbage, cauliflower	5 to 7 days
Cucumbers, summer squash, ripe tomatoes	1 week
Root vegetables *except* onions and potatoes	2 weeks
Vegetables — In a cool, dark, dry place	
Onions, potatoes	1 week
Dairy — In the fridge	
Eggs:	
Separated: whites in covered container, yolks covered with water	4 days
In shell, in carton	1 month
Milk, cream, buttermilk	1 week
Butter	1 to 2 weeks
Cheese, tightly wrapped:	
Fresh (cottage, cream, processed, ricotta, spreads)	1 to 3 weeks
Soft-ripened (Brie, Camembert, chèvre)	2 weeks
Semi-soft and veined (Gouda, Monterey Jack, blues)	1 month
Semi-firm and firm (Cheddar, Swiss, Parmesan)	2 to 4 months
Meat and poultry — In the fridge, loosely wrapped	
Ground meat, fresh sausage, stew chunks, organ meats	2 days

How Long Will It Keep?

Food — Where to Store	How Long
Poultry	2 days
Ham, sliced	3 days
Roasts, chops, steaks	5 days
Cold cuts	5 days
Bacon, unsliced ham, hot dogs	1 week
Dry sausage (salami)	2 to 3 weeks
Seafood — In the fridge, tightly wrapped	1 day
Leftovers and opened packages — In the fridge, tightly sealed	
Cooked meats and poultry (stuffing removed!)	2 days
Soups, stocks	2 days
Cakes or pies, dairy-filled	2 days
Stews, casseroles	3 days
Fruits, cut up	3 days
Wines, white	3 days
Coffee, airtight, in fridge:	
Beans	2 months
Ground	1 to 2 weeks
Leftovers and opened packages — At cool room temperature	
Wine, red	2 to 3 days
Home-baked breads and rolls	3 days
Oils (except nut oils)	3 months
Flour, white (other flours in freezer)	6 months
Shortening	6 to 8 months
Pasta	1 year
Rice:	
Brown and wild	1 year
White	2 years
Baking powder and soda	1 ½ yrs

Wrapping Tips

All wrapping must be moisture- and vapor-proof. Squeeze out the air. Trapped air dries food (the moisture it pulls out turns to frost) and causes freezer burn.

Spray foil with no-stick cooking spray before wrapping meat, fish and poultry so it will slide off without tearing or sticking. Pad sharp bone edges with several layers of foil so they don't puncture the wrapper.

Freezing Food

Freezing intensifies flavors, so go light on seasoning, especially garlic and curry powder, in soups, stews and casseroles.

You can freeze soufflés, casseroles, and fancy desserts in their dishes and still use the containers if you line them with foil before filling them. Once frozen, the blocks can be removed and you can put the dish back in the cupboard. At thawing time, take the foil off the frozen block and place it in the original container. If you plan to bake from the frozen state, be sure the container is the oven-to-freezer type.

When you rewrap prepackaged foods for freezing, cut off the original label with its record of the cut of meat or poultry, weight, purchase date, etc., and tape it to the new package.

Some things don't freeze successfully: Hard-cooked egg white gets hard and and rubbery. Aspics and gelatin get rubbery and weep. Raw salad ingredients go limp. Use this fact to your advantage when you want to soften cabbage leaves for stuffing. Just freeze, defrost, and use.

When frozen *in a liquid* such as soup or stew, cooked potatoes and rice get soggy and mealy. So omit them. Mayonnaise curdles, but a small amount mixed into a dish will be okay. Some people freeze homemade mayo and bring it back with a whirl in the processor or blender.

Plain, unsauced cooked meat or poultry gets dry and tasteless in the freezer. Boiled frosting gets sticky. Custard and cream pies get watery. Bananas die (but they're fine for banana bread).

Never refreeze previously frozen seafood. Check whether the seafood you buy has been "thawed for your convenience."

The chart below, which tells you how to freeze food you've prepared ahead, will improve the quality of your life. The first column notes how long food can remain in the freezer without losing quality. Don't let that time limit make you nervous. Food that stays longer is still safe, it just doesn't taste as good.

❦ Using Your Freezer ❦

There's a second quick-glance chart of maximum freezer times for a number of commonly frozen foods on p. 221.

Food (How Long to Freeze)	To Prepare for Freezing	To Thaw and Serve
Unsliced bread (4 weeks)	Wrap in heavy plastic bags.	Thaw in wrapper at room temperature (3 hours) or overnight in refrigerator. Or thaw in tightly-closed brown paper bag in a 300° oven for 30 minutes (sliced loaf at 325° for 5 to 6 minutes). Oven-thawed bread goes stale faster. Slices can be toasted frozen.
Unsliced bread and rolls, brown-and-serve (4 months)	Freeze immediately after buying: loaves in wrapper, rolls in plastic bag.	Bake frozen, unwrapped: rolls at 400° for 15 minutes, loaf at 425° for 40 minutes. Cool loaf before slicing.
Bread dough (3 weeks)	Mix, knead, and without letting it rise, flatten a 1-loaf quantity into a 2" thick brick. If it has risen once, roll into a tight cylinder that fits the bread pan. Freeze immediately before it starts rising.	Unwrap, place in greased bowl and let rise in warm place (4 to 6 hours) or in oven that was heated to 125° and turned off (2½ to 3 hours). Continue as usual: punch down, knead, shape or place in pan, let rise again, bake. If frozen in loaf shape, place in loaf pan, allow to rise, and bake.
Bread, quick (6 months)	Wrap in plastic bags.	Thaw *breads* in wrapping 2 to 3 hours at room temperature or place frozen unwrapped in 400° oven for 10 minutes or until thawed. Thaw *muffins and biscuits* 30 minutes at room temperature.

Using Your Freezer

Food (How Long to Freeze)	To Prepare for Freezing	To Thaw and Serve
Cakes (unfrosted, 6 months, frosted, 2 months)	Use less flavoring than usual. If desired, spread cream filling (but not jam) between layers before freezing. Wrap unfilled layers separately. Freeze frosted cakes unwrapped until frosting has set, then wrap and pack in a box to protect frosting.	Cream-filled cakes slice best while still frozen. Unwrap frosted cakes before thawing so paper won't stick to frosting. Thaw plain cakes in wrapping at room temperature. Thawing time: layers and small cakes, 1 to 2 hours; frosted cakes, 4 hours.
Cake batter (4 weeks)	Line pan(s) in which cake will bake with heavy-duty foil, pour in batter. Freeze. Remove from pan and wrap.	To bake, grease baking pan in which batter froze, unwrap frozen batter and place in pan. Bake frozen at recipe temperature, adding 5 to 10 minutes to baking time.
Casseroles: poultry, fish, meat with vegetables, or pasta (2 to 4 months)	Season lightly and undercook slightly. Cool quickly, turn into freezer container or foil-lined oven-to-freezer casserole. Cover or wrap tightly.	If frozen in casserole, bake from frozen state uncovered at 400° until heated through (1 hour for pint volume, 1¾ hours for quart volume). Cover for first half of baking. If frozen in freezer container, remove contents and heat, covered, in top of double boiler.
Cookies, unbaked, (6 months)	Dough: form 2" cylinders, wrap. Shaped cookies: form on paper-lined tray, freeze, pack in rigid containers with paper between layers.	Slightly thaw rolls, slice and bake at recipe temperature. Bake shaped cookies from frozen state at recipe temperature, adding 7 to 10 minutes baking time.
Cookies, baked (4 weeks)	Pack in rigid containers with paper between layers.	If necessary, crisp in warm oven (275°) after thawing.

Using Your Freezer

Food (How Long to Freeze)	To Prepare for Freezing	To Thaw and Serve
Crepes, unfilled (4 months)	Stack and wrap in packages of six, with wax paper between the crepes if you like.	Thaw in wrapping 2 to 3 hours at room temperature, overnight in the refrigerator. Gently peel off thawed crepes and use as recipe indicates.
Crepes, filled (1 to 2 months)	Choose fillings suitable for freezing. Underseason. Pack in foil containers, seal and overwrap.	Remove overwrapping. Place unopened foil container in 400° oven for 30 minutes or until thawed.
Croissants and Danish pastries, unbaked (6 weeks)	Prepare dough up to the final rolling. Wrap tightly in a plastic bag.	Unseal and retie the bag loosely to give dough room to rise. Thaw overnight in refrigerator or 5 hours at room temperature. Roll, shape, bake.
Croissants and Danish pastries, baked (croissants 2 months, Danish 1 month)	Wrap in foil or plastic bags.	Thaw in wrapping at room temperature for 1 hour. If desired, freshen for 5 minutes, unwrapped, in a 350° oven.
Meat dishes (2 months)	Underseason. Cook for a slightly shorter time than usual. Make sure meat is completely covered with gravy or sauce. Best to add potatoes, rice, noodles, garlic and celery *after* thawing. Freeze in rigid freezer container, or foil-lined casserole.	Remove frozen from rigid container into saucepan to reheat with a little water; if frozen in casserole and rewrapped, unwrap and place in casserole and reheat from frozen state, uncovered, for 1 hour at 400°. If edges darken too fast, reduce heat to 350° for last 40 minutes.
Meat loaves, pâtés, terrines (1 month)	Underseason and cook completely. Wrap in plastic, then foil.	Thaw in wrapper: 6 to 8 hours at room temperature, overnight in refrigerator.

Using Your Freezer

Food (How Long to Freeze)	To Prepare for Freezing	To Thaw and Serve
Mousses, cold soufflés (2 months)	Freeze in freezer-proof glass dishes or line dish with foil.	If removed from dish and re-wrapped, unwrap and place in dish to thaw. Thaw in refrigerator 6 to 8 hours or at room temperature 2 to 3 hours.
Pastry, unbaked (3 months). Don't freeze pecan pie.	*Bottom crusts:* Place in foil pie pans and freeze. Or place in foil-lined pie-pans, freeze unwrapped. Remove frozen crusts and wrap in plastic bags. *Top crusts:* Roll to desired size, separate with 2 sheets wax paper. Freeze on cardboard. Wrap. *Single or double-crust fruit pies:* Freeze ready for baking, but don't slash top. When solid, wrap.	*Pie shell:* Return to original pan and bake frozen at recipe temperature, adding 5 minutes to baking time. (If you bake in oven-proof glass, let stand at room temperature 10 minutes before baking). *Top crust:* Thaw at room temperature, then fit on filled pie. *Filled pie:* Replace in pie pan if wrapped separately. Unwrap, cover edges with foil and place frozen in 400° oven for 15 minutes, reduce heat to 350° and bake 15 minutes. Remove foil and bake 30 minutes or until done. *Slash top crust as soon as it begins to thaw.*
Pastry, baked (pie shells and fruit pies 6 months, meat pies 3 months) Don't freeze cream, custard or meringue-topped pies.	Bake pie in foil or foil-lined container, cool quickly. If desired, invert another foil pan over pie to protect the top. Wrap.	Thaw at room temperature (2 to 4 hours). Reheat meat pies in 350° oven.

USING YOUR FREEZER

Food (How Long to Freeze)	To Prepare for Freezing	To Thaw and Serve
Pizza, unbaked (3 months)	Prepare to baking stage. Wrap. Freeze and overwrap.	Remove all wrapping. Place frozen in *cold* oven, turn temperature to 450° and bake 30 to 35 minutes.
Pizza, baked (2 months)	Wrap, freeze and overwrap.	Remove wrapping, place frozen in 350° oven for 15 minutes.
Sauces, clear soups, stocks (2 to 3 months)	Cool completely, freeze in rigid containers.	Heat from frozen state to boiling point or thaw first at room temperature (1 to 2 hours).
Stews or soups (2 months)	Use only vegetables that freeze well (no potatoes). Undercook vegetables. Cool quickly. Pack in rigid container leaving head space.	Place in heavy saucepan over low heat, separating often with a fork, until thoroughly heated.

MAXIMUM STORAGE TIMES IN THE FREEZER (0°)

1 to 2 months:	Bread, cake, fish, gravy, ground meat, ice cream, pie, soup, stock.
3 to 4 months:	Casseroles, chops, cookies, shellfish, steak, TV dinners.
5 to 7 months:	Butter, citrus fruit, duck, nuts, roasts, turkey, vegetables.
8 to 12 months:	Chicken, game birds, juice concentrate, margarine, non-citrus fruit, rabbit.

Quick Hint

You can thaw poultry in the microwave. Like meat, it will lose a little juice. Watch carefully and turn often. Cover areas that start to cook with a little foil.

Defrosting

A friend who graduated from the Cordon Bleu works full time and entertains in the grand manner. She lives out of her freezer, buying elegant, expensive meats like rack of lamb and beef fillet when they are on sale. According to her, the trick to using frozen meat and poultry (most frozen food, for that matter) is very slow thawing, so there is no loss of juice or quality. She even freezes delicate cheeses, bringing them to the fridge a good day before she wants them.

Never thaw meat or poultry out on the counter at room temperature. You waste your meat (it loses its wonderful juices) and you risk your health (microbes wake up and flourish in the thawing meat.)

Meat

Frozen meat will keep most of its juices after thawing if thawed slowly, *in its wrapper, in the refrigerator.* In emergencies you can thaw meat, wrapped, in cold water. It will take about one third as much time as in the fridge and the meat will lose some juices. You can also thaw meat in the microwave; it will lose a little more of the juices. Watch it like a hawk, so one edge doesn't cook while the other end is hard as a rock. (If the meat does start to cook, cover the area with a small piece of foil.) *If you don't have time to thaw,* there are hints in Chapter 4 under the various methods of cooking meat for cooking from the frozen state.

Poultry

As with meat, flavor and texture are best when poultry is thawed in the refrigerator. However, when time presses, you can place a frozen, wrapped bird in a large kettle, cover with cold water, and let it stand at room temperature, changing the water often. It won't be as succulent, but you'll have dinner on time.

❧ THAWING MEAT AND POULTRY ❧

Meat	Thaw in Refrigerator
Large roasts and smoked meats over 4 lbs	4 - 7 hrs per lb
Steaks, chops, ham slices:	
1"	8 - 10 hrs total
1½"	9 - 12 hrs total
2 "	11 - 14 hrs total
Flank steak, whole	8 - 10 hrs total
Spare ribs, whole side	7 - 10 hrs total

Poultry	Thaw in Water	Thaw in Refrigerator
Cut-up pieces	1 - 2 hrs	3 - 9 hrs
Whole:		
Under 4 lbs	1 - 5 hrs	12 - 16 hrs
4 - 12 lbs	4 - 6 hrs	24 - 48 hrs *
12 - 16 lbs	6 - 9 hrs	2 - 3 days
16 - 20 lbs	9 - 11 hrs	3 - 4 days
20 - 24	11 - 12 hrs	4 - 5 days

* A 6-pound duck will take a full 48 hours to thaw. Be warned.

Seasonings

What Are Capers, What If I'm Out of Chives, and Does White Pepper Taste the Same As Black?

Sauces, spices and herbs should enhance flavors, not disguise them. Seasoned meats and vegetables should still taste like meats and vegetables. Season lightly and taste constantly. You can always add more, but you're stuck with an overdose.

TASTE, TASTE, AND TASTE

Start tasting before the cooking begins. It could make a big difference in how much of an ingredient you use. Lemons can be mild or sharp. So can onions. Hot peppers vary from gentle to fire-bomb. Old herbs and spices lose their punch and you have to use more of them. Cucumbers and zucchini are sometimes bitter. (Since there's no remedy for this, it's important to discover it in time so you don't use them.)

Cooking is a series of chemical reactions. Everything you do to food—beating, heating, chopping or chilling—alters its taste. See, for example, the comments in the Guide to Ingredients on how chopping and cooking affect the flavor of garlic. As soon as you add wine or an herb or spice to a sauce the taste changes. As that ingredient cooks, the taste changes again. You can give yourself a course in

Use Your Nose

A lot of the taste sensation is in your nose, so keep tabs on the flavoring and progress of a dish by fanning the vapors toward your face (safer than leaning into hot steam or spluttering fat).

RESCUE

It Doesn't Taste Right!

If a dish is too sweet, add a pinch of salt. In a main dish, add vinegar by drops, tasting as you go.

When a dish tastes too sharp or acid, add a little sugar. A spoonful of cream or butter can also smooth out an acid taste.

If cooked tomatoes or tomato sauce taste too sharp or acid, add a pinch of white or brown sugar, a little honey, currant jelly, grated carrot, or instant coffee powder. A friend who is a superb cook always puts instant coffee powder in her spaghetti sauce.

Also see box on p. 245.

food and cooking chemistry by tasting your way through a recipe.

You can judge the final result only when all the chemical changes have taken place, so start tasting in earnest near the end of cooking time. One more thing: the sense of taste dulls. After three tastes, wait 15 minutes before tasting again.

Don't let recipes bully you. Season to please yourself and the people you are cooking for. Who says hot chiles have to peel the skin off your tongue? If you don't like garlic, leave it out, and if you love it, add more than the recipe calls for. Just remember to move slowly. Add small amounts, tasting as you go, until you have what you like. It's your kitchen, after all; cooking is one of the few areas where you can do what you want. Make the most of it.

Things That Affect Seasonings

Age: Herbs and spices weaken as they age. If you aren't sure how old an herb is, crush a little in your hand and sniff to see if it still has flavor.

Heat: Most spices turn bitter if subjected to high heat for more than a few minutes. Remember this when you sauté, stir-fry, or fry spices "till fragrant" for curries, etc. (See hint, p. 228, on warming spices.)

Length of cooking time: Garlic and onions become more pungent the longer they are sautéed. If you allow garlic to color past a deep gold, though, it becomes bitter.

Temperature at which the food will be served: Flavors are strongest at room temperature. Next strongest are hot foods. Chilled foods need the most seasoning. After chilling, always taste a dish again to see if it needs perking up. Cold starches like pasta, rice and potato salads absorb a lot of flavor. Season them generously and count on adding still more when you do that last taste.

Freezing: Freezing changes some flavors and weakens most. When you cook for the freezer, hold back all or a part of the seasoning, and add it when you reheat the dish for serving.

When to Season?

The point at which you add seasonings affects the final dish. Garlic and most ground spices *except* paprika, chili powder, and bay leaf lose flavor during long cooking (more than 2 hours). Add them late or put in a little extra at the end of cooking.

Whole spices hold up well in long cooking. You can add them at the beginning. Many cooks enclose them in a piece of rinsed cheesecloth so they are easily fished out when the dish is done.

As a rule it's better to salt meats to be broiled, grilled, or sautéed after they have browned. The salt draws moisture to the surface and prevents browning. (See p. 122 for more on browning.)

Here's a rough guide as to when to add seasonings:

Dry cooking (roasting, grilling, broiling): Mix herbs and spices into oil or butter and spread on during the last 30 minutes of cooking.

Cooking in liquid (braising, stewing): If a dish will cook more than 1 to 1½ hours, add seasoning after the first half of cooking time. Remove bay leaves after the first hour; bay is one of the few herbs whose flavor intensifies as it cooks.

Frying and sautéing coated foods: Sprinkle seasonings on food before coating or mix them into the coating.

Uncooked foods like non-green salads improve the longer the seasoning is in them, so add seasonings early.

Shopping and Cooking Hints

Mark the date on your herb and spice bottles when you buy them, so you'll know how old they are. Buy them in small amounts so you can renew them often.

Organize your herbs and spices alphabetically on the shelf, or group them generally by beginning, middle and end of the alphabet.

Some cooks keep frequently used seasonings in bottles that look different from the others so they don't have to

All Taste Isn't In The Mouth

Tastebuds pick up bitter, sour, salty, and sweet flavors. All the others come through our senses of:

Smell—Food tastes like blotters when you have a cold.

Sight—Tests show that green mashed potatoes and blue hamburger don't taste like potatoes and beef.

Touch—A limp apple doesn't taste good; crispness is part of the taste.

— RULE OF THUMB —

Using Dried Herbs and Spices

Start with ¼ teaspoon dried herb or spice per pound of ingredients and taste as you add more. Or figure, for each four servings, ⅓ teaspoon powdered spice, ½ teaspoon crushed dried leaves or seeds, or 1 tablespoon chopped fresh herbs. Bear in mind that some herbs and spices have more dominant flavors than others.

The more cut surface you have, the more completely the herb will give out its flavor. So for maximum flavor, chop fresh herbs finely or grind them in a mortar.

read the labels.

Never shake seasonings directly into what you're cooking; instead, shake them into your palm so you see how much you're adding.

Always fish a bay leaf out before serving. It's not meant to be eaten: the hard, sharp spine can be dangerous if swallowed.

Dried Herbs: When you shop for dried herbs, buy whole leaves if possible; crushed and powdered herbs lose flavor fast. Powdered or ground spices are fine, although you will get a more intense flavor if you grind the whole berries and seeds yourself. There are various tools available for this: electric spice grinders, your coffee grinder, nutmeg graters, the mortar and pestle, and of course, the pepper mill.

To release the most flavor, crush dried herbs in your palm before adding; grind seeds in a mortar and pestle. Or, crush them in a saucer with the back of a spoon or the bottom of a jar.

Fresh Herbs: Store fresh herbs in the crisper drawer of the refrigerator in plastic bags with stems or roots wrapped in moist paper towels. Although dried parsley and chives are all but tasteless, they freeze well when fresh. Wash, shake, pat dry, and freeze in plastic containers.

Spices: Many spices should be warmed to bring out their flavor *before* you add them to a preparation. Asian recipes often call for **roasting or warming spices until "fragrant"**. To do this, place the spice in a dry skillet over medium low heat for 1 to 3 minutes. Stir, and watch carefully. When the color darkens one shade and you begin to smell it, it is ready. Don't let the spice burn or it will taste bitter.

Herbs and Spices

All too often we buy an unfamiliar herb or spice for a specific recipe and let it gather dust and die on the shelf. I am reminded that there is no excuse for such lack of imagination when I see my artist friend root through her ill-organized spices and herbs, pull out an orphan, sniff it, taste it, and create a delectable, unexpected dish. One time she pounded fennel seeds with butter and garlic, smeared the mixture over game hens and simmered them slowly in wine and more fennel. They were divine.

Most of us weren't born with that flair, but if you use the chart below, no one has to know. When you buy a new herb or spice, check the chart to joggle your creative juices. When someone applauds the whiff of cinnamon in the stew you can always say airily, "Oh just an idea that came to me as I stirred."

Quick Hint

Dried herbs to be used with uncooked foods will taste almost fresh if you mix them with an equal amount of fresh, chopped parsley and let the mixture stand for a few minutes. The added parsley will take on the flavor of the herb and the extra amount won't hurt a recipe.

🌿 Buying and Using Herbs and Spices 🌿

Name	Forms to Buy	Description
*Allspice	Whole or ground berries	Tastes like a mix of cinnamon, clove and nutmeg. Use for cakes, cookies, pie, pudding, breads, and Middle Eastern meat dishes.
Anise	Whole or ground seed	Tastes like licorice. Use for candies, liqueurs, Scandinavian and German breads, pastries, cookies. Use instead of ginger in cakes.
*Basil	Fresh or dried herb	Mild mint-licorice flavor. For meat, fish, seafood, tomato dishes, soups, stews, eggs, sauces, salads.

* Herbs and spices that should be in a basic pantry.

Buying and Using Herbs and Spices

Name	Forms to Buy	Description
*Bay leaf (Laurel)	Whole, dried herb	Aromatic, woodsy, bitter if you use too much. Good with veal, fowl, fish, stews, soup. Turkish bay leaves have better flavor than the California ones. Use 1 per quart of liquid.
Bouquet garni	Herb mixture	Aromatic herbs to season soups and stews. See pp. 346 - 7 to make.
Capers	Whole bud, pickled or in brine	Tart flower buds. Use with eggs, seafood, veal, tomatoes, piquant chicken dishes. Small are best.
Caraway	Whole seeds	Delicate licorice flavor. Use with beets, cabbage, bread, cookies, dips, organ meats, casseroles, cottage cheese, Sauerbraten, sauerkraut.
Cardamom	Whole pod or ground seed	Lemon-ginger taste. Good in pastries, pies, cookies, fruit dishes, sweet potatoes, pumpkin, Indian and Asian cookery.
*Cayenne	Ground spice	Hot red pepper blend. Use pinches in cheese sauces, soups, curries, Mexican recipes.
*Celery seed	Whole seeds	Tastes just like celery. Bitter if too much is used. Use in stews, soups, salads, poultry dishes.
Chervil	Fresh or dried herb	Delicate, sweet, parsley-licorice flavor. Use for soups, seafood, salads, eggs, fish, cottage cheese.
*Chili powder	Ground spice	Blend of chiles, cumin and oregano. Use in Mexican dishes, meats, stews, soups, cocktail sauces, eggs, seafood, relishes, dressings.
Chives	Fresh, freeze-dried or frozen herb	Delicate onion flavor. Ingredient or garnish for any dish complemented by onion flavor.
Cilantro (Fresh Coriander)	Fresh herb	Fresh leaves resemble flat-leaf parsley. Use in Mexican, Latin American and Indian dishes, dressings, and salsa. See also Coriander.

Buying and Using Herbs and Spices

Name	Forms to Buy	Description
*Cinnamon	Whole sticks or ground	Warm, spicy flavor. Use in pastries, desserts, puddings, fruits, spiced beverages, pork, chicken, beef (Greek and Mexican cooking), sweet potatoes, carrots, squash.
*Cloves	Whole or ground	Hot, spicy, penetrating. Use sparingly with pork, in soups, desserts, fruits, sauces, baked beans, candied sweet potatoes, carrots, squash. Poke two or three into an onion to flavor soups and stews.
Coriander	Whole or ground seed. Fresh herb is also called cilantro.	Seeds have a pleasant lemon-orange flavor. Use ground and whole seeds and fresh leaves in Latin American and Indian dishes, dressings, spiced dishes, cream and pea soups, pastries, cookies, cheese and meats.
*Cumin	Whole or ground seed	Warm, salty-sweet. For meat loaf, chili, fish, soft cheeses, deviled eggs, stews, beans, cabbage, fruit pies, Oriental, Indian and Mexican cookery.
*Curry	Powder	A combination of spices. Good with meats, sauces, stews, soups, fruits, eggs, fish, shellfish, poultry, creamed and scalloped dishes, salad dressings. Make your own. See p. 350.
*Dill	Whole or ground seeds, fresh herb	Aromatic, mild, sweet, caraway-like taste. Use with seafood, meat, poultry, spreads, dips, dressings, cream or cottage cheeses, potato salads, many vegetables, soups, chowders, or Scandinavian cuisine.
Fennel	Whole or ground seed	Licorice flavor. Try with breads, rolls, sweet pastries, cookies, apples, stews, pork, squash, eggs, fish, beets, or cabbage.

Buying and Using Herbs and Spices

Name	Forms to Buy	Description
Fenugreek	Whole or ground seeds	Red-brown seeds with a smoky-sweet taste. Use in curry mixes, Indian cuisine. Also makes a lovely tea to aid digestion.
Filé powder	Powder	Dried sassafras leaves. Woodsy flavor. Flavors and thickens gumbos and other Creole dishes.
Fines herbes	French herb mixture	Salads, chilled soups, eggs, sauces. See p. 351 to make.
*Ginger	Fresh whole root, ground	Aromatic, sweet, spicy, penetrating. Use in cakes, pies, cookies, chutneys, curries, stews, Indian and Oriental cuisine, yellow vegetables, beets, soups, dressings or cheese dishes.
*Horseradish	Fresh whole root, grated and bottled	Very pungent. Use to zip up sauces, dips, spreads, salad dressings, cocktail sauce, or as a condiment with ham and cured meats.
*Italian herb seasoning	Herb mixture	For Italian dishes, meats and poultry, salad dressings, marinades. See p. 357 to make.
Juniper	Dried whole berries	Used to flavor gin, game, salmon, goose, duck or pork.
*Mace	Whole or ground spice	Dried husk of nutmeg with nutmeg flavor but sweeter and milder. Try with chicken, creamed fish, fish sauces, cakes, cookies, pumpkin pie, spiced doughs, jellies, beverages, yellow vegetables, cheese dishes, desserts, or toppings.
*Marjoram	Fresh or dried herb	Mild cousin of oregano. Good with veal, lamb, poultry, potatoes, tomatoes or Greek dishes.
Mint	Fresh or dried herb	Cool, sweet. Good with lamb, veal, fish, soups, fruit desserts, cottage or cream cheese, sauces, salads, cabbage, carrots, peas, potatoes and Greek and Middle Eastern dishes.

* Herbs and spices that should be in a basic pantry.

BUYING AND USING HERBS AND SPICES

Name	Forms to Buy	Description
*Mustard	Whole or ground seeds, prepared bottled	Bitter and biting. Dijon-style is the best prepared mustard for cooking. Use in salads, dressings, eggs, sauces, fish, meats, and many vegetables.
*Nutmeg	Whole or ground seeds	A sweet spice. Use it in baking and custards. It picks up cheese dishes and creamed foods.
*Oregano	Fresh or dried herb	Strong, aromatic flavor—bitter if too much is used. Use with grilled meats, fish and poultry, stews, tomato based soups and sauces, vegetable soups or salad dressings.
*Paprika	Ground spice	Hungarian paprika has the best flavor. There are two varieties: *Sweet,* the kind that's labeled just "paprika", has a warm, musky-sweet flavor. It's good with veal, chicken, eggs, fish, stews, cream soups and sauces, vegetable or potato casseroles, salad dressings. *Hot* paprika is hot. It will be labelled "hot" or "sharp". Use it with caution in goulash and other Hungarian and Eastern European dishes.
*Parsley	Fresh or freeze-dried herb	Don't use dried. Fresh, mild flavor. Use the Italian flat-leaved for flavor, the curly kind for garnish. Use in soups, meats, fish stuffings, cream or cheese sauces, eggs, flavored butter, marinades, vegetables and salads, also to give dried herbs a fresh taste. See hint on p. 229.
*Peppercorns, black or white	Whole or ground spice, coarse, medium or fine grind	Black is rich and pungent; white is milder. Buy whole peppercorns and grind them in a mill. Use in most non-sweet dishes. Try with fruit like cantaloupe and strawberries.

* Herbs and spices that should be in a basic pantry.

BUYING AND USING HERBS AND SPICES

Name	Forms to Buy	Description
Peppercorns, green	Whole spice, packed in brine or vinegar	Soft texture, very pungent flavor. Use crushed in butters and sauces for meat, poultry and fish; use whole in place of black peppercorns in dishes like steak au poivre.
Pickling spice	Mixed seeds and herbs	Use for making pickles, for cooking preserved meats, and to season vegetables, relishes and sauces. See p. 357.
Poppy seed	Whole seeds	Rich, nutty flavor. Use in baked goods, salad dressings and Indian dishes.
Poultry seasoning	Herb mixture	Used to flavor poultry, stuffings and soups. See p. 358 to make.
*Rosemary	Fresh or dried herb	Vigorous, pungent flavor. Use sparingly with chicken, lamb, meat marinades, vegetable soups, broccoli, peas, potatoes. Always crush the needles when you add them.
Saffron	Whole or powdered threads	Threads are better than ground. Wonderful perfumy, bittersweet flavor. Gives food a golden color. Good with poultry, seafood, rice, breads, and South American and Mediterranean dishes.
*Sage	Fresh or dried herb	Determined, assertive flavor. Don't let it take over. Good with veal, sausage, poultry, pork, game, stuffings, lima beans and some corn dishes.
Sesame	Whole seeds	Rich, nutty flavor. Use in vegetables, baked goods, salads, and Middle Eastern, Indian, and Asian cookery.
Savory	Fresh or dried herb	Grassy, slightly peppery flavor. Lovely with vegetables, eggs, fish, poultry and meat.

* Herbs and spices that should be in a basic pantry.

Buying and Using Herbs and Spices

Name	Forms to Buy	Description
*Tarragon	Fresh or dried herb	Anise flavor. Use sparingly with veal, lamb, chicken, mild white fish, crab, shrimp, eggs, soufflés, soups, asparagus, mushrooms, béarnaise sauce and salad dressings.
*Thyme	Fresh or dried herb	Strong spicy flavor. Use sparingly with beef, pork, poultry, mild white fish, vegetable soups, tomato-based soups and sauces, carrots, green beans, mushrooms, salad dressings.
Turmeric	Ground spice	Musky, bittersweet flavor that turns bitter if scorched. Bright yellow color. Use in Indian cookery, chicken, pickles, relishes, salad dressings.
Watercress	Fresh herb	Fresh, peppery taste. Use for garnish or in salads, fruit and vegetable cocktails, soups and egg dishes.

* Herbs and spices that should be in a basic pantry.

❦ What's Good with What ❦

We buy a shelfful of herbs and spices, and then use the same comfortable few over and over. Look through this list of foods and vary your seasonings.

Baking

Breads	Anise, caraway, cardamom, cinnamon, cloves, fennel seed, mace, nutmeg, poppy seed, saffron, sesame seed
Cakes	Allspice, anise, caraway, cardamom, cinnamon, cloves, ginger, mace, nutmeg, poppy seed, saffron
Cookies	Allspice, anise, caraway, cardamom, cinnamon, cloves, coriander, cumin, ginger, nutmeg, poppy seed

What's Good with What

Doughnuts	Mace, nutmeg
French toast, muffins, pancakes, waffles	Cinnamon, nutmeg, poppy seed

Pies

Apple	Cinnamon, cloves, nutmeg,
Other fruit	Allspice, cinnamon, cloves, ginger, nutmeg
Custard	Nutmeg
Pumpkin	Allspice, cinnamon, cloves, ginger, mace, nutmeg

Beverages

Alcoholic	Mint (juleps), nutmeg (eggnog)
Chocolate	Cinnamon, nutmeg
Coffee	Cardamom seed, cinnamon or whole cloves
Milk	Allspice, cinnamon, cloves, mace, nutmeg
Tea	Cinnamon sticks or whole cloves

Cereals and Grains

Cream of wheat, oatmeal	Cinnamon
Rice, wheat berries	Chives, cinnamon, curry, saffron, tarragon, thyme, turmeric

Desserts

Custards	Cardamom, cinnamon, cloves, nutmeg

Puddings:
  Bread, rice
  Chocolate
  Indian
  Plum
	
	Allspice, cardamom, cinnamon, cloves, ginger, nutmeg
	Cinnamon
	Cinnamon, nutmeg, ginger
	Allspice, cinnamon, cloves, mace, nutmeg

What's Good with What

Eggs

Scrambled, shirred or creamed; omelets	Basil, chervil, chili powder, chives, cumin, curry powder, dill, fennel, fines herbes, marjoram, parsley, oregano, tarragon, thyme, turmeric
Deviled	Chives, cumin, mustard, parsley, turmeric

Fruit

Baked apples, bananas, peaches, pears	Whole or ground allspice, cardamom, cinnamon sticks or ground, cloves, nutmeg
Stewed apples, peaches, pears, prunes, cherries	Allspice, cardamom, cinnamon, ginger, nutmeg
Flamed bananas	Cardamom, cinnamon, nutmeg
Melons	Cracked black pepper, cardamom
Jellies and jams	Cardamom, mint
Preserves	Basil, cinnamon sticks, whole cloves, cracked dried ginger root, whole mace, dry mustard, black pepper, thyme

Meat, Fish and Seafood, Poultry

Beef:	
In general	Allspice, bay leaf, cayenne, cumin, curry powder, marjoram, mustard, nutmeg, black pepper, rosemary, sage, thyme
Boiled and corned	Horseradish
Game	Bay leaf, rosemary, sage, savory, tarragon, thyme
Ham, baked or boiled	Bay leaf, cloves, mustard, black pepper
Lamb	Basil, cumin, curry powder, dill, mint, oregano, rosemary, sage, savory
Liver, calf	Caraway, sage

WHAT'S GOOD WITH WHAT

Pork, fresh	Whole allspice, crumbled bay leaf, caraway, cinnamon, cloves, fennel, ginger, marjoram, mustard, poultry seasoning, rosemary, sage, thyme,
Poultry:	
In general	Basil, bay leaf, chives, cinnamon, cloves, cumin, curry powder, dill, marjoram, nutmeg, paprika, parsley, poultry seasoning, rosemary, saffron, sage, savory, tarragon, thyme, turmeric
Duck	Marjoram, sage
Goose	Ginger, marjoram, sage
Turkey	Marjoram, rosemary, sage, savory
Poultry stuffing	Basil, nutmeg, paprika, parsley, sage, tarragon, thyme
Seafood	Ground or whole allspice, bay leaf, cayenne, chervil, chives, cumin, curry, dill, fennel, marjoram, mint, mustard, nutmeg, oregano, paprika, parsley, saffron, sage, savory, tarragon, thyme, turmeric
Tongue	Whole cloves
Veal	Basil, bay leaf, curry powder, ginger, marjoram, sage, savory, tarragon, thyme

Salads

Beet	Whole mustard seed
Chicken, turkey	Cumin, curry, turmeric
Crab, shrimp	Cumin, turmeric
Potato	Chives, cumin, mustard, turmeric
Tomato	Basil, chives, parsley
Tossed	Basil, celery seed, chervil, chives, coriander, dill, horseradish, mint, mustard, whole mustard seeds, oregano, parsley, black pepper, poppy seeds, rosemary, savory, thyme, turmeric, watercress

What's Good with What

Salad Dressings

In general	Basil, celery seed, chervil, chives, curry, dill, horseradish, mustard, parsley, savory, tarragon, thyme, turmeric

Sauces

In general	Basil, bay leaf, celery seed, chervil, chili powder, chives, horseradish, mace, marjoram, mint, ground mustard, nutmeg, oregano, parsley, rosemary, savory, tarragon, thyme
Béarnaise	Tarragon
Cocktail	Horseradish
Tomato	Basil, bay leaf, oregano, parsley, rosemary, thyme

Soups and Stews

In general	Basil, bay leaf, bouquet garni, cayenne, celery seed, chervil, chili powder, chives, curry powder, dill, fines herbes, marjoram, mint, nutmeg, oregano, parsley, poultry seasoning, rosemary, saffron, savory, tarragon, thyme, watercress
Bean soup	Bay leaf, cloves, dry mustard, peppercorns
Bouillabaisse	Bay leaf, parsley, saffron, thyme
Chowder	Bay leaf, oregano, peppercorns
Cream	Dill, mace, nutmeg, watercress
Gumbo	Filé powder
Split pea soup	Bay leaf, coriander, parsley
Tomato soup	Basil, dill
Stew	Basil, bay leaf, cayenne, chili powder, chives, cinnamon, cumin, curry powder, fennel, ginger, marjoram, nutmeg, oregano, parsley, saffron, thyme

What's Good with What

Vegetables

Beans, green	Basil, marjoram, sage, savory, thyme
Beans, lima	Marjoram
Beans or peas, dried	Parsley, rosemary, thyme
Beets	Anise, basil, caraway, coriander, ginger, mustard seed, parsley
Carrots	Anise, basil, cinnamon, cloves, mint, nutmeg, parsley, savory, tarragon, thyme
Cauliflower	Chervil, chives, curry, nutmeg, parsley
Corn	Allspice, chili powder, sage
Creamed vegetables	Chervil, chives, curry, nutmeg, parsley
Eggplant	Basil, thyme
Peas	Allspice, basil, marjoram, mint, parsley, sage, savory
Potatoes, sweet	Cinnamon, cloves, mace, nutmeg
Potatoes, white	Chives, dill, saffron
Sauerkraut	Caraway, cumin
Spinach	Curry, nutmeg, thyme
Squash Winter	Allspice, cinnamon, cloves, fennel, mace, ginger, nutmeg, mace
Summer	Basil
Tomatoes	Allspice, basil, cayenne, chives, marjoram, oregano, parsley, sage, savory, tarragon, thyme
Pickles and relishes	Whole allspice, bay leaf, cardamom pods, celery seed, cinnamon sticks, whole cloves, coriander, cracked dry ginger root, mustard seed, pickling spice, turmeric

Substituting Herbs and Spices

When you substitute an herb or spice you can use one that *resembles* what you're replacing, or one that *complements the same flavors* and hence will suit the same dishes. The second will give a different taste, but it will still be good. You may find you prefer it. Start with half the amount you think you need, then add and taste until it's right.

For	Substitute
Allspice	Cinnamon + dash nutmeg + dash cloves*
Anise seed	Fennel seed*
Basil	Oregano, thyme
Caraway seed	Anise seed
Cardamom	Ginger
Celery seed	Minced celery tops*
Chervil	Parsley, tarragon
Chili powder	Hot red pepper or dash bottled hot pepper sauce + cumin + oregano*
Chives	Green onion*, onion*
Cilantro	Parsley
Cinnamon	Nutmeg or ¼ the amount of allspice
Cloves	Allspice, cinnamon, nutmeg
Cumin	Mexican chili powder
Fennel seed	Anise seed*, tarragon*
Ginger	Allspice, cinnamon, mace, nutmeg
Italian seasoning	Any combination of basil, oregano, rosemary, and ground red pepper*
Mace	Allspice, cinnamon, ginger, nutmeg*
Marjoram	Basil, oregano*, savory, thyme*
Mint	Basil, marjoram, rosemary

* *Resembles what it replaces (see introductory note)*

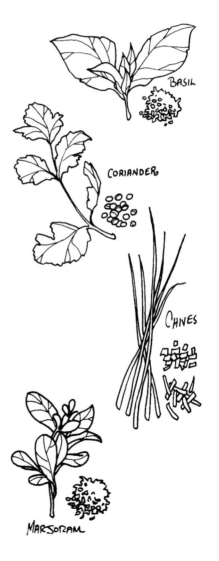

BASIL

CORIANDER

CHIVES

MARJORAM

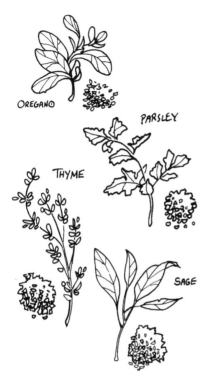

OREGANO

PARSLEY

THYME

SAGE

Nutmeg	Cinnamon, ginger, mace*
Oregano	Basil, marjoram*, savory, thyme*
Parsley	Chervil
Poultry seasoning	Sage plus a mix of any of these: marjoram, black pepper, rosemary, savory, thyme*
Red pepper, ground or flakes	Dash bottled hot pepper sauce*, black pepper
Rosemary	Savory, tarragon, thyme
Saffron	Dash of turmeric (will give the color, not the flavor)
Sage	Marjoram, poultry seasoning*, rosemary, savory, thyme*
Savory	Marjoram, sage, thyme
Tarragon	Chervil, dash fennel seed*, dash anise seed*
Thyme	Basil, marjoram*, oregano*, savory

❦ HERB AND SPICE EQUIVALENTS ❦

Cardamom pods, green	4 medium-size	=	½ t ground
Cinnamon	1-inch stick	=	1 t ground
Cloves	1 t whole	=	¾ t ground
Coriander	1 t seeds	=	1 t ground
Cumin	1 t seeds	=	1¼ t ground
Herbs, in general	1 T fresh	=	1 t dried

Herb and Spice Equivalents

Ginger	1-inch piece	=	1¼ t ground	=	1 tablespoon grated or crystallized, washed
Lemon grass (oriental herb)	1 T of the soft part, finely chopped	=	2 stalks	=	½ t finely shredded lemon peel
Mustard	1 t seeds	=	1½ t dry	=	1½ T prepared
Pepper, hot dried	2-inch long whole	=	1 t crushed red pepper	=	½ t cayenne pepper
Peppercorns	1 t whole	=	1 t ground		
Rosemary	Minced leaves from a 4-inch stem	=	¼ t dried		
Sage	10 thin fresh leaves	=	¾ t dried		
Thyme	1 sprig	=	1 t dried		

Beyond Herbs and Spices

Anchovies

I confess that I am not fond of anchovies, but I use them a lot for seasoning. A smidgen of anchovy paste or mashed anchovy fillet deepens and punches up flavors and performs a subtle magic: a dull little dish suddenly sings. An ⅛ teaspoon of paste or ⅛ of a fillet per cup of sauce will usually do it; any more lets the anchovy taste peek through and gives the game away.

Use anchovies to flavor robust tomato sauces, sauces for fish, salad dressings, roast lamb, grilled chicken. I mash a little anchovy with chopped parsley, garlic, lemon peel and sometimes capers. This is pure heaven sprinkled just before serving on lamb, Osso Bucco, or

RESCUE

Oops! I Oversalted!

Too salty? You can dilute the saltiness of soups or very liquid dishes by adding more of a saltless ingredient like water, pasta, or vegetables. When you can't dilute or add extra ingredients to a liquid dish, toss in a peeled, quartered raw potato and simmer 10 to 15 minutes. Then discard the potato along with the salt it absorbed.

An oversalty dish with a thick sauce can be remedied by adding more of an unsalted liquid ingredient from the recipe (tomato purée, water, milk, etc.) and more thickening, if necessary. A little cream (if it suits the dish) will often blunt the salty taste. Or stir in a little brown sugar and/or vinegar. Add by sprinkles and drops, tasting as you go, up to about a teaspoonful of either.

chicken cooked on the grill or in tomato sauce.

When you use whole anchovy fillets in salads, hors d'oeuvres, etc., soak them in cold water or milk for 30 to 60 minutes before using to remove some of the salt; when you use them to flavor a sauce, soak for up to 15.

Lemon Juice and Zest

Use it for more than the obvious pies, soufflés, cakes, ice cream and tea. Lemon brings out flavors, sharpens dim or blurred tastes. A slice of it in ice water is refreshing. My Greek friends squeeze it over cooked vegetables. Whisk 1 part lemon juice with 3 or 4 parts oil, salt and pepper until creamy and serve over grilled fish. Heaven. Squeeze a lemon over fresh and stewed fruit, squeeze one into and over a garlic-rubbed chicken before roasting, over sizzling shish kebabs. Add lemon zest to meat dishes—goulash, stews, meatballs and loaves, spaghetti sauce and my faithful *gremolata* seasoning (see p. 353).

Orange Peel, Dried

Keep it on hand to add wonderful flavor to Mediterranean dishes cooked in liquid. It's easy to dry it in the microwave: Peel an orange with a vegetable peeler, trying to get as little of the bitter white pith as possible. Scrape off any pith that remains with the edge of a regular teaspoon. Lay peel on wax paper. Microwave on high (100%) for 2 to 3 minutes or until dry. Store tightly covered.

Salt

A good cook salts at the beginning of cooking; too much added at the end gives a raw salt taste. Salt carefully. There's no good way to get it back out if you use too much. (See the box.) Soups and sauces that boil down should be salted lightly because the salt gets stronger as the liquid reduces. Remember that salty ingredients like ham, cheese or anchovies will season the dish. Coarse sea salt can be saltier than table salt. If you use it, taste as you go.

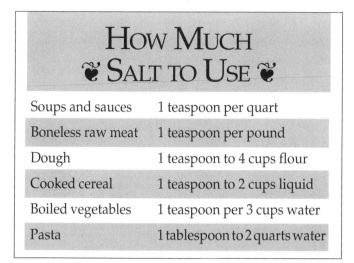

How Much ❦ Salt to Use ❦

Soups and sauces	1 teaspoon per quart
Boneless raw meat	1 teaspoon per pound
Dough	1 teaspoon to 4 cups flour
Cooked cereal	1 teaspoon to 2 cups liquid
Boiled vegetables	1 teaspoon per 3 cups water
Pasta	1 tablespoon to 2 quarts water

Salt is a must for flavoring breads and pastry. A pinch improves all sweet dishes (but never increase it when you double a sweet recipe). Salt draws liquid out of watery vegetables like cucumbers and softens them; it draws bitter juices out of eggplant. Because it draws water to the surface, don't salt meat, especially red meat, until just before cooking or you'll lose juices. If you're browning the meat, wait till after browning.

Sesame Oil

For Oriental cooking, use Chinese and Japanese sesame oil. The seeds for this dark orange-colored oil are toasted first, which gives the distinctive flavor. The pale sesame oils sold in Middle Eastern groceries are made of untoasted seeds and have little flavor. Oriental sesame oil is strictly a flavoring agent. It is used in small quantities—½ teaspoon or so per dish—and always added at the end of cooking. Unless a recipe specifically directs you to, don't use it as a cooking oil. The flavor is intense and because it is made of toasted seeds, it burns easily. The pale, tasteless Middle Eastern sesame oil is excellent for frying.

Fine Tune With Sugar

Sugar lowers the intensity of bitter, salty and sour flavors. For example:

Sugar softens the bitterness of black coffee or a burned sauce. Onions, sautéed apples, or a sweet wine like Madeira complement the slight bitterness of liver.

Sweet sauces and glazes soften and complement the saltiness of baked ham, a sugar cure smooths out the salt in bacon, and a pinch of sugar often saves an oversalted dish.

Sugar cuts and balances the sourness of lemons in lemonade and the acidity of tomatoes in a sauce.

Vinegar
Flavoring and Table Condiment

The fermenting agent in vinegar makes tastebuds sensitive to other flavors. Use a few drops to perk up listless soups, stews, sauces. A tablespoon or two of wine vinegar in cherry or apple pie will give a little sparkle.

Use it to deglaze a sauté pan. The sharpness will cook out leaving a piquant, slightly sweet, flavor.

Use it as a table condiment on fish and chips (The British prefer malt vinegar), french fries, Southern cooked greens. Fresh strawberries are heavenly sprinkled with top-quality (very sweet, very expensive!) balsamic vinegar.

Vinegar is the secret flavor in some cakes, candies and pies—old-fashioned Vinegar Pie is a treat.

Vinegar is volatile. The flavor dissipates when exposed to heat and air. To preserve the tang, add it after cooking. For a mellow, fruity sweetness, add it during cooking to let the sharpness cook out.

Soy Sauce
Light soy sauce is saltier, less sweet than dark. Japanese soy sauce is best for cooking because it's less salty.

Vinegar
Vinegar is one of the most common seasonings. It's indispensable in salads and marinades; with sugar it delivers the sweet-sour punch to pickles, preserves, Oriental and Italian sweet-sour dishes and barbecue sauce.

Vinegars vary in flavor and sharpness. Here's a rundown to help you choose the one to suit the dish.

Apple Cider Vinegar: From apple juice. Mild, fruity, slightly sweet. Use in salads, especially cabbage and fruit.

Balsamic Vinegar: From white grape juice. Aged 3 - 12 years. Dark brown, mellow sweet-sour to very sweet. Use small amounts in braises, stews, salad dressings.

Distilled White Vinegar: From grain alcohol. Too coarse for salad, good for pickling.

Herb Flavored Vinegar: From white wine and any herb. Delicate herb flavor. Use tarragon with shellfish, poultry, salads—especially potato; try rosemary in lamb stew.

Malt Vinegar: From beer. Rich, distinctive taste. Use in sauces, pickles, chutney and on fish and chips, french fries.

Raspberry Vinegar: From raspberries soaked in white wine. Subtle fruit flavor. Use with poultry, pork, liver, fish, salads that include fruit.

Rice Vinegar: From rice. Mild, slightly sweet. Use in delicate salads, cold noodle dishes, stir fries, chicken and fish marinades, oriental dipping sauces, sushi, pickles.

Sherry Vinegar: From Spanish sherry. Nutty flavor. Use in dressings for green beans, asparagus, poultry. Lovely to deglaze the pan after sautéing chicken or liver.

Wine Vinegar: From red or white wine. Pungent but not harsh. This is the most versatile of the vinegars. Use red with dark meat in marinades and salads where color doesn't matter; use white with fish, poultry, pork, pickles, salads—especially potato where color is matters.

CHAPTER 9

Changing Recipes

How Do I Double a Cake Recipe, What If My Store Doesn't Carry Jicama, and How Do I Cut Fat and Calories in My Recipes?

Once I quadrupled my sure-fire chicken curry for a big buffet. It cooked up grainy with a horrible, bitter flavor. My guests were waiting. Desperately I began stirring in yogurt. And more yogurt. I added almost as much yogurt as there was sauce before the screaming spices smoothed out. At which point it was delicious. I had learned an important lesson. You can't increase seasoning or fat at the same rate as other ingredients. Before you do much increasing and decreasing, read through the comments below.

INCREASING AND DECREASING

- Recipes you can increase and decrease with few problems are casseroles, sauces, cookies, muffins, most drinks and appetizers, most soups and vegetables.

- In top-of-the-stove cooking, a doubled recipe needs less liquid and a halved one needs more because of differences in evaporation. When you double one of these recipes, don't quite double the liquid; when you cut a recipe in half, add a little *more* than half the liquid.

- Never increase a recipe by more than 3 times. Now and then you can manage to quadruple, but you can't count on it working out.

RULE OF THUMB

> For even cooking, the larger the casserole, the lower the temperature.

- Instead of cutting a cake or bread recipe in half, make the whole thing, bake it in a large pan or two smaller ones (see the next section if you do this) and freeze the half you don't need.

- Don't double cake recipes or soufflés that use more than 6 eggs. Make them twice. Home kitchen equipment can't mix large quantities of delicate ingredients without overworking them. By the time a large amount of egg white has been folded in, it has lost its air.

- To increase a recipe that serves 4 to serve, for example, 22—divide 22 by the 4 of your recipe. Multiply each ingredient in the recipe by the answer you get. (Since 22 divided by 4 equals 5.5, you would multiply each recipe ingredient by 5.5.)

To Increase Seasonings

If everything else is multiplied by:	Multiply seasoning by:
2	1½
3	2
4 *	2½

* You're flirting with danger. Don't try it with a complex recipe.

Things you *never* double or triple when you increase a recipe:

Seasoning	Season to taste, slowly, tasting after each addition. See the box *for guidance only*. (Note how the proportion goes down!)
Sugar	Don't increase the small amount used to enhance flavor (in tomato sauce, for example.)
Salt	Don't increase the pinch or ¼ teaspoon used in sweet recipes. The pinch will still do it.
Fat	When you double a recipe, use only ⅓ more fat or oil. If you use more, the result will be greasy.
Yeast	If you double a recipe, use only 1½ times the yeast.

FIGURING COOKING TIME

When you alter a recipe, the original cooking time no longer applies. Use it only as a guideline, and cook toward the result you want—a browned cake that pulls away from the sides of the pan; a roast that has the right internal temperature; a casserole that is brown and bubbles around the edges.

If the grocery store doesn't have the size meat or poultry your recipe calls for, buy the closest thing. For example, if you need a 4 pound chicken and the meat counter has only 3 or 5 pound chickens, you're all right with either of those. Follow your recipe. Use all the other specified amounts of ingredients, but adjust the pot size and cooking time.

You may find the charts in Chapters 4 and 5 helpful; they provide estimated cooking times for a variety of foods and cooking methods, based on quantity.

❦ INCREASING OR DECREASING RECIPES ❦

Here's a chart that does the math:

Original	Double	Triple	Half	Third	Quarter
1 c	2 c	3 c	½ c	⅓ c	¼ c
¾ c	1½ c	2¼ c	¼ c + 2 T	¼ c	3 T
⅔ c	1⅓ c	2 c	⅓ c	3 T + 1½ t	2 T + 2 t
½ c	1 c	1½ c	¼ c	2 T + 2 t	2 T
⅓ c	⅔ c	1 c	2 T + 2 t	1 T + 2¼ t	1 T + 1 t
¼ c	½ c	¾ c	2 T	1 T + 1 t	1 T
3 T	¼ c + 2 T	½ c + 1 T	1 T + 1½ t	1 T	2¼ t
2 T	¼ c	¼ c + 2 T	1 T	2 t	1½ t
1 T	2 T	3 T	1½ t	1 t	¾ t

For other odd measures that might occur when you cut or expand recipes, see p. 68.

RULE OF THUMB

Timing Oddities

When the recipe says 45 minutes cooking time, *half the recipe* will be done in 30 to 35 minutes, and a *double recipe* will cook in an hour.

Pan Arithmetic

• A 7" pie pan holds half as much as a 9" pan.

• An 8" skillet holds half as many chops as a 10" skillet.

• An 8" ring mold holds half as much as a 9½" mold.

• A 2" muffin well holds half as much as a 3" muffin well.

CHOOSING THE RIGHT PAN SIZE

Choosing the right pan can mean the difference between a good dish and a not so nifty one. When you've doubled a recipe and need a different size pan, you may want to first check the chart on p. 58 to see what size container will hold the new amount. To find a pan for a doubled casserole that was originally cooked in a 1-quart baking dish, look in the left-hand column for 2 quarts. You'll see a number of possibilities, including an 11" x 7" baking pan and a 10" skillet.

The best choice is the container that comes closest to giving the ingredients the same depth as the pan originally called for. Such a pan will have the same *square inches of bottom surface* as the original. There's a chart in on p. 60 that will help you with this. When cutting or doubling a recipe, look up the area of the original pan, and then one that has approximately half or double the square inches. (When doubling or tripling, you may need to use more than one pan.)

Adjusting for New Pan Sizes

If it's not possible to keep the contents of the pan at the original depth, you often have to alter the recipe's baking time, temperature and amount of liquid. This is true of stove-top cooking as well as baking.

When the new pan makes the contents deeper than the original recipe (chicken tarragon cooked in a deep pot instead of a shallow skillet, cake baked as a loaf instead of a layer), there will be less evaporation and it will take longer to cook. So, for casseroles, braised dishes and sauces, increase the cooking time and hold back a little of the recipe's liquid. For baked goods, increase the time a little and lower the temperature slightly.

When the new container makes the contents shallower than in the recipe, (chili cooked in a skillet instead of deep pot, loaf cake in a layer cake pan) heat reaches the center more quickly and there is extra evaporation. For casseroles, braised dishes and sauces: shorten cooking time and add a little more liquid, either in preparation or as it cooks and you see it is drying. For baked goods, shorten baking time slightly and raise the temperature correspondingly.

If you don't know the temperature or timing for a baked recipe, try 350°, which is a good medium temperature. Then check for doneness at what you think would be the shortest possible time and keep checking every 5 minutes until it's done. The baking time for half a recipe of cake, bread or pie will always be more than half—probably two-thirds to three-quarters.

Don't worry about getting a temperature wrong when you're changing a recipe. Most things can bake at a wider range of temperature than you think. If there's a chance that you're guessing on the high side, stay near the oven and watch it closely; you'll be all right.

If you make a drastic change in the depth or surface measure of a cake, say you use a loaf instead of a layer pan, see the chart on p. 205 for the suggested baking temperature and time. A layer takes about ⅓ less baking time than a loaf.

To know when you've reached your goal, check the When Is It Done? sections of Chapter 4 (for meat, fish and poultry) and Chapter 6 (for baked goods).

RULE OF THUMB

How Full Should a Pan Be?

- Cake batter should fill the pan by at least half but never more than ⅔ so the cake has room to rise.
- Casserole and soufflé mixtures should fill a dish up to ¾" to 1" below the top.
- Jelly roll pans can be filled to the top.

The Big Cheesecake

When you double a cheesecake recipe, *always* keep the depth of the cake the same as the original. Since this means the pan will have a bigger surface, and will take longer to heat up and cook in the center, lower the oven temperature by 25° and increase the baking time up to double. Begin checking for doneness after the cake has baked half again the recipe's time.

Or, make your life easy. Divide the batter between two one-recipe pans and bake as directed in the recipe.

❦ JUDGING CAKE PAN SIZE ❦

When you alter a cake recipe, choose the pan according to the amount of egg and flour used. This chart will bail you out with old recipes that don't give pan size.

For	Use
1 to 2 eggs, 1 to 2 cups flour	1 8" x 8" or 2 8" round layer pans
2 eggs, 2½ cups flour	1 9" x 9" x 2", 1 10" x 10" x 2", or 2 9" round layer pans.
4 eggs, 2 to 3 cups flour	1 9" x 13" x 2", 1 10" x 12" x 2", 2 9" round layer pans, 3 8" layer pans or 3 dozen 2½" (medium) cupcake units
6 to 8 egg whites, 2½ to 3½ cups flour	1 10" x 14" x 2½", 2 9" x 3¼" tube pans, or 3 9" round layer pans

COOKING IN LARGER QUANTITIES TAKES MORE TIME

We often forget to allow more preparation time when we cook large quantities. Remember:

The extra slicing, chopping and measuring always take longer than you plan. Your magic machines can still only do only so much in one batch.

Flour in increased quantities takes longer to reach thickening temperature. Stirred custard, pastry cream and thick sauces like soufflé bases also take longer to thicken. Cook them until they reach an internal temperature of 165°.

When you have a large amount of sauce or liquid to reduce, speed evaporation by putting it in a pan that provides a lot of surface.

A full oven cooks more slowly. If you bake 3 or 4 cake layers at a time, or two casseroles, add extra oven time and raise the temperature by 25 degrees.

Delicate ingredients like fragile greens or soft vegetables are easily bruised if mixed in big batches. Divide them into smaller amounts and keep a light hand.

EQUIVALENTS AND SUBSTITUTIONS

A recipe calls for 1 large onion, chopped, and all you have are small ones. How much onion do you need?

What do recipe writers consider a "medium" eggplant or a "large" tomato?

You're hungry for hummus and don't have time to soak and cook chick peas. How much of the canned do you substitute?

How many egg whites substitute for whole eggs in a low-cholesterol soufflé? You're using cornstarch instead of flour; do you use the same amount?

How much chicken must you cook to get 3 or 4 cups of meat? How many potatoes make 2 cups of mashed?

A quickie magazine recipe catches your eye. It calls for biscuit mix, a can of soup, or a package of taco seasoning. What do you substitute to make it from scratch?

Using the chart below you can answer these and a thousand other questions. Look it over to get a notion of what it holds. Then dog-ear or put a paper clip on the page where the chart begins. It will be a daily reference whether you are a beginning or experienced cook, a leisurely or a busy one.

Also see the substitution and equivalent charts for herbs and spices in Chapter 8. And you may want to check the end of this chapter for ideas on how to substitute lighter, more healthful ingredients in your cooking.

Cake Pan Lore

Standard layer pans are 1" to 1½" deep and usually round. Square layer pans are not used for much besides brownies.

Square cake pans are usually 2" deep. An 8" one will hold the same amount of batter as 2 8" x 1½" round layer pans. This, of course, makes a thicker cake, which will have to bake longer.

❦ EQUIVALENTS AND SUBSTITUTIONS ❦

In this chart the symbol ~ means *approximately*. T = Tablespoon, t = teaspoon and c = cup.
All spice and herb equivalents are in the seasoning section on pages 242 and 243.

Item	Is Equal To	You Can Substitute
Almonds:		
In shell, 1 lb	¾ - 1 c shelled	
Shelled, whole		
1 c	5 oz	
3½ c	1 lb	
Ground, lightly packed		¼ t almond extract for 2 T ground, for flavoring only
4 oz	¾ cup	
1 oz	~3½ T	
Anchovy fillet, 1		½ t anchovy paste
Apple pie spice		To make, see p. 346.
Apples:		
Fresh, 1 lb	3 - 4 medium	Dried apples, reconstituted
	3 c sliced	Chayote
	1½ c sauce	Green papaya
Dried, 1 lb	3½ - 4 c raw, sliced	
	~ 10 apples	
	2 - 3 lbs for a 9" pie	
Apricots:		
Fresh, 1 lb	8 - 14	Dried apricots, reconstituted
	~ 2½ c halved, cooked, drained	
Dried, 1 lb	3 c	
	5 - 6 c cooked, drained	
Arrowroot, 1 T		2½ T flour
Asparagus, 1 lb	15 - 22 stalks	
	2 cups cooked, cut in pieces	

EQUIVALENTS AND SUBSTITUTIONS

Item	Is Equal To	You Can Substitute
Avocados: 1 lb	2½ c cubes ~ 1½ c puréed	
California, 1 medium	10 oz (unpeeled)	
Florida, 1 medium	1 lb (unpeeled)	

Bacon:
  1 lb
    Raw
	16 - 24 regular slices
	8 - 12 thick slices	

Diced and cooked	1½ c	
1 slice, cooked	1 T crumbled	
Baking mix, 1 c Also see p. 312.		¾ c flour + 1½ t baking powder + ¼ t salt + 2½ T fat
Baking powder, 1 t		¼ t baking soda with one of the following: • ½ t cream of tartar • at least ½ c sour milk, butter-milk or yogurt • ½ c applesauce, mashed bananas or tart jam • ½ T vinegar or lemon juice plus sweet milk to make ½ c • ¼ - ½ c molasses • 2 ounces chocolate
Baking soda, amount needed to neutralize acid ingredients—and to leaven	See above.	

Bamboo shoots:
  1 whole
  Canned
	¼ - ⅓ c chopped	

8 oz	~ 1 c solids	
15 oz	~ 2 c solids	

Equivalents and Substitutions

Item	Is Equal To	You Can Substitute
Bananas, 1 lb	~ 3 med 2 c sliced 1 - 1½ c mashed	
Barley: Medium size grain, 1 c Quick cooking, 1 c	3½ - 4 c cooked 3 c cooked	
Bean curd, 1 lb	2⅔ c 1" cubes 2 c crumbled 1¾ c beaten with mixer or puréed	
Beans, dried: 1 lb 15 oz can	2 c raw 6 - 7 c cooked 1¾ c drained	
Beets, 1 lb without greens	2 c cooked, diced	
Biscuit mix	See Baking mix.	
Berries, 1 pt box	2 - 3 cups	
Bouillon: Granulated, 1 t 10 oz can, undiluted Also see Stock.	1 bouillon cube	 4 t granulated bouillon + 1¼ c water
Bouquet garni		To make, see pp. 346 - 347.
Brandy or Cognac, in recipes		Scotch or bourbon
Brazil nuts, 1 lb in shell	1½ c nutmeats 8 oz shelled	

EQUIVALENTS AND SUBSTITUTIONS

Item	Is Equal To	You Can Substitute
Bread:		
16 oz loaf	14 - 18 regular slices	
	28 very thin slices	
1 slice	⅓ c dried bread crumbs	
	¾ c toasted cubes	
	½ c fresh bread crumbs	
	1 c fresh cubes	
Breadcrumbs:		
Dried		
8 oz pkg	2¼ c	
1 c	3¼ oz	¾ c fine cracker crumbs
Fresh		
1 c	1½ oz	
British mixed spice		To make, see p. 347.
Broccoli, 1 bunch	1½ - 2 lbs	
Brussels sprouts, 1 lb	1 qt raw	
	3 c cooked	
Buckwheat groats	See Kasha.	
Bulgur (precooked cracked wheat), 1 c dry	2 - 3 c cooked	
Butter or hard margarine:		
1 stick	½ c	
	4 oz	
	8 T	
1 c	16 T	1 c hydrogenated vegetable fat
	2 sticks	14 T lard
		For cooking, not baking:
		2 c diet margarine
		1 c vegetable oil less 2 T
		For margarine in baking see p. 33.

Equivalents and Substitutions

Item	Is Equal To	You Can Substitute
Butter or margarine, whipped, 1 lb	3 c	
Buttermilk, 1 c Also see Milk, sour		1 c sour milk 1 c yogurt 2 T cultured buttermilk powder + 1 c water
Cabbage, 1 medium	2 lbs 8 c coarsely grated 10 c coarsely sliced 5 to 6 c cut, cooked	
Cajun spice		To make, see p. 348.
Cantaloupe, 1 medium	2 lbs 3 c diced	

Carrots:
  1 lb
 	
  1 - 2 med
	12 - 14 thin
	6 - 8 medium
	2¼ c diced, uncooked
	2 c cooked
	1 c shredded
	½ c thinly sliced	

Cashew nuts, 1 lb	3¼ c	
Catsup, or tomato-based chili sauce, ½ c		½ c tomato sauce + 2 T sugar, + 1 T vinegar
Cauliflower, whole	~ 2 lbs 3 c cut, cooked	

Celery:
  1 med bunch
 	
  2 medium ribs
	~ 1¼ lb
	3 c diced, raw
	2 c cooked
	1 c sliced
	¾ c diced	

EQUIVALENTS AND SUBSTITUTIONS

Item	Is Equal To	You Can Substitute
Celery root, 1 medium	~ 1¾ lbs 4 c raw, grated 2 c cooked, mashed	
Cereal flakes, 3 c	1 c crushed	
Cheese		
Blue, 4 oz	1 c crumbled	
Camembert, 8 oz	1 small round	8 oz Brie
Cheddar, 4 oz	1 c shredded ¾ c small cubes	4 oz Edam* or Gouda*
Cottage:		
Creamed, 8 oz	1 cup	1 cup ricotta
Farmer's cheese, 4 oz		8 oz creamed cottage cheese, drained in a sieve
Cream:		
3 oz pkg	6 T	6 oz creamed cottage cheese, drained in sieve
8 oz pkg	1 c	
Feta		Muenster*
Mozzarella		Monterey Jack
Parmesan, grated, 3 oz	1 cup	Kephalotiri (a Greek cheese)*
Ricotta, 7½ oz	1 cup	1 c cottage cheese
Swiss, 4 oz	1 c shredded	Monterey Jack *These substitutes will work in recipes; results will be different, but good.
Cherries, 1 lb	3 c stemmed ~ 2½ c pitted	
Chestnuts, 1½ lb in shell	35 - 40 large 1 lb peeled 2½ c peeled 2 c purée	

EQUIVALENTS AND SUBSTITUTIONS

Item	Is Equal To	You Can Substitute
Chicken:		
Breast, whole, 10 oz	2 breast halves ¾ - 1 c cubed	
Broiler-fryer, 2 ½ - 3½ lb	2½ - 3 c diced, cooked meat	
Chile oil, hot Chinese, ¼ t		¼ t salad oil + ⅛ t cayenne pepper
Chinese Five Spice Powder,		To make, see p. 349.
Chocolate:		
Cooking, (Unsweetened), 1 oz	1 square 3 T grated	2 oz bittersweet less 1 T of the recipe's sugar 3 T cocoa + 1 T butter or 3 T carob powder + 1 T butter + 2 T water
Semisweet, 1 oz		3 T cocoa + 1 T butter + 3 T sugar
German's sweet, 8 oz		4 oz unsweetened + 2 T butter + 2 T sugar 8 oz semi-sweet
Milk, 3 oz		2¾ oz semisweet + 1 oz whole milk powder + 1⅓ T sugar
Chips, 6 oz pkg	1 c	6 oz semi-sweet cooking chocolate, chopped
Mexican, 2 oz cake		For hot chocolate: 1 oz unsweetened chocolate + 1 T sugar + ½ t cinnamon + 1 drop almond flavoring. In cooking, substitute an equal amount of American semi-sweet chocolate plus a tad of cinnamon.
Cinnamon sugar		To make, see p. 349.

EQUIVALENTS AND SUBSTITUTIONS		
Item	**Is Equal To**	**You Can Substitute**
Clams, cherrystone, 3½ qt in shell	36 small ~ 2 c 1½ c chopped 14 oz canned	
Coconut:		
Fresh, 1 medium	~ 5 c fresh grated or chopped ~ 3 - 4 c packaged shredded 1⅓ c packaged flaked, firmly packed	Equal amount sweetened, canned (baking only)
Shredded, 8 oz	2 ½ c	
Canned		Use canned coconut for baking.
3½ oz flaked	1⅓ c	Use fresh for cooking.
4 oz shredded	1⅓ c	
Milk		1 c whipping cream + ½ t each coconut extract and sugar
Coffee:		
Instant, 2 oz	1 c powder	
Ground, 12 oz can	60 - 80 c brewed, using 1 T per cup 5 cups ground	
Beans, 1 T	1 T ground coffee	
Brewed, as ingredient, ½ c strong		1 t instant coffee + ½ c water
Cognac	See Brandy.	
Cookies, crushed:		
Chocolate wafers		
20 2¼ inch	~ 1 c fine crumbs	
2½ oz pkg	scant ⅔ c crumbs	
Gingersnaps, 15	~ 1 c fine crumbs	
Vanilla wafers, 22	~ 1 c fine crumbs	

Equivalents and Substitutions

Item	Is Equal To	You Can Substitute
Corn:		
2 - 2½ lbs, on the ear	2 c kernels	
1 med ear	scant ½ c cream style	
	½ c kernels	
Frozen kernels, 10 oz	2 c	
Corn syrup, 2 c		1 c granulated sugar. Never use to replace more than half the sugar in a recipe.
Cornbread, 8" round or 9" square	4 c crumbs for stuffing	
Cornmeal:		
1 lb	3 - 3½ c cooked	
1 c	4 c cooked	
Cornstarch, 1 T		2 T flour
		4 t quick-cooking tapioca
		1 T potato flour or arrowroot
Couscous, 1 c dry	~ 2½ c cooked	
Crab:		
In shell, 1 lb	~ 1 c meat	
Meat, 7 ½ or 8 oz can	1 c	
Crab boil		To make, see p. 350.
Cracker crumbs (soda crackers):		
1 c coarse	18 - 20 crackers	
1 c fine	25 crackers	1⅓ c dried bread crumbs
Crackers, soda, 3½ lb pkg	33 2" squares	
Cranberries, 12 oz bag	3 c fresh	
	4 c sauce	

Equivalents and Substitutions

Item	Is Equal To	You Can Substitute
Crayfish, 4 - 5 lbs live	1 lb peeled tail meat	
Cream: Half and half, 1 c		Substitute for cooking and baking only: ½ c light cream + ½ c whole milk or ¾ c whole milk + 2 T heavy cream.
Cream: Light, coffee or table, 1 c		Substitute for cooking and baking only: ¾ c whole milk + 3 T melted butter or 1 c undiluted evaporated milk.
Cream: Whipping, 1 c	2 c whipped	For whipped: 4 oz frozen whipped dessert topping or 1 ¼ oz envelope dessert topping mix, prepared, or ⅔ c well chilled evaporated milk, whipped or 1 c nonfat dry milk powder whipped with 1 c ice water. For some cooking and baking, *never* whipping: ¾ c milk + ⅓ c melted butter.

Equivalents and Substitutions

Item	Is Equal To	You Can Substitute
Cream: Sour, 8 oz container	1 cup	For baking: ⅞ c buttermilk or sour milk + 3 T butter. For cooking cold sauces and dips: 1 c yogurt or 1 c buttermilk or 8 oz cream cheese + 3 T milk. Low-cal: see p. 285.
Crème fraîche	See p. 297 to make the real thing.	Equal amounts sour cream and heavy cream
Crenshaw melon, 3 lb	4½ c diced	
Cucumber, 1 medium	8 oz 1½ c chopped	
Currant jelly (in cooking)		Raspberry jelly
Currants: Dried, 10 oz pkg Fresh, 1 qt	~ 2 c 3¾ c	Raisins
Curry powder		To make, see p. 350.
Dates Unpitted, 1 lb Pitted, 5 oz	2½ c 1¾ c pitted 1 cup	
Eggplant: 1 lb 1 small	15 ⅓" slices 4 ½ c raw, diced 3 c raw, chopped 1 ¾ c cooked, diced ½ - ¾ lb 4 c 1" cubes	

EQUIVALENTS AND SUBSTITUTIONS

Item	Is Equal To	You Can Substitute
1 medium	11 ½" slices 4½ c raw, diced 1¾ c cooked, diced	
Eggs: 　Whole	See p.111 for egg sizes	
5 large	1 c	
1 large	4 T	For thickening: 2 yolks For custard: 2 yolks For leavening in batter: ½ t 　baking powder For cookies: 2 yolks + 1 T water For soufflés and custards: 2 egg 　whites
Fractions of 1 large	Beat lightly, then For ½ use 2 T. For ⅓ use 1 T.	
Hard cooked, 1 　Yolk	⅓ c finely chopped	
1 c	Yolks from 14 large	
1 large	1½ T	
White		
1 c	Whites from 7 large	
1 large	2½ T	
Stiffly beaten	6 times their unwhipped 　volume	
Egg substitute		
Liquid, ¼ c	1 egg, generally. (Check label.)	
Dry, 3 T	1 egg, generally. (Check label.)	
Endive, curly, 　1 medium head	12 oz 10 c loosely packed, torn	

Equivalents and Substitutions

Item	Is Equal To	You Can Substitute
Escarole, 1 medium head	8 oz 7 c loosely packed, torn	
Farina, 1 cup	~ 6½ c cooked	
Figs:		
Dried, 1 lb	2⅔ c chopped 4⅓ c cooked	
Fresh, 1 lb	4 small 2 c chopped	
Filberts (Hazelnuts):		
In shell, 1 lb	1½ c nutmeats	
Shelled		
1 lb	3½ c nutmeats	
1 c	5 oz nutmeats	
Ground, lightly packed		
4 oz	¾ c	
1 oz	~ 3½ T	
Flour:		
All-purpose		
1 T	¼ oz	For thickening: 1½ t cornstarch.
1 c	4 oz	These combinations can be substituted in most baking recipes: ½ c bran + ½ c all-purpose or ¾ c bran + ¼ c all-purpose or 1 c + 2 T cake flour or ⅓ c cornmeal + ⅔ c all-purpose or ½ c cornmeal + ½ c all-purpose or ½ c rice flour + ½ c all-purpose or 1 c rye or rice flour or ⅓ c soy flour + ⅔ c all-purpose or

Equivalents and Substitutions

Item	Is Equal To	You Can Substitute
		½ c whole wheat + ½ c all-purpose or ¾ c whole wheat + ⅓ c all-purpose.
1 lb	3½ c	
Cake, 1 c sifted		1 c sifted all-purpose less 2 tablespoons
Pastry, 1 c		¾ c + 1 T bread or all-purpose flour + 3 T cake flour or 1 c less 1 T all-purpose flour.
		Or add 1 teaspoon of lemon juice or vinegar *or* 2 tablespoons oil for each cup flour (these reduce gluten's elasticity).
Self-rising, 1 c		1 c all-purpose flour less 2 tablespoons + 1½ t baking powder + ⅛ t salt
Fruit:		
Canned, 16 oz drained	1½ c cut-up fresh	1½ c frozen loose-pack, drained
Frozen, 10 oz pkg, drained	1¼ c cut-up fresh	1¼ c frozen loose-pack, drained
Garam masala		To make, see p. 354.
Garlic:		
1 head	10 - 15 cloves	
1 small clove	¼ - ½ t minced	⅛ t garlic powder ¼ t garlic salt (reduce recipe's salt by ⅛ t)
1 medium clove (⅓" x 1")	¾ t minced	¼ t garlic powder ½ t garlic salt (reduce recipe's salt by ¼ t)

EQUIVALENTS AND SUBSTITUTIONS

Item	Is Equal To	You Can Substitute
1 large clove	1 t minced	¼ t garlic powder ½ t garlic salt (reduce recipe's salt by ¼ t)
Gelatin, granulated, 1 envelope	~ 1 T 4 sheets, 4" x 9"	

Glacéed fruits:
  5½ oz jar chopped fruit
  6½ oz jar whole cherries
	1 c
	1⅛ c	

Golden syrup (British recipes)		Equal amount light corn syrup

Graham crackers:
  12 - 15 squares
  1 packet
  1 lb pkg
	1 c fine crumbs
	1¼ c crumbs
	66 squares
		Vanilla wafers

Grapefruit, 1 medium	~ 1⅓ c sections 1 c juice	
Grapes, Thompson seedless or concord, 1 bunch	~ 1 lb 2 c halved	
Green onions (scallions, spring onions), trimmed, 1 bunch	~ 7 medium ½ c sliced ¼ c minced	Chives Mild onions
Green or wax beans, 1 lb	3 c raw 2½ c cooked	
Green pepper, 1 medium large	6 oz 1 c chopped	Red or yellow pepper
Guavas, 1 lb	4 medium 1 c chopped	

Equivalents and Substitutions

Item	Is Equal To	You Can Substitute
Ham, ½ lb, no bone or fat	1 - 1¼ c chopped or ground 1½ c sliced, loosely packed	
Herbes de Provence		To make, see p. 356
Herbs: Loosely packed leaves, 1 c Fresh, chopped, 1 T	½ c chopped ⅓ c minced 1 t dried	**See Substituting Herbs and Spices, p. 242.**
Hominy grits, 1 c	4½ c cooked	
Honey: 1 lb 1 c	1⅓ c	1¼ c sugar + ¼ c water
Honeydew melon, 2 lbs	1 medium 3 c diced	
Horseradish: 1 T grated fresh Bottled, 10 T	2 T bottled 6 T dried powdered	To make, see p. 356
Ice cubes, 3 2½" x 1" x 1"	1 c crushed ice	
Jam, 1 oz	1 T	
Jicama		Water chestnuts Jerusalem artichokes
Kale, 1 lb	1 ½ c cooked	
Kasha (buckwheat groats) 1 c	2½ - 3 c cooked	
Kohlrabi, 1 lb	4 med	
Kumquats, 1 lb	8 - 10 med 2 c sliced	

EQUIVALENTS AND SUBSTITUTIONS

Item	Is Equal To	You Can Substitute
Leeks, 2 medium, trimmed	1 c chopped or sliced	Onions
Lemons: 1 medium	5 oz 2 - 3 T juice 1½ - 2 t grated peel	Lime
1 dozen	~ 2½ c juice	
Juice, 1 t		½ t vinegar
Lentils, 1 c	~ 2½ c cooked	
Lettuce:	See also Measuring Salad Greens, p. 49.	
Butterhead, 1 medium head	12 oz 4 c loosely packed, torn	
Iceberg, 1 medium head	18 oz 10 c loosely packed, torn	
Leaf, 1 medium head	9 oz 8 c loosely packed, torn	
Romaine, 1 medium head	16 oz 8 c loosely packed, torn	
Lichees (Oriental fruit), 1 lb	6 medium ½ c chopped	
Lima beans, fresh: In pod, 1 lb Shelled, 1 lb	 ⅔ c shelled, uncooked 2 cups uncooked	
Lime, 1 medium	2 T juice 1 t shredded peel	Lemon
Lobster: Live 1 medium 4½ - 5 lbs	 1 - 1½ lbs 2 - 3 c cooked meat 5 c cooked meat	Monkfish

EQUIVALENTS AND SUBSTITUTIONS		
Item	**Is Equal To**	**You Can Substitute**
Lobster: Fresh or frozen meat, 8 oz	1 c	
Loquats (Oriental fruit), 1 lb	5 medium 1½ c chopped	
Macadamia nuts, 7 oz jar	~ 1½ c nuts	
Macaroni, elbow, 1 c dry	2 c cooked	
Mangoes, 1 lb	2 average 1½ c chopped	
Margarine, diet, 1 c		For cooking: ½ c butter or hard margarine Don't use for baking.
Margarine, hard	See Butter.	
Margarine, soft, 1 c		For cooking only: 1 c butter or hard margarine.
Marshmallows: 8 oz 1 large	4 c miniature 10 miniature	10 oz marshmallow cream
Matzohs, 6	1 c crumbs or meal	
Meat: Raw, boneless, 1 lb Cooked, 1 lb Ground, 1 lb	2 c packed 2 c cooked, cubed 3 c minced 2 - 2½ c diced or julienned 3 c raw 2¾ c cooked	

Equivalents and Substitutions

Item	Is Equal To	You Can Substitute
Milk: Whole, 1 c		½ c evaporated + ½ c water or ¼ c dry whole + ⅞ c water or 1 c skim + 2½ t butter or 1 c soy or almond milk (For those with allergies. Buy at health food stores.) 1 c coconut milk (in cooking) 1 c fruit juice or potato water (in baking)
Milk: Skim, 1 c		⅓ c instant nonfat dry + ¾ c water
Milk: Sour, 1 c		1 T vinegar or lemon juice plus sweet milk to make 1 c - let stand 5 mins
Milk: Buttermilk, 1 c		1 c sour milk (for cooking) 1 c yogurt
Milk: Evaporated, 5 oz can	⅔ c	
12 oz can	1⅔ c	
Condensed, 14 oz can	1¾ c	Place in blender or processor: 1 c instant nonfat dry milk, ⅔ c granulated sugar, ½ c boiling water, 3 T melted unsalted butter. Process until smooth. Store in fridge.

Equivalents and Substitutions

Item	Is Equal To	You Can Substitute
Milk:		
Instant dry		
1 - 1⅓ c	1 qt reconstituted	
¼ - ⅓ c	1 c reconstituted	
Millet, 1 c raw	3½ c cooked	
Molasses, 12 fluid oz	1½ c 1 c unsulfured = ¾ c sugar	In baking, decrease liquid by ¼ c for each cup of molasses. Eliminate the first 2 teaspoons of baking powder and add ½ t baking soda per cup molasses.
Mushrooms:		
Fresh, 1 lb	12 large 20 - 22 medium 30 - 40 small 6 - 7 c whole 5 c sliced 2 c cooked ½ c duxelles (minced fine and cooked)	
Canned, 8 oz, whole	¾ c mushrooms + 7 T liquid	
Dried, 3 oz	1 lb fresh	
Mussels in shell, 1 ½ lbs	1 qt 25 medium mussels 1 c meat	
Nectarines, 1 lb	3 - 4 medium 2 - 2½ c sliced	
Noodles:		
8 oz	6 c dry 4 c cooked	
1 c dry	1¾ c cooked	

Oriental mung bean
   or rice vermicelli
		Very fine egg noodles (but not
		   for deep-frying)

Oriental egg noodles		Any thin Italian *egg* pasta

EQUIVALENTS AND SUBSTITUTIONS

Item	Is Equal To	You Can Substitute
Oats:		
1 lb raw	5 c raw	
1 c raw	3 oz	
	1¾ c cooked	
Okra, 1 lb fresh	2½ c cooked	
Onions:		
1 lb, sliced	3½ - 4 c	Leeks
1 large	6 - 7 oz	2 T onion powder
	2 c chopped coarse	
	1 c chopped fine	
1 medium	3 - 4 oz	1 T onion powder
	1 c chopped coarse	
	½ c chopped fine	
1 small	2 oz	
	½ c chopped coarse	
	¼ c chopped fine	
¼ c minced		1 T instant minced, reconstituted
Oranges:		
1 medium	8 oz	
	⅓ - ½ c juice	
	¾ c diced flesh	
	2 - 3 T grated peel	
1 dozen	3 - 5 c juice	
Oysters, fresh, 1 pt	2 10-oz cans	Use equal amount scallops.
Pancake syrup		3 parts molasses or corn syrup + 1 part butter
Papaya, 1 med	1 - 1½ c chopped	
Parsnips, 1 lb	4 medium	
	2½ c cooked, diced	

EQUIVALENTS AND SUBSTITUTIONS

Item	Is Equal To	You Can Substitute
Pasta:		
Strands (spaghetti, fettuccine), 4 oz	1" diameter bundle, uncooked 1⅝ c cooked	
Small (elbow macaroni, noodles), 4 oz	1 c uncooked 1¾ c cooked	
Peaches, 1 lb	4 - 6 2½ c sliced 1 c purée	
Peanut butter, 8 oz jar	1 c	
Peanuts:		
Shelled, 2 c	Makes 1 c peanut butter in processor	
In shell, 1 lb	2 c nutmeats	
Pears:		
Fresh, 1 lb	3 medium 2 c chopped	
Dried, 1 lb	3 c 5½ c cooked	
Peas:		
Green, in pod, 1 lb	1 c shelled 5½ oz	
Frozen, 10 oz pkg	1½ c peas	
Dried, split, 1 lb	2¼ c 4 - 5 c cooked	
Pecans:		
In shell, 12 oz	1 c chopped nutmeats	
Shelled, 1 lb	4 c halves 3½ c chopped	
Persimmons, 1 qt	2 c pulp	

EQUIVALENTS AND SUBSTITUTIONS

Item	Is Equal To	You Can Substitute
Phyllo pastry leaves, 1 lb pkg	~ 25 sheets	
Pickling spice		To make, see p. 357.
Pineapple, 1 medium	3 lbs 2½ - 3 c cubed	
Pistachios: In shell, 1 lb Shelled, 1 lb	2 c nutmeats 4 c nutmeats	
Plums, 1 lb	2½ c sliced 2 c cooked	
Pomegranate, 1 med	4 oz ½ c pulpy seeds	
Popcorn kernels, ¼ c	4 - 5 c popped	
Pork fillet	12 - 16 oz	
Potato flour, 1 T		2 T flour
Potatoes: White, 1 lb	3 medium 3½ - 4 c sliced 2¼ c diced 2 c cooked 1¾ c mashed	
Poultry seasoning		To make, see p. 358.
Prunes, 1 lb	2½ c pitted 4 c cooked and drained	
Pumpkin See Squash.		
Pumpkin pie spice		To make, see p. 358.

EQUIVALENTS AND SUBSTITUTIONS

Item	Is Equal To	You Can Substitute
Purées, ½ c	4 oz fresh (or 1 c cooked and drained) berries, juicy fruit or fresh vegetables	
Quatre épices (French seasoning mixture)		To make, see p. 359.
Raisins, seedless, 15 oz pkg	2½ c ~ 5 c cooked	
Rennet, 1 tablet	1 T liquid rennet (Jells 2 c liquid.)	
Rhubarb, 1 lb	4 stalks 3½ c diced 2 c cooked	
Rice: White and brown, long and medium grain		Equal amount bulgur wheat or pearl barley
1 lb	1½ c dry	
1 c	3 c cooked	
5 oz pkg	2 c cooked	
Converted, 1 c	4 c cooked	
Short grain, 1 c	3 c cooked	
Instant, 14 oz pkg	4 c dry 5½ c cooked	
Long grain and wild, 6 oz pkg	1 c dry 4 c cooked	
Wild, 8 oz	1½ c 5 - 6 c cooked	
Rutabaga, 1 lb	2⅔ c cooked, diced 2 c mashed	
Saccharine, ¼ grain		1 t sugar
Salad greens	See p. 49	

Equivalents and Substitutions

Item	Is Equal To	You Can Substitute
Salt, coarse or kosher, 1 T		2 t table salt
Sausage, Italian, 1 lb	~ 8 sausages	
Scallions (green onions), 1 bunch	~ 7 onions ¼ c minced or ½ c sliced	Mild onions Chives
Seasoned salt		To make, see p. 359.
Shallots, 6 medium cloves (1" long)	¼ c minced	Finely chopped scallions

Shrimp:
  In shell, 1 lb
 	
  Shelled, 1 lb
	
	50 small
	25 - 30 medium
	20 jumbo
	8 oz
	2 c cooked	

Snails, 6	1½ oz	

Soup, condensed, 10½ oz can
  Cream of mushroom, chicken, etc.
  Tomato
	1¼ c	
		1¼ c medium white sauce with any seasoning
		1 c tomato sauce + ¼ c water

Soy sauce, ¼ c		3 T Worcestershire Sauce + 1 T water
Spice, whole, 1½ t	1 t ground	

Spinach:
  Fresh
    16 oz
 	
    10 oz pkg
	
	12 c, stems removed
	1½ c cooked
	12 c, stems removed
	½ c cooked, chopped, squeezed dry	

Equivalents and Substitutions

Item	Is Equal To	You Can Substitute
Spinach: Frozen, 10 oz pkg	10 - 12 oz fresh 1¼ c cooked 1 c well drained ½ c chopped and squeezed dry	
Squash: Acorn, 1 medium Butternut 1 medium 1 large Hubbard, 5 lb Pumpkin 3 lb whole 1 lb slice with peel Yellow, 1 lb Zucchini, 1 lb	12 oz 1 lb 2 lbs 5 c cooked, mashed 1 lb cubed meat 2 c cubed meat 1 c cooked, puréed ~ 3 medium 1 c cooked, mashed 3½ c sliced 3 c diced 2 c grated, squeezed dry	
Stock:		To make, including a quick version, see p. 294.
Beef, homemade, 1 c		1 t beef extract + 1 c boiling water *Never* use canned consomme— it's sweet.
Beef or chicken, homemade 1 c		1 bouillon cube + 1 c boiling water 1 heaping teaspoon bouillon granules + 1 c boiling water.
Fish		Bottled clam juice

EQUIVALENTS AND SUBSTITUTIONS

Item	Is Equal To	You Can Substitute
Strawberries, 1 pt	2 c sliced	
Stuffing mix, 8 oz pkg	4 c toasted bread cubes (enough for a 5-lb chicken)	
Suet, 3 - 4 oz	1 c grated	
Sugar:		
Brown, light or dark		
1 lb	2½ c packed	
1 c, packed		1 c granulated + ¼ c molasses (decrease liquid in recipe)
Demerara (British recipes)		Light brown sugar
Granulated		
1 T	~ ½ oz	
1 c	7 oz	¾ c honey (reduce liquid in recipe by ¼ c)
Powdered		
1 lb		
1¾ c	3½ - 4½ c	1 c granulated (in sweetening power) Never substitute for granulated in baking. To replace 1 c powdered, whirl 1 c granulated sugar + ⅛ t corn starch in blender or processor at high speed until fine enough, measure out 1 c.
Superfine (caster in British recipes), 1 lb	2⅓ c	
Turbinado, 1 c		1 c granulated
Sweet potatoes, 1 lb	2 medium ~ 2 c cooked, mashed	
Syrup:		
12 fluid oz	1½ c	
1 T	1 weighed oz	

Equivalents and Substitutions

Item	Is Equal To	You Can Substitute
Taco seasoning		To make, see p. 361.
Tangerines, 1 lb	4 medium 2 c sectioned	
Tapioca: Pearl, soaked, 4 T Quick cooking, thickening power	1½ - 2 T quick cooking For pudding: 3 T per 2 c liquid For 8" - 9" fruit pie: 1½ - 3 T For soup: ½ - 3 T per 4 c liquid	
Tea, 1 lb	125 cups brewed, using 1 t per 6-oz cup water	
Tofu	See Bean curd.	
Tomato juice, 1 c		½ c tomato sauce + ¼ c water
Tomato purée, 1 c	1 lb stewed and puréed 2 c whole, canned puréed	½ c tomato paste + ¾ c water
Tomato sauce, plain		Equal amount tomato purée plus desired seasoning
Tomatoes: Fresh, 1 lb Canned, with juice, 1 c Italian, 35 oz can	4 small 16 slices 1½ c peeled, seeded 1 cup canned with juice 1½ c fresh pulp 1 lb fresh 4 - 5 fresh 1⅓ c drained pulp	
Treacle (British recipes)		Equal amount light molasses
Tuna fish, 6 - 7 ½ oz can, drained	¾ c	

EQUIVALENTS AND SUBSTITUTIONS

Item	Is Equal To	You Can Substitute

Turkey:
  5 - 6 lbs
  12 - 14 lbs
	6 - 7 c cooked meat
	7 - 9 c sliced white meat
	8 + c cubed dark meat	

Turnips, white, 1 lb	3 - 4 medium	
Vanilla bean, 1" piece		1 t vanilla extract
Vanilla extract, ¼ t		1 T vanilla sugar. Reduce sugar in recipe accordingly.
Vanilla sugar		To make, see p. 362.
Vegetable shortening, 1 lb	2⅓ c	

Vegetables:
  1 lb canned, drained
 	
  Frozen, 10 oz pkg
		2 c cut-up fresh, cooked
		2 c frozen loose-pack vegetables, cooked, drained
		1¼ c cut-up fresh
		1¼ c loose pack frozen

Vinegar, 1 t		2 t lemon juice
Vinegar, rice, ½ c		⅓ c white (distilled) vinegar + 3 T water

Walnuts:
  In shell, 1 lb
  Shelled, 1 lb
	2 c nutmeats
	3½ c chopped nutmeats
	3¾ c ground, lightly
	    packed	

Water chestnuts		Jicama Jerusalem artichokes
Watermelon, 1 medium	10 - 12 lbs 20 - 24 c cubed	
Wheat berries, 1 c dry	2⅔ c cooked	

EQUIVALENTS AND SUBSTITUTIONS		
Item	**Is Equal To**	**You Can Substitute**
Whipped topping, frozen:		
4 oz	1¾ c	
8 oz	3½ c	
Whipped topping, mix, 4 oz pkg	~ 2 c whipped	
Wine:		
375 milliliters	1½ cups	
750 milliliters (usual size bottle)	3 cups	
1 liter	4 cups	
1 ½ liters	6 cups	
3 liters	12 cups	
Wine, white, ½ c		Equal measure dry vermouth For marinades: ¼ c vinegar + 1 T sugar + ¼ c water
Yeast:		
Compressed, ⅗ oz cake	1 pkg active dry	
Active dry, 1 pkg	1 T ⅓ of a 2 oz cake compressed yeast	
Yogurt, plain, 1 c		1 c buttermilk for cooking and marinades

Note: Herb and spice equivalents are on page 242.

Quick Hint

Elaine's meat loaf trick: For a lower fat loaf, shape an oval and lay it on a single layer of sliced bread in a shallow baking pan. The bread will soak up the fat and keep the bottom of the loaf from being soggy.

HEALTHY EATING

Nowadays we are all aware of the choices we make when we cook. Looking through some old magazines, I was amazed at the abandon with which we used to stir in butter and cream and eggs. I'm not knocking butter, cream and eggs, or fine, well-marbled beef. They're still part of good cooking—but probably we should use them with a bit of discretion. The chart that follows is designed to help you update rich old favorites or just lighten your diet.

❧ HEALTHY SUBSTITUTIONS ❧

Use this chart to lighten recipes by lowering their cholesterol or their calories.

For:	Substitute:
Bacon	Lean Canadian bacon
Basting fats	Wine Oil-free marinade Stock or fruit juice
Butter	Margarine made with liquid vegetable oil (soft margarine) Half the amount called for in recipe Equal amount unsweetened applesauce (baking only)
Buttered bread crumbs, to top casseroles	Wheat germ
Cheese: Cream	Half the amount called for in recipe Farmer's cheese Low-fat cottage cheese Part-skim ricotta

HEALTHY SUBSTITUTIONS

	For lower cholesterol, whirl 1 cup low-fat cottage cheese with ¼ cup soft margarine in the blender until smooth.
	Or use yogurt cheese: yogurt drained in a cheesecloth-lined sieve for 2 to 24 hrs until it is the consistency of cream cheese.
Creamed cottage cheese (4% fat)	Low-fat cottage cheese (1% fat)
	Pot cheese
	Farmer's cheese
	Yogurt cheese (See Cream Cheese).
Hard, like Cheddar	Low-fat Cheddar or Swiss, muenster, part-skim mozzarella
Melted, as topping	Mixture of equal amounts grated cheese and bread crumbs or crushed corn flakes
	A fine sprinkle of sesame seeds
Soft, high-fat	Camembert, feta, part-skim or regular mozzarella, Neufchatel
Chocolate, 1 ounce unsweetened	3 tablespoons unsweetened cocoa or carob powder + 1 tablespoon unsaturated oil or margarine
	If you use carob (it's sweet), reduce recipe's sugar slightly.
	If the chocolate is merely for flavor, substitute unsweetened cocoa powder.
Coconut milk or cream, 1 cup	1 cup evaporated skim milk or plain non-fat yogurt + 1 tablespoon dried coconut + ¼ teaspoon almond extract
Cream, heavy: For cooking	Whisk 2 teaspoons cornstarch or 1 tablespoon flour into 1 cup milk
For whipping	*Very cold* evaporated skim milk
Not for whipping	Evaporated low-fat milk, whole milk
Whipped	Mix ½ cup non-fat yogurt, ½ cup part skim ricotta and 2 tablespoons honey.
Cream, sour	1 cup low-fat cottage cheese + 1 tablespoon lemon juice + 2 tablespoons skim milk, whirled together in the blender
	Low-fat cottage cheese or part-skim ricotta plus enough yogurt or buttermilk to make the right texture
	1 can chilled evaporated milk whipped with 1 teaspoon lemon juice
	Low-fat yogurt or buttermilk
	Soft tofu

HEALTHY SUBSTITUTIONS

For:	Substitute:
	In baking or salad dressings: buttermilk or low-fat yogurt. In sauces: buttermilk or low-fat yogurt mixed with 1 tablespoon cornstarch per cup yogurt to prevent separating. Yogurt cheese (See Cream cheese.)
Egg, 1 whole	1 egg white + 2 teaspoons unsaturated oil For low cholesterol use 2 egg whites. For 2 whole eggs use 3 whites.
Evaporated milk	Evaporated skim milk
Fat: In baking	Substitute an equal amount of applesauce or puréed prunes. Cut recipe's butter in half and substitute beaten egg whites. (1 egg white = 2 tablespoons.)
For browning meat and sautéing vegetables	Non-stick spray Replace half or all the fat with stock, wine, vinegar, juice, or water, and sauté until liquid evaporates and food browns. Use about 4 times as much liquid as the amount of fat called for. You can sauté ground beef with an ice cube! (The steam created by melting helps keep the meat from sticking.)
Flour, white: 1 cup	1 cup unbleached flour or ¾ c whole wheat flour
2 tablespoons, for thickening	1 tablespoon cornstarch, arrowroot, or potato starch
Ground beef	Ground turkey
Luncheon meats	Turkey and chicken breast
Mayonnaise	Replace half with yogurt.
Meats, Prime or Choice grades	Good or Standard grades
Milk, whole, 1 cup	Low-fat milk (1 to 2%) Skim milk

Healthy Substitutions

For:	Substitute:
	For low cholesterol, combine 1 cup skim milk with 1 tablespoon unsaturated oil.
Nuts, ½ cup	¼ c toasted
Pie crust	Crumb crusts Phyllo pastry (brush melted margarine on *every other* layer).
Poultry, dark meat with skin	Light meat without the skin
Ricotta cheese	Part-skim ricotta cheese
Salad dressings	Absolutely dry greens need only half the dressing of poorly dried ones. Non-fat or low-fat yogurt with lemon juice, mustard, herbs, spices Oil-free dressing
Salt	Chiles, garlic Herbs, spices: basil, coriander, rosemary, nutmeg
Sauces: Thickened with flour and butter	Reduce sauce over high heat. Thicken with cornstarch. Purée some of the vegetables in the recipe in part of the liquid to thicken it.
Enriched with egg yolk and cream	Low-fat milk thickened with cornstarch
Sautéed onions, garlic, etc. as a base for dishes	Sweat these vegetables in very little fat in a covered, nonstick pan over low heat. Or do the same using stock or broth.
Sautéing or stir-frying	Steam or poach. Use a little broth and/or vinegar, or even fruit juice—start with a small spoonful and keep adding as it dries.
Shortening, solid: 1 cup, for baking	For cakes that cream fat and sugar: 1 cup firm margarine. For cakes using melted butter: ⅔ cup poly or monounsaturated vegetable oil.
1 tablespoon, for cooking	2 teaspoons oil

Healthy Substitutions

For:	Substitute:
Sugar, in baking	Except for sponge and angel food cakes, you can reduce sugar in most recipes by 50 to 75%. Use 1 cup honey for every 1¼ cup sugar and decrease liquid by ¼ cup or, if recipe has no liquid, add an extra ¼ cup flour plus a pinch baking soda to neutralize honey's acidity (not necessary if either sour cream or milk are used in the recipe). For every ¾ c sugar, use 1 cup unsulfured molasses and omit baking powder, using instead ½ t baking soda per cup molasses.
Tuna, oil-pack	Water-pack tuna
Turkey, self-basting	Regular turkey
Vegetable oil (type unspecified)	Olive, canola, corn, safflower, soybean, sunflower or peanut oil.
Vegetables cooked in butter	Vegetables steamed with herbs or chicken broth
Wine: Red, for cooking, ½ cup	½ cup red grape juice + 1 tablespoon strong tea + 1 tablespoon rice vinegar.
White, for cooking, ½ cup	½ cup white grape juice + 1 teaspoon rice vinegar.

Formulas for Everyday Cooking

A Tomato Sauce That Doesn't Come in a Can, a Salad Dressing That Doesn't Come in a Bottle and a Very Easy Soufflé

Most everyday dishes are based on short, simple formulas. A soufflé is 2 eggs per cup of thick white sauce plus flavoring ingredients; a quiche is 2 eggs per cup liquid plus fillings. With the recipe patterns in this chapter, you won't need to constantly run for the recipe book. Using these formulas you can cook up sudden inspirations or try to recreate the heavenly dish you had last week at that fancy new restaurant.

There's nothing sacred about any recipe. Someone put things together, liked the result and wrote it down. You can do that too. In your kitchen you are director and star of the production. It's the one place where you call all the shots.

In the past, one of a beginning cook's first lessons in the kitchen was a basic white sauce chart; my older British friends make pastry by the easily remembered 8 ounces of flour to 8 ounces of butter formula. But many of today's cooks were liberated from early kitchen learning and in these more complicated times, find that their heads are filled with more urgent sorts of information. So, in this chapter I give you the formulas cooks used to carry around in their heads, plus a lot more.

Lucky Me

Sometimes when I'm doing something repetitive and soothing like cutting cookies or kneading bread my mind wanders off. I get to thinking about how pleasant it is in my kitchen, how easy cooking is today, and I count my blessings. I'm so glad I don't have to:

Keep the ox turning on its spit in the fireplace...

Scour the pans with sand...

Worry about a mouse falling in the cream that's ripening for butter...

Worry about the kids falling into the cook fire...

Sort stones out of the rice...

Chase the chicken for tonight's supper...

...Or prepare oogruk flippers, which you must cut from the oogruk and place in fresh blubber for 2 weeks, at which time you remove the loose fur, cut the meat in small pieces and serve.

I purposely chose the simplest formulas. As long as you respect their basic structure, you can embroider them to your heart's content, making endless changes and adjustments. You can vary biscuits from no-fat to rich and buttery. You can cut as much as a third of the sugar in most baked foods with no problem.

Cakes are the one area where you have to temper your creative urge, because they depend on a chemical balance. Still, even the most delicate cake can take a change of flavor, or the addition of nuts or raisins. With the help of pan size, time and temperature charts, you can bake up a fat loaf or thin layers.

When you cook by inspiration you don't always get the result you intended, but that's how new dishes are born. When you create a real miss, you get the fun of turning it into a winner: the pudding that doesn't thicken becomes a velvety sauce; the raggedy pot roast gets shredded into its juices and zapped with tomato and herbs for a socko spaghetti sauce.

Unexpected results are food for the soul. They stimulate your juices. They make you feel clever. And that's the fun of cooking.

And when you produce the genuine disaster? If you're a real cook, you will now and then. It's no big deal. You should hear the tales the professionals tell on themselves.

THE BASIC BASICS

I put the recipes for stock, white sauce, mayonnaise and vinaigrette at the beginning of this chapter because they are the building blocks of cooking: culinary chameleons that turn up in slightly changed form in recipe after recipe.

Too many people think homemade stock is only for cooks with loads of time to fool around in the kitchen. And they're the losers. The actual working time needed to make stock is so little and the rewards so great that there's no reason for anyone to be without this culinary basic.

Stock is the base for soups and sauces and is an aromatic moistener for many dishes. By the way, in the past only chefs used the term *stock*. Home cooks called it *broth*. Stock is now the accepted cookbook term, but if you buy it in a can, it will be labeled broth—in a cube it's boullion.

White sauce is another basic. Whether you recognize it or not, you probably make this simple sauce in one of its guises many times a week.

The many forms of vinaigrette and mayonnnaise underlie, or perhaps I should say overlay, the go-withs and the side dishes.

Why not do what professional chefs do and make cooking easy and exciting? With the possible exception of mayonnaise, these basics can be prepared in quantity. With them at the ready in fridge or freezer you're never far away from really good eating.

Health Caution

Bacteria find warm stock a very comfy place to live and multiply, so cool your stock quickly. Set the pot in a stoppered sink (transfer microwaved stock into something metal) and add cold water to come halfway up the side. Refrigerate or freeze as soon as it is cool.

White Sauce Variations:

(All use *medium-thick* sauce.)

Cream: Add 1 part cream to 2 parts sauce.

Curry, Horseradish or Mustard: Add any of these to taste.

Mock Hollandaise: To 1 cup sauce add 2 slightly beaten egg yolks. Cook until 2 bubbles boil to the surface. Remove from heat and beat in 2 tablespoons each of butter and lemon juice.

Mornay (Cheese): Add ¼ cup grated cheese to 1 cup sauce.

Onion: Stir 1 to 2 tablespoons minced sautéed onion into each cup of sauce.

Tomato Cream: Add tomato purée or paste to taste.

Velouté Sauce: Substitute chicken or fish stock for milk. (Optional: Stir in 1 to 2 tablespoons light or heavy cream)

Basic White Sauce

This sauce (the French call it Béchamel) is the workhorse of the sauce repertoire. It is the base of thickened soups, creamed foods, puddings, croquettes, soufflés and a gamut of sauces from simple to spectacular. Below is the formula and at left, a few of the wonderful things you can do with it.

For 1 cup milk:

Consistency	Flour	Butter or Margarine
Thin (for soup-making)	1 T	1 T
Pouring (for accompanying food)	1½ T	1½ T
Medium-thick (for creamed food)	2 T	2 T
Thick, or *panada* (for soufflé base, pie filling)	3 T	3 T
Heavy (for croquettes)	5 T	3 T

Melt the butter. Stir in flour and cook and stir over moderate heat for 2 minutes. In a separate pan bring the liquid to a boil. Add it all at once, stirring steadily. Season with ¼ teaspoon salt and a little pepper. That's it.

Yield: About 1 cup sauce per cup of milk. Figure ¼ cup sauce per serving.

BASIC CHICKEN STOCK

(For beef, too—see variations!)

A stock recipe is basically bones, water and vegetables for flavoring. For a brown stock, which has a richer flavor and darker color, the bones are browned first. To draw out the maximum flavor, cook everything slowly: bring cold water *slowly* to the boil and simmer on the lowest heat so bubbles barely break the surface.

4 pounds chicken backs and wings cut into 2" pieces (use a cleaver)

4 quarts cold water

2 yellow onions, sliced

2 small carrots, sliced (make them large for beef variation)

2 ribs celery with leaves

1 teaspoon dried thyme, or 2 sprigs fresh

2 sprigs parsley

1 bay leaf

4 peppercorns

1 whole clove

Place chicken and water in a large pot. Bring slowly to a boil. Reduce to the lowest simmer (you should see a bubble rising only now and then). After 30 minutes, skim the foam and add the remaining ingredients. Simmer a total of 2 hours. Strain, cool quickly (see box on p. 291) and refrigerate. Lift off congealed fat before using or freezing.

Yield: About 3 quarts.

NOTE: Strip the meat off the bones. It'll be pretty bland, but with a well seasoned mayonnaise, it makes good sandwiches.

Chicken Stock Variations:

Beef or Veal Stock Substitute: I haven't made beef stock since I learned that several respected professional cooks and cooking teachers use this simple substitute: Add ½ teaspoon meat glaze (like Bovril) to each cup chicken stock. Depending on the recipe, for veal dishes I substitute ¼ cup white wine for ¼ cup of the recipe's stock and for beef dishes, ½ cup red wine for ½ cup of the stock.

Beef Stock: Instead of chicken bones, use 4 to 5 lbs beef marrow bones, sawed into 2" lengths. Simmer for 4 hours. (For microwave stock, follow the instructions below for chicken stock using the marrow bones. Timing is still 30 minutes.)

Microwave Chicken Stock: Use half the ingredients. Omit clove and peppercorns, cut thyme to ⅛ teaspoon. Place in an 8-cup microwave-safe container (a glass measuring pitcher is perfect). Cover tightly with plastic wrap, sealing well under the pitcher handle. Cook on high for 30 minutes. Remove from the oven but don't lift plastic until the liquid stops boiling (up to 8 minutes). Then lift it *on the side away from you*, being careful of escaping steam. Strain and continue as above.

Quick Hint

I freeze stock in usable amounts—2-tablespoon (ice cube tray compartments), 1-cup (yogurt cups or paper cups) and pints—then remove the frozen stock from the containers and pack it in plastic bags.

BASIC HURRY-UP STOCK

This is a handy recipe to have up your sleeve.

2 cans (10 ounces) low-salt broth or bouillon

1½ cans water

¼ cups white wine or vermouth

1 stalk celery, chopped

1 carrot, chopped

1 onion, halved

bouquet garni (½ bay leaf, 2 sprigs parsley, 1 celery leaf, pinch thyme)

1 teaspoon Bovril or meat extract (beef stock only)

Combine all ingredients in a heavy saucepan. Bring to a boil, lower heat, simmer uncovered for 30 minutes. Strain.

Yield: About 4 cups.

BASIC VEGETABLE STOCK

For more color don't peel the vegetables.

3 carrots, chopped fine

3 cups celery, chopped fine

3 onions, chopped fine

½ lb. mushrooms, or stems and pieces

3 leeks, sliced

3 quarts water

1 bay leaf

salt, to add at end to taste

Combine everything but salt in a large pot. Bring to a boil, reduce heat and simmer, covered, for 2 hours. Discard vegetables. Add salt to taste.

Yield: about 2 quarts

Basic Court Bouillon for Fish and Seafood

Seafood should always be poached in something flavorful and the traditional liquid is court bouillon. (See pp. 119 and 121 for poaching instructions.) Substitute clam broth when you're in a rush or out of the makings, but the real thing takes a mere 20 minutes and it's lovely. This is the one I learned in Madame Jacob's Brussels kitchen.

4 cups cold water

2 cups dry white wine

white part of 2 leeks, chopped, or 1 medium onion

3 small carrots, peeled and chopped

2 ribs celery, chopped

bouquet garni: a sprig of parsley, half a bay leaf and
⅛ teaspoon thyme

2 to 3 teaspoons salt

1 tablespoon butter

½ teaspoon black peppercorns

Combine everything in a large pan and simmer uncovered for 30 minutes. Cool and strain. You can reuse this stock. After poaching the fish, strain the stock, reboil and add a little water (1 cup or so) to compensate for what evaporated.

Yield: About 6 cups.

Mayonnaise Variations:

(Except for Rémoulade, each starts with one cup)

Aioli: Add 4 cloves garlic mashed with ⅛ teaspoon salt and ½ teaspoon lemon juice. Add 1 or 2 tablespoons olive oil, enough to make a soft consistency. Good with fish soups, fish, poached or boiled eggs, vegetables.

Creamy: Stir in as much as an equal amount of sour cream or unflavored yogurt. For salad dressing, use cream or buttermilk.

Green Goddess: Add 1 small clove garlic, chopped, 2 to 3 chopped anchovy fillets, 3 tablespoons chopped parsley, 6 tablespoons sour cream and lemon juice to taste. Serve on salad or with fish and shellfish.

Herb: Purée 2 tablespoons chopped fresh herbs with an equal part lemon juice. Press out liquid, stir into mayonnaise. Nice with fish, poached or boiled eggs, vegetables.

Horseradish: Add to taste. Serve with ham, beef, corned beef.

Rémoulade: Add to 1½ cups mayonnaise 1 finely chopped hard-cooked egg, 1 tablespoon chopped capers, 1 tablespoon chopped parsley, 1 teaspoon lemon juice. Classic accompaniment to cold poached or boiled eggs, fried fish, cold vegetables, cold meats.

BASIC MAYONNAISE

Given the concern about salmonella in raw eggs, it's best to use the commercial product which has been cooked. However, if you'd like to make your own, I'm giving you a basic recipe, with variations that include some of the favorite mayonnaise-based sauces.

1 large egg
1 teaspoon Dijon mustard
½ teaspoon salt
¼ teaspoon freshly ground white pepper
1½ teaspoons white wine vinegar
1 cup oil, peanut or corn
1 to 2 tablespoons lemon juice

Place everything but the oil and lemon juice in the blender or processor container. Process 5 seconds in the blender; 15 seconds in the processor. With the motor running, add the oil, first in a drizzle, then in a thin, steady stream. When all the oil has been added, stop the motor and taste. Add lemon juice to your taste. If the sauce is too thick, thin with hot water or lemon juice. If too thin, process a little longer.

Yield: 1¼ cups.

MAYONNAISE-MAKING TIPS

Here are a few mayonnaise-making tips:

- If you can't get your mayonnaise to thicken, beat in an equal amount of commercial mayonnaise and chill well.

- In general, use a good quality bland oil, like peanut or corn. To enhance flavor, use part olive oil, but no more than half.

- If the mayonnaise will stand, beat 1 tablespoon boiling water into the finished sauce to stabilize it.

Scandinavian Mustard: Add 2 tablespoons Dijon mustard, 4 teaspoons brown sugar, 2 tablespoons fresh dill. Sweet and luscious with smoked or fresh salmon, ham, cold meats.

Tartar Sauce: Add 1 tablespoon minced pickles, ½ tablespoon minced onion, 2 teaspoons parsley, 1 teaspoon lemon juice. I include a little dried tarragon, but that's up to you. Serve with fish and shellfish.

Thousand Island or Russian: Stir in ¼ cup chili sauce, 2 tablespoons chopped gherkins, 1 chopped shallot or green onion, 1 teaspoon grated horseradish. Serve with boiled eggs, fish, shellfish, cold meats, cold vegetables, green salad or a Reuben sandwich.

CRÈME FRAÎCHE

Here's the delicious velvety cream the French use. Use it in place of heavy or sour cream. It's ideal for cooking, because unlike sour cream, crème fraîche can withstand high heat without separating.

2 tablespoons sour cream or buttermilk

1 cup whipping cream

Mix ingredients in a glass pie plate, cover tightly with plastic wrap and leave at room temperature for 24 to 48 hours or until thickened. To test, tilt the pie plate. The cream should flow only slightly—like thick, half-set gelatin. It will keep for a week or two in the refrigerator.

Warning: If you use yogurt instead of sour cream or buttermilk, as some recipes recommend, your crème fraîche will curdle when heated just as yogurt does.

Vinaigrette Variations:

Cheese: To Basic or Creamy Vinaigrette add crumbled blue or feta cheese, or grated Parmesan.

Creamy: Replace the oil with cream, buttermilk, sour cream or unflavored yogurt.

Herb: Add 2 tablespoons fresh or a teaspoon dried herbs.

Italian: Add garlic and oregano to taste.

Mustard: Add 2 teaspoons Dijon mustard.

Quick Hint

When you hit on the combination of oil and vinegar you like, draw a line on your mixing jar showing the depth of the vinegar and the oil—the two will separate—so you'll know for next time.

BASIC VINAIGRETTE

The classic proportions for vinaigrette are 1 part acid (vinegar, lemon or lime juice) to 3 parts oil. This makes a sharp dressing which is delicious with sturdy greens like romaine but a little brutal on delicately-flavored ones. I prefer one part acid to four parts oil, which makes a more delicate dressing. With a gorgeously flavored oil such as walnut or a delicately perfumed olive oil, you can go to 1 part to 6. If you want an emulsion that holds for a few minutes, whip in a little Dijon mustard.

> *2 tablespoons wine vinegar*
>
> *1 teaspoon salt*
>
> *½ teaspoon black pepper*
>
> *½ cup olive or salad oil*

Beat vinegar, salt and pepper together with a fork in a small bowl. Then beat in the oil. Taste. Add more oil if too sharp, more vinegar if too bland.

Yield: About ⅔ cup.

Other uses for vinaigrette:

* Use to marinate meats, poultry and seafood.
* Brush onto meats and vegetables as they broil or grill.
* Drizzle over sliced vegetables and bake in a 450° oven until tender.
* Brush on cut side of French bread slices and bake like garlic bread, or toast under broiler.
* Toss with finely chopped raw vegetables for party appetizers.
* Pour over a block of cream cheese or over bites of firmer cheese for appetizers.

SAUCES

In this section you will find the vital finishing touches, the ornaments that make or break a dish. Brown sauce with its offspring, Madeira and mushroom; basic tomato sauce with its hundred ethnic faces that create a hundred different dishes; the elegant Hollandaise and her dainty daughters. You can keep many of these sauces in the freezer.

BASIC GRAVY

Although this is a variation of white sauce, it seems to deserve "Basic" status.

3 tablespoons fat

3 tablespoons flour

2 cups heated liquid (drippings topped up with water, broth or milk or light cream)

salt and pepper

For roasts: Remove meat from pan. Pour the drippings (fat and meat juices) into a bowl or large measuring cup. Place the pan over high heat, add a half cup stock or water, bring to a boil and scrape up all the browned bits. Add this to the reserved drippings.

Skim the fat off the drippings and return 3 tablespoons of it to roasting pan or saucepan. Add flour and cook and stir for 2 to 3 minutes, letting the flour brown with the fat. Gradually stir in hot liquid. Cook and stir until smooth and thickened. Season well with salt and pepper.

Yield: 2 cups. Enough for 6 to 8

For fried foods: Pour off all fat but 3 tablespoons, leaving the crisp bits in the pan. Add 2 cups hot liquid and proceed as above. Milk and cream are delicious with ham, chicken, pork and veal.

Pan Juices

These are the rich essence of cooking juices—what you serve with something that is "au jus".

Remove meat but leave any bones and vegetables in the pan. If the juices didn't brown during roasting, cook over medium high heat until they color nicely. Then pour off the fat. If it's poultry or veal, leave just a little fat for flavor. Pour into the pan twice as much liquid (stock or water plus a little wine or Cognac) as you want to end up with. (To serve four, use 4 cups.) Boil over high heat, stirring and scraping up the brown bits. When liquid has reduced to half, strain into a saucepan. Season and continue to boil until the gravy is concentrated and well flavored.

A half cup serves 4.

Variation: For steaks and chops, (for 4) remove meat, pour 2-3 tablespoons brandy into skillet, stir to scrape up brown bits and heat 1 minute. Pour over meat.

Mushroom Sauce

This brown sauce variation is delicious on beef, poultry, veal, eggs, pasta.

1 tablespoon olive oil
3 tablespoons butter
4 ounces mushrooms, chopped fine
¾ cup chopped green onions
⅓ cup dry sherry
1½ cups brown sauce
1½ tablespoons tomato paste
3 tablespoons minced parsley

In a saucepan heat the oil and 1 tablespoon of the butter and sauté the mushrooms and green onions for 3 minutes. Add the sherry. Cook over high heat until the liquid is almost gone. Stir in the brown sauce and the tomato paste. Cook over low heat for 5 minutes. Taste for seasoning. Just before serving, blend in the rest of the butter.

Yield: About 2 cups.

BASIC BROWN SAUCE

A lot of marvelous sauces use this base. Although brown sauces are usually served with dark meats, especially beef, lamb and duck, they're also good with poultry and eggs. A brown sauce or one of its kin should be thick enough to moisten the food, but not to cling to it. This is called Espagnole Sauce in fancy cooking. It has a deep, rich flavor.

3 tablespoons oil

2 tablespoons minced carrot

1 tablespoon minced onion

1 tablespoon minced celery

1½ tablespoons flour

2½ cups canned beef broth or bouillon (not consommé)

1 teaspoon tomato paste

bouquet garni: a sprig of parsley, half a bay leaf, ⅛ teaspoon thyme

salt and pepper

In a saucepan cook the minced vegetables in the oil until transparent and about to brown. Stir in the flour and brown it slowly, stirring. Cool slightly. Stir in 2 cups of the beef broth, the tomato paste, the bouquet garni and a little salt and pepper. Bring to a boil, whisking. Partly cover pan and simmer 35 to 40 minutes. Skim off the froth. Add another ¼ cup of broth. Bring quickly to a boil and skim. Simmer 5 minutes. Add the remaining ¼ cup of broth. Bring to a boil and skim again. Strain, pressing on the vegetables. Clean the pan and return the sauce to the pan. Partly cover and simmer until the sauce is very glossy and the consistency of heavy cream. Check for seasoning.

Yield: About 1½ cups.

QUICK BROWN SAUCE

This is a very good hurry-up sauce. I've often used it to make a quick Madeira Sauce (see box) to dazzle unexpected guests.

½ cup minced shallots or onions

1 bay leaf

2 tablespoons butter

1 tablespoon flour

2 cups canned beef broth (not consommé)

2 teaspoons tomato paste

⅛ teaspoon freshly ground black pepper

⅛ teaspoon thyme

Sauté the minced shallots and bay leaf in the butter for 5 minutes. Stir in the flour and cook and stir over low heat until browned. Slowly add broth, stirring until it boils. Add tomato paste, pepper and thyme. Cook over low heat 20 minutes. Strain.

Yield: About 1½ cups.

Madeira Sauce

This brown sauce variation is superb with beef. Also delicious with veal, chicken or turkey.

2 tablespoons butter
2 shallots
1½ cups brown sauce
2 tablespoons lemon juice
¼ cup Madeira

In a saucepan melt the butter over medium heat and sauté the shallots in it until they are tender, 3 to 5 minutes. Add the brown sauce and lemon juice. When the sauce boils, stir in the Madeira. Bring to boiling again and let simmer for 2 to 3 minutes.

Yield: 1½ cups.

Basic Tomato Sauce Variations:

Creole: Mince and sauté 2 seeded green peppers, 2 ribs celery and 1 carrot with onions. Add 1 teaspoon cayenne pepper. Purée finished sauce. Good with chicken, seafood, eggs.

Italian Marinara: Increase onions to 2 cups, add 1½ cups chopped carrots. After simmering 30 minutes, purée and simmer 10 minutes more.

Mexican: Increase onions to 2, garlic cloves to 4, add 1 hot green chile pepper. Purée together before frying. Omit bay leaf, add ½ teaspoon cumin, 2 teaspoons hot chili powder, 4 teaspoons vinegar. Use on tacos, enchiladas, fried eggs.

Provençale (my favorite): Substitute butter for oil, shallots for onion. Sauté vegetables in 2 tablespoons of butter. Use only 2 cups canned whole tomatoes. Cook until thickened. Swirl remaining butter into finished sauce. Delicious on shellfish, chicken, chops.

Yield: 2 cups

BASIC TOMATO SAUCE

Most of us use some sort of tomato sauce a couple times a week, so we need a quick, easy, versatile one that adapts to all types of recipes. Vary this one to suit your needs. Use more or less oil or onion, or make it with butter. Make a big batch and freeze it in 1-cup portions.

3-4 tablespoons oil

½ cup minced onion

2 cloves garlic, minced

1 bay leaf

1 large can (35 ounces) crushed Italian tomatoes with tomato purée added*

2 tablespoons chopped parsley

fresh or dried herbs, to taste**

salt and pepper

½ teaspoon sugar (optional)

1 tablespoon tomato paste (optional)

Heat oil in a saucepan and sauté onions until softened, about 10 minutes. Add garlic during the last 2 minutes. Break the tomatoes up and add. Simmer uncovered for 20 minutes over very low heat. Add herbs, salt and pepper to taste and the sugar, if it tastes too acid. Simmer uncovered over very low heat until it reaches the thickness you like—30 minutes or so. If the sauce needs perking up, add the tomato paste.

Yield: 4 cups.

***Or any one of the following:** 4 to 5 pounds ripe tomatoes, peeled and coarsely chopped, 4 to 5 cups canned tomatoes with their juice, chopped, 4 to 5 cups tomato purée, or 4 to 5 cups canned tomato sauce.

****Add any herbs you like:** basil, thyme, tarragon, oregano.

Basic Barbecue Sauce

When you make your own barbecue sauce you can adjust it until you've got a house special that makes you famous. Here is a good basic recipe to alter to suit your palate. Bake meatballs, meat and chicken in it, pour it over meatloaf before baking, add a little to baked beans, paint it on grilled foods during the last 10 minutes (no earlier because the sugar in it burns quickly) and, of course, serve it at table as a go-with.

> 2 tablespoons olive oil
>
> ½ cup minced onion
>
> 3 cloves garlic, minced
>
> 2 cups catsup, chili sauce, tomato sauce or tomato purée
>
> ¼ cup brown sugar or molasses (increase to ½ cup if not using catsup or chili sauce)
>
> ¼ cup vinegar
>
> 2 tablespoons Dijon mustard
>
> 1 tablespoon lemon juice
>
> 1 teaspoon crushed red pepper
>
> hot pepper sauce to taste

Heat oil in heavy, medium-size saucepan over medium heat. Add onion and garlic and sauté 8 to 10 minutes or until transparent. Add remaining ingredients. Simmer over low heat for 20 minutes or until thickened

Yield: 2½ cups.

Absolutely Instant Zingy Barbecue Sauce

Mix together equal parts catsup and Worcestershire sauce.

Hollandaise Variations:

Béarnaise: Omit the cayenne and make this essence of tarragon: In a small, heavy-bottomed pan place ¼ teaspoon black pepper, 2 tablespoons white wine vinegar, 3 tablespoons dry white wine, 2 chopped shallots, 3 tablespoons dried tarragon. Bring to a boil and cook until it looks thick and syrupy and less than 1 table-spoon remains. Whisk this into the finished Hollandaise. Delicious on beef, lamb, eggs or fish.

Choron: The gastronome's catsup. Into the warm Hollandaise slowly beat ¼ cup warm, *very thick* tomato sauce. (Cook the tomato sauce way down first if necessary). Yummy on steaks, fish, chicken breasts and eggs.

Maltaise: Whisk 1 teaspoon grated orange peel and 2 to 3 tablespoons orange juice into the finished sauce. The classic version is made with the juice of blood oranges. This is lovely on hot vegetables, especially aspara-gus.

Mousseline: Whip ¼ cup whipping cream and fold it into the warm sauce just before serving. Delicate elegance for fish, chicken, sweetbreads, or hot vegetables.

Also see **Mock Hollandaise**, p. 292, for emergencies and lower cholester-ol—it's delicious, too.

BASIC HOLLANDAISE

This elegant sauce makes a big impression and is dead easy. It glorifies asparagus, broccoli, fish, eggs—remember Benedict? It has superb variations. We can no longer make it with a quick zap in the blender or processor because that doesn't cook the eggs enough to eliminate salmonella risk, but that's no big loss. The traditional method is easy, almost as fast and very satisfying to the soul.

Hollandaise and its sister sauces should be served *warm*, never *hot*. Once they have cooled, never put them on hot food or the temperature difference will make them separate.

½ cup butter

3 egg yolks

3 tablespoons water

up to 1 tablespoon lemon juice

¼ teaspoon salt

pinch cayenne pepper

Melt the butter, reserving 1 tablespoon, over me-dium heat and set aside. Put egg yolks, water, lemon juice, salt and cayenne pepper in a small pan over low heat. Whisk the eggs until they turn pale and are thickened and smooth. Remove the pan from the heat. Whisk in the tablespoon of cold butter to cool the egg yolks and stop the cooking. Then whisk in the melted butter, which should now be about the tem-perature of the yolks, in half-teaspoon driblets until the yolks are thick as heavy cream. Then whisk in the rest in a steady stream.

Yield: 1 cup.

DOUGHS AND BATTERS

From dense bread, pie and cookie doughs to thickish cake and thinnish crepe batters, it's pure magic what you can do with flour and liquid just by adding, or changing the amount of, egg, fat and raising agent. Although it lacks flour, meringue batter is here because it shares with doughs and batters the remarkable ability to start wet and loose and end dry and puffed. These are recipes you can play with and put your own stamp on. You will find more information on doughs and batters in Chapter 6.

BASIC YEAST BREAD

This is the standard loaf I make several times a week. It has a soft, moist crumb and a crisp crust and is easy to vary. Bake it in a bread pan or a free-form loaf. Note: when I'm in a hurry I dump the dry yeast right in with the flour and get on with it.

Mix by hand or with a mixer; knead by hand or with a dough hook. Or opt for speed and no loss of quality by doing the whole thing in a food processor (see p. 307).

The instructions below cover all methods and all recipe variations.

1 package (¼ ounce, 1 tablespoon) dry yeast

1 tablespoon sugar

2 teaspoons salt

5½ to 6 cups flour

2 cups very warm water

1. **Prepare the yeast:** Stir it and the sugar into the water and let stand for 5 to 10 minutes until foamy.

Recipe Idea

Better Breads

How to change the character of your bread:

Add fat for a more tender, better-keeping loaf with a silky crumb.

Add egg for increased flavor, a fine crumb and tender crust.

Vary the liquid: Use *water* for a crisp crust. Use *potato water* for slightly coarse texture and a larger loaf. Use *milk* for a velvety texture, browner crust and longer keeping. Use *juices* like orange or tomato for color and flavor interest. These make a dryer loaf so add them mixed with and extra 2 or 3 tablespoons of melted butter.

Bread Variations:

Cinnamon Bread: When ready to shape the loaf, roll dough 1" thick. Spread with 2 tablespoons soft butter, sprinkle with 1 teaspoon cinnamon mixed with ½ cup sugar. Roll as for jelly roll. Place in bread pan and continue as in the basic recipe.

French Bread: Skip the second rising. Form two long loaves and place on a baking sheet sprinkled with cornmeal. Let stand 5 minutes. Paint with cold water, slash tops. Place in a *cold* oven with a pan of boiling water on the bottom shelf. Turn temperature to 400° and bake for 40 to 45 minutes or until well browned.

Nut Bread: Mix 1 cup coarsely chopped nuts into the last addition of flour.

Poppy Seed Bread: Use with the basic recipe or any variation. Soak 3 tablespoons poppy seeds and the grated rind of 1 lemon in 2 tablespoons hot water. Knead into the dough after the first rising.

Raisin or Currant Bread: Mix ¾ cup raisins or currants into last addition of flour. (Soak currants first for 30 minutes, then drain.)

Whole Wheat Bread: Substitute 2 or 3 cups whole wheat flour for an equal amount of white flour and increase the sugar to ¼ cup. For a moister loaf, substitute milk for water or add 2 tablespoons melted butter to the water.

BASIC YEAST BREAD CONTINUED

2. **Mix in the flour:** With a sturdy spoon or with mixer on low speed, beat in salt and enough flour to make a soft dough (usually a little more than half). Beat hard with the spoon or with mixer on high for 3 to 5 minutes until dough is stretchy. Beat in by hand or machine the rest of the minimum amount of flour until completely incorporated.

3. **Knead by hand...** Scrape dough onto a floured board, using some of the remaining flour. Knead briskly but gently enough to avoid breaking the dough's smooth surface. Add just enough flour as you knead to keep dough from sticking. See p. 182 for hints on kneading by hand. Knead for 8 to 10 minutes, or until dough is no longer sticky and feels satin smooth.

...or dough hook: Switch to the dough hook. Add remaining minimum of flour. Mix on low until flour is incorporated. Beat on high for about 8 minutes or until the dough pulls cleanly from the bowl sides and is no longer sticky. If dough still sticks, add flour, 1 tablespoon at a time, until it pulls free and is no longer sticky.

4. **Set to rise:** Place dough in well-greased bowl and roll it around to grease all sides. Cover, let rise until double (1 to 2 hours). Punch down. Knead for 1 to 2 minutes to get all the air out. Let dough rest 5 minutes and form a loaf. Place in a well-greased bread pan. Let rise until double (40 minutes to 1¼ hours). Slash the top, paint it with cold water for a crisp crust. Bake in a preheated 400° oven for about 40 minutes.
Yield: 2 loaves.

FOOD PROCESSOR METHOD

Prepare yeast in a small container with a pouring lip. Put minimum amount of flour in processor bowl. If variation recipe calls for fat and/or milk, add them to liquid. With motor running, pour yeast mixture rapidly into flour and process for 1 minute. If dough pulls from the sides of the bowl to bunch around the blade and doesn't feel sticky, it's ready. If not, add flour 1 tablespoon at a time, processing just to incorporate, until it is ready. Use a light touch. Overprocessed dough sometimes has trouble rising. Skip steps 2 and 3 and go to step 4.

Pizza Dough:

Make basic bread using only 1 teaspoon salt and no sugar. After first rising, punch down, cut dough in 4 pieces. Flatten on a floured surface. Roll to fit rimmed cookie sheet or pizza pan. Flour pans lighly and lay dough on them. Push up edges to make a slight rim. Brush lightly with oil. Add topping. (Try onions, garlic, coarse salt and rosemary and a drizzle of olive oil.) Bake at 450° for 20 to 25 minutes. Done when bottom and edges are golden and crisp.

Yield: 4

BASIC BAGELS

I agree, bagels aren't really basic; but this chewy bread is so special I'm tucking it in illegally.

1 recipe basic bread dough, made using 2½ table-
spoons sugar

3 quarts water

1½ tablespoons sugar

Punch down risen dough. Form 12 balls and push your thumbs through the center of each to create a ring about 3½ inches across. Let rise 20 minutes, covered, on a floured surface. Bring water to a boil in a wide 4 to 6 quart pan. Add sugar. Slide bagels in four at a time. Cook at a medium boil for 5 minutes, turning 3 or 4 times. Drain on a cloth towel. Place, not touching, on baking sheets. Bake at 400° until well browned, 30 to 35 minutes.

Yield: 12

Bagel Variations:

Sesame, Poppy or Salt: Before baking sprinkle with seeds or coarse salt.

Pumpernickel: Use molasses for sugar. Reduce flour to 1¾ cups and add 2 cups rye flour, 2 cups whole wheat flour. Mix in all rye and 1 cup of each of the other flours. Beat 3 to 5 minutes. Beat in all whole wheat and the reserved white flour as needed.

Whole Wheat: Replace sugar with honey. Reduce flour to 2¾ cups. Add 2 cups whole wheat flour and ½ cup wheat germ. Mix in all but 1½ cups white flour. Beat 3 to 5 minutes. Then beat in as much of the reserved white flour as needed.

Refrigerator Roll Variations:

Doughnuts: Substitute water for milk, increase sugar to ½ cup. Roll ⅓" thick, cut, place on greased cookie sheets to rise (30 to 40 minutes), fry in 1" of oil at 365° until light golden brown (45 seconds to 1 minute per side). Turn only once.

Swedish Raisin Ring: Decrease milk to ¾ cup and flour to 4½ cups. Add 1 more egg, 2 teaspoons vanilla and 1 teaspoon each nutmeg and cinnamon to the cooled milk. Knead for 8-10 minutes and let rise only 15 minutes. Roll out to a 17" x 17" square. Spread with 6 tablespoons soft butter. Sprinkle with 1 cup fine granulated sugar, ⅔ cup nuts, 1 cup raisins. Roll up and form a ring on the cookie sheet. Slash ring at 1" intervals and fan sections out slightly. Cover. Let rise until double (50 minutes). Glaze with an egg beaten with 2 tablespoons milk. Bake at 375° for 30 to 35 minutes. Wonderful!

Sweet Rolls: Decrease milk to ¾ cup. Add 1 egg and use 4 to 4½ cups flour. Eliminate butter. Mix as for rolls. Knead or not, as you like.

BASIC NO-KNEAD REFRIGERATOR ROLLS

I got this recipe in Zambia from a terrific baker. She always had a bowl of dough in her fridge, so a pan of rolls or a batch of doughnuts was never far off.

> 2 packages yeast
> ⅓ cup very warm water
> 2 cups milk
> 5 tablespoons sugar
> ½ cup butter or margarine
> 2 eggs, slightly beaten
> 1 teaspoon salt
> 6 to 7 cups flour

In a large mixing bowl mix yeast with warm water and 1 tablespoon of the sugar. Let stand until foamy. Heat milk with remaining sugar, salt and butter until butter melts. Cool 5 minutes. Stir into yeast mixture. Stir in eggs. With a sturdy spoon or with mixer on low speed, beat in flour 1 cup at a time to make a soft dough.

Place in a large, greased container, cover and let rise until doubled. Stir down and place in the refrigerator for 3 to 4 hours or overnight.

Divide into 24 pieces, shape into balls, place in greased muffin wells and let rise until double (30 minutes). Bake at 400° for 18 to 20 minutes.

Yield: 24 rolls

BASIC SWEET QUICK LOAF

Our grandmothers and aunties called this "tea bread" and always had a loaf on hand to slice thin when guests dropped in. There are so many wonderful quick breads: orange, lemon, nut, cranberry and of course, banana. Look through the variations and put a couple loaves in the freezer.

⅓ cup sugar

⅓ cup butter, margarine or vegetable shortening

1 cup milk

2 eggs

1 teaspoon vanilla extract

2 cups flour

2 teaspoons baking powder

½ teaspoon salt

Cream sugar and shortening. Beat in eggs and vanilla. Add milk alternately with sifted dry ingredients. Don't overmix. Pour into greased and floured 9" x 5" x 3" pan and bake at 350° for 45 to 50 minutes.

Yield: 1 loaf.

NOTE: Suite your taste. You can use up to 1 cup sugar, as little as 2 tablespoons shortening and only 1 egg. Flavor with lemon or orange rind. Fold in ¾ cup nuts or dates.

Quick Loaf Variations:

Apple: Toss 2 cups chopped apples with ¼ cup of the sugar and 1½ teaspoons apple pie spice. Either fold into the mixture or pour half the plain batter into the pan, top with half the apple mixture and then repeat the layering process. Yummy.

Banana: Increase sugar to ⅔ cup, replace milk with mashed banana pulp, decrease flour to 1¾ cups and add ¼ teaspoon soda and ¾ teaspoon lemon rind.

Cranberry: Increase sugar to ½ cup. Mix 1 cup coarsely chopped cranberries with 2 tablespoons sugar and fold in with 1 teaspoon orange extract and 1 teaspoon cinnamon.

Pumpkin: Use 1 cup brown sugar. Reduce milk to ¼ cup and add 1 cup canned pumpkin, ½ teaspoon soda and either 1 teaspoon pumpkin pie spice or a mixture of ½ teaspoon cinnamon, ¼ teaspoon cloves and ¼ teaspoon nutmeg.

Muffin Variations:

Bacon: Add 2 strips crumbled, crisp-fried bacon. Before baking, sprinkle tops generously with equal parts cinnamon and sugar.

Blueberry: Gently fold 1 cup washed and dried blueberries into batter.

Cornmeal: Use 1 cup cornmeal for half the flour. **For cornbread,** bake in a greased 8" square pan at 425° for 25 minutes or until it tests done.

Coffee Cake: Pour batter into a greased 8" or 9" square pan. Top with ½ teaspoon cinnamon, mixed with 5 tablespoons sugar and dots of butter (about 2 tablespoons). Bake at 350° for 30 minutes.

Cottage Pudding: Try a comforting, old-fashioned cottage pudding. Increase sugar to ⅔ cup, increase flour to 2¼ cups and add 1 teaspoon vanilla. Mix as for a cake by creaming butter and sugar, then add dry ingredients alternately with wet. Bake in a greased 8 or 9" pan at 350° for 45 minutes. Serve warm with a sauce.

Steamed puddings: fill 6 greased molds (custard cups are good) ⅔ full, cover tightly with foil and steam for 1 hour (see p. 88). Serve warm with lemon, orange or chocolate sauce.

Cranberry: In a bowl mix 6 tablespoons sugar and 1 teaspoon grated orange rind with 1 cup cut-up cranberries and use in place of the sugar in the recipe. Replace half the milk with orange juice.

BASIC MUFFINS

This is Mrs. Eddy's recipe. She sewed for us when I was a kid and she was also a terrific baker. When Mrs. Eddy brought over a batch of hot muffins we stopped everything and ran for the jam.

2 cups flour

2 to 4 tablespoons sugar

1 tablespoon baking powder

½ teaspoon salt

1 cup milk

1 egg, slightly beaten

2 to 4 tablespoons melted butter or margarine

In a medium bowl mix the flour, sugar, baking powder and salt. In a smaller bowl mix the milk, egg and melted butter. Add the wet ingredients to the dry, giving only enough stirs to wet the flour. Batter should stay lumpy. Fill greased muffin pans ⅔ full and bake at 400° for about 20 minutes.

Yield: 14 medium or 24 small muffins.

NOTE: Use less sugar and melted butter for an old-fashioned, bread-like muffin; use the higher amounts for a tender, cake-like muffin.

Buttermilk Muffins: Use ¾ cup buttermilk, reduce baking powder to 2 teaspoons and add ½ teaspoon soda.

BASIC BISCUITS

You should make biscuits more often. They dress up meals that need a little boost. Toss in a bit of cheese, herbs, ham or bacon. Change the shape. A Canadian friend bakes tea biscuits in muffin cups. They have a wonderful texture.

2 cups flour

3 teaspoons baking powder

½ teaspoon salt

¼ cup vegetable shortening, butter or margarine

⅔ cup milk

In a bowl mix the dry ingredients. Cut in the fat until the mixture resembles coarse crumbs. Add the milk and stir only until the dough clings together. Pat out ½" thick and cut. Bake on an ungreased baking sheet in a 450° oven for 10 to 12 minutes.

Yield: Twelve 2½" biscuits.

Biscuit Variations:

Buttercakes or Griddle Scones: Omit the fat. Substitute ½ teaspoon soda for the baking powder and 1 cup buttermilk or yogurt for the milk. Pat out ½" thick and cut in 3" rounds. Cook on a dry skillet or griddle over medium low heat until browned, about 4 minutes per side. Split while hot, butter and savor.

Cheese Biscuits: Add ½ cup grated sharp cheese to dry ingredients.

Cornmeal Biscuits: Replace half of the flour with cornmeal.

Drop Biscuits: Increase milk to 1 cup and drop on baking sheet by heaping tablespoons.

Dumplings: Add an extra tablespoon of milk to dough. Cook in simmering liquid for 10 minutes *uncovered* and for 10 more *covered*. (Don't peek until done.)

Herb Biscuits: Add ½ teaspoon dried herbs per cup flour.

Orange Biscuits: Add 2 tablespoons grated orange rind and 2 tablespoons sugar. Or dip a sugar cube in orange juice for 3 to 4 seconds and press into the center of each biscuit—good with muffins, too.

Rich Biscuits: Add 1 beaten egg and 1 to 2 tablespoons more fat and decrease milk to ⅓ cup.

Scones: Make **Rich Biscuits** (above), adding 2 to 4 tablespoons sugar and ½ cup raisins or currants.

A Basic Baking Mix

Home economists, who study such things, tell us that using a mix cuts preparation time by three-fourths. Make your own mix and you not only save time and money, you know what's in it. With a little imagination you can use a mix for more than the usual biscuits, pancakes and waffles. See the variations under those basic recipes for ideas.

9 cups flour

⅓ cup baking powder

4 teaspoons salt

2 cups shortening

Sift dry ingredients. Cut in the shortening until the mixture resembles fine crumbs. Store in a tightly covered container in the refrigerator. To use, add milk, egg and oil as shown below.

To Make	Mix	Milk	Eggs	Oil
Biscuits	1 cup	¼ cup		
Pancakes	2 cups	1 cup	2	
Waffles	2 cups	1½ cups	1	2 T

NOTE: To make only 1 cup mix see p. 255.

Basic Pancakes

Eat pancakes for breakfast, of course, but don't be too sophisticated to enjoy them for supper, too.

1 cup flour

1 to 2 tablespoons sugar

2 teaspoons baking powder

½ teaspoon salt

¾ cup milk

2 tablespoons melted butter or margarine or oil

1 egg, slightly beaten

In a mixing bowl combine the flour, sugar, baking powder and salt. Mix the milk, butter and egg in a small bowl. Quickly stir the wet ingredients into the dry ones, mixing with just a few strokes to moisten the flour. There will still be lumps.

Heat griddle or frying pan until a drop of water will bounce and sputter. Grease lightly. Spoon on batter, spreading cakes to the size you want. Don't crowd or they'll be hard to turn. Turn when the rims are full of broken bubbles and before center bubbles break (takes about 2 to 3 minutes). *Turn only once.* The second side won't take as long.

Yield: 12 small pancakes.

Pancake Variations:

Buttermilk: Reduce baking powder to 1 teaspoon and add ¾ teaspoon baking soda. Substitute 1 cup buttermilk for the ¾ cup sweet milk.

Chunky: Add ½ cup nuts or well drained berries or ½ to ¾ cup finely diced apple.

Feather-Lights: Substitute club soda for the milk—a plus for those who don't tolerate or want to use less milk. Soda water also works in muffins.

Whole Wheat: Substitute ½ cup whole wheat flour for ½ cup of the white flour. Increase milk to 1 cup.

German Apple: Fold into batter 1 cup grated tart apples, 1 tablespoon lemon juice, 2 tablespoons sugar. Serve with powdered sugar, cinnamon and a lemon wedge to squeeze over.

Cornmeal: Add 1 cup cornmeal, 1 cup boiling water. Reduce flour and milk to ½ cup each. Put cornmeal, salt and sugar in bowl. Slowly stir in boiling water. Let stand covered for 10 minutes. Add egg, milk and butter. Stir in flour sifted with baking powder.

Waffle Variations:

Chocolate: Increase sugar to ⅓ cup and add 1 ounce melted chocolate before folding in egg whites.

Fruit and Nut: Add ⅓ to ½ cup nuts to batter; scatter a couple tablespoons blueberries over each waffle before baking.

Hurry-Up: Don't separate the eggs.

Savory: Fold ½ cup grated cheese or 1 cup finely diced ham into the batter.

Corn: Add 1 cup drained canned whole-kernel corn. Lovely with ham or fried chicken.

Cornmeal: Replace 1 cup flour with 1 cup cornmeal, reduce fat to ¼ cup, cut sugar to 2 teaspoons. Good topped with chili.

Dessert Waffles: Top with fruit and whipped cream, or ice cream and caramel or chocolate sauce.

Waffle Iron Tricks

Cake batter bakes up crisp and delectable in the waffle iron. Try it when you have some extra batter.

If you bake French toast in the waffle iron you'll have all those wonderful holes to trap butter and syrup.

BASIC WAFFLES

Waffles are made from a glorified, lighter, richer pancake batter that bakes up crisp with little wells to trap butter and syrup. Serve them non-sweet and herby for supper, topped with something creamed.

> 2 cups flour
>
> 2 tablespoons sugar
>
> 1 tablespoon baking powder
>
> 1 teaspoon salt
>
> 2 eggs, separated
>
> 1¾ cups milk
>
> 6 tablespoons melted butter or margarine or oil

Sift dry ingredients into a medium bowl. In a smaller bowl mix egg yolks, milk and melted butter or oil. Add wet ingredients to dry, mixing with a few strokes until smooth. Beat egg whites until softly stiff and fold them in.

Heat the waffle iron as manufacturer directs. You don't need to grease because the batter has enough fat. When the iron is ready—if there's no indicator light, see p. 212—pour batter onto the center of the lower half until it covers about ⅔ of the surface. Close the lid gently. Cook until waffle stops steaming (about 4 minutes). Don't open during baking. Lift cover when waffle is done and loosen with a fork. If the lid balks, cook a little longer. Reheat before baking the next one.

Yield: 8 large waffles.

BASIC CREPES

Fill crepes with creamed chicken, meat, seafood, vegetable or cheese for a main dish, or with custard or whipped cream for dessert.

4 eggs

2 cups milk (use half water for lighter crepes)

2 cups flour

½ teaspoon salt

4 tablespoons melted butter

for dessert crepes add 2 to 4 tablespoons sugar

Mix eggs and milk. Stir in flour, salt, then melted butter. (Use a blender or processor). Let stand 30 minutes. Batter should be the consistency of light cream. Add flour or milk if needed.

Pour about 2 tablespoons of batter into a hot greased 6" or 7" crepe pan or skillet. (Non-stick pans work beautifully.) Tilt the pan quickly to spread the batter. As soon as it covers the pan bottom, pour all that doesn't adhere back in the mixing bowl. Cook over medium heat 30 to 40 *seconds* until the bottom is lightly browned. Turn and quickly brown the second side. Tip the crepe out onto wax paper.

Yield: Eighteen 6-inch crepes.

TO USE: **To roll:** place filling along 1 side, roll. **To heat:** place seam-down in one layer in pan or shallow ovenproof dish. **To fold:** bathe crepe in hot sauce, then fold in half, fold again. Serve with sauce poured over. **To stack:** spread 5 to 11 with filling, top with final crepe. Heat and/or top with sauce if desired. Cut in wedges.

Crepe variations:

Spring Salad Crepe Gateau: Make 8" crepes and layer them with a filling. A lovely cold one is 1 cup ham slivers, 1 cup tomato strips, 4 cups shredded lettuce in mayo tinted strawberry pink with catsup. Frost with more pink mayo, decorate with parsley, black olives. Serves 6.

Delices Savoyardes (Cheese-Ham Crepes): Make a thick Mornay sauce (page 92). Divide sauce among 12 crepes. Top each with a thin slice of prosciutto or Parma ham. Roll. Place in baking dish, drizzle each with 2 teaspoons cream. Sprinkle with ½ cup grated Swiss cheese. Bake at 350° until heated (10 - 15 minutes). Serves 6.

Ulla's Crepes: From a beautiful Swede who gave elegant dinners. Combine 8 oz. cream cheese, ¼ cup butter, ¼ cup sugar, 1½ teaspoons vanilla, 1 teaspoon grated lemon rind and beat until fluffy. Divide among 12 crepes and roll them up. Bake covered at 350° for 10 minutes. *Sauce:* Heat together ⅔ cup apricot juice, ⅓ cup orange juice, 2 tablespoons butter, 1 teaspoon lemon juice, 1½ teaspoons lemon rind, ¼ cup orange liqueur. Pour over hot crepes and serve. Serves 6.

Filling and Rolling a Crepe

1   2

Popover Variations:

Dutch Baby: Double the eggs, melt 3 tablespoons extra butter in a 10" skillet, pour batter into the hot butter and bake at 425° for 20 minutes. Serve for breakfast with lemon wedges and powdered sugar. Or top with any creamed mixture for a main dish.

Yorkshire Pudding: Put ½ teaspoon meat drippings in each of 12 muffin wells and preheat to bubbling before adding batter. Bake 8 minutes at 500°, then reduce heat to 400° and bake 8 to 10 minutes more.

Recipe Idea

Try a Gougere!

Beat ¾ cup grated Gruyere cheese into the cream puff dough. Form small, high mounds and bake at 425° for 15 minutes. Or drop spoonfuls of dough to form a large ring and bake at 425° for 20 minutes or until puffed and browned. Lower heat to 400° and bake another 10 minutes or until crisp. Serve both warm, the small puffs with cocktails, the big one as a lunch or supper dish with a crisp green salad.

BASIC POPOVERS

Popovers are just a crepe batter with less fat, baked in a hot oven until they pop. Eat them hot with jam, filled with creamed chicken or turkey salad, or, for a deadly sundae, with ice cream and chocolate sauce.

2 eggs

1 cup milk

1 tablespoon melted butter or margarine

1 cup flour

¼ teaspoon salt

Combine all ingredients in a blender or processor and whirl until smooth. Or, beat the eggs in a bowl with the milk, then beat in the flour, salt and butter. Preheat greased standard size muffin or custard cups, half fill and bake at 450° for 40 minutes. Puncture each popover with a toothpick when you take it from the oven to let steam escape.

Yield: 12 popovers.

Basic Cream Puffs

Cream puffs have the same ingredients as crepes also, but with more eggs and butter. What a difference it makes when you change the way you combine them!

Cream puff dough is easy and makes an elegant impression. It is the base for a lot of real show-stoppers. Take a look at the variations.

1 cup water

½ cup butter

1 cup flour

¼ teaspoon salt

4 eggs

In a saucepan, heat water and butter until the butter melts and the water boils. Take the pan off the heat, dump in flour and salt and stir hard. Return the pan to medium low heat and stir until the dough leaves the sides of the pan and forms a skin on the pan bottom (a few minutes only). Remove from heat and cool for 5 minutes.

Beat in the eggs one at a time, by hand or in the food processor. If you're beating by hand, the first egg will be hard to incorporate; the rest will go in easily. Hold out on the last egg, adding only as much of it as you need to make a stiff dough. On a greased baking sheet, shape into round puffs, using 2 tablespoons of dough for each. Bake at 400° for 30 to 35 minutes or until golden brown. Then pierce each one on the side with the tip of a knife, turn off the oven, leave the oven door ajar and leave them to dry out for 10 to 20 minutes.

Yield: Twenty-four 3-inch puffs.

Cream Puff Variations:

Cocktail or Dessert Puffs: These are tiny cream puffs. Use 1 tablespoon dough for each and bake at 425° for 20 minutes, then let them rest 10 minutes in a turned-off oven with the door ajar. Fill with warm, savory creamed chicken, or ham or cold salads.

Croquembouche: Fill tiny puffs with ice cream or whipped cream, dip their bottoms in caramel or chocolate sauce, pile them into a pyramid and pour a little more sauce over.

Dauphine Potatoes: Mix equal parts dough and mashed potatoes, drop by teaspoonfuls into 2 inches of hot (375°) frying oil and fry until golden. These will make your dinner party.

Éclairs: Use 2 tablespoons dough each, making them elongated.

Fritters: Use dough as is or add bits of savory things like cheese, ham or seafood. Or add 2 teaspoons sugar and something sweet if you like—Italians use raisins soaked in brandy. Fry by heaped teaspoonfuls in 2 inches of hot (375°) oil. You'll be famous for these.

Gnocchi: For these heavenly, light dumplings use cream puff dough as is or add grated cheese, chopped ham, chopped herbs or chopped cooked spinach or a combination. Drop by teaspoonfuls into simmering water. Poach uncovered for 15 to 20 minutes. Serve hot, topped with melted butter, maybe a dusting of cheese. Wonderful!

Cookie Variations:

Almond Date: Add ¼ teaspoon almond flavoring, ⅓ cup chopped dates and ⅓ cup chopped almonds.

Cereal: Reduce flour by ¼ cup. Add ½ cup any crushed, ready-to-eat cereal, ½ cup chopped dates, ¼ cup chopped walnut meats and ¼ teaspoon cinnamon.

Chocolate Chip: Use all brown sugar, substitute baking soda for baking powder and add ½ cup chocolate chips and ½ cup chopped walnuts.

Christmas Cookies: Substitute brown sugar for white. Add ½ cup golden raisins, ½ cup finely chopped glacéed cherries, ¼ cup sliced blanched almonds, ¼ cup finely chopped candied orange peel mixed with some flour and ½ teaspoon almond flavoring.

Cinnamon Coconut: Substitute ½ teaspoon cinnamon for the vanilla and add ½ cup coconut.

Fudgies: Add ½ cup cocoa.

Hermits: Use brown sugar instead of white. Add ½ teaspoon cinnamon, ¼ teaspoon cloves and ¼ teaspoon nutmeg and fold in ½ cup or more chopped nuts and ¼ cup raisins. Make big fat dunkers.

Marmalade: Add ¼ cup thick orange marmalade.

Oatmeal: Reduce flour to ¾ cup and add ½ cup quick cooking oatmeal, ½ cup raisins and ½ cup nuts.

BASIC COOKIES

Everyone loves the smell of baking cookies. Real estate agents tell us it even sells houses!

This cookie is very user friendly. It's simple, quick to make, bakes up crisp and buttery at 375° or chewy at 350° and welcomes all sorts of improvisations.

> *½ cup butter or margarine*
>
> *¾ cup sugar*
>
> *1 egg*
>
> *1¼ cups flour*
>
> *⅛ teaspoon salt*
>
> *¼ teaspoon baking powder*
>
> *½ teaspoon vanilla*

In a bowl cream the butter and sugar. Add the egg and mix thoroughly. In another bowl mix the flour, salt and baking powder. Add and mix well. Add the vanilla. Drop by teaspoonfuls on a greased baking sheet. For crisp cookies bake in a preheated 375° oven for 10 to 12 minutes or until well browned; for chewy cookies bake at 350° for 8 to 10 minutes or until light golden brown.

Yield: 2 to 3 dozen, depending on size.

Basic Layer Cake

With a basic cake and frosting in your repertoire, the creative horizons are limitless. Since cakes freeze well, keep a few layers on hand to whip out when the sweet tooth calls or when your spirits need jollying.

This is a light, delicate cake, my standby because it's easily made, foolproof *and* delicious. The Fudgy Chocolate variation is a favorite.

½ cup butter or vegetable shortening

1 cup sugar

1 teaspoon any flavoring extract

2 eggs

1¾ cups sifted cake flour (or 1½ cups + 1 tablespoon all-purpose flour)

2 teaspoons baking powder

½ teaspoon salt

½ cup milk

Cream butter and sugar until fluffy. Mix in flavoring, then beat in eggs one at a time. Sift dry ingredients together and add alternately with milk. Beat until smooth. Bake in two 8" or 9" greased layer pans at 350° for 25 to 30 minutes (9" layers will be thin), or one 8" square pan for 45 to 50 minutes.

Yield: 2 layers or 1 square cake.

NOTES: For a fluffier-textured cake, separate the eggs. Add the yolks after you cream the butter and sugar and fold in the stiffly beaten whites after adding the flour.

Check the chart on p. 58 for other pan sizes you can use and the one on p. 205 for the baking temperatures and times appropriate for them.

Cake Variations:

Blitz Torte: Top the uncooked batter in 2 pans with a soft meringue made of 4 egg whites, 1 cup sugar and 1 teaspoon vanilla (See p. 324 for how to make meringue). Sprinkle ⅓ cup chopped nuts over the meringue and bake. To serve, place the bottom layer meringue-side down, the top one meringue-side up and put a cream filling in the middle—and maybe some whipped cream and strawberries on top. You'll like it.

Caramel Cake: Substitute packed brown sugar for white. Good with any of the other variations.

Coconut Cake: Fold in ⅔ cup canned flaked coconut before baking.

Fudgy Chocolate Cake: After adding the eggs, beat in 3 1-ounce squares unsweetened chocolate, melted and increase the milk to 1 cup.

Nut Cake: Add ½ cup finely chopped nuts to the dry ingredients.

Silver Cake: Omit whole eggs and substitute 3 stiffly beaten egg whites. Fold them in at the end.

Spice Cake: Add 1 teaspoon cinnamon, ½ teaspoon allspice and ½ teaspoon nutmeg to the dry ingredients.

Frosting Variations:

Chocolate: Add three 1-ounce squares unsweetened chocolate, melted, or ½ cup cocoa.

Coffee: Dissolve 2 teaspoons instant coffee powder in 1 teaspoon of water and beat in.

Lemon or Orange: Substitute lemon or orange juice for the cream, omit vanilla and add 3 to 4 teaspoons grated orange or lemon rind.

Liqueur or Brandy: Add 2 teaspoons of your choice.

Mocha: Add to the coffee variation two 1-ounce squares unsweetened chocolate, melted.

—— *Recipe* ——

Upside-Down Cake

Prepare basic cake batter, p. 319. Melt ¼ cup butter in an 8" x 8" x 2" pan. Brush a little up the sides. Sprinkle the pan bottom with ½ cup brown sugar and on it arrange 8 canned pineapple rings, drained, or 8 cooked peach or pear halves or 12 apricot halves, cut-side down. Pour cake batter on top and bake as directed in recipe. Let cool 5 minutes, then carefully invert onto a serving platter. Spoon any remaining pan syrup over the top.

BASIC POWDERED SUGAR FROSTING

This makes enough to fill and frost a 2-layer 8" cake or top 24 cupcakes.

⅓ cup softened butter

1 pound confectioners sugar

5 to 6 tablespoons table cream

2 teaspoons vanilla or other flavoring extract

pinch salt

Place the butter in a mixing bowl. Starting with the sugar, beat sugar and cream alternately into the butter. Mix in the flavoring extract and salt. Beat until spreading consistency, adding more sugar or cream to get the right thickness.

Yield: 1½ to 2 cups.

BASIC PIE DOUGH

Of course you can buy ready-made pie crust, but the dough is so quickly done—10 minutes by hand, 10 seconds in the food processor—that it seems a shame not to make your own.

You can bake just about anything in a crust, from Beef Wellington to Grandma's chicken. Keep some crusts in the freezer so you can bake one up, warm and steamy, when the urge strikes.

We once had a cook who kneaded pie crust. Don't!

1¼ cups all-purpose flour

½ teaspoon salt

⅓ to ½ cup butter or shortening

3 to 4 tablespoons ice water

Sift the flour and salt together. Cut in the fat until it is the size of small peas for a flaky crust, or the consistency of cornmeal for a crumbly crust. Toss with a fork, adding only enough water to make the fat crumbles hold together. Chill 30 minutes. Roll. (See pp. 193-196 for hints on rolling and baking empty.)

To make your dough in the processor, have the ice water ready and use very cold fat. Put the flour and salt in the processor bowl. Cut the fat into small cubes and drop it on top. Process 2 to 3 seconds, or until the mixture looks like cornmeal. Leave the motor running and pour half the water down the tube. If the dough does not clump around the blade within a second, add the rest. Immediately turn off the motor. Remove the dough and form into a ball.

Yield: One 8" or 9" crust.

Pie Dough Variations:

Almond: Add ⅔ cup ground almonds to flour and use ½ cup butter. Use 3 tablespoons water to which you have added 1 egg yolk.

Cheese: Add ⅓ cup grated Cheddar or Swiss cheese per cup of flour, or 2 tablespoons grated Parmesan. Good with apple pie or savory pies.

Cream Cheese: Omit salt. Use ½ cup butter plus 4 oz cream cheese. Omit water. Nice for turnovers.

Nut: Toss in ¼ cup finely chopped nuts.

Orange: Use orange juice instead of water and add 1 teaspoon grated rind per cup of flour. Nice for fruit pies, especially apple and pear.

Spice: Add ¼ teaspoon each cinnamon, cloves and allspice and a pinch nutmeg per cup of flour.

Sesame, Caraway or Poppy Seed: Add 1 to 2 tablespoons seeds per cup of flour.

Crumb Crust Variations:

For sweet crumbs, use chocolate or vanilla wafers, ginger snaps or graham crackers. As flavoring, use melted chocolate, cocoa, toasted coconut, grated citrus peel, spices, or ground or chopped nuts.

For non-sweet crumbs, use any type of crackers such as wheat, cheese or plain. As flavoring, use ground or chopped nuts, herbs, spices or seeds (caraway, sesame, poppy).

BASIC CRUMB CRUST

Rich, buttery crumb crusts are for cold pies: use sweet crumbs for dessert pies, non-sweet crumbs for savory fillings like chicken or ham salad or salmon mousse.

1½ cups crumbs (see variations)

¼ cup melted butter

flavoring, as desired (see variations)

Mix crumbs with butter and flavoring. Press into a 9" pie plate. Chill for 30 minutes *or* bake for 10 minutes at 350°.

Yield: One 9" crust.

MULTI-CRUSTS

This recipe with its tenderizer is fool-proof, light and crispy. So fill the freezer.

4 cups all-purpose flour

1¾ cups soft vegetable shortening (no substitutes)

1 tablespoon sugar

2 teaspoons salt

1 tablespoon vinegar

1 egg

½ cup ice water

Work fat into sifted dry ingredients. Beat remaining ingredients lightly with a fork. Stir in until all is moistened. Form four equal-size balls.

Use after chilling or freeze in balls or flattened disks.

Yield: Four 8" or 9" crusts.

Basic Fruit Pie

Nothing tastes better than warm fruit oozing out of a flaky crust, with maybe a dollop of whipped cream or ice cream on top. Be creative with flavorings. Our cook, Louie, sprinkled vanilla over the apples for his pie—no cinnamon, no nutmeg—and put grated orange peel in the crust. Heaven. Madame Jacob put ground almonds in pear and cherry pie fillings. Ummmm. Try cinnamon and nutmeg in berry pies. Use more than one fruit. My friend Betsy mixes apples with blackberries and it's wonderful.

In this recipe you can use blueberries, boysenberries, loganberries, raspberries, cherries, grapes, sliced peaches, apricots, rhubarb or mincemeat. For apple pie, see the variation.

4 cups washed, cut-up fresh fruit or 3 cups canned, drained

¼ to ⅓ cup flour

1 cup sugar

pastry for a 2-crust, 9" pie

1½ tablespoons butter in thin slices (optional)

½ to 1 teaspoon spice (optional)

Mix fruit, flour and sugar. (Use the larger amount of flour for very juicy fruit like berries, sour cherries and rhubarb.) Line a 9" pie pan with pastry and fill with the fruit mixture. Put on the top crust, crimp edges and slash it. Bake at 425° for 35 to 45 minutes or until golden.

Yield: One 9" pie.

Fruit Pie Variations:

Apple: Use 6½ cups peeled, thinly sliced apples. Omit flour. Flavor with ½ teaspoon cinnamon, ¼ teaspoon nutmeg, ¾ teaspoon grated lemon rind and 1½ teaspoons fresh lemon juice—or try Louie's vanilla trick.

Mince: Omit flour, sugar and butter. Use 3¼ cups mincemeat and ½ cup chopped apple laced generously with brandy, rum, or vanilla.

Meringue Variations:

Brown Sugar: Substitute brown sugar for white.

Chocolate: Mix 2 teaspoons cocoa into the sugar before adding.

Coconut: Fold in ⅓ cup sweetened flaked or shredded coconut after beating in sugar.

Coffee: Dissolve 2 teaspoons instant coffee in 1 teaspoon water. Fold in after adding sugar.

Lemon or Orange: Beat in 1 teaspoon grated lemon or orange peel after adding the sugar.

Mont Blanc: On individual baked meringue shells make a nest of canned, sweetened chestnut purée (traditionally, you push it through a ricer making little spaghettis). Fill the nest with whipped cream and top with shaved chocolate. This is pure sin.

Nut: Fold in 3 tablespoons finely chopped nuts after adding sugar.

BASIC MERINGUE

This wonderful airy confection of sugar and egg white comes in two forms: **Hard meringues** that shatter deliciously in your teeth and **soft meringue,** the gold-tinged clouds that deck pies and puddings and dissolve silkily on your tongue.

This recipe makes both kinds. The difference is in the amount of sugar and the baking.

2 egg whites

¼ teaspoon cream of tartar

4 to 8 tablespoons sugar

1 teaspoon flavoring such as vanilla or almond extract (optional)

Beat egg whites until foamy, then beat in cream of tartar. Beat to soft peaks. Now beat in sugar 1 tablespoon at a time until you feel no grittiness when you rub a little between your fingers and meringue stands in stiff peaks. (Use 4 tablespoons sugar for **soft meringue;** use 8 tablespooons for **hard meringue shells**.) Beat in any flavoring.

Spoon **soft meringue** onto hot pie filling, making sure it touches all edges of crust or pan sides. Bake at 350° for 12 to 15 minutes.

Spoon **hard meringue** onto a cookie sheet covered with lightly buttered parchment or foil. Bake individual meringues at 275° for 45 minutes, then at 250° for another 15 minutes or until very light gold and hard to the touch. Bake larger, pie-size meringues at 275° for 1 hour. Cool in the turned-off oven.

Yield: Twelve 3" meringues. Double the recipe for a 9" pie shell.

PAVLOVA

There is another sort of meringue that falls between soft and hard: the Australian Pavlova—crispy outside, soft and chewy inside. This comes from Nona, whose Pavlova was famous.

4 egg whites

¼ teaspoon cream of tartar

¼ teaspoon salt

1 cup castor sugar (fine sugar)

2 teaspoons vinegar

2 teaspoons cornstarch

1 teaspoon vanilla

Beat egg whites stiff with salt and cream of tartar. Gradually beat in sugar. Fold in vinegar, cornstarch and vanilla. Butter an 8" springform pan and fill with mixture, hollowing out the center slightly. Bake for 1¼ to 1½ hours at 275° or until very lightly browned. Cool slightly, unmold onto serving plate and cool completely.

Just before serving top with filling.

Filling: In top of double boiler melt 1 tablespoon butter. Slightly beat 3 egg yolks and add to the butter with an 8-oz can crushed pineapple and 2 small, fresh pomegranates (or 1 8-oz can or 1 cup chopped mangoes or peaches). Cook and stir until it starts to thicken. Add a little cornstarch dissolved in cold water and cook until thickened. Cool.

Whip 1 cup whipping cream softly. Spread on the meringue. Top with 1 cup fresh strawberries and some kiwi fruit slices.

Or skip the cooked filling and: On the whipped cream place 3 cups mixed sweetened sliced tropical fruits—banana, mango, papaya, peach, pineapple, pomegranate; or all strawberries.

Make Meringue Ahead

You can make hard meringues 1 or 2 weeks ahead. When cool seal in a plastic bag and keep at room temperature or freeze.

Recipe Idea

Belgian Ways with Hard Meringues

Top with sweetened whipped cream and drizzle with chocolate sauce.

Top with coffee-flavored sweetened whipped cream (mix instant with a little water). Decorate with candied *marrons* (chestnuts) and slivered almonds.

Sandwich (flat sides facing) with whipped cream and a little crushed pineapple or strawberries. Cover with more cream and press on lots of shaved chocolate.

Main Course Soup Variations:

Barley: Use 2 cups each carrots, onions and celery and a pound of lamb cut in chunks. Brown everything in a tablespoon of oil and add 8 cups of water. Bring to a boil and add ½ cup pearl barley and a bouquet garni of parsley, thyme and a bay leaf. Cook until the barley is tender—1 to 1½ hours.

Minestrone: Use any combination of onion, carrot, celery, potatoes, green beans, cabbage, canned tomatoes and cooked kidney beans—about 10 cups total for 6 cups of stock. Sauté all the vegetables except raw cabbage in ¼ cup olive oil, starting with the onions and adding each one separately. Add two cloves of garlic, minced, to the sautéed vegetables and season the soup with oregano and thyme. Cook for 2 to 3 hours, adding the cabbage and ¾ cup small pasta 30 minutes before the end of the cooking time. If soup is too thick, add more stock. Serve with Parmesan cheese.

Vegetable Beef (or Lamb) Soup: Brown 1 pound of cubed or ground beef or lamb with some chopped onions and follow the basic recipe, using vegetables of your choice.

DINNER DISHES

Dinner here means everything that isn't dessert. The food you sit down to eat—or certainly ought to. If you bother to cook something, it deserves the honor of seated diners and a cheerfully appointed table. Here are the basic recipes for soup and soufflé, meat loaf and mashed potato, stew and stir-fry.

BASIC MAIN COURSE SOUP

Depending on how much you put in it, this soup can be light and elegant or robust and hearty.

> *2 cups stock (homemade, or canned broth)*
> *2 to 4 cups uncooked meat, chicken, or vegetables*
> *⅓ teaspoon dried herbs or 1 teaspoon fresh*
> *salt and pepper*
> *2 tablespoons cream or 1 tablespoon butter*

Cut the meat, chicken or vegetables into bite-size pieces. Add the solids directly to the broth or sauté first in a little oil. Add long-cooking vegetables and dried herbs at the beginning of the cooking time, short-cooking veggies and fresh herbs later. Simmer over low heat until everything is tender—anywhere from 30 minutes to 1 hour. Taste for seasoning.

Smooth the flavor and texture as necessary by adding 1 tablespoon cream or 1½ teaspoons butter for each cup of soup. Always add a little more herbs or seasoning just before serving.

For thick soup remove part of the solids from the finished soup, purée them in blender or processor and stir the purée back into the pot. Or stir a paste of equal parts flour and butter or cornstarch and cold water into the simmering soup.

For cream soup add milk or cream to taste.
Yield: About 4 cups.

BASIC PURÉED VEGETABLE SOUP

A beautiful, elegant soup, delicious hot or cold. I serve it often as a first course. It freezes perfectly.

½ cup minced onions

3 tablespons butter

3 tablespoons flour

4 to 5 cups diced vegetable (cauliflower, sunchokes, cucumber, broccoli, cabbage, carrots, zucchini, or turnips)

6 cups chicken stock

2 teaspoons white wine vinegar

2½ teaspoons fresh herbs or ¾ teaspoon dried

½ cup heavy or sour cream or crème fraîche

Cook onions in the butter until transparent. Stir in flour, cook 2 minutes. Then add chosen vegetable, stock, vinegar, herbs. Simmer partially covered for 20 to 25 minutes. Purée in the blender (see p. 375) and return to the pan. Taste for salt and pepper. If serving cold, chill in refrigerator. If hot, reheat but don't let boil. Stir in cream, heat (don't boil) and serve hot or cold.

Yield: 6 first course servings.

NOTE: When I want to make the soup a little more quick and easy, I often omit the flour and stir ¼ cup of farina or cornmeal into the broth when it comes to the boil.

Puréed Vegetable Soup Variations:

Curried Carrot: Use 4 cups carrots. Replace ½ cup of the liquid with orange juice and substitute 3 to 4 teaspoons curry and ½ teaspoon cinnamon for the herbs.

Spinach: Use shredded spinach, lightly packing the measure. Stir it into the sautéed onions before adding the flour and continue to sauté for about 5 minutes, until tender and wilted. Cook 5 minutes. Then add liquid. Omit herbs, season with nutmeg.

Soufflé Variations:

(Add all suggested ingredients before folding in the egg whites)

Crab: Add 2 tablespoons tomato paste, ½ teaspoon dried or 1½ teaspoons fresh tarragon, ¾ cup crabmeat and ¾ cup grated Swiss cheese, if that sounds good.

Feta: One of my favorite soufflés uses feta cheese and 8 egg whites instead of 4 whole eggs. Try it. (See box for egg white quantities)

Ham: Add 1½ teaspoons Dijon mustard, ½ cup minced ham and ¼ cup grated Jack cheese.

Mushroom: Sauté 1 cup minced mushrooms and 1 minced clove garlic in 1 tablespoon butter until almost dry. Add along with ¼ teaspoon dried or 1½ teaspoon fresh tarragon and ¾ cup grated cheese.

Nellie's Soufflé: Nellie Shanga, our Zulu cook in Lesotho, once stirred the eggs into the soufflé base whisked and *unseparated*. The result was dense and pudding-like and we loved it. It was a cheese soufflé and she topped it with a shrimp sauce. That was eating.

Rolled Soufflé: Make 1½ times the basic recipe (cheese or spinach is good). Line a jelly roll pan with wax paper, letting it overhang 2" at the short ends. Grease and flour the wax paper and pour in the soufflé. Bake for 12 to 15 minutes at 425°. When it comes from the oven, turn it out onto a piece of wax paper that has been sprinkled with ¾ cup bread crumbs. Spread with 1½ cups hot filling

BASIC SOUFFLÉ

Soufflés come in all sizes and shapes. You can bake one in a jelly roll pan, roll it around a filling and serve hot or cold, sauced or not. Heap uncooked soufflé on a fish and bake both in the oven (a real bit of glamour!), bake individual ones or serve the traditional soufflé sauced. To dazzle your guests, try a dessert soufflé. (Pop it in the oven when you sit down to eat.)

For this soufflé you need to make a thick white sauce—the directions are under Basic White Sauce earlier in this chapter, but I repeat them in this recipe. When making a soufflé, allow ¼ cup of thick white sauce and 1 egg plus an optional ½ egg white per person. For a low cholesterol soufflé, substitute 2 egg whites for each whole egg.

For the thick white sauce:

3 tablespoons butter

3 tablespoons flour

1 cup milk

salt and pepper to taste

For the soufflé:

4 eggs, separated, or 8 egg whites

additions: 1 cup grated cheese or ¾ cup other filler (see below)

seasoning: (optional) ½ teaspoon dried or 1½ teaspoons fresh herbs, 1 teaspoon dry mustard, or 2 teaspoons minced onion

Make the white sauce: Melt the butter, stir in the flour and cook 2 minutes. Add milk and whisk until thickened. Add salt and pepper to taste.

Stir the egg yolks into the sauce. Stir in additions, cheese, finely chopped chicken, ham, well-

BASIC SOUFFLÉ

drained minced cooked spinach or broccoli, drained canned tuna, clams or crab and seasoning. Beat the egg whites stiff and fold into the thick mixture.

Choose a dish that the uncooked soufflé will fill to within ¾" or 1" of the top. (Fill a jelly roll pan to the top.) This recipe fills a 6-cup dish. Bake in a preheated 350° oven for 30 minutes.

For other size dishes and their baking times, check the chart on p. 205.

Yield: 4 light servings.

NOTE: An extra egg white or two per cup white sauce makes a lighter soufflé.

Bake-ahead: Use 4 tablespoons butter, 8 tablespoons flour and 1⅓ cups milk and bake in a water bath. Cool and chill. Baked in a 350° oven for 30 minutes, it repuffs like magic.

(creamed meat, fish or vegetable) or with grated cheese. Roll and serve with a flourish. This is nice with a sauce. Sliced thin, it makes a lovely hors d'oeuvre.

Shrimp: Use ½ teaspoon dried or 1½ teaspoons fresh dill weed, 1 teaspoon Dijon mustard and ¾ cup chopped shrimp.

Spinach: Add ¾ cup drained, chopped spinach, ¼ teaspoon nutmeg and ¾ cup grated Gruyère cheese.

Tomato Cheese: Use ¾ cup grated medium sharp Cheddar, ½ cup tomato purée and 1 teaspoon dried or 1 tablespoon fresh basil.

Recipe Idea

Miniature Quiches

A fun party idea when you have time and feel frivolous and clever. Using the recipe for Basic Quiche on page 330, make miniature quiches in 2½-inch tart shells. Use three different fillings such as spinach, shrimp and plain cheese. Half a recipe of each would fill 8 to 10 pre-baked tart shells. Serve one of each to each guest. Bake for about 15 minutes at 350°.

Quiche Variations:

Broccoli Ham: In the pie shell, layer 1 cup each cooked chopped broccoli, ham and Swiss cheese. Pour on custard.

Greek: Replace the milk with a medium white sauce (see p. 292), which will give the custard a different texture. Add ¾ cup crumbled feta. Top the cooked pie with some black Greek olives. Try it. It's not Greek, but 2 cups cooked seafood or canned tuna or salmon makes a delicious addition.

Italian Sausage and Zucchini: Shred 1½ cups zucchini, sauté for 5 minutes in a tablespoon of butter. Remove the casings from 3 sweet Italian sausages and cook them in a skillet, breaking them up, until no pink remains. Drain on paper towels. (They should total 1 to 2 cups.) Spread the zucchini in the crust, then the sausage, then pour on the custard mixture.

Shrimp: Cooked shrimp and some fresh herbs make a wonderful quiche. Add cheese and it's denser and gooier and still wonderful.

Spinach, Mozzarella and Ham: Replace all the milk in the custard with 1½ cups ricotta cheese. Add ½ cup cooked spinach, chopped and squeezed dry and 1 cup each diced mozzarella and ham. Yum!

Basic Quiche

Twenty years ago quiche was the rage among sophisticates. Now it is standard in every kitchen—a surefire way to glamorize leftover tidbits. All you need is a custard made with egg and milk or cream, a filler and a pastry shell.

1 8" or 9" partially pre-baked pastry shell (See p. 321)

4 eggs, slightly beaten

2 cups cream, half and half or milk

1 to 2 cups meat, vegetables or cheese (see below)

seasonings such as herbs or 2 to 3 teaspoons minced onion, for non-cheese quiches

1 teaspoon Dijon mustard, for cheese quiches

In a bowl beat the eggs lightly with a fork. (Don't beat air bubbles into them.) Whisk in the cream or milk. Place the meat, vegetables or cheese in the pastry shell. Pour on the custard. You may not need it all if you use an 8" shell or have a lot of bulky additions. Custardy quiches like cheese or bacon will use most of the liquid mixture. Bake at 375° for 30 to 35 minutes for an 8" quiche, 35 to 50 minutes for a 9", or until a knife blade inserted 1" from the center comes out clean.

Ideas for Fillings: Use 2 cups grated cheese, cooked shellfish, cooked meat, chopped or puréed cooked vegetables, etc., or 1 to 2 cups of any filler plus ½ to 1 cup cheese—Cheddar and Swiss are good.

Yield: 6 servings.

BASIC STIR-FRY

The stir-fry is the darling of busy cooks who insist on eating well. A minimum of effort produces a show-off dish of browned but succulent meat, seafood or chicken and crisp-tender vegetables in a zesty sauce.

Here is the way I learned to stir-fry in Chinese cooking school. For a nice change, heap your stir-fry on noodles or Oriental rice sticks. Good!

For the stir-fry:

½ pound boneless lean meat, poultry or seafood

1½ to 2½ tablespoons oil

½ pound (about 2 - 3 cups) raw vegetables, thinly sliced

1 clove garlic, minced

For the marinade:

¼ cup soy sauce

1 clove garlic, crushed

½ teaspoon ginger root, minced (1 to 2 slices)

½ teaspoon sugar (optional)

1 tablespoon sherry (optional)

For the sauce:

½ cup chicken stock or water

1 tablespoon soy sauce

2 teaspoons cornstarch

pinch of salt

1 tablespoon sherry, optional

Slice meat thinly against the grain. Slice chicken thinly or cut in cubes. Leave shellfish whole. Place in a bowl with marinade ingredients. Turn to coat well and let sit for 15 minutes, turning occasionally.

In a wok or skillet over high heat, heat 1½ tablespoons of the oil. When it is very hot, slide the meat

Stir-Fry Variations:

Beef with Broccoli: Use flank steak, sliced ⅛" thick across the grain and broccoli. Omit the optional sherry in the sauce.

Pepper Chicken: Cut and marinate chicken as in the basic recipe, using only 2 tablespoons soy sauce. Sauté 1 onion, chopped very fine, in oil until translucent. Add 10 water chestnuts, sliced and 2 large green peppers, seeded and cut into ½ inch dice. Stir-fry until emerald green. Remove. Dust chicken with cornstarch. Stir-fry until it turns white. Return vegetables to the pan along with hot pepper flakes to taste. A handful of peanuts is a good addition. Mix and stir to heat thoroughly.

Hoisin Shrimp: Marinate shrimp as in the basic recipe, adding 1 table-spoon sherry. Heat the wok and stir-fry ½ cup (4 ounces) ground pork until it turns pale (about 2 minutes). Add 2 green onions, chopped fine and stir-fry 1 minute more. Remove the pork and onions from the pan. Heat the wok with 1 teaspoon of oil. On high heat, stir-fry the shrimp for 2 minutes or until they turn opaque. Remove. Mix ¼ cup chicken stock with ½ teaspoon cornstarch. Pour into the pan and cook until clear. Return the shrimp and the pork mixture to the pan with 1½ tablespoons hoisin sauce. Cook and stir for 1 minute. (You can do this ahead and reheat it in a covered casserole in a 250° oven.)

Vegetable Stir-Fry: Omit marinade and meat. Use 4 cups vegetables. Add 2 teaspoons grated ginger along with garlic. Add vegetables in order of cooking time (see below). When you add the last vegetables, add water and finish as in recipe.

Cooking Time (minutes):
4-5: broccoli, celery, onion
3-4: cauliflower, green onion
2-3: red/green pepper, squashes
1-2: bean sprouts, cabbages,
        mushrooms, pea pods, tomatoes

Quick Hint

Partially freeze meat or poultry to make it easy to slice thin.

BASIC STIR-FRY

along with the marinade, into the oil. Stir-fry for 2 to 3 minutes until brown but not quite done. Remove to a bowl.

If you are using vegetables, add another tablespoon of oil to the wok. When it is very hot add the vegetables, minced garlic and 2 to 3 tablespoons of water. Lower the heat, cover and cook until the water has evaporated and vegetables are brightly colored and crisp-tender.

Mix the sauce ingredients and add to the pan along with the meat. Cook and stir until thickened and clear, about 2 to 3 minutes. Taste for salt. Serve immediately.

Yield: 4 to 6 servings.

NOTES: Watch carefully and lower heat slightly if food starts to burn. Add oil to a hot wok in a thin stream around the edge of the pan. As it slides down it heats and oils the wok sides. If you add to much oil, don't pour it out, sponge out with a paper towel wad. When you stir-fry a mix of vegetables, add the slower cooking ones first, toss for a minute or so, then add the quicker cooking ones (see box at left).

For more on stir-frying vegetables see page 171.

BASIC CASSEROLE

Casseroles are the delight of the inventive cook and the gastronome. Everybody loves them; they fill the kitchen with the aromas of herbs, spice and browning cheese and they're natural make-aheads, perfect ways to send leftovers to heaven. Here's a good basic casserole pattern that will adjust to most any culinary flight of fancy.

The main ingredients:

1½ cups cooked meats, poultry, fish, egg and/or 1 cup any cooked vegetable

1 cup of a starchy ingredient such as cooked cubed, sliced whole small potatoes, cooked rice, cooked noodles or stuffing mix

The liquid binder:

2 to 2½ cups of gravy, medium white sauce, tomato sauce or canned cream soup thinned with milk.

Optional topping:

½ cup bread or cracker crumbs, or crumbled corn or potato chips

butter, to taste

Use a dish that the ingredients will fill to within ¾" or ½" of the top. Grease the dish and assemble the casserole to suit your whim: either mix everything but the topping; or make 2 or 3 alternating layers of meats, vegetables, starch and sauce, ending with sauce; or put all the dry ingredients in the dish and pour the sauce over. Top with crumbs, dot with butter if you like and bake at 350° for 25 to 30 minutes or until browned and bubbling.

Yield: 4 servings.

─ Recipe Idea ─

Custard-Topped Casserole

Try **custard** mixtures over any casserole that isn't too liquid: meat mixtures, drained cooked vegetables. Start with the egg/ milk mix you use for quiche: 1 cup milk with 2 eggs. For a yummy, puffy topping use 2 eggs with 3 tablespoons milk and 3 tablespoons heavy cream or yogurt. For a cheesy topping, 1 egg plus 2 cups ricotta or small curd cottage cheese.

Add salt, pepper and any extra flavoring you like. Spoon onto the casserole ingredients and bake as in the recipe—or at 350° until it tests done.

─ Recipe Idea ─

Crumble-Topped Casserole

Make a **crumble** topping, especially good on very moist mixtures or veggies in sauce. Cut 6 tablespoons butter or margarine into 1 cup flour until it resembles fine bread crumbs. Add grated cheese, chopped herbs, paprika, cayenne. Sprinkle on prepared ingredients. Bake at 400° for 20 to 30 minutes until browned and crunchy.

CASSEROLE TOPPINGS

Don't always reach for the cheese or crumbs to finish off your casserole. Check the topping ideas below and create a show-stopper. The suggested amounts will cover an 8-inch diameter dish (1- to 1½-quart capacity).

Bread Topping: Spread a couple of slices of bread with mustard or horseradish and fry in butter; cut into shapes and arrange over the hot casserole for the last 10 minutes of baking, raising the heat to 400°.

Crumb Topping: Mix ½ cup of bread crumbs in the recipe with herbs, grated cheese, chopped onion, nuts or spices. Or fry the crumbs, flavored or not, in 2 tablespoons butter until lightly browned. Sprinkle over the casserole and raise heat to 400° for the last 10 minutes.

Cobbler Topping: Make a cobbler topping. Use 1 recipe biscuit dough flavored with grated cheese, herbs or spices. Cut shapes or drop dough on the hot prepared mixture and raise heat to 425° for the last 10 to 15 minutes or until golden.

Mayonnaise Topping: Fold a stiffly beaten egg white into ⅔ cup mayonnaise. Spoon onto ingredients in dish for last 12 to 15 minutes of baking, with no temperature change.

BASIC MEAT LOAF

Don't knock meat loaf as PTA supper stuff. I know sophisticated hostesses who serve it for parties. You can even wrap your baked meat loaf in bread dough and bake a savory *coulibiac*. This always gets applause. Don't forget that meat loaf is delicious cold. Serve it plain or with an interesting cold sauce like mustard or horseradish, or mayo with a hint of Oriental sesame oil.

This recipe has served me for years as a standard loaf, a cold pâté (cool under a weight and slice the next day), meatballs and stuffing for peppers, tomatoes and eggplant.

The meat:

2 to 3 cups (1 to 1½ lbs) ground meat: all beef or any combination of beef, pork, veal and turkey

The binders:

1 ⅓ cups soft bread crumbs or cracker crumbs

1 egg

The liquid:

½ cup milk, broth, wine, gravy, tomato juice, tomato sauce or canned tomatoes

The seasonings (use any or all):

1 minced onion

1 tablespoon or more chopped green pepper

½ to 1 teaspoon salt

½ teaspoon dry mustard

2 to 3 tablespoons catsup

1 to 2 teaspoons horseradish

2 teaspoons Worcestershire sauce

1 teaspoon any herbs

½ teaspoon garlic salt

continued on p. 336

Meat Loaf Variations:

Cheese Filled: Pat half the meat mixture into a loaf pan. Mix 1 slightly beaten egg white with 1 tablespoon water, then with 1 cup soft bread crumbs and 4 ounces shredded Cheddar or crumbled blue cheese. Place this on the meat, then top with the rest of the meat.

Coulibiac: If the idea intrigues you, here's how to do it. Bake the meat loaf in a large, oven-glass bread pan, forming it a bit away from the sides. Cool and chill. Save the pan juices for gravy. Make or buy yeast dough for 1 loaf of bread. A tender loaf made with milk and a little butter is best. When you would normally shape the loaf, roll out a little more than half the dough and line the pan you baked the meat loaf in, lightly greased. Put the chilled meat loaf in the center.

Roll out the remaining dough, cover the meat loaf and tuck the edges down the pan sides with a knife. Cover and let rise 15 to 20 minutes. Brush the top with a little milk. Bake in a preheated 375° oven for 45 minutes. Reduce the heat to 350° and bake 20 minutes more. Remove from the oven, let sit 5 minutes, then loosen and tip the loaf out. Serve hot, sliced, with a gravy made from thickened meat loaf juices.

You can also wrap the loaf in pie crust (it will take a recipe for two 9" crusts) or with puff pastry. Bake at 425° for 15 to 20 minutes.

Ham: Substitute 1 cup ground ham for 1 cup of the meat, or use equal parts ground ham and ground pork.

Individual Loaves: Shape six ovals and place in a greased baking pan or fill muffin wells. Bake for 30 to 45 minutes.

Quick Hint

Elaine's meat loaf trick: For a lower fat loaf, shape an oval and lay it on a single layer of bread slices in a shallow baking pan. The bread will soak up the fat and keep the bottom of the loaf from being soggy.

BASIC MEAT LOAF

The optional extras:

cheese cubes, sautéed mushrooms, etc.

Mix all ingredients in a large bowl by hand.

Place the mixture in an ungreased loaf pan or, for a firmer loaf with crusty sides, shape an oval on a shallow baking dish 1 inch larger than the loaf on all sides.

Bake loaves at 375° for 1 to 1½ hours, or until firm.

Bake small meatballs on a sheet at 400° until brown, or drop into boiling soup, tomato sauce, barbecue sauce or a stroganoff sauce and cook until done. These make good hors d'oevres.

Yield: 6 to 8 servings.

BASIC MASHED POTATOES

The right potato and hot milk are the secrets to good mashed potatoes. Use baking potatoes, because their high starch content and mealy texture make them fluff up nicely.

1 pound baking potatoes

2 to 3 tablespoons butter

½ cup milk

salt and white pepper, to taste

Cook unpeeled potatoes in salted water to cover until tender. Drain and peel while hot. Mash or purée potatoes through a ricer directly into a pan in which you have melted the butter. In another pan bring milk to a boil. Start beating potatoes with whisk or fork, adding 2 to 3 tablespoons milk at a time. Keep adding until the potatoes have absorbed as much milk as they can without getting thin—potatoes will vary in this regard. If the potatoes are too thin, just put them back over the heat and stir. They'll thicken right up. Season to taste.

Yield: 4 servings.

Mashed Potato Variations:

Croquettes: Make the Duchess potatoes, below, using only 2 tablespoons milk. Cool, roll into a 1" thick cylinder and cut 1" lengths. Roll each in seasoned flour and brush with 1 egg mixed with ½ teaspoon salt. Coat with dry bread crumbs and fry in butter or deep fat (375°) until browned.

Dauphine: This is in the Cream Puff variations. (See p. 317.)

Duchess: Use 2 tablespoons butter and beat in 1 egg yolk. Pipe or spoon 4 rosettes or mounds onto a buttered baking sheet. Brush with 1 egg yolk mixed with a pinch of salt. Just before serving, bake at 400° for 10 to 12 minutes or until browned. Or warm them through at 325° and brown under the broiler. Small rosettes make a lovely border around a meat platter.

Italian: Halfway through adding milk, beat in ⅓ cup grated Parmesan.

Twice-Baked: Bake potatoes instead of boiling. Halve lengthwise or cut a lid off the top and scoop out pulp. Mash as in basic recipe, but don't make them too soft. Fold in ⅓ cup cheese if you like. Stuff potatoes with the mixture. Reheat in a 400° oven. Or put the cheese on top and broil at least 6 inches from heat until top is melted and potatoes are reheated.

Scalloped Potato Variations:

Decadent: Use whipping cream, omit flour and butter and layer with 1 cup grated Swiss cheese. Bake at 300° for 1 to 1¼ hours.

French Style (Savoyard): Substitute beef stock for milk and increase butter to a total of 4 tablespoons.

Main Course: Add chopped chives, onions and bacon, ham, salami (reduce the salt for these last three), or cheese to the layers.

BASIC SCALLOPED POTATOES

Just once, when you feel the urge to sin a little, try the whipping cream variation.

3 cups thin-skinned potatoes, thinly sliced

2 tablespoons flour

1½ tablespoons butter

1¼ cups milk or cream

1¼ teaspoons salt

Drop potatoes in boiling salted water and boil for 8 minutes. Drain well. Place a third of them in a greased 10" baking dish. Sprinkle on 2 teaspoons of flour and dot with ½ tablespoon butter. Make 2 more layers in this way. Heat the milk with the salt and pour over potatoes. Bake uncovered at 350° for 35 minutes or until tender when pierced with a fork.

Yield: 6 servings.

BASIC STUFFING

I bake my stuffing outside the bird in a covered casserole; I think it gives a moister bird. My friend Ellen argues that stuffing inside the bird soaks up all that tasty chicken juice. Try both ways and decide.

This is good old celery and sage—the stuffing most of us grew up with.

1 small onion, chopped

1 rib celery with leaves, chopped

⅓ cup butter

5 cups dry (3 to 4 days old) white or whole wheat bread cubes or crumbs

2 tablespoons chopped parsley

1 to 2 teaspoons poultry seasoning or sage

½ teaspoon salt

For a moist dressing: water, milk or broth

Sauté the onion and celery in butter until tender but not brown. Toss with the bread, parsley and seasonings. If you like your stuffing moist, or are baking it separately, add enough liquid to barely dampen the bread. If you don't bake this inside the bird, cook in a covered casserole in a 325° oven for 30 minutes.

Yield: Enough for a 5-pound bird.

NOTE: Figure ¾ cup stuffing per pound meat, poultry or fish; 1 cup if you're baking it separately.

Stuffing Variations:

Chestnut: Use only 3½ cups bread. Add 2 cups coarsely chopped boiled or canned chestnuts.

Cornbread: Substitute for all or part of bread crumbs. (A 9" square gives 4 to 5 cups crumbs.)

Fluffy Stuffing: Beat 1 egg with ¾ cup chicken stock or giblet broth. Stir into dry stuffing. Bake in a greased casserole, uncovered, along with the bird for the last hour of baking or until golden brown.

Giblet: Simmer giblets until tender. Chop and substitute for an equal amount of bread.

Mushroom: Sauté 8 ounces sliced mushrooms with the onions.

Nut: Add 1½ cups chopped pecans, walnuts, Brazil nuts, chestnuts or pine nuts.

Oyster: Use ½ cup butter and after sautéeing the vegetables add 1 cup drained oysters, chopped or whole. Sauté 1 to 2 minutes. Mix with remaining ingredients. Season with basil and ¼ teaspoon nutmeg. Moisten with milk and oyster liquor.

Sausage: Sauté 4 ounces crumbled sausage meat, drain and add. Substitute 2 tablespoons sausage fat for part of the butter.

Gelatin Custard Variations:

Bavarian Cream: Reduce milk to 1½ cups and sugar to ½ cup. Use egg yolks only. Cool custard until mixture mounds when dropped from a spoon. Beat ¾ cup whipping cream with 2 tablespoons confectioners sugar and fold in. Use any of the variations below.

Chocolate: Add 1-2 oz coarsely grated unsweetened chocolate to milk.

Butterscotch: Substitute brown sugar for white.

Eggnog: Substitute ½ cup whisky, rum, brandy or sherry for ½ cup of the milk.

FOR DESSERT

Here are all the wonderful sweet things that didn't fit into the batter and dough category: the delectations you were forbidden to eat until you'd finished your vegetables, back in the days when vegetables were supposed to build character and curl hair rather than taste good.

There's a lot of custard here. Soft custard turns up everywhere. It is a delectable pudding. It fills cream puffs and *gateaux*. It sauces the modest cottage pudding and it's the starting point for charlottes and Bavarians. The homey old-fashioned puddings—bread, rice, cornstarch—are all custards. I give basic recipes for them because in one guise or another, they have become popular again with everyone who knows what's good.

BASIC GELATIN CUSTARD

Sometimes called Spanish Cream, this is the silky mother of the elegant Bavarian Cream.

1 package (1 tablespoon) unflavored gelatin
⅔ cup sugar
¼ teaspoon salt
2¼ cups milk
3 eggs, lightly beaten
1 teaspoon vanilla

Mix gelatin, sugar and salt in the top of a double boiler. Slowly stir in milk. Cook and stir over simmering water until well heated and sugar is dissolved. Blend a little hot mixture into the eggs, then stir them into the milk. Cook and stir until slightly thickened (4-6 minutes). Add vanilla. Strain into mold or individual dishes. Top with fruit, chocolate or caramel sauce, or line your mold ahead with rum-dipped lady fingers.

Yield: Serves 6

BASIC BAKED CUSTARD

Custards are the base of so many desserts. With this basic recipe you can make the velvety cup custards beloved by our grandmothers plus a host of elegant variations. For a richer custard, substitute 2 yolks for one of the eggs, or replace up to ½ cup of the milk with cream.

2 cups milk

3 eggs

⅓ c sugar

1½ teaspoons vanilla

Heat milk until little bubbles appear around the sides of the pan. Remove from heat. In a bowl whisk the eggs with the sugar until well mixed but not frothy. Stir into the hot milk and let mixture cool slightly. Add vanilla. Pour custard into a 1 quart dish or 4 individual dishes. Bake in a water bath: Place the dishes in a shallow pan in the oven. Pour in boiling water to a depth of 1½ inches. Bake uncovered at 350° for 20 to 25 minutes for small dishes, 40 to 50 minutes for a large one.

Yield: 4 servings.

Baked Custard Variations:

Apricot: Substitute 1 cup unsweetened apricot purée for 1 cup of the milk. Taste and add more sugar if needed. If you make pulp from canned apricots, omit all sugar in recipe.

Bit O' Irish Heaven: Replace 2 tablespoons of the milk with Bailey's Irish Cream. Divide ½ cup raisins that have soaked in brandy or cointreau among 4 individual dishes before pouring in the custard. And you thought custard was for kids!

Chocolate: Melt 1 square semi-sweet chocolate and add to ¼ cup of the recipe's scalded milk. Stir into custard.

Coconut: Add ¼ to ½ cup grated coconut.

Coffee: Add 2 to 3 teaspoons dry instant coffee to scalded milk.

Crème Caramel: Make a caramel syrup with ¼ cup water and ½ cup sugar (see p. 78). Immediately pour ¼ of the caramel into an individual dish and turn the dish to coat the base and part way up the sides evenly. Work quickly because the caramel will set at once. Repeat with 3 more dishes. Pour custard into the prepared dishes and bake as in recipe.

Bread Pudding Variations:

(You can also use the variations for baked custard):

Fresh Bread Crumb Pudding: Substitute 2½ cups fresh bread crumbs for the 1 cup dry crumbs.

Gingerbread: Substitute crumbled, stale gingerbread or gingersnaps for bread and add an extra egg and ½ cup raisins.

Meringue Topped: After the baked pudding has cooled, cover it with a soft meringue (2-egg size—see p. 324) and bake in a 300° oven for about 15 minutes, or until browned and set.

Queen of Puddings: The wonderful British pud. Use cake crumbs and add an extra egg yolk. After the crumbs have soaked, add the grated rind of a lemon and 1 to 2 tablespoons brandy or Madeira. When it's baked, spread the pudding with strawberry jam and top with meringue as in the version above.

Holiday Eggnog: Use cinnamon-raisin bread. Substitute commercial eggnog for the milk and replace 3 tablespoons of the eggnog with brandy.

BASIC BREAD PUDDING

Custard jazzed up with bread or cake crumbs, bread pudding has suddenly become fashionable. Little wonder.

> 2 cups milk
>
> 1 cup dry bread or cake in crumbs or cubes
>
> 1 egg
>
> 2 tablespoons sugar
>
> ½ teaspoon vanilla or ⅛ teaspoon nutmeg
>
> ¼ teaspoon salt
>
> 2 tablespoons melted butter

Scald milk, add crumbs and soak for ½ hour. Whisk the egg with the sugar, vanilla and salt until well mixed but not frothy. Stir into the milk mixture and add butter. Pour into a one-quart greased casserole or 4 individual dishes. Bake in a water bath for 45 to 50 minutes for either size dish. Serve warm with cream, lemon sauce, hard sauce, or sweetened crushed berries.

Yield: 4 to 6 servings.

BASIC RICE PUDDING

Another variation on the custard theme. Remember A. A. Milne's Mary Jane, who had nice rice pudding for supper again? Everyone should be so lucky. Try it once with half and half instead of milk and a splash of rum or bourbon. **Note:** *Do not* use converted rice.

½ cup short or medium grain rice

3 eggs

⅓ cup sugar

½ cup raisins

2 teaspoons vanilla

1½ teaspoons grated lemon rind

¼ teaspoon salt

3½ cups milk

1 teaspoon nutmeg

2 tablespoons butter

Cook rice as directed on package until tender. Beat eggs lightly with a fork. Stir in sugar, raisins, vanilla, lemon rind and salt, then the milk and cooked rice. Pour into greased 1½ qt casserole. Sprinkle the top with nutmeg. Dot with butter. Bake at 300° without a water bath for 1 hour and 25 minutes. After ½ hour, you can stir the pudding once or twice to keep the rice from sinking to the bottom (insert the spoon at the edge and draw it across the bottom of the dish). Serve slightly warm with regular or whipped cream, maple syrup, hot fudge or butterscotch sauce.

Yield: 6 to 8 servings.

Rice Pudding Variations:

Same as for baked custard, omitting raisins, lemon rind and nutmeg.

You can also:

Use ½ cup brown sugar in place of white.

Use dates instead of raisins.

Use cake or cookie crumbs to coat greased bottom and sides of dish. Top mixture with more crumbs.

Boiled Custard Variations:

Chocolate: Add 2 to 3 ounces chopped semi-sweet chocolate to the milk after it has been heated.

French Pastry Cream: Use to fill cream puffs, pies and cake. Add an extra yolk and whisk 3 tablespoons flour into the whisked yolks and sugar. Use any of the variations here, but use double the chocolate.

Liqueur: Add 2 tablespoons kirsch, rum, Cointreau, etc., to the finished custard.

Orange: Omit vanilla and infuse milk with the grated zest of 1 orange. Flavor finished custard with 1 to 2 tablespoons orange liqueur. Good on cooked fruit.

BASIC BOILED CUSTARD

Thick like whipped cream but denser, it can be used as a sauce or a pudding. My mother poured it over sliced oranges and let it cool.

2 cups milk

5 egg yolks

¼ cup sugar

few drops vanilla

Scald milk in the top pan of a double boiler. In a bowl, whisk yolks and sugar until thick and light (3 to 4 minutes). Very slowly, stir in hot milk. Return custard to pan and heat over (not touching) simmering water, stirring constantly until it coats a wooden spoon. (If you draw a finger across the back of the spoon it will leave a clear trail that won't fill back in.)

Yield: 2¼ cups.

Cornstarch Sauce Variations:

Brandy or Kirsch: Omit vanilla and add brandy or kirsch to taste. Good on steamed and plum pudding.

Fruit Juice: Make the sauce using ½ cup sugar, 1 tablespoon cornstarch and 2 cups fruit juice. Omit butter and vanilla.

Lemon: Add juice and rind of 1 lemon. Omit vanilla.

CORNSTARCH SAUCE

Serve over plain cake, apple dumplings, hot waffles or pancakes jazzed up with berries and nuts.

1 cup sugar

2 tablespoons cornstarch

2 cups boiling water

2 tablespoons butter

2 teaspoons vanilla

dash nutmeg

Mix sugar and cornstarch; add boiling water gradually, stirring constantly. Cook 8 to 10 minutes. Add butter, vanilla and nutmeg. Serve hot or cold.

Yield: 2 cups.

Basic Vanilla Pudding

Every cook should make this simple pudding instead of relying on the box. If you think Vanilla Pudding sounds too plain Jane, call it by its Victorian name: Blanc Mange—was it Amy or Beth who made it in Little Women?

2 cups milk

3 tablespoons cornstarch

⅓ cup sugar

¼ teaspoon salt

1 teaspoon vanilla

In a heavy-bottomed pan scald 1¾ cups of the milk. In a small bowl mix the cornstarch, sugar and salt and gradually stir in the remaining milk. Add this to the scalded milk and cook and stir over low heat until thickened. Then cook and stir for another 3 to 5 minutes or until the cornstarch has lost all raw taste.

Remove from heat. Stir in vanilla. Pour into serving dishes. Serve cold with whipped cream, or fresh or puréed fruit.

Yield: 4 servings.

Pudding Variations:

A Sort of Trifle: Make little jam sandwiches with pound cake or any stale cake. Cut into cubes and place in serving dish or 4 small dishes—you'll need about 1 cup of cubes. Sprinkle with sherry. Top with any fresh or canned fruit you have around, sliced thin. Pour hot vanilla pudding on top and let it cool so the cake soaks it all up. Serve with cream.

Chocolate Pudding: Reduce sugar to 2 teaspoons, replace ¼ cup of the milk with whipping cream. When pudding is done, remove from heat and stir in 6 ounces finely chopped bittersweet chocolate until melted. Heavenly!

Vanilla Custard Sauce: Thin the pudding with an extra half cup of milk.

Most of the variations for Baked and Boiled Custard are also delicious with Vanilla Pudding.

Quick Hint

When you make Bouquet Garni make 2 or 3 extra bouquets while you're at it. Store them in a covered container in the refrigerator. As long as they stay completely dry they'll last up to 10 days.

SEASONING MIXTURES

You don't use most seasoning mixtures daily, so commercial sizes tend to go dead before they're used up. If you make them yourself in small quantities, the flavors are always bright and you can tailor the mix to your taste.

APPLE PIE SPICE

This makes enough for one pie.

½ teaspoon ground cinnamon

¼ teaspoon ground nutmeg

⅛ teaspoon ground cardamom

Combine all ingredients. This is also good in applesauce and crust for fruit pie.

SMALL BOUQUET GARNI

The French use this savory herb bouquet in dishes cooked with liquid.

5 fresh parsley stalks (omit the leaves because of their dark color)

2 sprigs fresh thyme or 1 teaspoon dry

1 large bay leaf

To give a luscious Provençal (southern France) taste, add a small strip of orange peel. Tie the herbs up with a string, or wrap them in cheesecloth and tie.

NOTE: Some people put the herbs in a tea ball instead of cheesecloth.

LARGE BOUQUET GARNI

This is usually used in soups.

To the small *bouquet garni,* add:

1 rib celery with its leaves

1 carrot

1 leek or onion

1 sprig thyme or other herb

1 sprig parsley

Tie everything up in a bundle with string. The French call this a *faggot.*

BRITISH MIXED SPICE

You see this often in British recipes for baked goods, meat dishes and casseroles. Allspice is a satisfactory substitute, but the real thing is better.

1 tablespoon cloves

1 tablespoon mace

1 tablespoon ground nutmeg

1 tablespoon coriander seeds

1 tablespoon allspice berries

a small piece of cinnamon stick

Grind the spices to a fine powder. Keep in an airtight jar.

Recipe

British Rock Cakes

These gems are a cross between a big, fat cookie and a scone. Savor them with a cup of tea or coffee.

In a large bowl, whisk together 2 cups sifted flour, 2 teaspoons baking powder, ½ teaspoon mixed spice, ½ teaspoon nutmeg and a pinch of salt. Cut in ¼ cup of butter and 2 tablespoons solid vegetable shortening until mixture looks like bread crumbs. Stir in ½ cup firmly packed brown sugar, 2 tablespoons chopped, mixed candied peel, ½ cup raisins and the grated rind of ½ a lemon. Add a lightly beaten egg and 6 tablespoons milk.

Divide the dough into 8 portions. Shape each into a slightly flattened ball. Place on a greased baking sheet 1½" apart. Bake at 400° for 15 minutes or until pale golden and firm. Cool on a rack. Enjoy!

What is Filé Powder?

Filé powder, made from ground sassafras leaves, is used as a thickener. It's available in the spice section of the supermarket or in specialty shops.

CAJUN SPICE

Rub this sassy mix into meat, poultry or fish to be roasted or grilled, or use it in gumbo and jambalaya.

3 bay leaves, crushed or ground

1 teaspoon salt

1 teaspoon gumbo filé powder

½ teaspoon each black and white peppercorns

½ teaspoon dried thyme

¼ to ½ teaspoon cayenne pepper (or to taste)

¼ teaspoon dried, crumbled sage

¼ teaspoon dry mustard

Mix everything. If your recipe doesn't already provide for onions or garlic, add ½ teaspoon each garlic and onion powder. Or, if you're among those who think onion powder tastes artificial, crush ½ medium onion with a mortar and pestle or in the processor, mix well with the spices and keep the mixture in the refrigerator.

Chile Pepper Sauce Variation:

Cover 4 tablespoons coarsely cracked black peppercorns with ½ cup Cognac and proceed as in recipe.

CHILE PEPPER SAUCE

When we lived in Africa we all made our own hot pepper sauce, called Piri Piri, Pili Pili, or Hell Fire Sauce, depending on the country.

Fill a small bottle loosely with fiery little hot chile peppers, dried or fresh. Cover completely with sherry or Cognac. Let stand uncorked for 2 weeks, shaking occasionally. Cover tightly to store.

CHINESE FIVE SPICE POWDER

Pungent and slightly sweet, besides being good in Chinese dishes, this is delicious on roast meat and poultry and in stews and spice cake.

3 tablespoons ground cinnamon

6 whole star anise (available at Oriental groceries)

1½ teaspoons whole Szechwan peppercorns or whole black peppercorns

1½ teaspoons fennel seeds

¾ teaspoon ground cloves

Grind all ingredients to a powder. Store in a tightly closed jar.

CINNAMON SUGAR

Keep a shaker of cinnamon sugar on hand to make cinnamon toast, sprinkle on hot cereal, baked apples, muffins, cakes, or pancakes.

4 teaspoons cinnamon

¾ cup sugar

Mix well and store in a tightly closed jar.

Recipe

Five Spice Wings

In a large skillet brown 12 to 16 wings in 2 tablespoons oil, removing them as they brown. Pour the fat out of skillet and add 2 cups sliced leeks (white part only). Place wings on top of leeks. Add ¼ cup sherry, ¼ cup soy sauce, 1 tablespoon honey. Bring to a boil over high heat. Add 2 cups of water. Return to the boil, cover and simmer gently for 20 minutes, basting once or twice. Uncover, sprinkle with 1 teaspoon five spice powder. Cook uncovered for 15 minutes more (there should be only about ¼ cup of liquid left). Taste and add salt if they need it.

Serves 4.

Recipe

Steamed Crabs

If you want to make your reputation as someone who knows crabs, steam them this way.

Use a large pot with a rack that stands 2 inches above the bottom. Add equal amounts of water and vinegar to reach just below the rack. Layer the crabs on the rack and sprinkle each layer with a mixture of Crab Boil and salt. (Use 2½ tablespoons of crab boil and 3 tablespoons salt for each dozen.) Cover the pot. Bring quickly to a boil, steam until crabs are red.

CRAB BOIL

As well as using it to flavor crab water, toss in a little when you sauté crabs or shrimps in the shell. Put it in chowders and beef or chicken stew, in crab cakes and in water for boiling pasta.

3 bay leaves

1 teaspoon black peppercorns

1 teaspoon mustard seeds

1 teaspoon dill seeds

1 teaspoon coriander seeds

1 teaspoon whole cloves

1 teaspoon whole allspice

1 small piece dried ginger

Tie the spices in a muslin bag to use.

Recipe

Nippy Mayo for Seafood Salads

Make this delicious dressing herby or spicy to suit your whim. Mix ½ cup mayonnaise, 2 teaspoons Crab Boil, ¼ cup chopped scallions, ⅓ cup chopped celery, 2 teaspoons lemon juice. Add any of these: ½ teaspoon dried dill, 2 teaspoons paprika, or ¼ teaspoon cayenne pepper plus a drop of hot pepper sauce. Mix with 1 lb cooked seafood and chill.

CURRY POWDER

Curry powder, which is a mixture of spices, has as many formulas as there are Indian households. I like this all-purpose one from my friend Neena Sahai, who is a heavenly cook. Add hot pepper if you like. I prefer to add it separately to each dish so I can vary hotness to suit the dish and the guests.

¼ cup ground coriander

2 tablespoons ground cumin

2 tablespoons ground turmeric

1 tablespoons ground ginger

Mix all ingredients. Store in a tightly closed container.

FINES HERBES

Use this delicate mixture in salads, chilled soups, sauces and fish and egg dishes.

1 tablespoon dried chervil

1 tablespoon dried tarragon

1 tablespoon dried chives

Mix. When you use it, add an equal measure of fresh minced parsley. Fresh herbs are even better: use equal parts chives, tarragon, chervil and parsley.

FLAVORED BUTTERS

Shape these quickly-made butters into logs and store them in the freezer. To add a touch of magic to the ordinary, just slice off a pat and let it melt over a hot steak, chop, or fish. Toss flavored butter with steamed vegetables or pasta, whip it into mashed potatoes, or swirl it into sauces, soups and stews.

Mix any of the ingredients below with ½ cup butter which you have creamed until soft. Fresh herbs, at your option, can be first chopped finely or pounded to a paste. Same with the shallot and garlic. If you use a processor, whirl the ingredients first to chop them, then drop in softened butter and process to mix.

Anchovy: *6 fillets rinsed in cold water, dried and pounded to a paste.*

Chive: *8 tablespoons, minced.*

Garlic: *4 cloves, chopped or put through the press.*

Horseradish: *4 tablespoons, grated.*

Flavored Butter Log

Flavored Butters

Lemon: *1 teaspoon grated rind.*

Maître d'Hôtel: *1 tablespoon minced parsley, salt, pepper, few drops lemon juice.*

Mustard: *1 tablespoon Dijon.*

Ravigote: *1 tablespoon each fresh chervil, chives, parsley, tarragon and chopped shallot.*

Shallot: *4 tablespoons, minced.*

Snail: *1 tablespoon chopped shallot, 1 teaspoon chopped parsley, 1 clove garlic, crushed, salt and pepper.*

Tarragon: *¼ cup fresh leaves.*

Tomato: *2 tablespoons tomato paste.*

Flavored Vinegar

Use this in salads, of course. But also use it in marinades and to deglaze a pan in which chicken, veal or pork was sautéed.

one bottle white wine or cider vinegar, less ¼ cup

a large sprig of aromatic herbs

a few strips of lemon peel

1 tablespoon green peppercorns

2 cloves garlic, bruised

Add any of the above seasonings you like to the bottle of vinegar and put on the cap. Set the bottle in a sunny windowsill for 3 weeks. Then strain. Now you can add more fresh herbs or flavorings, but it's not necessary. Store in a cool dark place. Keeps a maximum of 6 months.

French Seasoning Mixture

An all-purpose seasoning for just about everything.

1 cup salt

2 tablespoons cinnamon

1 tablespoon broken bay leaves

1 tablespoon dried thyme

1 tablespoon mace

1 tablespoon dried basil

2 teaspoons paprika

1½ teaspoons ground clove

1 teaspoon crushed dried rosemary

1 teaspoon freshly ground pepper

½ teaspoon nutmeg

½ teaspoon allspice

Whirl this in the blender or pound in a mortar. Then sift through a sieve, crushing any lumps. Store in a tightly closed jar.

Garlic-Parsley Mix

The Italians call this **gremolata.** Delicious on meat, poultry, fish or vegetables.

1 large clove garlic, minced fine

¼ cup parsley (packed measure), minced

grated rind of 1 lemon

Mix well. Sprinkle on top of dishes or stir into sauce and/or juices just before serving. Enough for four servings.

Gremolata Variations:

Anchovy: Add 1 flat anchovy, minced. (Won't taste fishy but will deepen the flavor.)

Caper: Add 2 tablespoons capers, minced if large.

Persillade: The French standby. Omit lemon rind. Optional, add 1 tablespoon any French herbs. Wonderful stirred into pan juices of quick-fried meat, poultry or fish.

Salsa Verde: Italian. Delicious on hot or cold poached fish, chicken or meat. Instead of lemon zest, use 1 tablespoon lemon juice. Add 2 tablespoons minced capers, 1 to 6 chopped anchovy filets. Beat in ½ cup olive oil. Serves six.

Salsa Verde with Egg: Add 1 minced hard-cooked egg to Salsa Verde.

Recipe

Indian Meatballs

Use as much or as little hot pepper as you like in these tasty treats.

Mix 1 lb ground lamb or beef, ½ cup soft bread crumbs, 1 slightly beaten egg, 1 teaspoon garam masala, ¼ teaspoon red pepper (or to taste), ½ teaspoon salt and ¼ cup chopped, fresh coriander leaves (cilantro).

Over medium heat sauté 1 sliced onion and 2 - 3 minced cloves of garlic in 1 tablespoon oil until deep gold—don't burn! Add water if the onion starts to stick. Add 4 chopped tomatoes, 1 tablespoon finely chopped ginger, ½ teaspoon salt, ¼ teaspoon red pepper (or to taste), ¼ teaspoon turmeric, ½ teaspoon garam masala. Cook and stir for 2 - 3 minutes. Add ½ cup yogurt.

Form the meat into 1" balls and drop them into the mixture. Reduce heat and cook covered for 10 minutes or until meatballs are firm. Uncover. Add 1½ cups of water, raise heat and bring to a boil. Lower heat and simmer uncovered 15 - 20 minutes or until the sauce is thickened. Garnish with fresh coriander leaves.

Serves 4

GARAM MASALA

The Indians add this aromatic seasoning near the end of cooking time and sprinkle a little extra on finished dishes. Our cook in Nepal, Surja Lal, taught me this one. I keep it in a jar by the stove the way he did and sprinkle it on meats, stews and chicken to give a little exotic oomph.

2 tablespoons cumin seeds

1 tablespoon black peppercorns

5 small bay leaves

1½ sticks cinnamon, broken up

5 small green cardamom pods

4 large black cardamom pods

7 whole cloves

Grind all the spices in a coffee or spice grinder or blender and store in a tightly covered jar. Good with onion-based sauces for meats and poultry. Sprinkle a little on grilled fish.

HANDY HERB MIXTURE

This is recipe friendly. Use it wherever a mix of herbs would taste good.

6 bay leaves, crushed

1 tablespoon dried thyme

1 tablespoon dried savory

1 tablespoon dried marjoram

1 tablespoon grated lemon peel

Put these in a wooden bowl and crush them with the back of a spoon. Store in a tightly closed jar.

Herb Paste

Here's how to add fresh herb flavors to soups and sauces long after the garden has gone to bed for the year.

Wash 3 to 4 cups tightly packed fresh basil, marjoram, oregano, sage or tarragon leaves—or a mixture—under cold running water. Blot very dry with paper towels. Put in the blender with just enough fruity olive oil to make a smooth purée. Refrigerate tightly covered or freeze in small quantities.

Herb Rub

Nice and herby. Each time you use it, grind the herbs with a mortar and pestle or rub them fine in your palm to release their flavor.

4 teaspoons dried thyme

1 tablespoon garlic powder

1 tablespoon dried oregano

1 tablespoon dried rosemary

1 tablespoon dried basil

1½ teaspoons dried marjoram

1 teaspoon dried sage

¾ teaspoon salt

½ teaspoon cayenne pepper

⅛ teaspoon pepper

Combine all ingredients and store in a tightly covered jar. Use a teaspoon for every pound of meat, poultry or fish.

How Rubs Work

Rubs are often called dry marinades, but they season in a quite different way. Since they are not diluted by liquid—or by very little if you make a paste of them—their flavor is stronger and they stick to the surface better than marinades. Unlike a marinade, the rub does not penetrate and join with the flavor of the food it coats. Instead, during the cooking process it forms a browned crust of concentrated flavors which contrast gloriously with the juicy, unadorned taste of the food beneath.

Rub them on meat, poultry or fish before sautéeing, grilling, broiling or roasting.

HERBES DE PROVENCE

There are a lot of formulas for this seasoning of southern France. Here's a lovely one. It's delicious in stews or rubbed into roast or grilled chicken, meat and fish.

4 tablespoons crushed bay leaves

3 tablespoons dried basil

3 tablespoons nutmeg

3 tablespoons dried rosemary

3 tablespoons dried thyme

2 tablespoons ground clove

2 tablespoons dried savory

2 tablespoons ground white pepper

1 tablespoon ground coriander

1 teaspoon dried lavender, optional

Mix and store in tightly covered jar.

Recipe

British Horseradish Cream

Fold ¼ cup prepared horseradish into ½ cup softly whipped cream. Season to taste with salt, pepper, a teaspoon or so of sugar and a touch of vinegar. Use on roast beef.

HORSERADISH

It used to be that you had to cry a lot to have freshly grated horseradish. Now that we have blenders and processors the relish is painless—and so much better than the commercial variety.

2 cups cubed horseradish

1 teaspoon salt

white vinegar

Grate horseradish root in the blender with a little white vinegar. Fill a pint jar ⅔ full. Add 1 teaspoon salt and fill jar to the top with white vinegar. This keeps a long time in the fridge.

ITALIAN HERB SEASONING

Use this in Italian dishes, meats, poultry, salad dressings and marinades.

4 teaspoons dried oregano

4 teaspoons dried marjoram

4 teaspoons dried basil

2 teaspoons rubbed sage

Mix and store in a tightly covered jar.

PICKLING SPICE

Obviously used in making pickles, this can also be tossed in the water when you boil ham, corned beef and shellfish.

¼ cup mustard seeds

¼ cup dill seeds

¼ cup coriander seeds

6 small, dried red chile pods, crumbled

2 tablespoons crumbled bay leaves (about 6)

1 tablespoon celery seeds

1 tablespoon white peppercorns

Mix and store in a tightly covered jar.

Recipe

Brown Rice Stuffing Casserole

Cook 1 cup brown rice. Chop ½ cup onion and 6 tablespoons celery. Sauté until soft in 2 teaspoons oil. Add to rice with 3 tablespoons chopped parsley, 2 slices whole wheat bread torn into small pieces, ½ cup chopped roasted nuts. Mix ¾ cup milk, ½ teaspoon salt, 1 teaspoon onion powder, 1 tablespoon soy sauce, ¾ teaspoon poultry seasoning. Add to rice. Bake in covered, greased casserole 1 hour at 350°.

Serves 6 - 8.

POULTRY SEASONING

When you use this, why not add a little nutmeg or grated fresh ginger or even both? Yummy and it keeps you out of the rut.

4 teaspoons dried sage

4 teaspoons dried thyme

4 teaspoons dried marjoram

Mix and store in a tightly covered jar.

As a spice rub: Use 1 teaspoon for a 5-pound roasting chicken. Rub it all over the bird, inside and out.

For stuffing: Use ¼ teaspoon per cup of bread cubes.

As a seasoning: Toss a little poultry seasoning in sauces for creamed things, polenta and biscuits to top pot pies.

PUMPKIN PIE SPICE

This is enough for one pie. Try it in custards, cookies and cakes, too.

½ teaspoon ground cinnamon

¼ teaspoon ground ginger

⅛ teaspoon ground allspice

⅛ teaspoon ground nutmeg

Combine all ingredients.

QUATRE ÉPICES

The French use this aromatic mixture in pâtés, sausages and long-simmered stews. Some add a whiff of cinnamon to the mixture, which makes it very Mediterranean and very good. But of course with a fifth spice it would become *Cinq Épices*—another seasoning!

1 tablespoon freshly grated nutmeg

1 tablespoon ground ginger

1 tablespoon freshly ground cloves

2 teaspoons ground white pepper

Mix and store in a tightly closed jar.

SEASONED SALT

This is good in just about everything. I keep it close at hand.

1 cup salt

2½ teaspoons paprika

2 teaspoons dry mustard

1½ teaspoons dried oregano

1 teaspoon garlic powder

½ teaspoon onion powder

Mix and store in a tightly closed jar.

Recipe

Savory Braised Chicken

Season a cut-up 3-lb chicken with salt, pepper and about ½ teaspoon quatre épices. Brown chicken in 2 tablespoons of oil. Cover and cook over low heat for 25 to 30 minutes.

Uncover and add to the pan ¼ teaspoon coarsely crushed peppercorns, ⅛ teaspoon dried thyme, ½ bay leaf, 1 chopped shallot and 2 tablespoons chopped parsley. Stir to coat the chicken evenly. Add enough dry white wine to cover ⅓ of the chicken's depth. Bring to a boil. Lower heat and simmer uncovered, turning now and then for 15 minutes. Discard bay leaf, remove chicken to a plate.

Turn heat to high and boil until the sauce is thickened and glossy, about 2 to 3 minutes. Pour sauce over the chicken.

Serves 4

Flavor with Smoke

On hot charcoal lay hard wood chips (hickory, alder, mesquite, apple), soaked 30 minutes in water; dried rosemary or fennel branches; or, toss on wet fresh herbs or lemon or orange rinds just before you put on the food.

SPICE RUB

This has hints of the Orient in the ginger and clove. Divine on roast chicken, mysterious on fish—try it. This makes enough for three roast chickens.

4 broken up bay leaves

¾ teaspoon celery seeds

1½ teaspoons dry mustard

1 teaspoon black pepper

1 teaspoon salt

1 teaspoon paprika

¾ teaspoon ground nutmeg

½ teaspoon ground cloves

½ teaspoon ground ginger

¼ teaspoon hot paprika or cayenne pepper

Grind bay leaf and celery seeds in a coffee mill or blender, or with a mortar and pestle. Mix with the remaining ingredients and store in a tightly covered jar.

Use ¾ to 1 teaspoon per pound of meat, chicken or fish.

See How Rubs Work on p. 355.

SPICED COFFEE

This is one of my party coffees.

8 whole cloves

3-inch stick cinnamon, broken up

8 tablespoons coffee beans or ground coffee

Grind the spices in the coffee grinder or blender along with the coffee (French roast is best). Brew as usual. You will love it. Makes 8 cups coffee.

Recipe

Joy's Iced Coffee

Put 1 cup cold milk in a blender with 4 teaspoons instant coffee, 2-3 teaspoons sugar, 2 ice cubes. Blend until smooth. Serve in sugar-frosted glasses. I like this for summer coffee parties.

Serves 2.

TACO SEASONING

Not just for tacos, but for most Mexican dishes, tomato sauces and dips.

For 1 pound beef:

1 teaspoon salt

½ teaspoon chili powder

¼ teaspoon pepper

¼ teaspoon cumin

¼ teaspoon oregano

pinch crushed red pepper

Mix and use.

Recipe

Cocktail Tarts Olé

Combine 1 lb lean ground beef with ¼ cup dry bread crumbs, 3 tablespoons taco seasoning and 2 tablespoons cold water. Press into 24 2" muffin cups to make a shell. In a small bowl mix 1 cup sour cream, 2 tablespoons mayonnaise, 2 tablespoons salsa, 2 tablespoons *each* chopped ripe olives and green peppers, and ¾ cup crushed tortilla chips. Heap a little mound in each meat shell. Sprinkle tarts with grated Cheddar cheese (use 1 cup). Bake at 425° for 8 minutes.

Makes 24 tarts.

Recipe

Frau Dietrich's Vanilla Kipfels

These are superb the first day, but to experience pure cookie bliss, follow Frau Dietrich's advice and let them mellow for two weeks. They are treasures!

⅔ cup butter

⅓ cup sugar

1⅓ cups flour

pinch salt

½ cup ground almonds

½ cup vanilla sugar

Grease and flour a baking sheet. Preheat oven to 325°. Cream butter. Gradually add sugar, beating until soft and light. Stir in flour and salt, then the ground almonds. Mix until smooth. Chill 30 minutes or until firm.

Pinch off tablespoonfuls and shape into 3" long rolls. Bend ends to form crescents. Bake on a prepared baking sheet for 20 to 25 minutes, or until lightly browned. While still hot, roll in vanilla sugar. Cool on a rack. Store tightly covered.

Yield: About 3 dozen.

VANILLA SUGAR

To make vanilla sugar, bury a vanilla bean in 1 cup granulated sugar in a tightly covered container. Replace the bean every 6 months, replenishing the sugar as necessary. For every ¼ teaspoon of vanilla extract called for in a recipe, substitute one tablespoon of vanilla sugar for an equal amount of plain sugar.

Use this instead of regular sugar in baking, in puddings and custards in addition to the vanilla in the recipe. The flavor is delectable.

CHAPTER 11

Using the Microwave

Why Do I Have to Keep Moving Things Around, What Do I Have to Know about Watts and Can I Really Use It to Dry Herbs?

The microwave is handy for melting, defrosting, reducing liquids, and other preparation steps as well as for basic cooking of things like vegetables. It reheats delicate foods like quiche beautifully. (Use a mid-range power setting.) But it's tricky to use for thawing meat and poultry; if you're not careful some parts start cooking before the rest thaws.

This chapter contains a few basic hints. If you use your microwave a lot, you'll want to get a good microwave cookbook. The manual that came with your oven will also provide useful information.

POWER LEVELS

Microwave ovens come in different power strengths, measured in watts:

650 to 700 watts	=	Full power oven
500 to 650 watts	=	Medium power oven
400 to 500 watts	=	Low power oven

Microwave Power Levels

High	100%
Medium-High	70%
Medium	50%
Medium-Low or Defrost	30%
Low	10%

Quick Hints

Not all glass cookware is microwave-safe. To test, fill a glass measure with 1 cup of water, set it in the dish you're testing and put both in the microwave. Heat at high for 1 minute. Touch the dish. If it's hot, it's not microwave safe. If the *water* is hot but the dish is cool, it is microwave-safe.

Microwaved food is still cooking when it leaves the oven, so allow 5 to 10 more minutes outside the oven for it to finish.

The lower your oven's power, the longer it takes to cook at each setting. Most recipes, and also the hints in this chapter, are for full power ovens. If you don't know what you have, find out this way. Put exactly 1 cup of lukewarm water (test it on your wrist) in a 1-cup glass measure and place it in the oven. Press the highest (100%) power setting. Set the timer for 10 minutes. The minute you see the first bubble rising, note the time it took. Repeat the process, starting each time with fresh lukewarm water, at all the power settings your oven offers. The box will help you identify power levels.

A full-power oven will take 2 to 3 minutes to boil the water at high, 3½ to 4½ minutes at medium and 4½ to 5 minutes at low.

If your oven takes longer than 2 or 3 minutes to boil water at its highest setting, you know you have something less than full power. So when a recipe calls for high, cook on high but for a *longer time* than the recipe says. When a recipe calls for medium power, cook on high for a *shorter time* than in the recipe. You should be able to establish a setting on any oven that corresponds to low. Write down your adjustments and tape the note to the oven door.

Here are suggested power levels to use for various foods:

High	Medium	Low
Cereals	Cakes	Eggs
Fish	Defrost frozen	Cheese
Liquids	*cooked* food	Defrost frozen
Puddings	Pie crust	*uncooked* food
Sauces	Poultry	Large roasts
Soups	Small roasts	Melt butter
Small cuts		Melt chocolate
of meat		Soufflés
Vegetables		Yeast breads

Keys to Microwave Cooking

The key to success is remembering that **microwaves heat food unevenly.** They heat the edges while the center stays cool. They zap one side harder than another. So the secret is to keep moving the food and changing the areas getting the most heat.

If the food can be stirred, do it at intervals. When you are cooking pieces of chicken or fish, switch center and edge pieces. Foods like potatoes and corn on the cob should be turned over halfway through cooking. Unless the recipe says to do differently, give casseroles and other things that can't be stirred or rearranged a 180° turn at the halfway point .

It is easy to overcook food in the microwave, so **test for doneness at the minimum time** given in the recipe or, when you are winging it, a bit before you think it might be done.

Aluminum foil can be used in limited quantities as long as it doesn't touch the oven wall or rack. Use foil to avoid overcooking the thinner parts of food—the tail of a fish, the two thin ends of fish steaks—and to cover any spots that start to cook when defrosting. Bend it loosely around the area so it is easy to remove part-way through cooking.

Adapting Recipes

It is not difficult to adapt conventional recipes to micro-wave cooking. Here are some guidelines.

Liquid: If the recipe has a large amount, reduce the liquid by about half. If a dish is covered with plastic wrap, very little liquid evaporates. When you decrease liquid, remember to decrease the amount of salt.

Seasoning: Wine, garlic, and fresh herb flavors *cook out quickly*, so use more than the recipe specifies. Dried herbs and pepper flavors *are intensified*; reduce the amount of those.

Things That Affect Cooking Time

Temperature: The colder or denser the dish, the longer it takes.

Size: A pound in one piece takes longer than a pound in small pieces.

Quantity: As a rule, a double amount takes 50% longer.

Shape of Container: Beware of very deep or very shallow containers. With both, by the time the center cooks the edges may be overdone.

Quick Hints

The edge of the dish gets the most microwave energy, so place the densest part of the food (broccoli stem) near the outside, and the less dense part (broccoli head) toward the center.

Round dishes are best. Square corners get double microwaves and cook faster. If you use a square dish, shield the corners with foil.

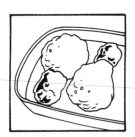

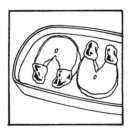

Shield quicker-cooking parts of meat or fish with foil

REHEATING

The microwave is wonderful for reheating. Food stays moist and fresh tasting. The secret is to halt the process the second the food is heated, before it starts to cook again. In general, set the power on medium or a little higher. Give the food a short zap, check, turn or stir, zap again, check, etc.

Reheat:

- Cereals, pasta, and rice tightly covered on *high*.
- Eggs and casseroles containing eggs at *medium* to *medium-high*.
- Large casseroles that can't be stirred at *medium* to give the center time to warm before the outside starts cooking.
- Meat slices at *medium* to *medium-high*. Don't try to reheat large pieces of meat. The outside will cook and toughen before the inside warms.
- Hot dogs, hamburgers, meat loaf and sausage patties covered lightly with wax paper on *high*, but watch very closely.
- Vegetables on *medium-high*. Watch closely.

DEFROSTING MEAT AND POULTRY

When I bought my microwave oven, I thought defrosting meat would be one of its major jobs. It hasn't worked out that way. Unless I give the defrosting constant attention, one end cooks and sizzles while the other remains frozen. I use the microwave to thaw soups and casseroles, but thaw meat and poultry overnight in the refrigerator.

When I get into a desperate pinch, I do defrost meat in the microwave, but I hover over it like an anxious hen. Here are a few rules:

Wrap the food loosely in wax paper and shield quicker-cooking parts with foil (see the note on aluminum foil on p. 365). Microwave on low for 5 to 10 minutes. Let it stand for the same amount of time. Check. If it's still frozen, rearrange or turn it. Zap it for a shorter time—maybe 4 to 5 minutes. Let it stand that amount of time. Check again. Continue this way, decreasing defrosting time until the meat is *almost* thawed. Then exhale and let the meat finish its last few minutes of defrosting at room temperature.

❧ USING THE MICROWAVE TO MAKE LIFE EASIER ❧

Crisp:
  Stale crackers or chips by zapping them on *high* for 45 to 60 seconds.

Defrost:
  Bread.
  Frozen stock, egg whites, pie dough.

Dry:
  Fresh herbs. Place between paper towels. Microwave on *high* for 4 minutes or until dried. Let stand 10 minutes. Store in a covered jar.
  Orange peel. See p. 244.

Extract:
  More juice and flavor from lemons, oranges, limes, grapefruit. Warm on *high* for 15 seconds and let stand 3 minutes before squeezing.

Freshen:
  Brewed coffee leftovers (keep them in the fridge) by reheating a cup at a time for ½ to 2 minutes on *high*.

Heat:
  Baby food in the jar. Remove the top and warm on *high* for 15 to 20 seconds.
  Brandy and liqueurs for flaming foods on *high* for 15 seconds. Ignite and pour over food.
  Brandy in the snifter, as gastronomes do, to bring out its flavor: on high for 10 seconds in lead crystal; for 15 seconds in glass.
  Crepes. Wrap 1 to 12 in a cloth towel or napkin. Heat on *high* for 1 to 2 minutes. Keep covered so they remain soft.
  Plates. Moisten 4 paper towels and place between microwave-safe plates. Microwave 4 plates on *high* for 2 to 3 minutes.
  Tortillas. See Crepes.

Using the Microwave to Make Life Easier

Liquify:
Honey that's gone to sugar. Heat on *high* for 30 to 45 seconds.

Loosen peels:
On fresh peaches, tomatoes. Heat on high 10 to 30 seconds, depending on the fruit. Let stand for 10 minutes and peel.

Melt:
Butter. Place in glass measuring cup. Zap on *high*: 15 seconds for 2 tablespoons; 30 seconds for ¼ cup.
Chocolate squares or chips at *medium* for 1 to 3 minutes.

Plump:
Dried fruits. Cover with water or other liquid. Heat on *high* for 5 to 6 minutes. Let stand 5 minutes.

Pre-cook:
Meat and poultry to be barbecued to speed cooking and keep pieces from drying out on the grill. Cook for half the cooking time in microwave instructions (or figure about 3 minutes per pound on *high*). Sear and finish cooking on the grill. This is especially useful if you're using a barbecue sauce with a high sugar content, which burns easily.

Remove:
Stuck-on freezer paper from frozen packages. Heat on *high* for 15 seconds. Let stand 2 to 3 minutes.

Scald:
Milk. Heat on *high* for 1½ to 2½ minutes per cup.

Separate:
Cold bacon slices. Warm the package on *high* for 15 to 20 seconds. Let stand 3 to 5 minutes.

Serve:
Dinner to family members at different times by dishing up the plates, covering them and letting each microwave his or her own.
Perfumed hot towels after a meal of ribs or barbecued chicken. Heat rolled, dampened wash cloths, scented with a few drops of after-shave, on *high* for 1 to 2 minutes until steamy hot.

Using the Microwave to Make Life Easier

Soften:

Brown sugar. Put it in a microwave safe container with a slice of bread or apple. Cover. Heat on *high* for 30 to 45 seconds.

Butter or margarine, but *carefully* or you'll have liquid. Open the wrapper. Heat on *medium* or lower for 15 seconds. Repeat in 5 second increments until softened.

Cream cheese: For mixing with other ingredients, place on a plate (tightly covered) and heat 3 ounces on high for 30 seconds, 8 ounces for one minute. To serve at room temperature, soften 3 ounces on high for 5 to 15 seconds, 8 ounces on high for 20 to 30 seconds.

Gelatin that set too soon on *medium* so you can fold solids into it. For a recipe using 2 cups of liquid, reheat for 1 to 1½ minutes; for a 4-cup recipe, reheat for 1 to 2 minutes.

Marshmallows and caramels, to mix with other ingredients, on *high* for 60 seconds.

Ice cream that's too hard to scoop. Warm it unopened as follows:

Package Size	Power	Time
Pint	Medium	15 to 30 secs
Quart	Medium	30 to 45 secs
Half-gallon	High	10 secs *or*
	Medium	30 secs

(Let the half-gallon stand for 2 to 3 minutes and if necessary reheat for 5 seconds more.)

Toast:

Nuts or seeds. Place shelled nuts in single layer on a plate. Heat on *high* for 3 to 6 minutes per cupful. Stir. Repeat until toasted to taste—up to 10 minutes.

Warm:

Fruits like apples to eating temperature.

Pie slices one at a time for 15 seconds on *high*.

Syrup and honey for serving in a pitcher on *high* for 30 to 45 seconds.

— RULE OF THUMB —

Don't Microwave Everything

The microwave oven doesn't give a dry heat, so don't use it for:

Roasts. They won't cook evenly (see right) and their outsides won't brown and crisp.

Steaks. They will steam, turn greyish and taste boring.

Standard cake and pie recipes that aren't formulated for microwave. They won't work right—cakes will be pale and have funny layers in them; pies will have cooked filling and raw crust because the microwaves make a bee line for the moist filling and ignore the crust.

Breaded or batter-coated things that haven't been made especially for microwaving. They won't crisp.

Standard yeast bread recipes. Yeast breads get wet and spongy.

A FEW USEFUL "DON'TS"

After all those nifty "do's", here are a few important "don'ts."

Don't microwave meats on the bone like drumsticks and chops **or large cuts of meat** like chuck roasts and briskets. Bones don't absorb much microwave heat, so meat near the bone is often still raw when the outside meat is cooked. Microwaves cook large pieces of meat unevenly, leaving raw patches in roasts. Harmful bacteria like salmonella can stay alive and vigorous in the undercooked spots.

Don't cook in deep fat. You risk causing a fire or burning yourself when you deal with the boiling-hot fat.

Don't use recycled paper products like towels, plates, or brown bags. Some recycled paper has metal flecks which make sparks that can ignite the paper—as my husband discovered when an innocent looking paper towel turned into a fireball.

Don't cook eggs in their shells. The little pocket of air inside the shell will expand and explode your egg into a mess. In fact, **anything cooked in the skin** can explode if no vent is provided (steam from the moisture expands). So prick unskinned fruits and vegetables (like potatoes)—and the membranes of whole egg yolks too! The same principle applies when you cook in a plastic bag. Don't force the steam to blast its way out.

Equipment

Should I Buy That Set of Copper Pots and Pans, Do I Need Both a Food Processor and a Blender, and What Kind of Knife Will Cut Bones?

Of course you *can* turn out a good meal in beat-up pots on a cranky stove. The best cook I ever knew was a Yugoslav friend in Zambia. She had about 4 battered pots. Her hand-operated eggbeater was missing one of the beaters and she propped her oven door shut with a chair. Under these conditions Dana turned out gossamer puff pastry, fluffy cakes, and Hollandaise that was buttery velvet. It's the old truism: the equipment doesn't cook, the cook does.

So never think you can't make a soufflé because you don't have a soufflé dish. Or that you *must* beat egg whites in a copper bowl, or that you *can't* simmer something slowly without a heavy bottomed pan—you can, for example, set a thin pan on a skillet to achieve a heavy bottom. If you know the result you want, you can usually figure out a way to achieve it no matter what equipment sits on your shelf.

That being said, cooking is infinitely easier and more fun when you have the right tools. Here is some information to make it easier to choose kitchen equipment.

Quick Hint

For stove-top cooking, use a slightly larger pot than necessary if you'll be doing a lot of stirring. This avoids spills and boilovers and lets you stir more thoroughly.

POTS AND PANS

It's usually not a good idea to buy a matched set: most include pieces you'll never use. (However, check the price. I once bought a set that included a huge pot I didn't want because the price of the set was less than if I had bought the pieces I wanted separately!)

Pieces of a set all have the same construction and material. You don't necessarily want that. Different constructions and materials do different things. For slow cooking you want heavy bottoms and materials that hold the heat, whereas for delicate, quickly cooked foods, thin-bottomed pans and materials that change temperature quickly are best. For cooking in water—boiling pasta, making stock, poaching fish—thickness and heat conduction don't matter. Any pot will do if the size is right.

When you buy cookie sheets, make sure they are the right size for your oven. If they're too big, they don't allow the air to circulate.

Handles

Heavy handles make pans tippy. Wood handles are lightweight and stay cool, but they can't go in the oven unless wrapped in several thicknesses of aluminum foil.

Covers

You need two kinds of covers for two purposes.

Domed covers hold in steam and make a tight seal— some actually create a vacuum seal. If you can't get a sealed lid off, run a little lukewarm water over it or return the pan to the heat for a moment.

Flat covers let a little steam escape. You can set them askew to allow extra evaporation.

Materials

Aluminum heats fast, distributes heat evenly, and responds quickly to temperature change. It's inexpensive, easy to clean and maintain, and excellent for baking.

Unclad, untreated aluminum can discolor foods like white sauces and egg whites if you stir or whisk vigorously with a metal utensil, and can give acid foods like wine and tomatoes an off taste. Heavy, commercial-weight aluminum is ideal.

Treated aluminum (like Calphalon) is even better but expensive. It is non-reactive, meaning that it isn't bothered by acids like vinegar, and resists sticking. To fry without fat, however, you have to use a cooking spray.

Cast iron heats slowly, holds heat better than most materials, diffuses heat well at very low temperatures, and is cheap. It's not good for high-heat cooking like stir-frying because it doesn't cool down quickly and you have to get the food out the instant it is done to prevent further cooking. It's also heavy to handle. Some claim it discolors acid foods, but that doesn't seem to be a problem with well seasoned iron. (All cast iron must be seasoned. See box p. 374.) Health advantage: people who want to boost their iron intake cook in cast iron because some of the iron leaches out into the food.

Clad combinations offer the best of two worlds: easily maintained stainless steel joined to copper or aluminum bottoms for heat conduction. To be effective, the bottom must be at least⅛" thick. It's expensive, but lasts a lifetime, which is more than you can say for your running shoes.

Copper is the best heat conductor. Copper pans must be tin-lined because copper reacts with egg yolks and with acids like wine and tomato. Copper is expensive, needs constant polishing, and dents easily. The lining is easily scratched.

Enameled iron has all the advantages of cast iron (*and* you can cook acid foods in it), and one disadvantage: it doesn't brown food well. Always brown first in aluminum or cast iron, then transfer to the enameled pot. It is rather expensive and can scratch or chip if dropped, and crack if exposed to intense heat or sudden temperature change. Treated with consideration and respect, it lasts forever.

How To Season Cast Iron

Rub cast iron pans with oil. Place in a 350° oven for 2 hours. Cool to room temperature. You can wash the pan *briefly* with a little soapy water. Rinse and dry with a towel—never air dry.

Non-Stick Pans

Non-stick surfaces like Teflon or Silverstone are not porous. An egg will slide right off. They are excellent for omelets, crepes, low-fat frying and baking. Metal or sharp utensils will scratch them.

For baking, even non-stick pans must be greased unless the recipe says otherwise.

Stainless steel offers poor heat conduction: it heats slowly, distributes heat unevenly and cools down slowly. Food tends to scorch. Stainless steel is good for small pots, for pans used to boil, pan-fry or deep-fry, and is excellent for mixing bowls. It's inexpensive, a dream to keep clean and unlikely to warp.

Glass, earthenware, porcelain and ceramic are for oven cooking. They can't take sudden temperature changes; never set a hot dish on a cold surface. *Glass* heats slowly, then holds the heat determinedly, so lower oven temperature by 25° when using it. *Earthenware* spreads heat unevenly. In an oven hotter than 350°, you will have hot spots that burn food.

Don't use these materials on the stove top. They will crack or explode. Some newly marketed materials are safe and are marked as such.

Types of Pans

Heavy, flat-bottomed pans and Dutch ovens heat and cool slowly, hold a steady, even heat and meet burner surfaces evenly (important for electric ranges). Use them for sauces that contain flour or have to cook a long time in order to reduce, and for long, slow, stove-top cooking (braising and stewing).

Materials: Cast iron, enameled cast iron, treated aluminum, clad combinations.

Light thin-bottomed pans heat and cool quickly, helping you to avoid overcooking. Use them for delicate egg dishes and for sauces that don't have a flour base.

Materials: Lined copper, treated aluminum, clad combinations.

Frying pans must be able to hold a steady, high heat. Use them for frying and for cooking where quick cool-down is not important. **Chicken fryers,** big, deep, covered skillets, are the American equivalent of the French *sauteuse.* Use them for stews and braises, and for cooking large recipes of meat or chicken on top of the stove.

Materials: Heavy, commercial-weight aluminum (preferably treated), heavy stainless steel, uncoated cast iron.

Lightweight bakeware must absorb a lot of heat quickly in order to produce baked goods that are dry and crusty outside, moist and soft inside. Use it for cakes, pastries and sturdy cookies.
Material: Dull-finish aluminum is best.

Heavy bakeware won't buckle in high heat. Shiny metal doesn't absorb heat as well as dark, dull-finish metal, so it doesn't get as hot and delicate cookies won't burn. Use for delicate cookies.
Material: Shiny metal.

Insulated cookie sheets sandwich air between two metal layers, protecting delicate cookie bottoms from burning.
Material: Bright-finish aluminum.

Pie plates with dark or dull-finish metal get hotter and give the best crust. Glass lets you see how the bottom crust is browning.
Materials: Dull-finish aluminum, glass. Avoid shiny pans.

Casserole dishes are used for deep-dish pies, casseroles, and other foods whose insides must cook thoroughly and evenly before the outside gets too brown. These should heat up slowly and then hold the heat tenaciously.
Materials: Glass and earthenware.

Maybe Your Pan Was

...Too Square

Food baked in a round dish browns more evenly. Ever notice how the corners of a square cake are always darker than the edges or center?

...Too High

The sides of a container should be just high enough to hold the contents after rising. Sides that are too high shield food from the heat and prevent browning. They also hold in moisture. Meats and chickens roasted in high-sided pans will steam, not roast.

USING KITCHEN EQUIPMENT

Blender
Blenders are good for very wet or very dry ingredients. They are *better* than the processor for making velvety soups and grinding spices.

Food Processor Alternatives

I still chop small amounts by hand—or by fist, using a nifty little whacking gadget made by Zlyss. You set it over the food to be chopped and punch a spring handle which rotates the blade with each chop.

To grate or cut a small amount into julienne I use a salad shredder called Mouli Julienne. It stands on 3 legs and has a choice of disks offering a range of small to large cutting holes, which you turn around with a handle like a food mill. A little more muscle power, but quick cleanup.

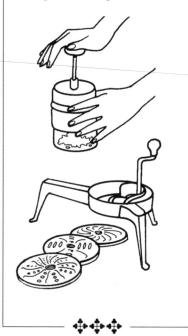

Deep Fryer

Although it's easy to deep-fry using a saucepan, a mesh skimmer and a thermometer, electric deep fryers are useful because they hold a steady temperature. Useful if you do a lot of frying.

Food Processor

I love my food processor, but I don't use it the way I thought I would because it is pesky to clean. (See the box for some of my favorite alternatives.)

Why then the processor? Because it chops, slices and shreds and juliennes large amounts in minutes. I use it weekly to knead bread. I zap up wonderful biscuits in it, and turn out tender, flaky pie dough in 3 minutes. I purée in the processor when I don't mind a slightly granular result, but I still prefer the blender for velvety soups. (To get a smooth purée in the processor, let it run and run—two minutes isn't too long.) I grind meat in the processor for Greek, Middle-Eastern and Indian dishes because it effortlessly produces the desired pasty consistency. And for fun and fussy things like quenelles you can't beat it.

Here are a few tips on using the processor:

Mincing small things like *garlic, shallots, ginger, hot peppers:* Put the metal blade in a *dry* bowl. Turn on the machine, drop the pieces through the tube, and keep the blade whirling until all the tiny pieces are stuck to the sides of the bowl.

To chop or mince bigger things like *onions*, don't overload the work bowl. A standard bowl holds about 2 cups of ingredients at a time. Cut pieces roughly 1" square. Don't over-process.

The first time I chopped onions, I turned on the machine and watched it blast them to a watery sog in 10 seconds. I quickly learned that you control chopping by pulsing, or turning the motor on and off. Most machines now have a pulse control button.

To pulse: put the cut-up food in the work bowl, run the motor for half a second, stop the motor and wait a second while the food falls to the bottom of the bowl. Give it another half-second whirl. Continue until the food is chopped the way you want it.

To pulverize (finely grate) *cheese* and *citrus peel*, run the motor continuously, don't pulse. Pulverize citrus peel with a little sugar from the recipe and the peel won't clump.

To get long slices or shreds, lay the food down in the feed tube; to get short ones, stand the pieces up, filling the tube tightly so they stay erect. When you slice round things like potatoes, cut a bit off the bottom so they don't roll. Hard cheeses like Parmesan should be at room temperature for good shredding. Watch the amount of pressure you apply. Generally, firm foods need firm pressure and soft foods need light or medium pressure. Use light pressure on all cheeses.

To knead dough, see p. 307.

If the motor overheats, a food processor may stop automatically. Don't be alarmed. Once it cools, it will carry on.

Mixer

Good for mixing pastry, for whipping cream and egg whites. With attachments it grinds meat and kneads dough.

Knives

Blades can be high-carbon steel, stainless steel, or a mix of the two. The mix is best. High-carbon takes a sharp edge but rusts, can stain food, and loses its edge quickly. Stainless steel won't rust or stain food, but doesn't take a good edge. High-carbon stainless won't rust or stain, sharpens well and can be reground. It's expensive, but you'll have it forever so it's by far the best buy.

Buy knives with flat-ground edges; they can be sharpened, honed and reground. Hollow-ground edges can't be reground and machine-ground edges have no strength. Serrated edges are ideal for slicing easily crushed foods.

Mini-Choppers

I grate small amounts of Parmesan cheese and grind hard spices in a little electic mini-chopper that holds less than ¼ cup. (Parmesan must first be in ¼" cubes and all chopping must be done with a very light touch).

Sometimes I mini-chop garlic and parsley—but it's not much faster than a few quick knife strokes and there's more to clean, so I only do it to vary the routine.

Types of Knives

Asian knife (Chinese cleaver): Has a wide, rectangular blade like an American cleaver and a ranges of sizes. The #1 is a heavy, bone-whacking cleaver. The most useful sizes are medium-weight (#3 and #4). It has all the uses of the chef's knife plus a wooden handle whose butt end can be used to pound peppercorns and the like.

Boning knife: Has a sturdy handle and a narrow, curved 5" to 7" blade of varying degrees of stiffness. The flexible blade cuts easily around small bones and is probably the one you would use most.

Chef's knife: Has a broad, stiff, slightly curved blade. The blade runs anywhere from 6" to 13" long and up to 3" wide. I find the 6" and 9" blades the handiest sizes. This and the Asian knife are ideal for chopping, slicing, dicing and mincing. Use the broad side to crush garlic and ginger and to flatten chicken breasts, also to scoop up whatever you have cut and ferry it to bowl or pan.

Cleaver: Technically not a knife because it doesn't cut, but breaks bones by impact. You can also use it to chop meats and vegetables coarsely. To be useful, a cleaver must be big and have plenty of weight.

Paring knife: A small chef's knife with a 2" to 5" blade. Use it for peeling and slicing fruits and vegetables and chopping small amounts of herbs and such.

Serrated knife: Blade should be of stainless steel and long enough to slice bread. Use for bread and soft, delicate foods like tomatoes.

Utility knife: A medium-size paring knife. Many cooks consider it a compromise that doesn't do anything well.

Using an Asian or Chef's Knife:

To slice, (for making thin slices and shreds) hold the item flat with the fingertips of one hand. Hold the knife in the other hand, blade parallel to cutting surface. Cut horizontally between the cutting surface and your fingers, moving slowly, feeling the movement of the blade with your fingertips.

To crush, make sure your cutting board is at the edge of the counter so you won't bang your fingers. Cover the item with a piece of plastic wrap or wax paper, place the flat side of the blade over it and whack the blade with your fist.

To tenderize: The Asian knife is best for this. Hold the knife with the cutting edge up and pound the meat with the blunt side, making parallel and crisscross lines.

Using a Chef's Knife:

To chop, grasp the handle with one hand, rest the fingertips of the other hand lightly on the spine of the blade at the pointed end, and rock the blade over whatever you are cutting.

To slice, grasp the handle near the blade with your thumb on the side of the blade to steady it. Hold what you're cutting with your fingers, tips curled under and away from the blade so that it can be guided by the knuckle of your middle finger. Keep the cutting edge slightly angled away from your knuckles.

Using a Cleaver

Place thumb and index finger against either side of the blade and wrap your remaining fingers around the handle. This gives you a sure grip.

Using Paring or Utility Knives

Grasp the handle near the blade, your thumb resting on the side of the blade near you, your index finger curved against the opposite side, and the heel of your hand resting on top of the handle. This way your hand can swivel from the wrist, and you control both tip and edge of the blade.

Protect Your Knife's Sharp Edge.

Give it a couple of quick passes over a sharpening steel every time you put it away and you'll always have a sharp knife. Never scrape food off a cutting board with the sharp edge; you'll dull it fast. Use the back of the blade instead.

Chopping Techniques

Dicing

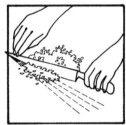
Mincing

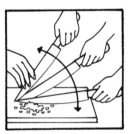
Chopping

Using Other Equipment

Bulb baster: Use this syringe to suck up liquid from the roasting pan and release it over the meat.

Colander: To drain food and wash vegetables under running water. Invert it over the skillet when you fry, to control spatters.

Custard cups or small soufflé cups: In addition to their use as baking dishes, they're handy for holding small amounts of ingredients measured out for a recipe.

Egg slicer: Chop eggs by turning the sliced egg crosswise and slicing again. Also good for slicing mushrooms and cooked beets.

Food mill: Purées things with small seeds (like raspberries and tomatoes) better than a processor because it strains out the seeds instead of grinding them into the purée. A food mill won't make food watery or gluey; the processor sometimes does.

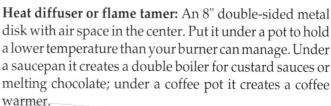

Heat diffuser or flame tamer: An 8" double-sided metal disk with air space in the center. Put it under a pot to hold a lower temperature than your burner can manage. Under a saucepan it creates a double boiler for custard sauces or melting chocolate; under a coffee pot it creates a coffee warmer.

Jelly roll pan: Use it for rolled cakes and soufflés, as an in-a-pinch cookie sheet or to assemble ingredients for cooking in one handy place.

Kitchen scissors have a million uses! Use them to cut bacon, and raw meats for stir-fry; to trim fat from cooked or uncooked meat and fins from fish. They halve Cornish hens (cooked or raw), slash Swedish tea rings or loaf tops before baking, and cut pizza into slices, tortillas into chip-size pieces and pita bread in wedges. They're also handy for trimming crusts off bread slices (for pretty sandwiches), cutting phyllo dough leaves to size, and cutting up canned tomatoes while they're still in the can. Mince fresh herbs and parsley with them, cut dates, marshmallows and dried and candied fruit (dip blades frequently in hot water to prevent sticking) and use them to trim the tops off artichoke leaves before cooking.

Measuring cups: You'll need different cups for wet and dry ingredients. (See p. 55 for the difference.) Large glass measuring cups (2-cup and 4-cup sizes) are good for rapidly measuring large amounts of liquid. They double as mixing bowls that you can pour from.

Mixing bowls: Buy large, medium and small ones, in glass, stainless steel or plastic. You can bake in ovenproof glass ones. Plastic bowls are not good for beating egg whites.

Spoons: Wooden or plastic ones don't scratch non-stick pans. You'll also need a slotted spoon to lift food out of its cooking liquid.

Parchment paper is very useful in the kitchen. Buy it in sheets or rolls at kitchenware and fancier grocery stores. It is far better than wax paper for lining cake pans and cookie sheets because it doesn't need greasing, will stand high temperatures without discoloring or scorching, and is easy to cut and fit in the pans. Sugary baked foods like meringues lift off parchment easily.

   To cut parchment for cake pans, set the pan on the paper, bottom down, and draw around it. To line several layer pans, fold the paper into layers and cut them all at once. Always grease the pan first so the paper adheres. When you've baked cookies on parchment, you can slide the whole thing onto the rack for cooling.

Pastry blender: Besides using it to blend shortening or butter into flour, use it to mash soft foods like avocadoes and bananas, or heavy mixtures like liver pâté or cream cheese which are too stiff for the blender or processor to handle easily.

Pepper mill: Buy one and throw away your ready-ground pepper. Wooden mills don't break, and glass or clear plastic mills show you when to refill. Decide which you like.

Mortar and Pestle

Salad spinner: If you get a covered one you can store greens in it for 1 or 2 days.

Scale: I find a scale is a must. I use it daily to weigh out 4-ounce portions of spaghetti, to check the size of a roast whose wrapper label is gone, measure 8 ounces of mushrooms, or establish the weight of something to decide how long to microwave it. It's much faster to weigh out flour for baking than to measure cup by cup. (A cup of flour weighs 4 ounces.)

Get a scale that measures up to 5 or 10 pounds in increments no larger than ½ ounce and one that measures in both pounds and kilos. It should have a measuring tray that holds a quantity of liquid or dry ingredients. You should be able to reset the scale at zero *after* placing an empty tray or bowl on it so you are weighing only what is *in* the tray or bowl. The reset also allows you to measure 4 ounces of an ingredient, return it to zero, and measure in 5 ounces of a second ingredient without having to remove the first one.

When I make a recipe for the first time I measure each dry ingredient by cup onto a piece of wax paper on my scale and note the weight on the recipe. Next time I make it, instead of digging out cups, filling them, then levelling off over box/bag/canister, I heap each ingredient on the scale until the pointer hits the right weight, and dump it in the bowl. No pain, no strain.

Sieves: You need at least two: one with coarse mesh and one with fine. There are times when you have to strain several times; use the coarse one first, then the fine.

Skimmers: Use to lift food from deep fat or boiling water.

Spatulas: Rubber ones fold in ingredients and scrape out bowls. You'll also need a metal one, long, narrow and flexible. They're good for removing cookies from the baking sheet.

Swivel-blade parer: To peel vegetables and fruits, cut lemon peel for drinks, make chocolate curls. Get one with

Chinese Skimmer

a carbon blade, which cuts best. It will rust, but parers are inexpensive to replace.

Thermometers: They make the cook's life a lot easier. There are thermometers for deep fat, for sugar syrups, and for taking the temperature of foods to know when they are done.

Springform pan

The meat thermometers that stay in the roast during cooking create a nifty path for juices to escape out of. If you still have one, consider replacing it with an instant-read thermometer that you pop into the food for a few seconds and remove. Of course, it also makes a hole, but one that is small and quickly sealed. Another advantage of this type of thermometer is that you can test-probe foods at more than one place.

Timer: The only way to make sure you don't overcook the sauce or roast. Always use it when finishing up dinner for guests so you don't get engrossed in conversation while dinner burns.

Tongs: To lift hot food from water, skillet or oven, and to turn meats without puncturing.

Whisks: The longer, more flexible ones are for thin sauces like Hollandaise which you beat a long time; the shorter, stiffer ones for thicker sauces like Béchamel (white sauce).

Zester: A little tool with 5 small holes at the squared-off blade end. You pull it across citrus rinds and threads of peel come out. You then chop them. Get one with a stripper hole to make lemon peel strips for drinks.

Tools from Around the House

Dental floss: Keep unwaxed floss in the kitchen. Use it with a sawing motion to cut chiffon or angel food cakes and to cut cakes through their middles into layers; to cut cheesecake and semi-soft cheese like feta. Run it under cookies or pastry that sticks to the baking sheet. Truss poultry with it.

Vegetable Steamer

Large paper clips: Use to mark the page in the recipe book you're using.

Hands, The Ultimate Tool

For some things, hands are your best tool. Use them to:

- Scoop, sprinkle, knead, pat out, shape, funnel, tear or pound.

- Mix, beat and fold batters to get a feel for texture and consistency, as James Beard's students did.

- Toss salad, for evenly coated greens and less flying lettuce.

- Separate eggs—break the shell, slide the egg into your palm, let white run between your fingers. No sharp, yolk-cutting edges.

- Poke and prod doughs, meats and cake tops to judge their stage of readiness.

- Check temperature of soup, sauce and custard.

Ruler: To check pan sizes, diameters of rolled crusts and cookies, width of phyllo dough strips and bar cookies, and thickness of fish and steaks to figure broiling time.

Toothbrush: Keep one in the kitchen for cleaning things like graters.

Tweezers: To pull bones out of fish fillets. Always run your fingers over fillets. Many fish sellers just cut across the bones when they fillet fish, leaving the stubs in place.

EQUIPMENT CHECKLIST

You don't need everything in this list. Consider the way you cook before you buy. If you don't bake much, ignore the cookie sheets and cake pans. If you cook for a big family or entertain a lot, get all the sizes of pans and skillets. If your family is small and you prefer intimate dinners, small and medium pots and pans are all you need. Build up slowly. Don't invest in an expensive kitchen machine until you are sure you will use it more than once a year.

Pots and Pans

Cake pans
    8" round
    9" round
    8" or 9" square
    9" x 12"
Casserole with cover
    (2- quart)
Cookie sheets
Custard cups or small
    soufflé cups
Double boiler (See p. 386.)
Jelly roll pan
Loaf pans
    9" x 5" x 3"
    8½" x 4½" x 2½"
Muffin tins

Pie pans
    8"
    9"
Roasting pans
    Buy 2 sizes to fit your needs, for holding anything from a Cornish game hen to a turkey.
Saucepans
    Large (3-quart)
    Medium (2-quart)
    Small (1-quart)
Shallow baking dishes

Pots and Pans continued

Skillets
  Large (12")
  Medium (10")
  Small (8")

Soufflé dish (2-quart)
Springform pan
Stock pot
Tube pan

Appliances

Blender
Coffee grinder
Coffee maker
Deep fryer
Food processor
Juicer
Microwave oven

Mixers:
  Hand-held
  Counter-top
Toaster
Toaster oven
Waffle iron

Knives

Carving knife
Chef's knife, 6" to 9" blade
Paring knife

Serrated bread knife
Sharpening steel

Other Equipment

Basting brush
Bulb baster
Colander
Cookie cutters
Cutting board
Egg beater
Egg slicer
Fork, two-pronged
Funnels
  Narrow (½") opening
  Wide opening
Grater/shredder
Juicer or reamer
Ladle
Measuring cups for wet
  and dry ingredients
Measuring spoons

Mixing bowls
Nutcracker
Openers
  Bottle opener
  Puncture-type opener
  Corkscrew
  Jar opener
  Rotary can opener
Pancake turner (plastic if
  your pan is nonstick)
Pastry bag
Pastry scraper
Pepper mill
Ring molds
  Large
  Small
Rolling pin

TECHNIQUE

How to Use a Pastry Bag

Slide the tip inside the bag and push it down to the end. You may have to cut the opening a little bigger—that's okay. Twist the bag a few times just above the tip and push the bag against the tip to seal it in place.

Place the bag in a tall jar or measuring cup and fold it down half way to make a cuff that drapes over the sides. Fill the bag no more than ⅔ full or it will be difficult to squeeze.

Unfold the cuff and twist the unfilled bag fabric tightly against the filling to force it down into the tip. Gently twist the top part of the bag and press down. The mixture will squeeze out of the tip.

If you decide to become known for your piping skills, copy the professionals and practice with mashed potatoes. Why not? It's fun to be famous for something.

Light-weight nylon is the best pastry bag material; a 16-inch bag is probably the most useful size. If you use too small a bag the filling will ooze out of the top and you'll have a mess.

Salad shredder
Salad spinner
Scale
Scissors
Sifter (See p. 387.)
Skewers
Skimmer
Spatulas
    Metal
    Rubber
Spoons
    Mixing
    Slotted
Spring-activated hand-
    held chopper

Strainers (sieves)
    Large, coarse mesh
    Medium
    Small, extra fine mesh
Swivel-blade parer
Thermometers:
    Candy/deep-frying
    Meat
    Oven
Tongs
Whisks
Wire cooling rack
Zester

Storage, Cleanup and Convenience

Apron
Canisters, airtight
Kitchen towels, cloth

Potholders—get *thick* ones
Refrigerator and freezer
    containers

❧ SUBSTITUTING EQUIPMENT ❧

Remember I said you didn't have to own everything in the kitchenware store in order to cook well? Here is a list of what some people use for substitutes.

Don't have?	Use
Cookie cutter	A drinking glass.
Double boiler	Most professional cooks don't use a two-piece double boiler. They prefer cooking in a small, heavy pot or ovenproof glass or earthenware bowl set in a skillet containing ½ inch of water. This way the sauce is surrounded by an even heat rather than cooked above the heat. Try it. I like it because you have more control. You can see what the water is doing, lower the heat when it starts to boil, and add to it when it runs low. If the heat is too intense, it's easy to lift out the bowl while you continue whisking.

SUBSTITUTING EQUIPMENT

Don't have?	Use
Egg beater	A whisk. When you are desperate, two forks (held in one hand, tines facing inward) will do the trick, but it will take a bit longer.
Funnel	Just about any paper except a paper towel, rolled into a funnel shape.
Heavy-bottomed pan	When I've been caught in furnished quarters with lousy pans, I set a thin-bottomed pan on a skillet for stove-top use and on a cookie sheet for oven use.
Heavy or insulated cookie sheet	Stack one cookie sheet on another of the same size.
Mortar and pestle	Pound with the bottom of a heavy bottle or heavy-bottomed drinking glass, or crush with the rounded underside of a spoon.
Rolling pin	An empty bottle (like a wine bottle) or a wide dowel rod.
Sifter	A sieve and a wooden spoon to stir flour through. This is all I ever use.
Slow cooker or crock pot	1) A tightly-closed casserole set in a 200° oven for 8 hours, or 2) A heavy, tightly-covered pot on 2 bricks placed over a very low burner to simmer for 8 hours.
Steamer	Set a custard cup, heatproof mug, or empty tuna fish can in a pot. Top it with a heatproof plate containing the food to be steamed. Add boiling water—don't let it touch the plate. Cover and steam.
Strawberry huller	Beer can opener.
Snug-fitting lid	Top the pot with a sheet of foil, then press the cover on.

Keeping Your Kitchen Safe and Clean

How Do I Handle a Grease Fire, Why Is Raw Poultry So Dangerous, and How Long Can I Keep Things at Room Temperature?

This chapter should probably have a sexier title. Safety has no glamour, but neither do bloody fingers, burned wrists or twisted ankles. So stop turning pages and read this section now, while you are still undamaged. It will help keep you that way so you can continue having fun in the kitchen.

Like all exciting pursuits, cooking has its hazards. If you are unwary, it can be dangerous to your health. Here are some precautions good chefs keep constantly in mind.

SHARP THINGS

Store knives carefully. Never leave a knife where you can't see it. A knife in a pan of soapy water is waiting to be grabbed by the blade. Never wash a knife blade with your finger. When you dry a blade, turn the sharp edge away from you. If you drop a knife, jump out of the way. Don't try to catch it!

Be careful when you slice piles of things. The knife can skid off. Cut away from yourself, especially when cutting

—— RESCUE ——

The Oil Caught Fire!

If the fire is in the pan, smack a large lid on it pronto! If the fire has spilled onto the burner, *don't lift the pot!* Clap on the lid and shake lots of salt or baking soda on the fire.

something with a surface that resists like a tomato, or—worst of all—a shiny-topped hard roll. Attack these stubborn surfaces with a serrated knife.

When a glass breaks in a sink filled with water, drain the sink; don't paw around for the glass.

Don't pour cold liquid into hot ovenproof glass dishes or place them on a cold surface or a wet cloth. They will shatter.

HOT THINGS

Don't fill pots or serving dishes too full of hot ingredients. They'll spill and someone will get burned.

Keep pot holders handy for lifting lids. Beware of the wet pot holder or towel. Use one and you'll get a nasty burn.

Speaking of lids, when you lift one, raise the side away from you so you don't get a gust of hot steam in the face.

If your pans don't have wooden handles, buy a couple of those leather sheaths that slide on. I have two hanging next to my stove. It's so easy to forget and grab a hot pan handle.

Keep handles turned toward the back of the stove so you don't bump them and knock the pan over. Get in the habit of doing this if you have small children who might reach up and grab a pot handle and pull its contents down on their heads.

Water and hot oil are a treacherous mix. Keep water away from a grease fire; keep it away from hot grease, period. Always dry food you plan to drop into hot fat so the moisture won't spit up hot grease in your face.

When you flame food, stand back and turn your face away. Warmed alcohol ignites instantly with a plume of fire. Calvados is especially incendiary.

Tiny Growing Things

Probably the most important food safety rule is to avoid giving bacteria cozy places to hatch and grow. Bacteria love food rich in fat and protein, like meat, poultry, fish, eggs and milk. They enjoy temperatures between 40° and 165°. So keep protein-based perishables chilly.

Another growing thing to be aware of is mold. Penicillin may be good for you, but most molds aren't.

All moldy foods should be thrown out because you can't see and remove all the tiny filaments. Never taste moldy food; for that matter, don't smell it—some molds cause respiratory problems. Hard cheese is the one thing you don't have to discard. But be sure you cut off the mold *plus an inch of good cheese.*

Safe Storage

Refrigerate or freeze perishables as soon as possible after you get them home. Place meat, poultry and seafood in the coldest storage area (usually at the lower back).

Freeze meat or poultry you won't use within 5 days; freeze ground meat and seafood after 2 days.

Never leave perishable foods out of the refrigerator for more than two hours.

Thawing

Don't thaw meat, poultry or seafood at room temperature. Bacteria set up shop on the thawed outsides while the insides are still rock hard. Thaw in the refrigerator (see the chart of thawing times on p. 223) or in the microwave using the defrost setting (medium power, usually). Watch the microwave carefully, and turn often so one spot doesn't overheat and cook while the rest is still frozen. See p. 366 for other microwave thawing tips.

Good Work Habits

After you work with raw meat, poultry or seafood wash with soapy water *everything* that touched them: your hands, surfaces (including the sink), utensils, plates, etc.

Fashion in the Kitchen

Wear low heeled shoes—you'll be hefting pots and pans. No bare feet—imagine spattering hot grease on them! Tight slacks can conduct hot spilled liquid directly to your skin. Loose overblouses and dangling sleeves can catch fire when you lean over a burner.

The best apron is a full-length chef's apron with long strings that wrap around your waist. Pull a towel through the strings—you'll use it constantly.

Safety Caution

Never run water into a hot pan or skillet to rinse it out. Cool the pan first by running luke-warm water over the *back* where it won't provoke grease to splat up in your face.

Never return cooked food to any plate or surface that held it uncooked unless you wash the plate or surface first.

Cook meat, poultry, seafood and eggs to the point where bacteria are killed.

Because of the danger of salmonella in eggs, **don't serve foods prepared with raw egg**—homemade mayonnaise, mousses, Caesar dressing, chiffon pies, Christmas egg nog. Since to knock out salmonella, eggs must be cooked to the firm stage—no runny whites *or* yolks—the following foods are risky: eggs sunny-side up, soft-boiled or soft-scrambled; soft custards; French toast with a yummy, squidgy center. But take heart. Scientists are making real progress toward eliminating this problem. While we wait, stick with commercial mayo and eggnog and try the new, safe methods for making mousses and custards. You'll see them in newspapers and magazines.

Never stuff poultry until you are ready to put the bird in the oven and always, always remove the stuffing to a separate container before you refrigerate the leftover roast poultry. Stuffing is bacteria's favorite stamping ground.

If you partially cook a dish in advance, don't stop the initial cooking until the main ingredient (meat, fish or fowl) has reached 160°. Then chill quickly (set the pan in cold water) and refrigerate until you are ready to continue cooking.

Reheat leftovers thoroughly (to at least 165°). Make sure gravies and soups boil for an entire minute before you serve them.

If you cook food from the frozen state, allow 1½ times the normal cooking time to ensure that the center gets cooked. Refrigerate all cooked food you won't eat immediately—stocks, casseroles, etc. First cool it quickly in a sink filled with ice water, so the fridge or freezer won't have to work overtime.

BUMPS AND SPILLS

Wipe up spills on the floor immediately so you don't slip.

Close doors and drawers. How often have you barked your shins on the opened door of the dishwasher or a low drawer? An open upper cupboard door can give your head a nasty whack, too.

CLEAN-UP TIPS

Clean up as you go. A tidy kitchen is so much easier to work in. When pans pile up in the sink and counter surfaces disappear, you can feel as out of control as the kitchen looks. That's why professionals wash up as they go.

One cook I admire marches to the sink still gripping the pot she just emptied and scrubs it there and then. Done so soon, skillets need no detergent, just hot water, a good scrub, and a wipe-down with paper towels. I keep a soapy sponge in the sink—I love the thick ones covered with nylon mesh—and wash just about everything as I use it, either drying it immediately or setting it to drain.

Or, before you start a cooking project, fill a sink (if yours is a double) or a plastic basin with hot, sudsy water so dirty utensils have a place to soak the minute you're finished with them. Rinse and put things away at intervals so the pile doesn't get discouragingly large. This is a great nerve soother.

Quick Hint

Deep-frying generates a lot of spattering. Put a couple layers of newspaper on the floor in front of the stove before you begin. It will save mopping up afterwards and eliminate tracking grease around or, heaven forbid, slipping.

A Nifty Spoon Holder

I glued a small square of heavy metal—part of some dead gadget—to the bottom of a clean, empty soup can, and I keep it next to the stove to hold drippy stirring spoons. It keeps the counter clean and is more practical than the porcelain rests spoons can bounce out of.

The Pantry

What Condiments Should I Have, What Do I Need to Bake a Cake at a Moment's Notice, and What's in a Well Stocked Bar?

When I was starting out in the kitchen, I was fascinated by what seasoned cooks kept in their pantries. The idea of a cupboard of staples that could meet any recipe's requirements, that could handle unexpected guests with aplomb—even elegance—enchanted me. It still does. There is something deliciously soothing in the knowledge that you are prepared to meet whatever comes along.

Here is what you might find in the pantry of a kitchen prepared to handle most everyday needs. Look through the list and revise to suit your tastes, the way you live, and your storage space.

Remember that your freezer can extend your pantry space. Keep extra breads and bread crumbs there. That's also the place to store flour made from whole grains (the germ and bran turn rancid at room temperature). My freezer always has a supply of homemade things: crepes, tomato sauce, stock in 2-tablespoon and 1-cup amounts, fresh lemon juice and tomato paste in 1-tablespoon amounts, spaghetti sauce, and a couple hearty soups and casseroles.

Unexpected Guests?

If unexpected guests descend, your pantry can be a life saver.

For a quick antipasto:
Marinated artichokes and mushrooms
Roasted red peppers
A variety of olives
Tuna, sardines, anchovies
Garbanzo beans, drained, with Italian dressing

Fast first courses:
Shrimp or crab in seasoned mayonnaise
Same heaped in canned artichoke bottoms
Caviar with toast, sour cream and minced onion

BAKING NEEDS

Baking powder
Baking soda
Chocolate: bits, semi-sweet, unsweetened, unsweetened cocoa powder
Coconut
Condensed and evaporated milk
Corn syrup
Cornmeal

Cornstarch
Extracts: almond, vanilla
Flour: all-purpose, cake, self-rising, whole wheat
Honey
Phyllo or strudel dough
Pie shells
Pizza bases
Puff pastry shells
Yeast

BEVERAGES

Coffee: beans, instant coffee powder
Frozen lemonade concentrate

Frozen orange juice concentrate
Tea

BREADS, CEREALS, GRAINS AND PASTA

Biscuits
Bread: French, Italian, pita, rolls, sourdough, whole wheat
Bread crumbs
Cereals: farina, grits, oatmeal
Crackers

Grains: barley, couscous
Pasta and noodles: spaghetti, fettuccine, egg noodles, tube pastas
Rice: brown, white
Tortillas: corn, flour

CONDIMENTS

Catsup
Chili Sauce
Chinese sauces: chili oil, hoisin, plum, soy
Dijon mustard
Horseradish
Hot pepper sauce
Mayonnaise
Salad dressing
Steak sauce
Worcestershire sauce

COOKING NEEDS

Anchovies or anchovy paste
Clam juice
Gravies: beef, mushroom
Green chiles
Maple syrup
Molasses
Nuts: almonds, hazelnuts (filberts), pecans, peanuts, pine nuts, pistachios, walnuts
Oil: olive, peanut, vegetable
Olives: green, black, Kalamata
Peanut butter
Pesto (in the freezer)
Solid vegetable shortening
Spaghetti sauce
Stock: canned beef bouillon and chicken broth, instant bouillon granules or cubes
Sugar: brown, granulated, powdered
Tomato paste
Tomato sauce
Vinegar: cider, raspberry, red wine, tarragon, white, white wine
Unflavored gelatin

DAIRY PRODUCTS

Butter
Cheese: Cheddar, cream, Monterey Jack, mozzarella, Parmesan, Romano, Swiss
Cream
Eggs
Egg substitutes
Ice cream
Milk: fresh, extended-life (shelf-stable)
Sour cream
Yogurt

Unexpected Guests?

If unexpected guests descend, your pantry can be a life saver.

Canned soups:
Black bean with sherry
Chicken broth with soy sauce, ginger and green onions
Cream of potato with half and half and sherry
French onion, topped with bread rounds and cheese and broiled.

Main dishes:
Pasta with butter or olive oil, herbs and Parmesan
Antipasto with cold meat and cheese added
Shrimp, crab or tuna, creamed or in a soufflé or quiche

— *Recipe* —

Pasta with Tuna in Roasted Pepper Sauce

This orange-gold sauce has the seductive flavors of the garlicky Mediterranean rouille sauce. A quick supper dish and one of my standbys for unexpected guests.

In a food processor or blender, place a 7-oz jar roasted red peppers and their liquid, 2 flat anchovies, 2 large cloves garlic, 2 teaspoons dried oregano, ¼ teaspoon salt, ½ teaspoon pepper, 1 teaspoon sugar. Process until smooth. Add ¼ cup olive oil and process just to blend. Scrape into a bowl. Add a 7-oz can tuna, drained and flaked, 1 tablespoon drained capers and hot red pepper flakes to taste. Cook 1 lb. pasta, drain and immediately toss with the sauce. Serve on *hot* plates. Serves 4

FRUIT

Canned:
 Your family's favorites plus mandarin oranges, Hawaiian fruit, guava shells and mango.

Dried:
 Dates
 Raisins

HERBS AND SPICES

See Buying and Using Herbs and Spices, p. 229. Note the starred items and choose your favorites.

JAMS, JELLIES, PRESERVES

Apricot (for baking)
Red currant (for sauces and gravies)
Your favorites.

MEAT

(You can keep these in the freezer.)
Bacon
Salt pork

SEAFOOD

Clams   Sardines
Crabmeat   Tuna
Salmon

SOUP

Canned chicken broth, if you don't make your own.
Your favorite canned or frozen varieties.

Cream of celery and cream of mushroom soups for emergency sauces.

Vegetables, Beans and Legumes

Artichoke hearts
Bamboo shoots
Beans and legumes:
cannellini (white kidney beans), garbanzo beans (chick peas), kidney beans, lentils, navy or pea beans
Bell peppers, chopped and frozen in bags
Broccoli
Corn: cream-style, whole kernel
Hearts of palm
Lima beans
Peas
Spinach
String beans, green and yellow
Tomatoes (Italian)
Water chestnuts

Stocking the Bar

Soft drinks and mixers:
Club soda
Cola and diet cola
Ginger ale
Juice
Mineral water
Non-alcoholic beer
Tonic
Alcoholic Drinks:
Beer and light beer
Bourbon
Brandy
Campari
Canadian blended whiskey
Champagne
Gin
Liqueurs, especially Crème de Menthe and Cointreau
Madeira
Port, white and ruby
Rum, light and dark
Sherry, sweet and dry
Scotch
Tequila
Vermouth, sweet and dry
Vodka
White Dubonnet or Lillet
Wine, white and red

Unexpected Guests?

For dessert, your freezer might have ice cream, sherbet, meringues, cake, brownies, pie or frozen fruit.
Desserts:
Brownies with mocha ice cream and caramel sauce
Hot apple pie with Cheddar
Pumpkin pie with ginger whipped cream
Ice cream topped with liqueur and puréed berries
Toasted pound cake with ice cream
Puréed rasberries on barely thawed peaches

Entertaining

How Soon Should I Start Cooking for a Party, How Many Hors D'Oeuvres Should I Make, and What's the Easiest Way to Serve a Crowd?

The sort of entertaining most of us do is uncomplicated and relaxed. You don't need much advice for that, although a few hints are always welcome.

However, the time always comes when you have to give a *real* party: it's your turn to honcho the family Thanksgiving banquet, you got promoted and have to do a Christmas party for the whole office, it's the right moment to impress a client with an elegant sit-down dinner, or you decide to give a bash for your parents' 50th anniversary. Now you need help, because who gets much chance to practice that sort of party?

In the lists and hints below, I tried to anticipate questions on big and small parties, formal and informal ones. The last thing you want is a surprise—the 11th hour discovery that you're out of pepper, that you left the tomatoes out of the casserole because you were making the recipe from memory or, heaven forbid, you forgot to polish the silver.

We Eat With Our Eyes

Enock, our Zambian cook, served onion soup in earthenware bowls, their tops golden and oozing cheese down the sides. As it was set before her, one guest exclaimed, "Oh! This is delicious!" And she hadn't even picked up her spoon.

Your Party List

Keep your list in the kitchen (a party-giving friend tapes hers to the fridge) and check things off as you do them. Glance at it now and then while you toss the family's salad or wait for the oven to heat. It will make you feel more confident.

A PARTY TIMETABLE

When you plan any party, no matter the size, look through this timetable. Pick out and write down whatever applies to your party. A small do will mean a couple of notes; a big bash will produce a page. This list is your security blanket; it lets you sail serenely into a small gathering of friends or navigate a giant New Year's affair with the confidence that you are in charge.

Two to Three Weeks Ahead

Write out the guest list.

Decide on theme, party favors, dress, etc.

Phone or send invitations.

Plan the menu.

Make a shopping list, including all condiments and staples as well as non-foods like candles.

Shop now for non-perishables and ingredients for dishes you'll cook early and freeze.

Start cooking for the freezer: pastry or other doughs, cakes, cookies, appetizers, soup, stocks. Remember, you can prepare and freeze *parts* of dishes such as sauces, grated cheese or chopped onions.

Make a list of the dishes and serving pieces you will need. You may have to borrow or buy some things.

Check the house for small repairs and special cleaning jobs that are needed.

The Week before the Party

Polish silver.

Wash seldom used serving pieces.

A Party Timetable

Check bar supplies and note wine and liquor needed.

Shop for the wine and liquor.

Start making ice cubes and bagging them for the freezer. See How Much Serves How Many on p. 406 for quantities you'll need.

Two Days Ahead
Clean the house.

Shop for all the food except seafood. (Buy this the day you prepare it or see p. 20 on holding fish in crushed ice.)

Wash and dry salad greens and store them in plastic bags.

Trim and store meat, or set it to marinate.

One Day before the Party
Do all day-before cooking.

Set the table or tables and set up the bar if you can trust children and pets to leave them undisturbed.

Buy flowers or, if it's summer and you don't have a garden, ask a gardening friend for raiding privileges.

Gather platters and serving pieces and arrange them on the table or buffet the way they'll be for the party so you don't have to fuss with that at zero hour.

Fill sugar bowls, salt shakers and the like.

Write place cards, if you use them.

In cold weather, prepare closets for coats. If closet space is limited, decide whose bed gets the coats and tidy that room.

Outdoor Party Tip
Always have a bad weather plan. Have the living room tidied and the dining room ready to go if it is suddenly too wet or too hot outside.

House Checklist

- House number visible?
- Driveway clear?
- Is the car in the garage or outside taking up parking space?
- In winter, are the walks clear?
- Exterior lighting—all bulbs working?

A Party Timetable

Rearrange furniture if necessary.

Unclutter table tops so guests will have a place to set glasses and plates.

If you're expecting bad weather, dig out something to hold umbrellas and a runner or mat for boots.

Clean and set up the grill, if you're giving a barbecue.

On Party Day

Arrange flowers.

Do touch-up cleaning.

Freshen the bathroom, put out guest towels, fresh soap, tissues.

Add final touches to recipes.

Set out kitchen service items.

Check the bar.

Chill white and rosé wines at least 2 hours ahead. For a big party, pack them in ice in a picnic cooler.

Chill water and drink mixes if you have the fridge space.

If the dog sheds, give the rug a last minute vacuuming.

If you use your fireplace, start the fire at least 15 minutes ahead so there's time to clean up if it smokes.

Near zero hour, fill ice buckets, picnic cooler, laundry tub, or plastic trash can with ice.

Put out dry nibbles. If you have pets or munchy children, do this just before the guests arrive.

> ## A Party Timetable
>
> Decide on your music, but keep it soft enough so guests can hear each other.
>
> For outdoor parties, set off a non-scented insect repellant (many people are allergic to scents), and ready the grill.

Planning Your Menu

Plan do-ahead menus so when you answer the doorbell you are ready to enjoy the guests.

When planning your menu take into consideration:

1. **Color.** A one-color meal of poached fish, rice and cauliflower is depressing and won't taste good. Jazz it up with some bright greens or reds.

2. **Variety** in flavors and textures. Don't put cream or tarragon in every dish. If you serve several soft, creamy things, offer something crisp to set them off. If several dishes are sweet, include a salad nippy with lemon or vinegar.

3. **Balance.** Don't overload your oven's circuits by planning more dishes for it than it can hold, or your own circuits by having more than one dish that needs last minute attention, or your guests' by serving too many or too rich dishes. If the main course is heavy, choose a light opener and a light dessert.

If you serve cheese as a separate course, offer a selection. I like to include one of each of the following: a **blue-veined cheese** (Roquefort or Danish blue); a **soft creamy cheese** (Brie or Camembert) or a **fresh one** (goat or Petit Suisse); and a **hard cheese** (Cheddar or Gruyère). Serve them with butter and a loaf of good French bread. Figure one ounce of each type of cheese

A Menu Caution

Be careful with iffy foods and exotic dishes. Invite guests for "a curry dinner" or "steamed mussels" so they can regret if they can't eat spices or hate mussels. You might also include fish in this warning. Despite its current popularity, it's amazing how many people are less than enchanted when you bring out fish.

How Many Mouthfuls?

For appetizers or snacks figure:

Cocktail party: 10 mouthfuls per person

Before lunch or dinner: 4 or 5 mouthfuls

Tea: 4 small sandwiches and 2 cookies or other sweet items

Receptions: 8 cocktail mouthfuls and 4 sweet ones

Wine and cheese party: 3 to 4 ounces cheese per person

How Much Bread?

An 18-inch baguette (French bread) serves 15.

Allow 1 to 2 slices of bread per person from a regular loaf.

per person. If you serve only one cheese, and that's good too, allow three ounces per person.

As soon as you have decided on it, post your menu on the refrigerator door along with the number of diners (include yourself!). Strange but true: several experienced party givers have told me that at one time or another they forgot to count themselves! This will keep you from forgetting the salad or some other item that's not in your line of sight at serving time. The number of diners will remind you how many plates, forks, etc. to set out.

How Much Serves How Many?

Everybody knows a pie serves six very nicely, but how much spinach do you prepare for 16? How much catsup or mustard do you need for a barbecue for 40? How much cream do you whip to top eight desserts?

When you are serving a small number, it's not a serious problem. You can always pare down portions for the family if you buy too little, and enjoy a couple of cooking-free days if you buy too much. But a mistaken guess for a big party can leave you with a vat of leftover spinach or a table of grumpy, still hungry guests.

Our cook in the Congo, a cranky old dear, once prepared his famous salmon mousse for a buffet honoring a travelling American woodwind quintet. He figured badly and one quintet member, who visited too long before attending the buffet, got no mousse at all. With fine artistic temperament, he made it clear that he felt ill-treated.

I overcompensated from then on, emulating the Middle East where hospitality demands that platters are still heaped when the last guest eats his last bite. This proved extravagant and impractical and led to the development of the chart below, which handily estimates what the average diner will eat.

Note that the amounts recommended for vegetables assume that they are plain and buttered. If you prepare them in a rich sauce, diners will eat less.

HOW MUCH FOOD TO ALLOW PER PERSON

Artichokes: 1 large or 2 small

Asparagus: 6 to 10 spears

Avocado: ¼ to ½ large

Bacon: 2 slices

Beans:

 Green or wax: ⅓ pound

 Lima and broad: ½ pound unshelled

  (⅓ cup shelled)

 Dried (incudes peas and lentils):

  ⅙ to ¼ pound dry

Beets: ¼ pound

Berries: ¼ to ½ pint

Brains: 4 ounces

Broccoli: ⅓ pound, untrimmed

Brussels sprouts: ¼ to ½ pound

Butter: 1 tablespoon

Cabbage:

 As a side dish: ⅓ pound

 For coleslaw: A small cabbage, finely

  shredded, serves 10 to 12

Cake

 A 13" x 9" x 2" cake serves 12

 A 10" torte or angel food or bundt cake serves

  12

 A 9" round layer cake serves 10

 An 8" round layer cake serves 8

How do I Figure a Chinese Meal?

At a Chinese meal, guests share a number of main dishes. To know if you have enough, add the total weight of boneless meat, poultry, and seafood in *all the main dishes* you plan to serve. You need a total of ¼ to ⅓ pound meat per guest.

How Much Dip?

One cup serves 8 if other food is provided.

One quart provides 150 teaspoon-size servings.

How Much Ice?

For a cocktail party, allow 8 to 10 ice cubes per person. In hot weather, provide 24 to 30 cubes (1 to 1½ pounds) per person.

HOW MUCH FOOD TO ALLOW PER PERSON

A 9" square cake serves 6 to 8.

An 8" square cake serves 6.

Candies: Eight ounces of small candies serves 25.

Cantaloupe: ⅓ to ½ melon for dessert or first course

Carrots:

    Served fresh: ¼ to ⅓ pound

    Served cooked: ½ pound

Casseroles: ½ to 1 cup

Catsup: ½ to 1 tablespoon

Cauliflower: One medium head serves 5.

Chicken:

    Boned and skinned: ⅓ to ½ pound

    Parts: ½ to ¾ pound

    Whole: ¾ to 1 pound

    Also see Sandwiches box p. 412.

Clams:

    On the half shell: 10 to 12

    Shucked: ¼ to ⅓ pint

    For steaming: 1½ pounds

Coffee: One 12-ounce can brews 60 to 80 cups.

Cookies: 2, as an accompaniment

Corn:

    Cream-style: ⅓ cup

    On the cob: 1 to 2 ears

    Whole kernel: ½ cup or ⅓ package frozen

Crab:

    In the shell: 4 to 6 large whole crabs or 4 Alaskan crab legs

    Meat: ¼ to ⅓ pound

    Soft-shell: 3 small

Crayfish: 10 to 12

Cream:

    For coffee: 1 tablespoon

HOW MUCH FOOD TO ALLOW PER PERSON

For whipping to top a dessert: 2 tablespoons unwhipped

Creamed dishes: ⅔ cup (allow extra for seconds)

Cucumber:

As a side dish: ½ medium split lengthwise

For salads: 1- to 2-inch piece

Desserts, puddings—very generally: ½ to ¾ cup

Duck: 1¼ pounds

Eggplant:

As a main dish: ½ to ¾ pound

As a side dish: ⅓ pound

Eggs: 2

Endive, Belgian,

As a side dish: 2 medium

Raw, for salad: 1 medium

Escarole: ¼ medium bunch

Fennel: 1 medium bulb

Fish:

Fillets, steaks or chunks: ½ pound (less if in a rich dish)

Dressed (gutted, head and tail removed): ½ to ¾ pound

Whole, undressed: 1 pound (weight before gutting)

Fruit, cut up: ½ cup

Goose: 1 pound

Gravy: ¼ cup

Greens, to be served cooked,

Stemless: ¼ to ⅓ pound

With stems: ⅓ to ½ pound

Grouse:

Roasted: ½ bird

Casseroled: ⅓ bird

Ice cream or sherbet: ⅔ cup

Cucumber Garnishes

Have to Serve Tea to 25?

You'll need: 4 ounces tea, 8 ounces sugar cubes, 1½ cups milk and 2 sliced lemons. Pour 3 cups of *rapidly boiling* water over the tea. Let it steep for 5 minutes. Strain into serving pot. Dilute 1 part tea with 8 parts freshly boiling water and serve with sugar, milk and lemon.

Lemon Rose

Lemon Cups

❖❖❖

How Many Sandwiches?

For hors d'oeuvres: Use a ½-ounce slice of meat or cheese for each.

A 3½ to 4 pound chicken will make chicken salad for about 70 small sandwiches.

Full-size: For each: 2 to 3 ounces sliced meat or cheese or a combination; 2 tablespoons peanut butter or other spread; 1 hard-cooked egg.

❖❖❖

How Much Food to Allow Per Person

Jam, jelly: 1½ to 2 tablespoons

Jerusalem artichokes (Sunchokes): ¼ to ⅓ pound

Jicama: ¼ pound

Kidneys: 4 ounces

Kohlrabi: 1 medium or 2 small

Leeks: 1 medium

Lettuce: ¼ medium head, or one loose handful
Also see the chart on p. 49.

Liver: 4 ounces

Lobster:
Meat: ¼ to ⅓ pounds
Tail: 1 large
Whole: 1½ to 2 pounds

Mayonnaise: As a condiment, allow 1½ tablespoons per person. One cup dresses 10 salad servings or 10 to 15 sandwiches.

Meat:
Cold cuts: ¼ pound
Ground: ¼ to ½ pound
Small amount of bone (round steak, pot roasts, ham slices, rib roasts): ⅓ pound
Large amount of bone or fat (most steaks, shoulder cuts, leg of lamb, short ribs, neck, chops, breasts, plate, brisket): ½ pound
Mostly bone (spare ribs, oxtail): 1 pound serves one generously.
Also see Sandwiches box this page.

Mushrooms: ⅓ to ½ pound

Mussels: ½ to 1 pound in the shell

Nuts: A 12-ounce can serves 20 to 25.

Okra: ¼ to ½ pound

Olives: 2 to 4

How Much Food to Allow Per Person

Onions: 1 medium
Oysters:
    On the half shell: 6 to 12
    Shucked: ⅓ to ½ pint
Parsnips: 1 medium
Partridge: 1 bird
Pasta, dry:
    As a first course or side dish: 1 to 2 ounces
    As a main dish: 3 to 4 ounces
Pasta, fresh:
    Double dry pasta amounts.
Peas:
    In the pod: ½ pound
    Shelled: ⅓ to ½ cup
    Sugar snap or snow peas: ¼ pound
Pheasant: ½ bird
Pickles: 1 medium
Pie:
    An 8" pie serves 4.
    A 9" pie serves 6.
    A 3½" tart serves 1.
Pigeon (squab): 1 bird
Potatoes:
    For potato salad: ⅕ pound
    For mashing: ¼ to ⅓ pound
    Plain: ⅓ to ½ pound
Poultry stuffing: ½ cup
Punch: 1 cup
Quail: 2 small or 1 large, stuffed and served on a crouton
Rice, dry:
    White or wild: ⅓ cup
    Brown: ¼ cup

Radish Garnishes

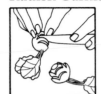

Serving Buffet Style

If you want to serve buffet style, plan a menu of fork food. Casseroles and pasta dishes are easy on the host and the guests.

Leave enough room on the buffet table so guests can put down their plates while serving themselves.

Be sure to have plenty of chairs and trays or folding tables so guests have a place to perch while eating.

To keep traffic moving, put beverages and silverware on a separate cart or small table.

HOW MUCH FOOD TO ALLOW PER PERSON

Rock Cornish hen: A 1-pound hen (hard to find now) serves 1.

A 1½-pound hen serves 1 or 2.

Rutabagas: ¼ to ⅓ pound

Salsify (Oyster plant): ⅓ pound

Sauce:

    White: ¼ cup

    Tomato: 1 cup

Scallops: ¼ to ½ pound, depending on richness of dish

Shrimp:

    In the shell: 1 pound serves 2 as a main course, 4 as a first course.

    Without shells: One pound serves 2 to 3 as a main course, 4 to 6 as a first course.

Soups: ½ to 1 cup, depending on richness

Squash, untrimmed:

    Summer: ¼ pound

    Winter: ½ pound

Squid: ⅓ pound

Stews and braised dishes: 1 to 2 cups

Sweet potatoes: 1 medium

Sweetbreads: 4 ounces

Tomatoes: ⅕ pound

Tongue: 4 ounces

Tripe: 4 ounces

Turkey:

    Boneless (turkey roll, breast): ⅓ to ½ pound

    Meaty parts (thighs, legs): ½ to ¾ pound

    Whole, over 12 pounds: ½ to ¾ pound

    Whole, less than 12 pounds: ¾ to 1 pound

    Bony parts (wings, backs): 1 pound

Turnips: ¼ pound

HOW MUCH FOOD TO ALLOW PER PERSON

Vegetables, in general:
  Fresh, untrimmed, unpeeled: ¼ to ⅓ pound
  Frozen, peeled, trimmed: 3 to 5 ounces
Vinaigrette: 1 tablespoon
Watercress, for salad: ¼ bunch
Watermelon: slice 1" thick and 6" in diameter

MAKING PREPARATION EASIER

If you photocopy the recipes you plan to use, it makes it easier to do the grocery list, frees counter tops of open cookbooks, and lets you scribble notes in the margins such as: the parts of the recipe you can do ahead (check off each as you do it); any changes you make; garnishes and serving pieces you plan to use. After the party, if you decide to keep the changes, note that, too. If you don't photocopy, make these notes on a piece of paper for later reference.

Before you start any cooking, *read the recipe through—* especially if you haven't prepared it within the last month. Measure ingredients onto wax paper or into small containers. Then you're ready to start cooking.

Cooking Ahead Tips

Desserts are usually time-takers. Make them as early as possible.

Most casseroles and braised dishes improve if made 1 or 2 days ahead so flavors have time to ripen. Take advantage of this.

You can pre-cook vegetables up to 24 hours ahead. At serving time, reheat them quickly either in a sauce or by tossing in butter.

Any food to be fried in a dry coating (flour, breading—but not batter!) can be coated up to two days ahead.

Coffee Tricks

When I brew coffee for a party and it comes out weaker than I intended, I stir in a spoonful or two of instant.

If you're caught short and have to serve *instant* coffee, it will taste almost like the real stuff if you boil it for 30 seconds, turn off the heat, and let it steep for 2 to 3 minutes.

Keep a Party Log

A party log becomes a wonderful reference. For each party note the guests, what you served, how much food you prepared and whether it was the right amount. If it was a buffet, sketch a quick diagram of the buffet, noting what you placed where. At the end of your log book, keep a list of the loves, hates, and allergies of your guests.

See the sample log on p. 416 and photocopy the one on 418-419 to make your own log.

What an Honor!

A boardinghouse hostess in Alaska honors guests by piping their names in mashed potatoes on the steak or roast!

An Elegant Touch

Perfumed hot towels are a nice touch after you've served finger food. Dampen washcloths, scent with a few drops of after-shave, roll, and heat in the microwave on *high* for 1 to 2 minutes.

Make a timetable for last minute tasks: Counting backward from the time you have set to start eating, calculate when to start defrosting and when to start heating and final cooking for each dish. You can also write this down on the recipes *and* on the menu taped to the fridge door.

If you plan to finish a dish or reheat a casserole after the guests arrive, *always* set a timer so you don't get engrossed in conversation while dinner burns.

See the Cooking Ahead section on p. 96 for help with holding and reheating food.

SERVING

Buffet style service is easiest for large groups. When you set up the buffet, put dinner plates at the near end of the table, and napkins and silverware at the far end.

You can easily serve groups of 8 or fewer at the table. Have bread, butter, salt, pepper and the soup or first course, if you're serving one, on the table before the guests sit down.

For informal service, put the food in attractive bowls and let the guests pass them. For more formal service, fill plates in the kitchen. Or place serving dishes in front of you or on a cart next to you and serve each guest yourself. If plates are in front of the guests

Informal Place Setting

Formal Place Setting

because the first course sat on top of them, invite each to pass his or her plate to be served. Otherwise, have the plates stacked in front of you when guests sit down.

I like to use a combination of at-table and buffet service for more than six seated guests. After the first course is cleared, guests rise and serve themselves from a buffet. I hate to have all the women get up and go to the buffet, then all the men. It wrecks conversation. Instead, I invite one side of the table to serve themselves, then the other.

Serve hot food on hot plates. A cold plate chills food in minutes. There are lots of ways to heat plates: in a 175° oven for 5 minutes; on a warming tray; in a covered electric skillet set on "warm". You can heat a large quantity of plates in a styrofoam picnic cooler. Put them on a towel-covered heating pad and press on the lid. The plates will warm in about 4 hours.

If you work outside the home, consider hiring a helper for big parties. Teenagers like the extra money and generally are good workers.

Reminders

Keep centerpieces low: at table, guests need to see each other; on a buffet, a tall arrangement is asking to get knocked over.

Refrigerate candles for a few hours before the party and they'll drip less. Use votive candles on the dinner table. They give a flattering light, don't look tired when they burn low, and can't drip.

Quick Hint

Use the high setting of your microwave to warm brandy right in the snifter: 10 seconds for lead crystal, 15 seconds for glass.

Buffet Table Against a Wall

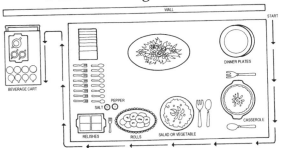

Buffet Table in Center of Room

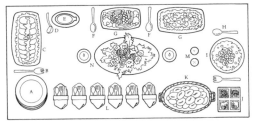

PARTY LOG

Function   *Dinner Party*
Reason   *Hank & Joan's Anniversary*
Date   *August 25th*
Time   *7 PM*

Invited	Phone	Yes	No
Phil & Margery Blain	737-0428	X	
Hank & Joan Martin	632-1333	X	
Betsy Carpenter	737-2175	X	
Richard Miller	731-8546	X	
Sally & Fred Dixon	737-2594		X
Max & Leah Sanders	737-2224	X	

Seating

Margery · Richard · Leah · Phil
Host · Hostess
Joan · Max · Betsy · Hank

Allergies, Food Preferences

Richard allergic to nuts & seafood
Hank adores anything chocolate
Betsy hates mushrooms

Menu—Recipe Source   Wine

Camembert Puffs - Canadian Book   Wine: St. Joseph Piesporter
Cucumber Soup - Nelly's recipe   1969
Spanish Chicken with Olives -   (Mosel - Saar - Ruwer)
     Thoughts for Buffets
Rice
   Grilled Garlic - Parmesan Tomatoes - card file
Fresh Green Beans
French Bread - notebook
   Chocolate - Raspberry Roll - D. Lucas basic recipe

Table Arrangement and Decoration

Dark brown round straw mats
Brass place plates with smoked glass liners
Covered pottery soup bowls on wooden trivets
Chocolate napkins with the brass napkin rings
Green ivy plant in brass cachepot with four
     African brass figurines
Brass candlesticks w/ green candles

Notes

Did everything ahead except broiling tomatoes. (Chicken
day before, blanched beans and cooked rice in a.m.)
   Surrounded beans with tomatoes on oval platter. Looked
good. 2 lbs. beans just right for ten
1½ chickens just about right using double the recipe's
sauce.

Party Log

Function

Reason

Date

Time

Invited	Phone	Yes	No

Seating

Allergies, Food Preferences

Menu—Recipe Source   Wine

Table Arrangement and Decoration

Notes

Sometimes Water Is Best

Some foods actually fight with wine and give it an off taste. Serve only water with asparagus, artichokes, vinegar-dressed salads, and soups. If the soup has an added wine such as sherry, though, serve that.

Place cards are useful at parties where guests don't know each other well. They can be informal, or a part of the table decoration. If place cards don't suit the mood of your party, give a little thought to who would enjoy sitting next to whom. Then, before people start hesitating and looking uncomfortable, you can suggest that Jane sit here and Fred there.

People visit better when they're close to each other. A slightly crowded table is generally more animated than one where guests have lots of space. The same goes for cocktail parties. Keep the area limited.

Don't let guests help unless you really need it or enjoy the chitchat and commotion. I like to be alone so I can concentrate on last minute details. Just before dinner and at table clearing time I ask one guest to help. If you leave it to guests to offer, everyone jumps up to be useful, the table empties and conversation lurches to a halt.

If the party is large, don't have a fire in the fireplace. It uses up oxygen and dries out the air.

DRINKS

Nowadays more and more people are ignoring the old rules about wine and are drinking what they like with meals rather than what they were told is "correct". Here is a little guidance in choosing wines in case you haven't settled on any preferences.

The standard rule always works: red wine with red meat like beef and lamb; white wine, which is lighter flavored, with white meats like poultry, veal and fish. Red wine also goes well with cheese, duck and goose. Champagne goes with everything, at any time of day.

If you use wine in a sauce, serve the same one with the dish. Creamy or delicate herb-scented sauces go well with fruity white wines. Tomato-based sauces, whose acids can overpower a white wine, are complemented by crisp-edged red wines like Beaujolais or Chianti.

With seafood-based cuisines like Japanese, try clean, non-fruity white wines. Robust red wines like Zinfandel or fruity, spicy white wines like Gewürztraminer go well with the highly spiced foods of India, Southeast Asia, China or Mexico. On the other hand, many people who know about such things prefer beer with these zesty dishes.

A few words of caution: You probably wouldn't enjoy a sweet wine with a meal. The French make an exception for pâté de foie gras, which tastes best with a sweet, white wine. In general, sweet wines are best with dessert.

Serve white and rosé wines lightly chilled and red wines at a cool room temperature.

Here's a guide to how much wine and other spirits to buy for your party.

Buying Beverages for a Party

Aperitif wines
Allow 3 ounces per serving of sherry, port, etc. A 24-ounce bottle provides eight glasses.

Beer
For a picnic, barbecue, etc., allow three bottles per person.

Carbonated drinks
Allow one 28-ounce bottle for every two people.

Cocktails
For martinis and manhattans, you need 1 bottle of vermouth for every 3 quarts of liquor.

If you're making tall drinks, figure 2 ounces of liquor per 8-ounce drink.

Liquor
For a cocktail party for twelve, the following will give you a well-stocked bar:

> 1 pint scotch
> 1 pint bourbon

Still Some Wine in the Bottle?

A Belgian wine merchant recommended the following way to save unfinished bottles of wine: Since air is the enemy, drop in glass marbles (the small ones children use) until the wine enters the neck. Recork, refrigerate, and drink sooner rather than later.

1 quart vodka
1 quart gin
1 quart rum
2 to 3 bottles white wine
1 to 2 bottles red wine
6 to 8 beers

Liquor bottle sizes and number of 1½-ounce drinks each will make:

Pint	16 ounces	10
Fifth	25 ounces	17
Quart	32 ounces	21

Wine

For a substantial meal, allow about half a bottle per person if you are serving a single wine. If you are serving two wines, count on 2 glasses of each per person. Fill wine glasses about two-thirds full, no more, so you can enjoy the bouquet.

Wine bottle sizes and number of glasses each holds:

Split	6 ounces	2
Half	12 ounces	3
Bottle	24 ounces	6
Magnum	48 ounces	12
Jeroboam	96 ounces	24
Gallon	130 ounces	32

TIPS FOR LARGE PARTIES

Get extra seating with large pillows on the floor. Get extra table or bar space with cloth-covered dressers or bureaus. Get extra kitchen counter space with trays or cookie sheets placed over opened drawers. Set up the ironing board.

A small plastic trash can is perfect for chilling wine or beer in ice. If chilling space is limited, place bottles and cans in ice in the washing machine or the laundry room sink. Leave the stopper out so melted ice can drain away.

Here's a checklist to help you get organized:

LARGE PARTY
❦ CHECKLIST ❦

Bar:
>   Bar table
>   Bottle openers
>   Coffee, for those who like it
>   Garnishes: olives, lemon slices, limes,
>   pickled onions and cherries
>   Glassware
>   Ice cubes, crushed ice
>   Mixers
>   Napkins
>   Non-alcoholic drinks
>   Stirrers
>   Wines, spirits

Coasters
Coat racks and hangers

Serving:
>   Candleholders, candles
>   China
>   Cloth or place mats, napkins
>   Collection trays for wandering cups, plates,
>   napkins, etc.
>   Flowers
>   Glassware
>   Serving trays and platters
>   Silverware and serving pieces
>   Warming devices

Trash receptacles
Parking space

CLEAN-UP

Drop dirty silverware in a bowl of hot, soapy water. After the party you can either wash and dry it, or drain and re-cover it with plain hot water to wait until morning. Don't let washed silver drain dry or it will spot.

Wash and dry wine glasses or crystal by hand. A friend taught me the trick of washing things harmed by dishwasher detergent—dishes with gold or silver trim and sterling silver. Do them in the dishwasher *without detergent*. The scalding water cleans them beautifully.

Soak napkins overnight in a basin of hot water with pre-wash solution added. Next day you can dump them in the machine. Treat red wine stains before you go to bed. Rub them with wet salt and leave them till morning (they need at least 6 hours). Club soda is also good for removing red wine stains.

❦ ARRANGE A PRETTY PLATE ❦

Think of the plate as a design. Mentally divide it in quarters. A long main item (a fish fillet, a steak) will fill two of them. Don't use up the other two with another long item (an ear of corn, a baked potato), especially if the long item is a similar color (a brown-skinned potato with steak). Instead, put brightly colored vegetables in one quarter and a mound of parsleyed rice or crispy, diced potatoes in the other. If a main item fills one quarter of the plate (a square of lasagne, a chicken breast or couple chops), it leaves you three to fill with brightly colored vegetable, starch, and salad.

Or do a target arrangement. Put a round, square or triangular main item (fish, chicken breast) in the center and arrange sauce and accompaniments around it.

Or ladle sauce over the plate first and arrange the foods on top.

Make the plate look generous. When you can see a lot of empty plate the serving, no matter how big, looks skimpy. Remember when nouvelle cuisine cooks served giant plates decorated with a few artistic bites?

ARRANGE A PRETTY PLATE

Provide contrast in color, size and shape. Vegetables offer great possibilities for dressing up the plate.

- whole (*round* beets, broiled tomatoes; *long* asparagus spears, corn, green beans)
- in *mounds* (greens, purées—2 or 3 in contrasting colors is beautiful)
- *chunks and irregular pieces* (carrot, celery, zucchini)
- *pebbles* (peas, lima, corn kernels)
- *disks* (eggplant slices, corn cakes)
- *diced* (carrots, turnips)
- *little sticks* (potato straws, julienned zucchini).

Look at the food photos in books and magazines. Once you see them as design patterns they are easy to copy.

Glossary of Cookbook Terms

Cooking has its own jargon, which sounds intimidating until you learn that sauté just means fry, braise is quick-speak for cook-covered-with-a-small-amount-of-liquid, and blanch—well, it's here in the glossary along with all the other terms peculiar to kitchens.

For many of these terms, see the index for further information.

Acidulated water: Cold water with a little lemon juice or vinegar added. You put cut-up fruits like apples in it to keep them from turning brown.

Aioli (eye-oh-LEE): A garlic mayonnaise made in southern France.

Al dente (al DEN-tay): Describes pasta or rice cooked only to the point where your teeth can still detect some firmness.

Au jus (oh ZHU): Unthickened cooked meat juices.

Bake blind: Bake pastry such as pie crust before adding the filling.

Bard: Wrap meats like roasts and game in thin sheets of pork fatback to keep them moist during cooking.

Baste: Pour liquid over food as it cooks—usually hot fat during roasting. Adds flavor and keeps food from drying out. Use a spoon, brush or bulb baster.

Enock, our Zambian cook who moonlighted as a tailor, was convulsed when I announced that we should baste the chicken.

Batter: A mixture thin enough to pour, made of flour, liquid, and often eggs and sugar.

Béarnaise (bay-are-NEZ): Tarragon-flavored Hollandaise.

Beat: Mix vigorously in order to work air into a mixture. Cut spoon or whisk down energetically into the mixture, lift, flicking the mixture over the spoon, and plunge it down again.

Beurre manié (burr mahn-YAY): Flour/butter paste used to thicken sauces.

Blanch: Cook food in boiling water for a very short time to prepare for further cooking or freezing.

Boil: Cook food in liquid at a temperature that makes bubbles rise steadily and break on the surface.

Bouquet garni (boo-KAY gar-NEE): Herb bouquet used to flavor liquid dishes.

Braise: Cook meat or vegetables by first browning in hot fat, then simmering in a small amount of liquid in a heavy, covered pot.

Bread: Coat food with bread or cracker crumbs before cooking to give them a crusty coating when cooked.

Brown: Cook food until the surface browns, by sautéing or placing under the broiler.

Capon: A male chicken that has been desexed so it will grow fatter than it would otherwise and yet remain tender. Excellent for roasting.

Chop: Cut into rough pieces about the size of a pea.

Choron (sho-ROAN): Tomato-flavored Hollandaise.

Chunks: Irregularly shaped pieces, larger than cubes and thicker than slices.

Clarify: Remove solids from a liquid such a stock or melted butter, making it clear.

Coulibiac (koo-LEE-bee-ak): A Russian dish, originally salmon and rice enclosed in pastry.

Court bouillon (koor bwee-YON): Broth made with water, root vegetables, white wine or vinegar, herbs and seasoning. It is simmered and strained, then used to poach fish or veal.

Cream or cream together: Work fat or fat and sugar until light and creamy in texture and color. Fat for creaming should be soft and at room temperature.

Crème fraîche (Krehm FRESH): Thick, cultured cream very like sour cream but milder.

Cube: Cut into cubes ½" thick (larger than if you were dicing).

Cut in: Mix a fat like shortening or butter with flour using a pastry blender or two knives. The pieces of flour-coated fat become smaller and smaller until they are the size of small peas or the texture of coarse crumbs, or whatever the recipe specifies. For good results, both fat and utensils should be chilled.

Deep-fry: Cook food by submerging it in hot oil or fat.

Deglaze: Pour water, stock or wine over brown and caramelized pan drippings in order to loosen them by stirring and scraping. The flavor-rich liquid is then used for sauce.

Dice: Cut into cubes ⅛" to ¼" thick (smaller than if you were cubing).

Dot: Distribute small of pieces of butter uniformly over the top of a food before cooking or baking to keep the surface moist and encourage browning.

Dough: A thick, pliable mixture of flour and liquid that is firm enough to be shaped or kneaded, as opposed to a batter, which can be poured.

Dredge: Sprinkle food with flour, sugar, bread crumbs or seasoning. An easy way to dredge a solid piece of food is to put it in a bag with the dry coating, close tightly and shake.

Emulsion: Two substances that normally won't mix, usually oil and liquid, forced into a creamy suspension.

A friend called to say his cookie dough was misbehaving. "I creamed the butter carefully," he said. "That means melting it to a cream, doesn't it?"

The French Have a Lovely Cooking Language:

When water simmers, they say it *smiles*, when it boils, they say it *laughs*—and when you add just the teeniest touch of something, that's a *soupçon*, a suspicion.

En papillote (ahn pah-pee-YOT): A method of cooking in a wrapper, usually parchment or foil.

Espagnole (ess-pah-NYOHL): French for "Spanish", generally referring to a sauce or style of cooking.

Fines herbes (feenz AIRB): An aromatic mixture of finely chopped herbs.

Flour: Coat a food lightly with flour or another powdery, dry coating. Always shake off the excess. Use the dredging technique.

Fold: Blend a delicate, easily damaged substance like beaten egg whites into a sturdier one like a batter or custard. Use a spoon, rubber scraper or whisk. Dip, lift the mixture, and turn it over lightly to avoid crushing the fragile ingredient.

Fry: Cook in a skillet with fat.

Gnocchi (NYO-kee): Italian dumplings, generally made from semolina, potatoes or cream puff dough.

Grate: Cut food such as cheese or cabbage into shreds, flakes or tiny particles using a tool with sharp-edged holes, a knife or a food processor.

Gratin (grah-TAN): A casserole with a topping of bread crumbs and/or cheese. It is best cooked in a gratin dish—a shallow, ovenproof baking dish, usually round or oval, that can tolerate being placed under the broiler.

Gratiné (grah-teen-AY): Having a browned topping of crumbs or cheese.

Grill: Roast in the open air, uncovered, on a grate—usually over charcoal. In British usage, it means "broil".

Heavy cream: Whipping cream

Hydrogenated fat: The solid, always soft fat you buy in a can and store in the cupboard. It is made by treating liquid oils like corn oil with hydrogen.

Julienne (ju-lee-ENN): Cut food into uniform pieces about the size and shape of a kitchen match: 1" long by ⅛"

I had a friend who always cut things Julie Anne. I rather liked that.

x ⅛". Small julienne would be 1" long by 1/16" x 1/16"; large julienne 2" long and ¼" x ¼".

Leavening: Anything that lightens and increases the volume of a batter or dough when heated: air beaten into egg whites, yeast, baking powder. Each adds gases that expand when they heat and make the substance rise.

Light cream: Heavier than milk, lighter than whipping cream. In a recipe it usually means table or coffee cream. If you're watching your fats, substitute half and half, which is lighter still.

Maltaise (mal-TEZ): Orange-flavored Hollandaise.

Marbling: The small white lines and specks of fat in the meat of animals—and sometimes fish. A lot of marbling insures moist, tender (and rich) meat.

Marinate: Tenderize and flavor a food by soaking it in a seasoned acidic and/or oily solution.

Mince: Cut food into bits about ⅛" thick (smaller than if you chopped them).

Pan-broil: Cook meat briefly and rapidly in a pan with very little or no fat. To prevent sticking, salt is sometimes sprinkled into the dry skillet beforehand, or the warm skillet is rubbed with a piece of the meat's fat.

Pan-fry: See Fry.

Pan juices: The drippings, fat and browned, caramelized crust that accumulate in a pan which has been used to fry meat or poultry. See also Deglaze.

Parboil: Cook food briefly in boiling water to prepare for further cooking by another method. Parboiling is similar to blanching (see above), but the cooking lasts slightly longer.

Phyllo (FEE-lo): Tissue-thin dough sheets used in Middle Eastern cooking.

Pinch: The teeny amount you can hold between thumb and forefinger—about 1/16 teaspoon.

Pith: The soft, white, often bitter skin between the peel and flesh of citrus fruit.

Poach: Cook food in a liquid heated to just below the boiling point.

Proof: Test yeast for its rising capacity. You generally do this by mixing the yeast with warm liquid and a little sugar and letting it stand 5 to 10 minutes.

Purée: Reduce food to a smooth, velvety pulp by pressing it through a sieve or food mill, or processing in an electric blender or food processor.

Reduce: Boil a liquid so some of the water content evaporates and the liquid becomes thicker and more concentrated.

Refresh: Quickly cool hot cooked food by rinsing or immersing it in ice cold water.

Render: Slowly cook pieces of animal fat until they liquify and only crisp solids, or cracklings, remain.

Roux (roo): A briefly cooked mixture of flour and fat used to thicken sauces. See p. 93 for complete directions.

Sauté (so-TAY): French for "pan-fry". The term means "to jump"; when you sauté, you toss the food to keep it from sticking or burning.

Scald: Heat a liquid such as milk to a temperature just below the boiling point. Tiny bubbles should just start to fizz around the sides of the pan.

Score: Make shallow or deep cuts in a decorative pattern with a sharp knife. Ham fat is often scored in diamond shapes. You score the thickest part of whole fish with 2 or 3 slashes so that part will cook as fast as the thin areas.

Sear: Quickly brown the surface of food (usually meat) over or under very high heat to seal in juices and give a rich flavor.

Shortening: A white, almost tasteless, solid fat made by hydrogenating (see above) vegetable oils to make them solid. Shortening is also a general term for all solid vegetable or animal fats that give the "short", crisp quality to pastry and cakes. Lard, the fat with the least liquid, has the greatest shortening power.

Shred: Cut or grate into long, even, thin strands.

Simmer: The gentlest possible boil. A continuous stream of small bubbles should rise *slowly* to the surface.

Skim: Remove fat or scum from the surface of a liquid. Meats cooked in water usually need this attention. Easiest done with a slotted spoon, ladle, or skimmer.

Slice: Cut into thin pieces.

Steam: Cook in steam, on a rack above (never touching) boiling liquid, in a tightly covered container.

Steep: Soak a food such as tea, mint leaves or saffron in liquid that is just under the boiling point, to soften the food or flavor the liquid.

Stew: Cook food slowly in a simmering, well-seasoned liquid in a covered pan.

Stir-fry: Sauté small, uniform-sized pieces of food quickly over high heat in a Chinese wok or skillet, tossing the food constantly.

Stock: A flavored broth made by simmering the bones, skin and scraps of meat, poultry or fish with vegetables in water. It is strained and used instead of water in soup, sauces, etc.

Strain: Place food in a sieve to separate liquid from solids, or force a soft food through a sieve to purée it and remove hard particles. Read the recipe carefully to know which process is required.

Sur le plat (soor luh PLAH): Literally, "on the dish." Generally used for eggs cooked in the oven.

Sweat: Cook sliced or chopped ingredients in a little fat and no liquid over very low heat, covered, until they ooze their juices and begin to brown. Often a preliminary step for stewing, braising, soup making.

I have a wonderful recipe from a Cambodian diplomat's wife which directs the cook to mix until the flavor is "exquisite". I can't define that one for you!

Tabbouleh (tah-Boo-luh): A Middle Eastern salad made with bulgur, parsley and mint.

Triticale (trit-ih-KAY-lee): A hybrid of wheat and rye.

Whip: Incorporate air into a mixture by beating.

Whisk: Whip using a wire whip or whisk.

Zest: The outermost surface of the peel of a citrus fruit. Also, to remove that outermost skin in tiny strips.

Index

For recipes, see the contents at the front of the book.

About The Author

Polly Clingerman is the author of four cookbooks: *Fast and Fabulous Hors d'Oeuvres, Holiday Entertaining, A Passion for Pasta,* and *Red Raspberry Recipes*. She has written articles on cooking and travel for Vogue, Mademoiselle, The Washington Post, The Chicago Tribune, The Stars and Stripes and The Foreign Service Journal. In 1987 she was a featured cook in Bon Appetit's Great Cooks series. Polly graduated from Michigan State University with a BA in English Literature and studied for a year at the Sorbonne in Paris. As the wife of a foreign service officer, she spent thirty years traveling the world, living, cooking and entertaining in the capitals of Nepal, Zaire, France, Benin, Belgium, Zambia and Lesotho, where her husband, John, was the Ambassador. After John retired the Clingermans lived for two years in Germany, England and Greece where John taught foreign affairs on air force bases and Polly wrote travel articles and began work on *The Kitchen Companion*—a book that grew out of the notebooks she kept during her years as cook and hostess. The Clingermans now make their home in Northern Virginia and spend part of each year abroad.